CHICAGO-AREA ITALIANS IN WORLD WAR I

CHICAGO-AREA ITALIANS IN WORLD WAR I

A Case Study of Calabrians

PETER L. BELMONTE

AMERICA
THROUGH TIME®
ADDING COLOR TO AMERICAN HISTORY

America Through Time is an imprint of Fonthill Media LLC
www.through-time.com
office@through-time.com

Published by Arcadia Publishing by arrangement with Fonthill Media LLC
For all general information, please contact Arcadia Publishing:
Telephone: 843-853-2070
Fax: 843-853-0044
E-mail: sales@arcadiapublishing.com
For customer service and orders:
Toll-Free 1-888-313-2665

www.arcadiapublishing.com

First published 2019

ISBN 978-1-63499-176-6

Typeset in 10pt on 13pt Sabon
Printed and bound in England

In honor of Pvt. Luigi Santelli, 159th Depot Brigade,
and Pvt. Benedetto Sicilia, 158th Depot Brigade,
who got me started.

Acknowledgments

Many people and institutions helped by providing information and photographs of some of the men: Geoff Gentilini (Golden Arrow Research); Russ Horton (Wisconsin Veterans Museum, Madison, Wisconsin); Lori Berdak Miller (Redbird Research); Andrew Woods and J. Perkins (First Division Museum at Cantigny, Wheaton, Illinois); Illinois Adjutant General's Office (Springfield, Illinois); and Kenosha Public Library (Kenosha, Wisconsin). Thanks also to Matthew Rodriguez and Alan Sutton at Fonthill Media for agreeing to publish this book. I would especially like to thank the kind and thoughtful members of the Marano Marchesato-Marano Principato Cousins Google Group (most of whom are my cousins). I have heavily researched immigrants from these two villages, and they are well represented here.

Individuals who provided information, stories, and copies of photographs of their ancestors include Beverly Adamski (Silvio Aiello and Francesco Miceli); Frank Aiello (James Aiello); Gail Cannova and the Nino family (Frank Nino); Paul Ferraro (Serafino Ferraro); Rudolph Ferraro (Eugenio and Serafino Ferraro); Louise Juliani (Antonio and Joseph Giorno and Filiberto Morelli); Andrea Koprcina McGuire, Mark Koprcina, and the Pellegrini family (Pasquale, Francesco, and Luigi Pellegrini); Margo Metegrano and the Metegrano family (Michael Metagrano); Anthony Morrone (Fred Morrone); Rosemary Presta Pennington (Vincenzo Presta); Robert R. Porcaro and Deena Porcaro Hill (Benjamin and James Potesta); Mary Jane Ruffolo (Serafino Ruffolo); Albino Santelli (Luigi Santelli); Christine Chiappetta Thorsen (Carmine Chiappetta); Theresa Van Landuyt (Giuseppe Covelli and Carmine Chiappetta); and Vickie Zagame (Angelo Biscardi). If I have missed anyone, I sincerely apologize; a book like this requires help and encouragement from a great many friends and fellow researchers.

Lastly, I thank my wife, Pam, and my family for their love and support during the times I was living in virtual training camps and trenches.

Contents

Introduction

At dawn on October 4, 1918, on a cold, damp hillside near the Argonne Forest in France, Private Giuseppe Covelli, a member of Company "G," 18th Infantry Regiment, in the much-heralded 1st Division, left his foxhole and charged into a hail of German machine-gun fire. Private Covelli, along with his regiment, was part of the Meuse-Argonne Offensive, the final Allied drive to end the war. Before the end of the following day, Pvt. Covelli was lying grievously wounded, shot through the neck and bayonetted in his side.[1] He is just one of perhaps as many as 400,000 Italian Americans who served in the United States military during World War I.[2] To date, no comprehensive history of these men exists; indeed, it would require a Herculean effort and many volumes to fully tell that story. This book, however, seeks to tell a small portion of that story. It relates the story of 389 men, like Covelli, from the southern Italian region of Calabria who entered military service from the Chicago area (a complete list of the men appears in Appendix II).

Hundreds of Calabrian men from the Chicago area served in the United States military during the Great War. Many of them would, like Pvt. Covelli, end up with life-changing wounds, while others were killed in action, died of wounds, or died of a disease or an accident. Others managed to serve in combat and escape the bullets, shells, and poison gas that claimed so many lives. Still others served overseas but, assigned to support roles behind the lines, did not see combat. Finally, others served stateside, either undergoing training prior to deployment or, deemed unfit for combat service because of physical or mental limitations, assigned to depot brigades or development battalions.

But why focus on Calabrians? Italian immigration to the United States from the 1880s to the 1910s had a strong regional and local flavor. Groups of Sicilians, Campanians, or Calabrians came to the United States together and, very often, settled together in the same locale. In fact, many lived and worked together. Thus, to fully understand Italian immigration history, one must examine these regional and local immigration groups discretely. Referring to the tendency among scholars and others to lump immigrants together as "Italians," "Poles," or "Germans," historian Rudolph Vecoli asserted:

Pvt. Giuseppe Covelli, 18th Infantry Regiment, 1st Division, with friends, *c.* January 1919. Interestingly, he is wearing an early form of the 1st Division patch on his left shoulder. (*Theresa Van Landuyt*)

> Our literature on ethnic groups is replete with generalizations about Irish Americans, Polish Americans, and Italian Americans as if these were homogeneous entities. In fact such labels often disguise at least as much as they reveal.... If we are to advance the study of immigration beyond the level of facile generalizations, we need a series of microstudies which trace particular contingents of immigrants from their specific origins to their specific destinations.[3]

This book can be considered as one such micro-study. While not pretending to be a complete history of Italian Americans in World War I, it gives the military history of a small segment of the larger cohort. It will add to the historiography of Italian immigration and of the United States military during World War I. The data and the biographies presented here lean heavily toward military history while also touching on social and immigration history and genealogy. For most biographies, I have kept pre- and post-war material to a minimum; in some cases, I have omitted it entirely. Many of the biographies illustrate "typical" military service among these men. I have included examples of many types of military units, and some of the biographies highlight interesting aspects of some men's military service. Taken as a whole, these biographies help us to better understand U.S. military service during World War I.

Most of the men were single when they entered the service; some were married. Some men had a wife and children in Italy; this, of course, compounded the problems of communication and support, with a corresponding increase in anxiety among those left at home. After the war, most of the men who had been single later became husbands and fathers, but I have not delved deeply into that aspect of their history. The reader should bear in mind the importance of family in Italian American society a century ago. In this respect, one should consider the burden born by the wives of those men who were already married when they were called into military service. In some cases, these women had to maintain a household on a drastically reduced budget while at the same time being engulfed in a cloud of anxiety over the fate of their husband. Their sacrifices should not be forgotten.

Sources and Methods

For the purposes of this book, I have defined the Chicago area as Cook and Lake counties in northeastern Illinois; Lake County in northwestern Indiana; and Kenosha and Racine counties in southeastern Wisconsin. I have also included some neighboring counties in northeastern Illinois. This is the Chicago metropolitan area, and the communities in this area historically share economic and social ties. The inclusion of the two Wisconsin counties is not arbitrary. Calabrians first settled in Chicago during the early 1870s; from there, immigrants founded smaller sub-colonies as far north as Kenosha and Racine. Even later, Chicago was often a stopover point for men who eventually made their way north to other cities. Indeed, from the very beginning, Calabrian railroad laborers living in Chicago were sent to work on railroad construction and maintenance projects in Michigan, Wisconsin, and as far away as Montana and Colorado. Many men, especially in the case of those working north of Chicago and in southeastern Wisconsin, chose to settle in the area where they worked on these projects. On the other hand,

I have excluded several men from outlying areas of Wisconsin, Illinois, Indiana, and Michigan. These men probably had ties to Chicago, but it seemed best to limit the focus geographically.[4] I chose immigrants from the province of Cosenza in Calabria because they settled in the area in large numbers; many of them came to the area early in the immigration period, and a careful study of them and their children reveals much about Italian settlement in the Chicago area.

This book is a combination of military, social, and immigration history. As such, research involved the pursuit of many types of records; much of the data is available online in databases such as Ancestry.com. Information as to place of residence at the time of their entry into the military is taken from draft registrations, service records, or passport applications. Of course, residence could change between the time of registration and the time of entry on active duty, but for the most part, this gives an accurate portrayal of each man's place of residence. Date of immigration is taken from documents such as census records, passport applications, or naturalization documents. Many men made more than one trip between Italy and the United States.

In many cases, military service information for World War I veterans is difficult to find. Individual personnel records for men who served in the U.S. Army were stored at the National Personnel Records Center (now the National Archives) at St. Louis, Missouri. Most of them were destroyed in a 1973 fire, but a few have been salvaged and reconstructed. From this repository, it is still possible to obtain copies of final pay vouchers and sometimes Veterans Administration claims index cards. The records of World War I U.S. Navy veterans, however, are still intact and easily available. For information on other sources, see Appendix I.

Occasionally there are differences in data between; for example, an individual's statement of service card and their veteran's bonus application. Usually those differences are small, such as a slightly different date of discharge or a different home address. In most cases, I have not bothered to point out each difference but have done my best to reconcile the two (or more) differing pieces of data. This is, of course, the case with all historical and genealogical research.

In most cases, I have given information as it appears on the various documents. I have given the names here just as they appeared on whatever records are extant; with a fairly good working knowledge of surnames from this area, I have reconciled differences to the best of my ability, but I also wanted to keep surnames actually used by men who might have changed their name. Also, the reader will note that I have used the phrase "he was assigned as a private, serial number XXXXXX" in most biographical sketches. In fact, serial numbers were first issued to U.S. servicemen in February 1918. Thus men who entered the Army before then did not receive their serial number until February 1918, sometimes a matter of a few months after their enlistment. When reading sketches of men who entered service in 1917, it should be understood that the men did not immediately receive their serial number. Also, when discussing men who were drafted, I have often used the phrases "drafted into the Army," "inducted into the Army," or "entered the Army." Of course, being drafted was not a one-day process. Typically, once a man's draft number was drawn, he, along with many others from his draft precinct, would be ordered to report to the draft board for a physical examination and interview to determine his eligibility to serve in the military. If he passed, he was later notified to get his affairs in order and to report back at a given date, along with many others from his draft precinct. At that time, the man was sworn in and officially inducted into the Army; he and his comrades were then sent to a training base to begin military service. But, in order to simplify the sketches, I have opted for the shorthand terms described above.

I have tried to document the military history of many of the men as thoroughly as possible. By showing each transfer of unit assignment, I hope to give some idea of the turbulence and confusion that could easily disrupt and confound any attempt at successful military training. For example, after many transfers—each of which might require varying amounts of time for transportation to another camp—a recruit might be sent overseas with only a minimum of actual, effective training.

I have described my approach to citations and sources in Appendix I; the reader would do well to consult the Appendix before reading the biographies. For well-known cities such as Chicago, and for cities such as Kenosha and Racine (both in Wisconsin), that occur frequently throughout the narrative, I have not identified the associated state. Also, to avoid repetition, I have not identified the state associated with each training camp except as they appear in individual biographies; a list of the commonly used camps appears below. The camps were technically cantonments, but were and are mostly referred to as "camps:" Camp Custer, Michigan; Camp Devens, Massachusetts; Camp Dix, New Jersey; Camp Dodge, Iowa; Camp Funston, Kansas; Camp Gordon, Georgia; Camp Grant, Illinois; Camp Greene, North Carolina; Camp Greenleaf, Georgia; Camp Humphreys, Virginia; Camp Jackson, South Carolina; Camp Johnston, Florida; Camp Kearny, California; Camp Lee, Virginia; Camp Lewis, Washington; Camp Logan, Texas; Camp MacArthur, Texas; Camp McClellan, Alabama; Camp Merritt, New Jersey; Camp Mills, New York; Camp Sevier, South Carolina; Camp Sherman, Ohio; Camp Stuart, Virginia; Camp Taylor, Kentucky; Camp Travis, Texas; Camp Upton, New York; Camp Wadsworth, South Carolina; and Camp Wheeler, Georgia.

Research Limitations

Historians and researchers are at the mercy of census takers and draft board clerks who wrote down names as they heard them. These are, of course, not always accurate; likewise, even correctly spelled names are sometimes incorrectly transcribed to databases and indices. However, most surnames appear properly recorded and transcribed. As stated above, I have, for the most part, spelled names as they appear on the original civil or military documents.

Because veteran status was shown on the 1930 U.S. census, it is an important source for finding men who were World War I veterans. Men who were killed in action or otherwise died before 1930, or those who went back to Italy soon after the war, will, of course, not appear in the 1930 census. I suspect that there are many men from Cosenza villages who fall into one of these categories, and their stories might be lost forever. If a man moved from his wartime state of residence before the 1930 census, tracking him in the census was more difficult. Likewise, men who changed their surnames from the common Cosenza names would be overlooked.[5] Also frustrating are the number of men who are identified as World War I veterans on the 1930 census but for whom no other service information could be found. In these cases, I have reluctantly opted to omit them from the list. Certainly some of them were, indeed, veterans.

Ultimately, I have no way of knowing exactly how complete this list is. There are certainly men who served who are not included here, but this book probably covers a major portion of the group.

Finally, it should be noted that a work of this size and scope involves often-complex research in an enormous variety of sources. It is inevitable that errors are present; I apologize for these and hope that they do not take away from the value of the historical record presented here. It is hoped that this work of military and social history will give due honor to not only these men, but also all immigrants who served in the U.S. military during the Great War.

1

Immigration Background

The so-called Great Migration from Italy to the United States, which lasted from the 1880s to the mid-1920s, saw as many as 4 million Italians come to the United States. This migration had a strong regional characteristic to it; groups of Calabrians, Sicilians, or Campanians journeyed together from their villages to America. The regional composition of the migration is based further on the phenomenon of "chain migration" whereby pioneers from given villages or areas started the migration and, in turn, provided the impetus and necessary support for others from their own area to come to America. Once started, these chains, based upon locale and kinship, branched and spread out to form a base of support for interrelated groups of immigrants. Thus, when studying Italian migration, it behooves us to examine the basic components, or "chains," from a given region. The southern Italian region of Calabria, the "toe" of the Italian boot, sent a great many immigrants to the United States. At the time, Calabria was divided into three provinces, each named after its provincial capital: Cosenza in the north, Catanzaro in the middle, and Reggio Calabria, in the south. With about 5,800 square miles of territory, the region's population was round 1,300,000 during the 1890s. The Province of Cosenza has supplied tens of thousands of immigrants to America since the mid-1800s. The history of migration from this area is a history of chain and kinship migration.

Immigration from the Province of Cosenza to the U.S. had been established by the 1870s. Francesco Principe and Luigi Spizzirri came to the U.S. from the area near the city of Cosenza in that decade (as early as 1872 in Spizzirri's case) and settled in Chicago, where they functioned as leaders among their compatriots, loaning money for steamship tickets, providing job guidance and boarding, etc. These men spurred immigration into Chicago from the Cosenza area.[1]

Most of the early Cosenza immigrants were men seeking jobs; these pioneer immigrants usually worked in the United States for a number of years and then returned to Italy. Typically, they would start a family and then return to the United States for more work. By the turn of the century, more women and children began to join their husbands in the United States. By the 1880s, many Cosenza immigrants were destined for Chicago; from there, they worked on railroads throughout the Midwest, Northwest, and West. But many immigrants stayed in the Chicago area, drawn by industrial jobs in cities such as Kenosha and Racine, Wisconsin, or by railroad jobs in Lake County, north of Chicago.[2] It is these Chicago-area men who are the subject of this book.

Others Cosenza immigrants settled in New York and Pennsylvania and in eastern cities that were experiencing growth in industries. Still others settled in the American West, usually working in railroad or mining jobs. Immigration from Italy in general, and Calabria in particular, slowed to a relative trickle during the war years, but it resumed shortly after the Armistice. Notably, in 1920, many of the men who had left the U.S. to serve in Italy's armed forces in 1915 returned to the U.S. to resume their lives here.

During the 1920s, many Cosenza-area immigrants returned to Italy. In many cases, men were returning to visit aged, ailing parents; in other cases, men were returning to bring their wife and children to the United States. When, as apparently happened quite frequently, men had to get to Italy quickly to visit sick family members, they often visited a local Italian consulate to obtain an Italian passport to allow them to travel to Italy. These men, who, in many cases, had become American citizens while in military service, then had to apply to an American consulate in Italy in order to obtain an American passport to enable them to return to the United States. The variety of letters and affidavits appended to applications paint a rather poignant picture of men who sought to visit their loved ones as quickly as they could.

A number of men returned to Italy to live soon after the war; some of these men had become American citizens while in the U.S. military. Often the U.S. State Department considered these men as having expatriated themselves, and in some cases, they stripped them of their U.S. citizenship.

Calabrian immigration to the United States continued at a trickle through the 1930s; by 1941, friends had become enemies, and Italian immigration to the U.S. ceased during World War II. After the war, Calabrian immigration resumed; families were reunited and new immigration chains, often to the old Calabrian colonies established during the preceding half-century, started. The Calabrian men who served in the U.S. military during World War I were not necessarily the pioneers of Calabrian immigration, but they came to the U.S. during the high tide of immigration, and they sustained close ties with the old country even after serving their beloved new county.

Some of the selected biographies that appear later in this book will illustrate the chain migration pattern and how it served to attract people to the U.S.; many of these immigrants would serve in the U.S. military during the war. Given the nature of immigration from the Cosenza area, it is not surprising that many brothers and cousins served in the military. There were at least eighteen pairs or sets of brothers and several cousins who served during the war: Frank and Silvio Aiello (Chicago), Bruno and Ippolito (also known as Filippo or Paul) Andrea (Kenosha), Fred and James Baratta (Chicago), Louis and Enrico Bruno (Chicago), Dominick and William Cara (Chicago), Beniamino and Louis Chiappetta (Kenosha), Sam and Mariano Conforti (Springfield, Illinois, and Chicago, respectively), Alessandro and Eugenio DeBartolo (Highwood, Illinois), Anthony, Charles, and Louis Desmonie (Kenosha), Fiore and Salvatore Docimo (Chicago), Eugenio and Serafino Ferraro (Kenosha), Antonio and Giuseppe Giorno (Kenosha), Eugenio and Salvatore Greco (Highwood), Alessandro and Salvatore Guido (Kenosha), Pasquale, Francesco, and Luigi Pellegrini (Chicago), Benjamin and James Potesta (Indiana Harbor, Indiana), Pietro and Serafino Ruffolo (Detroit and Kenosha, respectively), and Francesco and Pietro Spizzirri (Chicago). There were surely other pairs or sets of brothers among these men that research has yet to establish.

Furthermore, several sets of cousins also served. Eugenio Aiello and Pasquale Aiello (Racine and Kenosha) were cousins, and they, in turn, were distant cousins of Giuseppe Loizzo (Chicago). Brothers Beniamino and Louis Chiappetta were cousins of Bruno and Ippolito Andrea, and brothers Sam and Mariano Conforti were cousins of Luigi Santelli (Kenosha). Other cousins include Francesco Bartucci and Beniamino Caira (both from Chicago) and Frank Capparelli and Frank Sam Capparelli (both from Chicago). There were, of course, other sets of distant cousins who served. For example, no less than five descendants of Giuseppe Palermo and Carmina Spizzirri, both born in Marano Marchesato in the late 1700s, served during the war: Pasquale DeFranco, Antonio Giorno, Joseph Giorno, Francesco Loizzo, and Luigi Santelli.[3]

The Sons of the Pioneers

In many ways, the story of the immigration, settlement, and military service of these men can be illustrated by examining the story of some men who were born in the United States from immigrant parents. Their history demonstrates the chain migration prevalent during the period of heavy immigration from Calabria, from roughly the 1880s to the start of World War I. For example, many of the sons of pioneer immigrants to Chicago served during the war.

Three sons of Luigi Spizzirri, who has been discussed earlier and who was possibly the earliest immigrant to Chicago from the Cosenza area, served during the war. All three men were working as railroad clerks in Chicago when they entered the Army on the same day, June 24, 1918. Raymond "Ray" C. Spizzirri, born in Chicago in 1888, joined the Enlisted Medical Corps Reserve in 1917. After his entry on active duty in June 1918, he was assigned to the 70th Company, 18th Battalion, Infantry Replacement and Training Troops, probably at Camp Grant, Illinois. He was promoted to private first class during his service and was discharged at Camp Grant on January 10, 1919. Albert Anthony Spizzirri was born in Chicago in 1890. He served as a private in Company "B," 138th Engineer Regiment, a railroad construction unit at Fort Benjamin Harrison, near Indianapolis, Indiana. He was discharged on December 4, 1918. Frank Charles Spizzirri was born in Chicago in 1893. He served as a private in the 106th Ordnance Depot Company and was discharged on February 4, 1919.[4]

Carmine DeSimone, another early immigrant from the Cosenza area, arrived in Chicago in 1880. In 1887, DeSimone married Caterina Coia, and shortly thereafter they moved to Kenosha. Eventually, the DeSimone family was known for their many children. When Carmine died in June 1912, a Kenosha newspaper notice read: "Survived by a widow and 14 children, Carmen Desimone, the head of the biggest family in Kenosha, died at his residence here, death resulting from heart failure [*sic.*]."[5]

Three of the DeSimone's sons served during the war. By that time, the sons had begun spelling their surname "Desmonie." Louis "Louie" Desmonie was born in Kenosha in 1888; by June 1917, when he registered for the draft, Louie, a teamster, was "in custody of Deputy U.S. Marshal" in Omaha, Nebraska. Louie still listed Kenosha as his place of residence, and the circumstance of his detention are unknown. At some point, Louie was drafted into the Army. He was a private first class in Supply Company, 342nd Field Artillery Regiment, 89th

Division, when he boarded the *Justicia* with his regiment for shipment to France on June 28, 1918. As a teamster, his skills handling horses and mules probably came in very handy in the regimental supply company, as most of the supply wagons were animal-drawn. The 89th Division, which was made up initially of draftees from Missouri, Nebraska, and neighboring states, saw combat during the Meuse-Argonne Offensive, and it participated in the Army of Occupation of Germany after the war. By the time Louie returned to the United States on May 27, 1919, he had been demoted to private. He probably was discharged early in June.

Charles Joseph Desmonie was born in Kenosha in 1892. He was working for the city of Kenosha when he entered the Army on February 26, 1918. Charles was a private in Company "B," 318th Engineer Regiment, 6th Division, when he left for France on May 18, 1918. The 6th Division arrived in time to participate in the Meuse-Argonne Offensive. Charles returned to the United States and was discharged in June 1919.

Anthony Jerry Desmonie was born in Kenosha in 1898. Although precise information is not known, Anthony served in the Army during World War I and World War II.

Another brother, Joseph George Desmonie, born in Kenosha in 1900, served as a private in Battery "D," 16th Field Artillery Regiment, 4th Division, from March 1920 to March 1921. Joseph registered for the draft in Kenosha in September 1918, but it is possible he entered service just before the end of the war and reenlisted afterwards.

There were other native-born Americans of Calabrian ancestry who served in the U.S. military during the war. These are early examples of the immigration pattern in which wives joined their husbands in the United States after the men had established an economic base. Other American-born men who served include Fred Louis Baratta (born in Chicago in 1895); James D. Baratta (born in Chicago in 1893); Nicholas Benedetti (or Nicola Benedetto, born in Chicago in 1894); Eugene Joseph Chesrow (Cesario, born in Chicago in 1894); Emilio Cosentino (born in Chicago in 1896); Joseph Fucilla (born in Chicago in 1897); Antonio Giorno (born in Kenosha in 1895); Joseph Giorno (born in Kenosha in 1897); James Greco (born in Chicago in 1896); Robert D. Imbrogno (born in Hazelton, Pennsylvania, in 1891); Arthur Frank Lucchetti (born in Chicago in 1897); Michael Metagrano (born in Chicago in 1892); Michael Molinaro (born in Beach Park, Illinois, in 1896); Salvatore Morelli (born in Chicago in 1894); Benjamin E. Potesta (born in Chicago in 1899); James Potesta (born in Chicago in 1892); Sam Potesta (born in Chicago in 1897); Fred Ruffolo (born in Kenosha in 1897); Louis Raymond Ruffolo (born in Kenosha in 1894); Louis Joseph Ruffolo (born in Racine in 1900); Peter F. Serpe (born in Chicago in 1897); Anthony Francis Spizzirri (born in Chicago in 1895); Dominick J. Volpentesta (born in Chicago in 1890); and Frank L. Ziccarelli (born in Chicago in 1890).[6]

Examination of non-military aspects of these men's lives falls into the categories of immigration and social history. The data gleaned from records can give us a good idea of the general background of these men and the immigration cohort from the province of Cosenza during this period. For the following data, conflicting information sometimes exists. A man's occupation and residence, for example, might differ as reported on his draft registration and his statement of service card. This is due to the fact that during this time many men did change jobs and residences with some regularity. Indeed, several men moved to a different state after registering for the draft and before their induction. The data presented here is certainly an accurate overall picture. A careful reading of the individual biographies will reveal patterns of chain migration, settlement, and occupational attainments among these men and their families.

2

War and Military Service

When the world war erupted in August 1914, Italy was actually a part of the Triple Alliance with Germany and Austria-Hungary. However, Italy did not join in on the side of Germany because she felt that the war was not a defensive war on the part of Germany and Austria-Hungary, but rather that they were the aggressors. So Italy remained neutral while, at the same time, engaging in talks with France and England that would result in the promise of lost Italian territory being returned to Italy after the war. With this promise, Italy came into the war on the side of the Triple Entente (England, France, and Russia) on April 26, 1915. Soon some 90,000 Italian men left the United States and returned to Italy to fight in her armed forces. Among these were some men from the subject villages.[1]

The United States officially remained neutral until a series of provocations, including the resumption of unrestricted submarine warfare, and German duplicity in attempting to stir Mexico into war against the United States, prompted President Woodrow Wilson to ask Congress for a declaration of war on April 2, 1917. Congress granted the president's request on April 6.

After the declaration of war, one of Congress's first orders of business was to pass a military conscription law—the draft—to build the small U.S. Army to a size big enough to fight a modern was such as was being fought in Europe. On May 18, 1917, Congress passed the Selective Service Act. This allowed the president to call men to increase the size of the Army. The draft was administered locally, with 4,648 boards scattered throughout the country. By war's end, there had been three registration periods: the first, on June 5, 1917, was for all men between the ages of twenty-one and thirty-one; the second, on June 5, 1918, registered those who attained the age of twenty-one after June 5, 1917 (a supplemental registration was held on August 24, 1918, for those becoming twenty-one years old after June 5, 1918. This was considered a part of the second registration); and the third registration was held on September 12, 1918, for men aged eighteen through forty-five. Approximately 24 million men registered during these periods.[2]

In the meantime, President Wilson called up the National Guard, and these units, many of them only recently returned from their federal service on the Mexican border, began to assemble in the respective states. Following the initial draft registration, the actual calls for selected men to report for service commenced, with the first men reporting to their newly built (and in some cases still unfinished) training camps in early September 1917. The War Department called men throughout the war. The draftees, combined with voluntary enlistments and the federalization of the National Guard, resulted in an Army of more than 4 million men by November 1918.[3]

During the course of the U.S. involvement in the war, some 2 million men were sent to France, England, and Italy as part of the American Expeditionary Forces (A.E.F.). Other men went to North Russia or Siberia in an effort to aid pro-Allied forces in those areas. A detailed account of U.S. participation in the war is outside the scope of this work; what follows is an examination of the contribution of the Cosenza men from the Chicago area to the Allied victory.

An Analytical Overview of the Men Who Served

Of the 389 men recorded, 358 were born in the province of Cosenza, while thirty were born in the United States. The following Cosenza area villages are represented among all the men: Albidona (two), Alessandria del Carretto (two), Altomonte (four), Belsito (four), Bisignano (two), Carolei (seven), Carpanzano (one), Castiglione Cosentino (two), Castrolibero (eighteen), Castroregio (one), Celico (two) Cerisano (two), Cervicati (one), Corigliano Calabro (one), Cosenza (twenty-eight), Diamante (one), Dipignano (one), Domanico (one), Fagnano Castello (two), Falconara Albanese (six), Fiumefreddo Bruzio (three), Grimaldi (three), Lappano (nine), Lattarico (three), Longobardi (one), Longobucco (two), Luzzi (three), Malito (two), Malvito (one), Marano Marchesato (ninety-three), Marano Principato (thirty-six), Mongrassano (five), Montalto Uffugo (one), Panettieri (one), Paola (two), Paterno Calabro (two), Pedace (two), Piane Crati (five), Plataci (three), Rende (forty-three), Rogliano (three), Rose (four), Rota Greca (seventeen), Rovito (fourteen), San Fili (fourteen), San Giovanni in Fiore (two), San Lorenzo Bellizzi (three), Lucido (one), San Marco Argentano (three), San Pietro in Guarano (two), San Vincenzo la Costa (sixteen), Santa Caterina Albanese (one), Trenta (one), and Zumpano (one). The men born in the United States were born in the following locales: Beach Park, Illinois (one), Chicago (twenty-one), Kenosha (six), Hazelton, Pennsylvania (one), Racine (one), and unknown (one).

Of the men in this study, 380 served in the Army, eight served in the Navy, and one served in the Coast Guard. Most of the men who served in the Army were drafted, and all of the men who served in the Navy or Coast Guard enlisted voluntarily, as did the few men in the Students' Army Training Corps (S.A.T.C.).

As might be expected, the Cosentino men who served were all relatively young men. The oldest man, Frank Scola, was born on July 15, 1886; he was two months shy of this thirty-second birthday when he was drafted in May 1918. The youngest man, Silvio Aiello, was born on October 17, 1900; he was four months shy of his eighteenth birthday when he enlisted in the Navy in June 1918. The table below shows the year of birth for each of the men who served.

Birth Year	Number of Men
1886	6
1887	19
1888	26
1889	13
1890	25
1891	24
1892	40
1893	58
1894	47
1895	60
1896	33
1897	25
1898	4
1899	2
1900	3
Unk	3

Pre-War Service

At least seven Chicago-area Calabrians entered the U.S. military or National Guard prior to World War I. Below is a list of these men; more detailed biographies appear later in this book.

Damiano Candelise served from 1911 to 1913 in the 8th Infantry Regiment, including a tour of duty in the Philippines.

William Cara served in the Navy from 1914 until 1920.

Francesco Costabile served in the 2nd Cavalry Regiment from 1913 to 1915.

Andrea Morelli served in the Illinois National Guard from 1911 to 1916, including service on the Mexican border in 1916.

Pasquale Pellegrini served in the Illinois National Guard from 1911 to 1916, including service on the Mexican border in 1916.

Luigi Pellegrini served in the Illinois National Guard on the Mexican border in early 1917.

Frank Prete served in the Illinois National Guard in 1916, including service on the Mexican border.

Other men enlisted in the National Guard shortly after America's declaration of war and before the draft began. For example, three of the men from Kenosha enlisted in the Wisconsin National Guard in the five months between American entry into the war and the first draft call. Bruno Bombi, Dominick Parise, and Antonio Perrone all enlisted in Company "M," 4th Wisconsin Infantry Regiment, between June and August 1917 (Bombi on July 23, Parise on August 10, and Perrone on June 30). All were transferred to Battery "A," 121st Field Artillery Regiment, 32nd Division, and served overseas in combat. The 32nd Division was initially comprised of Wisconsin National Guard units.[4] Still others enlisted in the Regular Army in the spring and summer of 1917. For example, James Potesta enlisted in the Army on April 17, just eleven days after the declaration of war, and Frank DeRango enlisted on June 22. The last man to be inducted during the war was Fred Morrone, who reported for duty on November 6, 1918, only five days before the armistice. A close runner-up is Gennaro "Jean" Rizzo who entered the Army on November 5, 1918.

Entry into the Military

Dates of entry into military service are not available for all of the men; however, the table below shows that information for most of the men from Marano Marchesato and Marano Principato. Although only a sampling, this will give an idea of the general trend. It reflects the draft days when large numbers of men reported for duty.[5]

1917		
April: 0	July: 0	October: 4
May: 0	August: 1	November: 2
June: 2	September: 13	December: 2

1918			
January: 2	April: 11	July: 15	October: 8
February: 1	May: 30	August: 7	November: 1
March: 14	June: 9	September: 8	

A study of the dates of induction for draftees reveals that there were several big "draft days." The first increment reported to training camps in mid-September 1917, with others trickling in throughout the rest of the year. There were a few men who arrived at their camps in early September 1917; these men were the "first five percent" of the National Army to report. The men coming in mid-September were the "first fifty percent" to report. Together, these September men formed the training cadre for the new divisions. Officers, themselves in a mad rush to learn, stayed one step ahead of the September men. These men, in turn, helped train the follow-on men, and so on through the rest of 1917. March and April 1918 saw another batch of men inducted, and perhaps the largest group reported to their training camps in late May 1918. Other induction days followed, notably in late June, late July, September, and late October 1918.

It is interesting to note that as early as the draft registration day, men were under scrutiny in order to determine whether they were fit for service. The registration clerk had to annotate whether the man was missing a limb or was otherwise physically disabled. Once the man was notified that he had been drafted, he had to report to his local board for more questioning and a fairly thorough exam. Once accepted for service, he reported to his training camp where he was subjected to still more physical and psychological exams.

Despite such close examination, the sheer volume of men proceeding through induction centers meant that some men who should have been rejected for service

Pvt. Carmine Chiappetta (right) with his brother, Pasquale, at a stateside training camp, *c.* July 1918. (*Christine Chiappetta Thorsen*)

would fall through the cracks and be inducted. A few examples will suffice to illustrate the problem as it manifested itself among these men: Eugenio "James" Aceto who was inducted on August 26, 1918, and discharged at Camp Sherman, Ohio, only twelve days later; Aceto suffered from "Flaccid flat feet with abduction and eversion which existed prior to induction and was not incurred in line of duty."[6] Paul Tenuta served at Camp Taylor, Kentucky, for only eight days in July 1918 before being discharged for being under weight. Pietro Tenuta served from April 27 to May 10, 1918, before he, too, was discharged because of physical disability. Gaetano Presta served at Camp Taylor for only four days in August 1918 before he was discharged with a hernia. It should be noted that these examples are cited not to belittle any man's service. On the contrary, these men were called and reported for duty as required. Rather, as stated, they illustrate a problem that occurred nationwide during the war.

An examination of the military history of these men will reveal certain patterns. In addition to the draft or induction days, mentioned previously, one can discern certain geographical patterns to assignments. Men were assigned initially to the camp and unit nearest to their residence. Thus we find that groups of men traveled together to become part of a common unit, and they began training at the same time. Throughout 1917 and into most of 1918, the War Department transferred men from one unit/camp to another in order to fill the manpower requirements of units going overseas. This often appeared random and capricious; such transfers served to interrupt training and rupture unit cohesion. Again, one can discern a pattern whereby groups of men, sometimes in the thousands, were sent from their initially assigned camp and unit to another camp and unit; thus even the gaining units had pockets of men serving together who had come to the unit from an "outside" geographical location.

Most of the men in this study reported to a training camp near their home for initial training. For men from the Chicago area, the two most common training camps, especially for draftees in 1917 and early 1918, were Camp Custer, Michigan, and Camp Grant, Illinois. In the summer of 1918, some inductees reported to Camp Taylor, Kentucky, and Camp Sherman, Ohio, for training. Thus, at least initially, even National Army divisions had a regional characteristic to their personnel. But the transfer of men from camp to camp resulted in a dilution of whatever regional character a division may have had. Not even National Guard divisions were immune to this phenomenon, and men from other states began to salt the ranks of the 33rd (Illinois National Guard) Division, for example. Once a division went to France and saw combat, it received replacements from a variety of depot divisions; this further served to dilute regional characteristics. Even Regular Army divisions were, by war's end, "Regular" in name only.

At least 195 of the men in this study served overseas during the war, most of them in France, but at least three in England and six in Siberia. Most, if not all, of the rest of the men served stateside only. An examination of the types of service, both overseas and stateside, follows in subsequent chapters.

Most men were in more than one military unit during their time in service; the individual biographies reflect each transfer and unit, as far as possible, to give the reader an idea of the turbulence some men experienced as they entered the military.

An impromptu patriotic boxing match at a training camp, 1918. Some of these soldiers are Cosenza-area men from Kenosha. (*Theresa Van Landuyt*)

Types of Units

Cosenza-area men served in all types of units during the war: infantry regiments, artillery regiments, trench mortar batteries, machine-gun battalions, pioneer infantry regiments, engineer regiments, railroad construction regiments, transportation and truck companies, field hospitals, evacuation hospitals, base hospitals, supply depots, cavalry regiments, depot brigades, development battalions, limited service regiments, coast artillery batteries, veterinary units, ammunition trains, supply trains, replacement centers, recruit depots, U.S. Guards Battalions, training schools, aero squadrons, headquarters troops, bakery companies, and a butchery company are all represented here. In order to help the reader understand the structure of the Army as experienced by these men, a brief outline of World War I U.S. Army divisions and regiments follows.

A U.S. Army Division

The basic, self-contained fighting unit in the U.S. Army was the division. At this time, a division in the U.S. Army consisted of about 28,000 men, double the number of men found in divisions in Allied or German armies. The main combat component of the division was infantry; each division had two brigades of infantry, with two infantry regiments in each brigade. There was one artillery brigade in the division; in it were three artillery regiments, two of which were equipped with 75-mm cannons and one of which was equipped with larger, heavier 155-mm howitzers, and one trench mortar battery. The division also had one engineer regiment assigned to it, along with an engineer train that hauled engineer supplies for the regiment. Each division had three machine-gun battalions assigned, one to each infantry brigade and one to the division at large. The division sanitary train included four ambulance companies and four field hospitals. Other support units included a supply train, which consisted of animal-drawn wagons or motor trucks, an ammunition train to supply all elements of the division, military police troops, and signal troops. Smaller, attached units included ordnance repair shops, bath and laundry units, a bakery company, and veterinary troops to care for the many horses and mules assigned to a World War I division. The Headquarters Troop consisted of the division commander and his staff, including administrative personnel. The brigades each had similar headquarters troops.[7]

Upon arrival overseas, two or more divisions would be grouped into a corps (sometimes called an army corps). These corps were numbered (e.g., I Corps, III Corps) and their composition changed as divisions and other support units were transferred in to and out of them depending upon the tactical situation. Two or more corps were then assigned to an army. The 1st Army was formed, solely of American units, in August 1918; later, the 2nd and 3rd Armies would be formed.

A U.S. Army Infantry Regiment

Each infantry regiment consisted of twelve rifle companies divided into three battalions. The 1st Battalion consisted of Companies "A," "B," "C," and "D." The 2nd Battalion consisted of Companies "E," "F," "G," and "H." The 3rd Battalion consisted of Companies "I," "K," "L," and "M." Each company consisted of four platoons; each platoon had about fifty-eight men led by a lieutenant. The platoons each had several squads or sections, each one with a specialization: riflemen, auto-riflemen, rifle grenadiers, and hand bombers (grenade throwers). Each battalion had a small headquarters staff. There was also a Machine Gun Company and a Supply Company in each regiment. The Headquarters Company consisted of the regimental commander and his staff, along with support platoons. These platoons consisted of support troops that would be assigned to various regimental units during an assault; they included the signal, trench mortar, 37-mm (or 1-pounder) cannon, pioneer, personnel, intelligence, and mess platoons. During combat, the men in these platoons would perform their various functions in support of the regiment at large or would be assigned to the battalions as necessary. Also the regimental band was in Headquarters Company; during combat, these men often functioned as litter-bearers. A medical detachment rounded out each regiment. There were about 250 men in a rifle company, 1,000 in a battalion, and about 3,700 in a regiment.

Although the infantry regiment and the division were the backbone of U.S. Army fighting forces overseas, there was a plethora of types of units in the U.S. Army. Modern war required the use of large number of specialized troops and units, both stateside and overseas. Subsequent chapters give a brief look at the types of units in which some men served stateside.

Promotions and Rank

Enlisted men entered the Army with the rank of private, the lowest rank. If a private did a good job and followed orders, he might be promoted to the next level, private first class. A private first class had more responsibilities than a private, and they might be in a higher position such as auto-rifleman. The next step, promotion to corporal, brought the soldier into the ranks of the non-commissioned officers. A corporal had still more responsibilities, and, in an infantry regiment, he could be a squad leader in charge of six or eight men. Next came the rank of sergeant, and after that, sergeant major and battalion sergeant major. Higher than this were the officer ranks; these were reserved for college-educated men who would be leaders of platoons, companies, and battalions.

In addition, there were some specialist ranks that fell above private first class and below corporal. These required special skill and duty, such as bugler, musician, cook, mechanic, wagoner, and horseshoer. These titles were ranks as well as duty descriptions, and they carried with them extra pay and responsibilities. Most regiment-sized units had an assigned band made up of enlisted men who played various types of instruments. Bands performed at parades, and during other times, they provided entertainment to their own or nearby units. In combat, the men would often function as stretcher-bearers. Most company-sized units had at least one bugler assigned. The bugler would blow the various calls for whatever formation the commander desired the company to attend to. There were calls for meals, sick call, mail call, retreat, taps etc. Of course, the bugler was universally hated for blowing reveille to arouse sleeping soldiers at some unfortunate hour.

Rank information is known for 330 of the men who served in the Army. There was, as might be expected among a group of more than 380 mostly immigrant men, only one officer, First Lieutenant (Doctor) Eugene Joseph Chesrow (Cesario) of Graves Registration Service Unit 304. The rest of the men attained ranks that were probably typical for most foreign-born World War I soldiers: eight men attained the rank of battalion sergeant major, first sergeant, or sergeant; sixteen men held the rank of corporal; seven men were cooks; four were buglers; four men were musicians; and two men were mechanics. Fifty-four men attained the rank of private first class, and 235 men remained at the rank of private. Most of the rest of the men, for whom rank is not known, were probably privates, but there certainly could have been men among them who had attained higher rank. Below is a list of some non-commissioned officers:

Battalion Sergeant Major: Serafino Ruffolo, Army Service Corps, A.E.F.; and Frank L. Ziccarelli, Ambulance Company 344, 86th Division, A.E.F.

Sergeant First Class: Gilberto Loratto, Service Park Unit 515, Motor Transportation Corps, A.E.F.

Sergeant: Giacomo Bilotti, Machine Gun Troop, 311th Cavalry Regiment; Frank P. Prete, 122nd Field Artillery Regiment, 33rd Division, A.E.F.; Mike Salerno, Quartermaster Corps, A.E.F.; Gabriel Tarsitano, 4th Infantry Regiment, 3rd Division, A.E.F.; and Louis R. Rochetto, Detachment 8, Army Air Service.

Corporal: Enrico Bruno, 346th Infantry Regiment, 87th Division, A.E.F.; Ignazio Conforti, 9th Machine Gun Battalion, 3rd Division, A.E.F.; Emilio Cosentino, Motor Transport Company 318, A.E.F.; Frank A. Costabile, 34th Engineer Regiment, A.E.F.; Lawrence Covelli, 49th Infantry Regiment, 83rd Division, A.E.F.; Emilio Marrazzo, 18th Infantry Regiment, 1st Division, A.E.F.; Gaetano Miceli, 18th U.S. Guards Battalion; Frank Middono, 132nd Infantry Regiment, 33rd Division, A.E.F.; Giuseppe Misurelli, 3rd Battalion, Chemical Warfare Service; Clemente Morrone, Quartermaster Corps; Eugene Potente, Prisoner of War Escort Company 65, A.E.F.; James Potesta, 18th Infantry Regiment, 1st Division, A.E.F.; James Rocco Savaglio, 47th Infantry Regiment, 4th Division, A.E.F.; Anthony F. Spizzirri, 311th Supply Train, 86th Division, A.E.F.; Benedetto Turco, 42nd Machine Gun Battalion, 14th Division; and Mike Zicarelli, 312th Engineer Regiment, 86th Division, A.E.F.

Cook: Frank Aiello, Mechanical Repair Shop 301, Quartermaster Corps, A.E.F.; Joseph Alfano, 306th Motorcycle Company, A.E.F.; Joseph Bagnuola, 149th Field Artillery Regiment, 42nd Division, A.E.F.; Ferdinando Bartucci, 25th U.S. Guards Battalion; Salvatore Greco, 18th Infantry Regiment, 1st Division, A.E.F.; Joseph Ritacca, A.E.F. University; Giuseppe Stellato, Cook Company 7, Army Service Corps, A.E.F.

Bugler: Damiano Candelise, 56th Infantry Regiment, 7th Division, A.E.F.; Mariano Conforti, 5th Corps Artillery Park, A.E.F.; Louis Pellegrini, 130th Infantry Regiment, 33rd Division, A.E.F.; and Tom Scarpelli, Columbus Barracks, Ohio.

Musician: Frank Conforti, 124th Field Artillery Regiment, 33rd Division, A.E.F.; Vincenzo Conforti, Coast Artillery Corps, Fort Williams; Agostino Morelli, 27th Field Artillery Regiment, 9th Division; Vincent Presta, 340th Infantry Regiment, 85th Division, A.E.F.; and Emil Sicilia, 27th Field Artillery Regiment, 9th Division.

Mechanic: Salvatore Docimo, 103rd Engineer Regiment, 28th Division, A.E.F.; and Bartolo Scarpelli, 130th Infantry Regiment, 33rd Division, A.E.F.

Citizenship and the U.S. Military

The early years of the Italian migration can be described as the sojourner phase. The immigrants during this phase were primarily concerned with making enough money to live in Italy and better support themselves and their families; consequently, these men made several trips to the United States and each time obtained jobs that offered quick, temporary employment before returning to Italy. Few of these men sought to avail themselves of the benefits of United States citizenship. Later, as more men desired to remain in the U.S. and transplant or start families here, they began to formalize their status by becoming U.S. citizens. In order to do this, the prospective citizen appeared before one of any number of courts at any level of government to formally declare their intention to become a United States citizen. Then, after a minimum of five years, the declarant would appear before a judge to take the oath of allegiance to become a U.S. citizen. Thus the process of becoming a U.S. citizen required a minimum of five years of U.S. residency.

In May 1918, Congress passed a law waiving residency requirements for alien servicemen who wanted to become United States citizens. No longer would they have to appear in a court and file a declaration of intention and reside in the United States five years before taking the oath of allegiance. Now a serviceman was required to have two witnesses who could attest to the man's loyalty, and a certificate of naturalization would be issued after a mass oath of allegiance. When servicemen took advantage of this opportunity it was usually in a civilian court near their training or embarkation camp, and the witnesses were almost always fellow soldiers or even officers in their unit; dozens, perhaps hundreds of men would take the oath of allegiance at one time. Many Cosenza-area immigrants availed themselves of this important opportunity, as will be seen from the biographical listings.

There were not more than 339 men in this group who were eligible to become U.S. citizens when the law was passed in May. Of these, at least 191 men became naturalized U.S. citizens while in military service in 1918, 1919, or sometime after discharge, in some cases as late as the 1930s. This means a minimum of 56 percent of the eligible men took advantage of the law to more easily become a U.S. citizen. Most of the wartime naturalizations occurred from May to August. A large number of men became naturalized in June and July, often at Camp Merritt, where they paused in their transit from their training camps to the port of embarkation. The number decreased after that, with a spike in November as stateside men, about to be discharged, sought to take advantage of the law. More men were naturalized throughout 1919 as they returned from overseas. Interestingly, many men took advantage of the opportunity years later, presenting evidence of their military service in order to bypass the requirement to file a declaration of intention and instead proceed directly to a petition of naturalization. Many, if not most, of the men who were naturalized after the war used their war service in this manner, but the records omit inclusion of the appropriate documentation in many cases. Furthermore, it must be stressed that records for citizenship are not complete. On the 1920 and 1930 U.S. census lists, many of these men were recorded as being a naturalized citizen, but no other record could be found. Given the verifiable statistics, it is reasonable to assume that many of those men became naturalized citizens using their wartime service, perhaps more than 70 percent.[8]

A few of the men seem to have obtained citizenship twice, first during their military service and then again afterward. Filiberto Settino, for example, became a citizen at Camp Mills, New York, on July 30, 1918; he also underwent naturalization proceedings a year after discharge, on June 18, 1920, in Chicago. Ferdinando Chiappetta became a U.S. citizen while stationed at Camp Wadsworth, South Carolina, in August 1918 and then went through the process again in Chicago in 1924. It is possible that Luigi Santelli became a citizen during his military service and then repeated the process in Chicago in 1928. Interestingly, several men who used their military service to facilitate their attainment of U.S. citizenship lost that citizenship in the 1920s, 1930s, or 1940s because they returned to Italy and took up residence there.

One unusual example is Luigi Mandarino who obtained his citizenship while in the Army but then lost it when the U.S. State Department determined that he had moved back to Italy to live in 1947. Mandarino eventually returned to the U.S. and reapplied, obtaining U.S. citizenship again in 1953 (see Mandarino's entry in Chapter 6).

TO WHOM IT MAY CONCERN:

This is to certify that August Diego Buccierri, Seaman, enrolled in the United States Naval Reserve Force on August 6, 1918 at Chicago, Ill., reported for active duty on August 13, 1918 at the Naval Training Station, Great Lakes, Ill., and was honorably released from active duty on February 15, 1919 from the USS KEARSARGE.

(Signed) H. J. Fanning
H. J. Fanning
(NAVY DEPT.SEAL) Ensign, USN

Detail of a copy of an affidavit filed for August Buccieri's naturalization, Chicago, 1920, showing his service in the Navy during the war. U.S.S. *Kearsarge* sailed the eastern seaboard while training Armed Guard crews and Navy engineers during the war. (*Ancestry.com*)

ORIGINAL

UNITED STATES OF AMERICA No. 4554

PETITION FOR CITIZENSHIP

To the Honorable the Circuit Court of Kenosha County at Kenosha, Wis.

The petition of Emil Sicilia, hereby filed, respectfully shows:

(1) My place of residence is 2009 - 61st Street (2) My occupation is Laborer

(3) I was born in Rende, Italy on March 29, 1897 My race is S. Italian

(4) I declared my intention to become a citizen of the United States on Omitted pursuant to Act of May 25, 1932

~~Court of~~ ~~at~~

(5) I am not married. ~~The name of my wife or husband is~~ ~~we were married on~~ ~~at~~ ~~; he was born at~~ ~~on~~ ~~entered the United States at~~ ~~on~~ ~~for permanent residence therein, and now resides at~~ I have no children, ~~and the name, date, and place of birth, and place of residence of each of said children are as follows:~~

(Enlisted July 21, 1918. 1st.cl musician Battery G 27 F.A. Army Serial #3715473. Honorable Discharge Feb. 10, 1917.)

(6) My last foreign residence was Rende, Italy I emigrated to the United States of America from Naples, Italy My lawful entry for permanent residence in the United States was at New York, N.Y., under the name of Emil Sicilia on Nov. 16, 1921, on the vessel unknown ~~as shown by the certificate of my arrival attached hereto.~~

(7) I am not a disbeliever in or opposed to organized government or a member of or affiliated with any organization or body of persons teaching disbelief in or opposed to organized government. I am not a polygamist nor a believer in the practice of polygamy. I am attached to the principles of the Constitution of the United States and well disposed to the good order and happiness of the United States. It is my intention to become a citizen of the United States and to renounce absolutely and forever all allegiance and fidelity to any foreign prince, potentate, state, or sovereignty, and particularly to Victor Emmanuel III, King of Italy of whom (which) at this time I am a subject (or citizen), and it is my intention to reside permanently in the United States. (8) I am able to speak the English language. (9) I have resided continuously in the United States of America for the term of five years at least immediately preceding the date of this petition, to wit, since Nov. 16, 1921 and in the County of Kenosha this State, continuously next preceding the date of this petition, since Nov. 21, 1921, being a residence within said county of at least six months next preceding the date of this petition.

Emil Sicilia's Petition for Naturalization, dated 1932. Of interest is the fact that Sicilia's Declaration of Intention is "Omitted pursuant to the act of May 25, 1932." This was one of the several acts that modified the May 1918 act that permitted alien U.S. soldiers to apply directly for citizenship without first filing a Declaration of Intention. Even fourteen years after the war, as in Sicilia's case, men were still becoming U.S. citizens based upon their wartime service. In this case, the clerk erred in typing Sicilia's year of discharge, showing 1917 instead of the correct 1919. (*Area Research Center, University of Wisconsin, Parkside*)

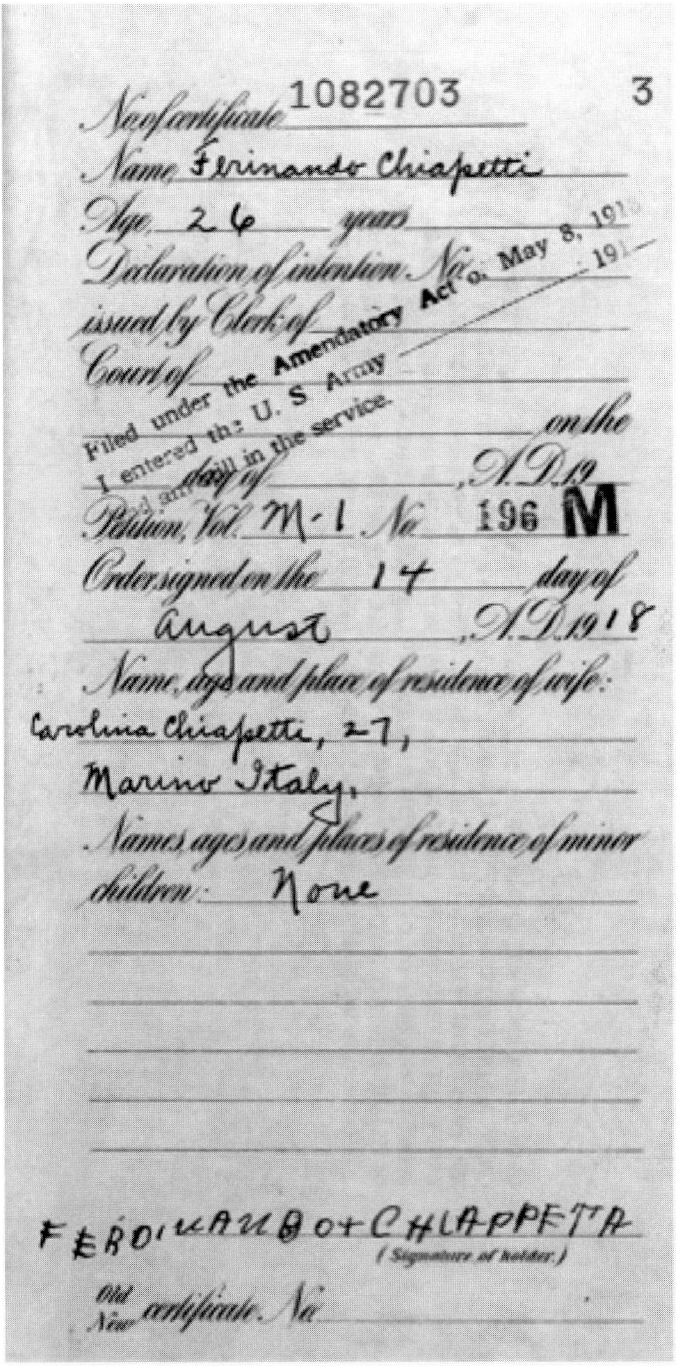

No. of certificate 1082703 3

Name Ferinando Chiapetti

Age 26 years

Declaration of intention No. Filed under the Amendatory Act of May 8, 1918

issued by Clerk of I entered the U. S Army

Court of and am still in the service.

on the day of , A.D. 19

Petition, Vol. M-1 No. 196 M

Order signed on the 14 day of

August , A.D. 1918

Name, age and place of residence of wife:

Carolina Chiapetti, 27,

Marino Italy.

Names, ages and places of residence of minor children: None

FERDINANDO CHIAPPETTA
(Signature of holder.)

Old / New certificate No.

Part of Pvt. Ferdinando Chiappetta's naturalization paperwork, Camp Jackson, 1918. (*National Archives via Ancestry.com*)

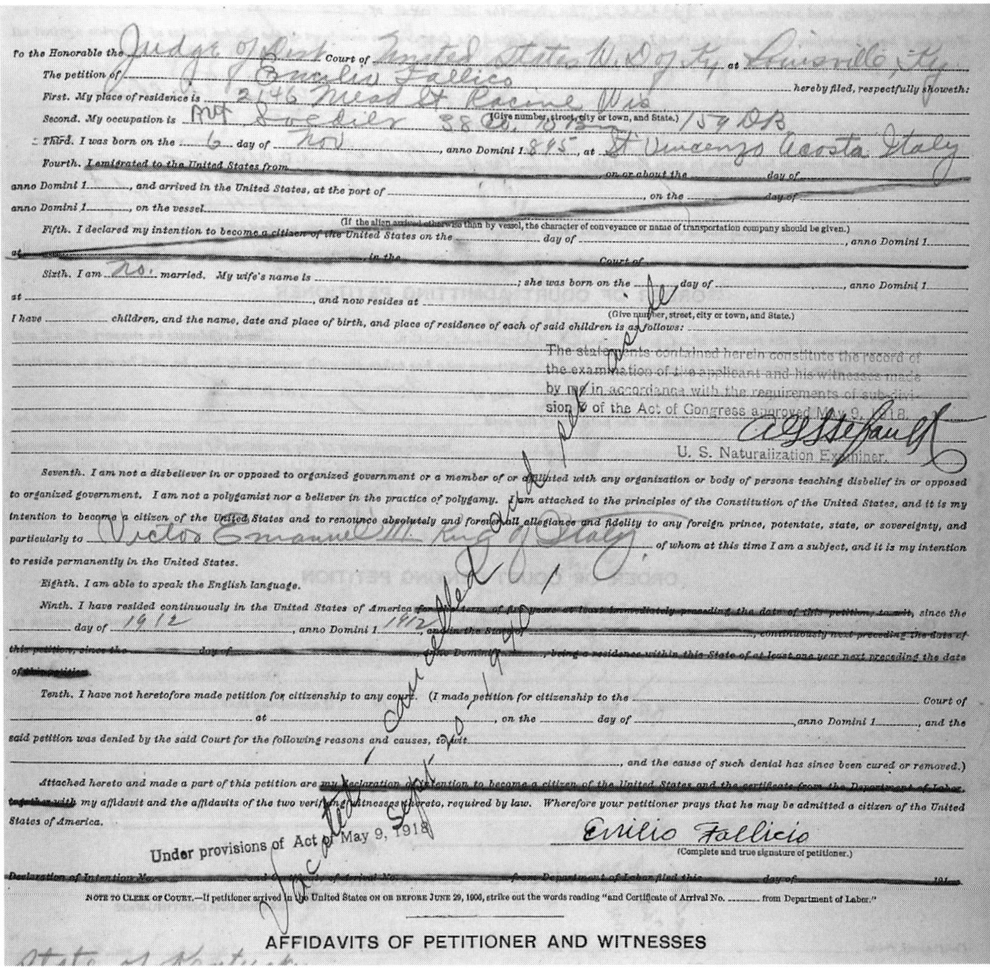

To the Honorable the Judge of Dist Court of United States W. D of Ky at Louisville, Ky

The petition of Emilio Fallico hereby filed, respectfully showeth:

First. My place of residence is 2146 Mead St Racine Wis (Give number, street, city or town, and State.)

Second. My occupation is Pvt Soldier 38 Co. ... 159 DB

Third. I was born on the 6 day of Nov, anno Domini 1895, at St Vincenzo Acosta Italy

Fourth. I emigrated to the United States from ..., on or about the ... day of ... anno Domini 1..., and arrived in the United States, at the port of ..., on the ... day of ... anno Domini 1..., on the vessel ...

(If the alien arrived otherwise than by vessel, the character of conveyance or name of transportation company should be given.)

Fifth. I declared my intention to become a citizen of the United States on the ... day of ..., anno Domini 1... at ... in the ... Court of ...

Sixth. I am no married. My wife's name is ...; she was born on the ... day of ..., anno Domini 1... at ..., and now resides at ... (Give number, street, city or town, and State.)

I have ... children, and the name, date and place of birth, and place of residence of each of said children is as follows:

The statements contained herein constitute the record of the examination of the applicant and his witnesses made by me in accordance with the requirements of subdivision 7 of the Act of Congress approved May 9, 1918.

U. S. Naturalization Examiner.

Seventh. I am not a disbeliever in or opposed to organized government or a member of or affiliated with any organization or body of persons teaching disbelief in or opposed to organized government. I am not a polygamist nor a believer in the practice of polygamy. I am attached to the principles of the Constitution of the United States, and it is my intention to become a citizen of the United States and to renounce absolutely and forever all allegiance and fidelity to any foreign prince, potentate, state, or sovereignty, and particularly to Victor Emmanuel III King of Italy, of whom at this time I am a subject, and it is my intention to reside permanently in the United States.

Eighth. I am able to speak the English language.

Ninth. I have resided continuously in the United States of America for the term of five years at least immediately preceding the date of this petition, to wit, since the ... day of 1912, anno Domini 1912, and in the State of ..., continuously next preceding the date of this petition, since the ... day of ..., anno Domini 1..., being a residence within this State of at least one year next preceding the date of this petition.

Tenth. I have not heretofore made petition for citizenship to any court. (I made petition for citizenship to the ... Court of ... at ..., on the ... day of ..., anno Domini 1..., and the said petition was denied by the said Court for the following reasons and causes, to wit: ..., and the cause of such denial has since been cured or removed.)

Attached hereto and made a part of this petition are my declaration of intention to become a citizen of the United States and the certificate from the Department of Labor, together with my affidavit and the affidavits of the two verifying witnesses thereto, required by law. Wherefore your petitioner prays that he may be admitted a citizen of the United States of America.

Under provisions of Act of May 9, 1918

Emilio Fallicio (Complete and true signature of petitioner.)

Declaration of Intention No. ... and Certificate of Arrival No. ... from Department of Labor filed this ... day of ... 191...

NOTE TO CLERK OF COURT.—If petitioner arrived in the United States on or before June 29, 1906, strike out the words reading "and Certificate of Arrival No. ... from Department of Labor."

Vacated cancelled and set aside Sept 20 1940

AFFIDAVITS OF PETITIONER AND WITNESSES

Pvt. Emilio Fallico's Petition for Naturalization, Camp Taylor, August 1918. The annotation, "Vacated—cancelled and set aside, Sept 20, 1940," refers to the court action that stripped Fallico of his U.S. citizenship because he had returned to Italy to live sometime after the war. (*Ancestry.com*)

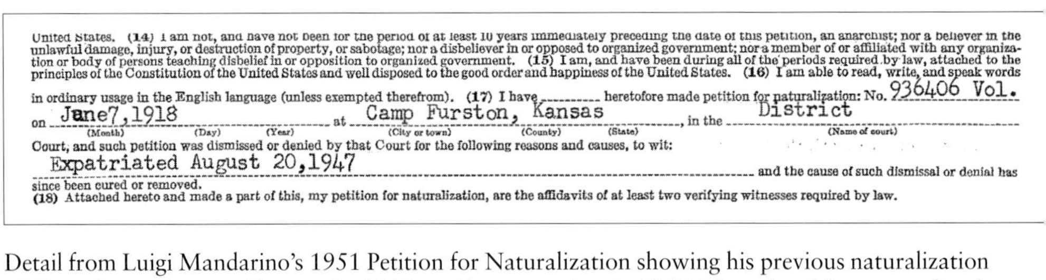

United States. (14) I am not, and have not been for the period of at least 10 years immediately preceding the date of this petition, an anarchist; nor a believer in the unlawful damage, injury, or destruction of property, or sabotage; nor a disbeliever in or opposed to organized government; nor a member of or affiliated with any organization or body of persons teaching disbelief in or opposition to organized government. (15) I am, and have been during all of the periods required by law, attached to the principles of the Constitution of the United States and well disposed to the good order and happiness of the United States. (16) I am able to read, write, and speak words in ordinary usage in the English language (unless exempted therefrom). (17) I have ... heretofore made petition for naturalization: No. 936406 Vol. on June7,1918 (Month) (Day) (Year) at Camp Furston, Kansas (City or town) (County) (State), in the District (Name of court) Court, and such petition was dismissed or denied by that Court for the following reasons and causes, to wit: Expatriated August 20,1947 and the cause of such dismissal or denial has since been cured or removed.

(18) Attached hereto and made a part of this, my petition for naturalization, are the affidavits of at least two verifying witnesses required by law.

Detail from Luigi Mandarino's 1951 Petition for Naturalization showing his previous naturalization while at Camp Funston, Kansas, in 1918, and its revocation in 1947. Note that "the cause of such dismissal or denial has since been cured or removed." Mandarino was granted U.S. citizenship again in 1953. (*Ancestry.com*)

Awards and Decorations

Distinguished Service Cross

The Distinguished Service Cross is the second highest U.S. military award for gallantry in action. It was first awarded in January 1918. Sergeant Frank Prete (122nd Field Artillery Regiment, 33rd Division) earned the D.S.C. (see Prete's entry in Chapter 6).

Silver Star

Men who were cited in higher headquarters special orders (division or brigade orders, for example) were authorized to wear a small Silver Star device affixed to the ribbon of their Victory Medal. Typically, such citations involved specific acts of heroism or gallantry in action. In 1932, Congress authorized the award of a separate Silver Star Medal to be awarded to those men who had been so cited. As with the Purple Heart, men would have had to apply for the Silver Star after 1932. Seven of these men are known to have earned a Silver Star citation: Luigi Barbieri (132nd Infantry Regiment, 33rd Division), Carmine Chiappetta (18th Infantry Regiment, 1st Division, Saint-Mihiel Offensive), Giuseppe Covelli (18th Infantry Regiment, 1st Division, Meuse-Argonne Offensive), Antonio Giorno (26th Infantry Regiment, 1st Division, Meuse-Argonne Offensive), George Imbrogno (16th Infantry Regiment, 1st Division, Soissons), Frank Muto (26th Infantry Regiment, 1st Division, Meuse-Argonne Offensive), and James Potesta (18th Infantry Regiment, 1st Division, Soissons). It is probable that some of the other men, especially those who served in infantry units in combat, earned a Silver Star citation, and it is hoped that those records will come to light.

Purple Heart

In 1932, Congress authorized the award of the Purple Heart Medal to those who had been wounded in action. Posthumous awards to next of kin were authorized later. The men would have had to apply for award of the Purple Heart sometime after 1932.

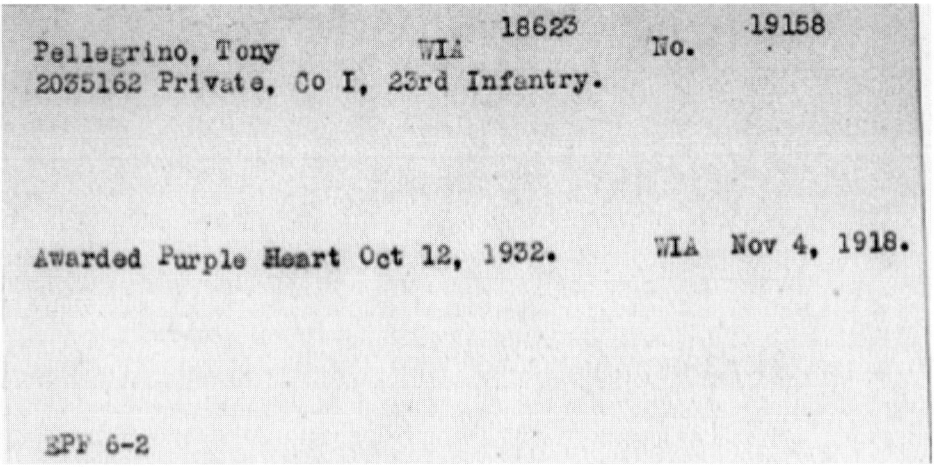

18623 19158
Pellegrino, Tony WIA No.
2035162 Private, Co I, 23rd Infantry.

Awarded Purple Heart Oct 12, 1932. WIA Nov 4, 1918.

BPF 6-2

Award card showing the award of the Purple Heart to Pvt. Tony Pellegrino, 23rd Infantry Regiment, 2nd Division. He was wounded in action on November 4, 1918, during his regiment's drive toward the Meuse River. (*National Archives*)

World War I Victory Medal and Clasps
All men and women who served in the United States military between April 6, 1917 and November 11, 1918 received the Victory Medal after the war. Those who left the continental United States also received recognition in the form of a small bronze star upon the ribbon bar, representing a clasp upon the ribbon of the actual medal. Men who served in combat were awarded battle clasps, each clasp bearing the name of a battle or campaign in which the recipient participated (for example, "Meuse-Argonne"). The "Defensive Sector" clasp was awarded to men who served in areas subject to enemy action during periods not covered by the other battle clasps. Those men who went overseas but did not see combat were awarded a service clasp designating the country in which they served (for example, "France" or "England"). Men who were awarded a battle clasp were not entitled to a service clasp.

Army of Occupation of Germany Medal
In 1941, Congress authorized the creation and award of the Army of Occupation of Germany Medal to those men who had served in that capacity anytime between 1918 and 1923.

Mexican Border Service Medal
On July 9, 1918, Congress created and authorized the Mexican Border Service Medal for those men who served on the border in 1916–1917. Another medal, the Mexican Service Medal, was authorized for service within the country of Mexico during this same period. Andrea Morelli, Charles Pellegrini, Louis Pellegrini, and Frank Prete served on the border with the Illinois National Guard. These men, and perhaps others, earned the Mexican Border Service Medal.

Post-War: Discharge and Reenlistment

Following the armistice on November 11, 1918, the A.E.F. began to disband. Although some units such as the 1st through 6th Divisions were destined to become part of the Army of Occupation in Germany, most units awaited their turn to return to the United States. Several of the Cosenza-area men were part of the Army of Occupation in Germany, but most men simply waited their turn to join the flow of men back to America. Those men who were most severely wounded returned ahead of their units; other men stayed with their units until discharge from the service. Of the combat veterans, Carmine Chiappetta and Giuseppe Covelli, both of whom were seriously wounded while serving in the 18th Infantry Regiment, 1st Division, returned home the earliest, in November and December 1918, respectively. Angelo Biscardi, who was seriously wounded while serving in the 4th Infantry Regiment, 3rd Division, Benjamin Potesta, who lost a leg while serving with the 7th Engineer Regiment, 5th Division, and Potesta's brother, James Potesta, who was wounded while serving with the 18th Infantry Regiment, 1st Division, also returned to the U.S. ahead of their units. Michael Metagrano was wounded while serving with the 47th Infantry Regiment, 4th Division, and returned home early. Louis Pellegrini, who was gassed while serving along the banks of the Meuse River with the 130th Infantry Regiment, 33rd Division, returned to the

Pasquale Chiappetta (left) greets his brother, Pvt. Carmine Chiappetta, at a stateside training camp, *c.* July 1918. Six months later, *c.* January 1919, the brothers strike a similar, more joyous pose when Carmine returned home after suffering a near-fatal wound and being declared killed in action. (*Christine Chiappetta Thorsen and Theresa Van Landuyt*)

U.S. before the rest of his regiment. The other men, including some who had been only slightly wounded, followed throughout the spring and summer of 1919, with the last combat soldiers, members of the 1st Division who were the last men to leave the Army of Occupation of Germany, returning to the U.S. in August 1919.[9] A few other men, in support roles, returned in the autumn of 1919, with Serafino Ruffolo, a battalion sergeant major in the Army Service Corps, being perhaps the last of these men to return from Europe in October 1919. Some of the men in the Siberian Expeditionary Forces returned to the U.S. in November 1919; these men were the last of this cohort to return to the U.S. and be discharged.[10]

Most of the men who were stationed in the U.S. were discharged within a few months after the end of the war. The first to be discharged were the recent draftees who were in training. Many men from the depot brigades and development battalions were discharged beginning in late November 1918; most were out of the service before the start of 1919. The men in the Students' Army Training Corps were all discharged by mid-December. Although the Army needed to retain men in the various training camps in order to facilitate the paperwork and other administrative requirements for discharging the almost two million men projected to return from Europe in the first half of 1919, most of the stateside men were out of the service by early spring 1919.

Some men reenlisted in the Army either immediately or shortly after their discharge. Luigi Baratta, Mariano Conforti, Frank Costabile, Lawrence Covelli, Sam Giordano, and Antonio Perrone each reenlisted shortly after their discharge (their biographies appear later in this book). In addition, Leopoldo Conforti and Anthony Jerry Desmonie reenlisted for service during World War II.

Not every man experienced success and happiness after the war. In those difficult times, men struggled to make ends meet, and others experienced physical and personal tragedy including an early death. In this regard, attention is called especially to the stories of Ferdinando Bartucci, Angelo Biscardi, Ignazio Conforti, Moris Costabile, and Benedetto Sicilia. Other men struggled with the physical effects of their wounds for the rest of their lives. This is documented for Carmine Chiappetta and Giuseppe Covelli, and it is probably true for some of the others; many men sought treatment in veterans' hospitals in the 1920s and 1930s. There is no gauging the psychological effects of military service and combat upon these men. This was a different era, when such things were not discussed; indeed, it was probably a rare man who privately sought medical treatment for such a condition.

3

Stateside Service

As the U.S. Army rapidly expanded from its somnolent peacetime size and state to its wartime size and state, the need for training camps was apparent. Thirty-two new camps were constructed beginning in August 1917. This was one of the most massive construction projects ever undertaken by the U.S. government. Each camp was to be regionally located so as to receive and train men from the various regions throughout the United States. Since the National Guard units had already had some degree of training, most of their camps were situated in the south, usually with tents rather than wooden buildings. It was presumed that these units would require less training and be in camp for a shorter period of time before departure for France. Furthermore, the southern location of these camps would allow for the use of tents instead of heated wooden buildings. Of course, in the actual event, things turned out differently; the fall and winter of 1917–1918 turned out to be unseasonably snowy, cold, and miserable throughout the south. Meanwhile, the men began to arrive at training camps while those camps were still under construction in most cases. Often the early draftees would be required to help clear land, haul lumber, and otherwise participate in construction activities, usually while still in civilian clothes.[1]

As stated above, the basic fighting unit in the Army was the division, and the U.S. had varying and changing plans as to the number of divisions she could raise, train, transport, and supply in the A.E.F. The divisions numbered from 1 through 20 were to be made up of Regular Army soldiers, men who were already on active duty when the U.S. entered the war, coupled with men entering service through subsequent voluntary enlistments. The National Guard divisions were numbered from 26 through 42; each of these divisions was comprised of a state's or a region's National Guard complement. The drafted men were slated to go into divisions numbering 76 through 100; these were to make up the National Army. In actual practice, these lines blurred and, in many cases, disappeared. Early in the training phase, men were transferred from one unit to another in what seemed to be a most capricious manner. Large drafts of men from the 86th Division (part of the National Army) were sent to the 85th Division (another National Army division) and to the 33rd Division (an Illinois National Guard division), for example. Once divisions were engaged in combat in France, they suffered casualties and received replacements from depot divisions without regard to the distinctions discussed above. At least 184 of these men served in stateside units only, including a few who served in the Navy stateside.

Depot Brigades

Most men who served in the U.S. Army during the Great War spent some of their early enlistment in a depot brigade. It was originally intended that a depot brigade would be assigned to each division; later, a single depot brigade was assigned to each camp or cantonment. The depot brigade functioned as an initial reception, processing, and training point for draftees and enlistees. From its personnel pool, drafts were made for filling the various units stationed at that particular camp. Often, as was the case with several men in this study, men would be initially assigned to a regular infantry regiment and spend time training with that regiment, only to be transferred to a depot brigade prior to the regiment's sailing for France. This usually resulted when the men in question were unable, for whatever reason, to attain the proficiency required for active front-line service.

By September 1918, the War Department further codified the duties of depot brigades in its Training Circular Number 23. According to the circular, the functions of depot brigades were as follows:

> (a) Receiving depots involving the issue of clothing and equipment, physical examination involving the segregation of the physically unfit, and the assignment of the men to training battalions.
>
> NOTE—Preparation of preliminary records and occupational classification of the men is conducted by the camp headquarters, personnel office.
>
> (b) The organization of development battalions for the rehabilitation of all men who, for any reason, are not immediately fit for full military duty.
>
> (c) The separation and organization of all skilled men and their careful allotment under orders from the War Department.
>
> (d) The assignment, distribution and shipping of men to organizations under orders from the War Department.
>
> (e) Incidentally the providing of efficient basic training for the recruit, suitable and proportional to the length of time he is retained in the depot brigade.[2]

Some spent their entire time in a depot brigade. These men performed unpopular and unsung service. A list of depot brigades and their location follows: 53rd, Camp Hancock, Georgia; 57th, Camp MacArthur, Texas; 151st, Camp Devens, Massachusetts; 152nd, Camp Upton, New York; 153rd, Camp Dix, New Jersey; 154th, Camp Meade, Maryland; 155th, Camp Lee, Virginia; 156th, Camp Jackson, South Carolina; 157th, Camp Gordon, Georgia; 158th, Camp Sherman, Ohio; 159th, Camp Taylor, Kentucky; 160th, Camp Custer, Michigan; 161st, Camp Grant, Illinois; 162nd, Camp Pike, Arkansas; 163rd, Camp Dodge, Iowa; 164th, Camp Funston, Kansas; 165th, Camp Travis, Texas; 166th, Camp Lewis, Washington; 167th, Camp McClellan, Alabama.

A Cosenza-area soldier enjoys a brief smoke break at his training camp, 1918. (*Theresa Van Landuyt*)

At least forty-seven men in this study spent most or all their time in the service in a depot brigade. Probably several more did so, at least for some of their time in service, and some of these men were in development battalions (see below) within depot brigades. A breakdown of their distribution reflects the regional character of the draft calls and formation of the National Army divisions. Eighteen men each were at Camp Grant and Camp Taylor, two each at Camps Custer and Sherman, and one each at Camps Devens, Dodge, Gordon, Hancock, Jackson, MacArthur, and Travis.

Development Battalions

With so many men entering military service, it was inevitable that some men would be below acceptable physical or mental standards to be a soldier. Such men, ideally, would be screened and "weeded out" during the draft registration or induction process. But some men slipped through the cracks. Thousands of men were physically unfit and many more could not speak or understand English well enough to function as an American soldier. With this in mind, the War Department, perhaps belatedly, devised military units to accommodate such men, with the first "development battalions" being formed at training camps across the U.S. in May 1918. Many of these men no doubt had trouble with the English language; although perhaps willing to serve in combat, their lack of understanding hampered their ability to perform well enough to function in a combat unit. They spent their term of service in these development battalions drilling, reading, learning, and attending lectures, all in an effort to make them better soldiers. At least twelve men in this study spent their service time in development battalions, three men at Camp Grant, two men each at Camps Gordon and Taylor, one man each at Camps Jackson, Logan, and Shelby, and two men at unknown camps. Many of the men recorded as serving in depot brigades probably spent most, if not all of their time in a development battalion.

Without more complete service records, it is difficult to evaluate the efficacy of development battalions for these men. Certainly some men moved from development battalions to other units during their service. For example, Giuseppe Salvatore Loizzo went from a development battalion to an infantry replacement regiment at Camp Logan, Texas; Clemente Morrone served in a development battalion before being sent to a quartermaster unit at Camp Knox, Kentucky, where he was promoted to corporal;

Soldiers enjoying a break from training, 1918. (*Theresa Van Landuyt*)

and Beniamino Chiappetta served in a United States Guards battalion after a stint in a development battalion. Surely there were others, and it is not known how many development battalion *alumni* were able to serve overseas in any capacity. Since the development battalions were formed only in early 1918, and given the challenge of training vast numbers of foreign language-speaking men, it is perhaps no surprise that more men did not make the transition from development battalion to overseas service.

Newly Forming Divisions

The War Department sent forty-two complete divisions and elements of three others overseas before the end of the war.[3] Stateside, the War Department was still drafting and training men and forming divisions at the war's end. Sixteen divisions were in various stages of training in preparation to being sent overseas; some of these were Regular Army divisions, made up of volunteers and draftees, and some were National Army divisions, made up of draftees. Among the men in this book there were several who served in one of these newly forming divisions. Men and units represented include:

Pasquale DeFranco, Salvatore Presta, and Frank Ruffolo, 9th Trench Mortar Battery, 9th Division, Camp McClellan, Alabama.

Francesco Marrazzo, Agostino Morelli, Giuseppe Salerno, and Emil Sicilia, 27th Field Artillery Regiment, 9th Division, Camp McClellan, Alabama.

Rocco Valente, 46th Infantry Regiment, 9th Division, Camp McClellan, Alabama.

Salvatore (Sam) Aiello, 41st Infantry Regiment, 10th Division, Camp Funston, Kansas.

Antonio Aceto, Field Hospital 246, 12th Sanitary Train, 12th Division, Camp Devens, Massachusetts.

Eugenio (James) Aiello, 38th Machine Gun Battalion, 13th Division, Camp Lewis, Washington.

Benedetto Turco, 42nd Machine Gun Battalion, 14th Division, Camp Custer, Michigan.

James Mazzuca, 80th Infantry Regiment, 15th Division, Camp Logan, Texas.

Luigi Ruffolo, 21st Infantry Regiment, 16th Division, Camp Kearny, California.

Mike Frank Arnone and Joseph Greco, 19th Infantry Regiment, 18th Division, Camp Travis, Texas.

Filippo Gammuto, 48th Infantry Regiment, 20th Division, Camp Sevier, South Carolina.

Pasquale Morelli, 67th Field Artillery Regiment, 95th Division, Camp Taylor, Kentucky.

Giuseppe Ricchio and John Trotta, 66th Field Artillery Regiment, 96th Division, Camp Kearny, California.

A look at the 9th Trench Mortar Battery of the 9th Division will reveal the regional characteristic of even Regular Army units forming late in the war. The drafts of men in late July 1918 netted perhaps hundreds of men from southeast Wisconsin, including Milwaukee, Racine, and Kenosha. These men were sent to Camp Taylor, Kentucky, for initial training, and many of them were afterwards sent to Camp McClellan, Alabama, to become part of the newly forming 9th Trench Mortar Battery, part of the 9th Division. Although the 9th Division was technically a Regular Army division, it received a large influx of drafted men. By the time of the Armistice, the 9th had completed training and was preparing to depart for France; in fact, the advanced school detachment had already departed for the port of embarkation. In early 1919, the 9th Division was disbanded.[4]

In addition to having a regional flavor, the 9th Trench Mortar Battery had a large number of foreign-born men in its ranks. Twenty-seven of the twenty-eight men sent from Kenosha were foreign-born; sixteen of these were Italian, five were Russian, two were Lithuanian-Russian, one was Lithuanian, one was Russian-Polish, one was Armenian, and one was Dutch. Only two of the fourteen men from Milwaukee were foreign-born, one each from Russia and Belgium. The man from Belgium soon was commissioned as a first lieutenant. Thus, out of the men from southeastern Wisconsin, at least twenty-eight were foreign-born. When one considers that, at this time, a trench mortar battery consisted of approximately 170 enlisted men, one can see that this particular unit would have had a fair percentage of foreign-born soldiers. At least twenty-three of the foreign-born men from Kenosha became U.S. citizens at Camp Taylor, in August 1918, just prior to transferring to Camp McClellan to join the 9th Trench Mortar Battery. One, and probably both, of the foreign-born Milwaukee men were already naturalized citizens.

Unattached Infantry, Artillery, and Cavalry Units

In addition, there were numerous unattached infantry, artillery, and cavalry units, especially in the Southwest and West, which were associated with defense of the mainland. Infantry regiments and cavalry troops still patrolled areas of the U.S.–Mexican border and other areas stateside during the war. These units were never made a part of divisions for the purpose of going overseas to join the A.E.F. in combat. Some men assigned to these units might have felt the disappointment common among those men who served stateside, ready, willing, and able to go overseas to do their part but who were denied that opportunity.

Among the men in these regiments were Antonio L. Bianco, 302nd Cavalry Regiment, Camp Harry J. Jones, Arizona; Giacomo Bilotti, Machine Gun Troop, 311th Cavalry Regiment, Fort Riley, Kansas; Eugenio DeBartolo, 14th Infantry Regiment, Washington and Montana; Frank Nino, 17th Cavalry Regiment, Camp Harry J. Jones, Arizona; and Peter Spizzirri, 3rd Infantry Regiment, Camp Eagle Pass, Texas.

Coast Artillery

Coastal defense has always been an important part of U.S. military policy. During World War I, there were still many coastal forts that contained batteries of guns capable of fending off foreign warships.

Men who served in Coast Artillery units stateside during the war include Vincenzo Conforti, Fort Williams, Maine; Eugenio Rossi, Portland, Maine; and Giuseppe Savaglio, New Orleans, Louisiana.

Training and Replacement Units, Automatic Replacement Drafts

In addition to depot brigades and development battalions, there were many other training and replacement-type units to which men could be assigned. Most common were the engineer training regiments at Camp Humphreys, Virginia, or one of the many infantry replacement and training units at various stateside camps. The War Department tended to group men who were being slated for duty as replacements together by month; many men went overseas as part of the "August Automatic Replacement Draft" for a given camp, for example. Upon arrival in France, such men were sent to one of the depot divisions (see Chapter 4) where they were processed, equipped, and trained; from there, they were eventually sent to a combat unit as a replacement. Many of the men who were drafted late in the war were assigned to one of these automatic replacement drafts at war's end; many of them ended their service as part of the November Automatic Replacement Draft (N.A.R.D.).

Men were assigned to a variety of training and discharge units at war's end, including Eugene Belmonte, 2nd Recruit Battalion, Camp Forrest, Georgia; Ralph Cairo, N.A.R.D.; Leopold Conforti, N.A.R.D.; John DeBartolo, 1st Recruit Battalion, Camp Forrest, Georgia; Giuseppe Giorno, Recruit Depot, Camp Shelby, Mississippi; Fred Morrone, 2nd Recruit Battalion, Camp Forrest, Georgia; Gasparo Ritacca, N.A.R.D.; and Luigi Savalio, N.A.R.D.

U.S. Guards Battalions

The U.S. Guards were established by the War Department on December 22, 1917, and eventually consisted of forty-eight battalions of soldiers whose duty was to guard various installations deemed essential to the defense of the United States. The men in these battalions were mostly those who were over age or otherwise deemed unfit for more active military service. The battalions guarded military and key infrastructure installations.

At least eight men served in U.S. Guards Battalions: Francesco Amadeo, Company "B," 25th U.S. Guards Battalion, at Long Beach, California; Ferdinando Bartucci, Company "D," 25th U.S. Guards Battalion, Camp Taliaferro, California; Frank Sam Capparelli, 3rd U.S. Guards Battalion, Allston, Massachusetts; Giovanni Caputo, 22nd U.S. Guards Battalion, Camp Stanley, Texas (temporarily); Beniamino Chiappetta, Company "A," 46th U.S. Guards Battalion, at Camp Funston, Kansas; Gaetano Miceli, Company "D," 18th U.S. Guards Battalion, at Fort Brady, Michigan; Angelo Naccarato, Company "A," 19th U.S. Guards Battalion, at Orange, Texas; and Francesco Spallato, Company "D," 20th U.S. Guards Battalion, at Fort Sam Houston, Texas.

Students' Army Training Corps

The members of the Students' Army Training Corps (S.A.T.C.) were college students who had enlisted in the Army and were allowed to continue their schooling. They took their normal academic courses while at the same time taking military training, including military drill and radio maintenance and use. Three men were in S.A.T.C. units: Joseph Fucilla (born in Chicago in 1897), University of Wisconsin, Madison; Rudolph Eugene Monaco (born in Paola, Calabria, in 1899), University of Chicago; and Fred Ruffolo (born in Kenosha in 1897), University of Wisconsin, Madison. All three men enlisted in October 1918 and were discharged by the end of the year. Monaco became a U.S. citizen while in the S.A.T.C. on November 9, 1918.[5]

U.S. Army Air Service

The U.S. Army Air Service was the forerunner of the Army Air Corps, Army Air Forces, and, finally, the U.S. Air Force. Air Service units served in the U.S., England, France, and Italy during the war. There were flying squadrons, support squadrons, repair squadrons, construction companies, and other types of units.

At least two men served in Air Service units stateside: Albert Bonaretti (25th Construction Company, Henry J. Damm Field, New York) and Louis Rochetto (Detachment 8, U.S. Army Air Service, in Chicago).

Miscellaneous

The stateside military needed personnel to man their supply depots, embarkation centers, and arsenals. There were, of course, hospitals in all major military camps in addition to separate regional hospitals. Most camps had Guard and Fire Companies to protect government personnel and property.

Some of the men who supported the vast wartime Army in unheralded stateside units include Francesco Gaudio, 809th Motor Transport Company; Giuseppe Misurelli, 3rd Battalion, Chemical Warfare Service, Edgewood Arsenal, Maryland; Michael Molinaro, 6th Ordnance Supply Company; Clemente Morrone, Quartermaster Corps, Camp Henry Knox, Kentucky; Giuseppe Napolitano, School for Bakers and Cooks, Camp Gordon, Georgia; Carmine Noto, Guard and Fire Company 336; Albert Anthony Spizzirri, 138th Engineer Regiment (Railway Construction); Frank Spizzirri, Guard and Fire Company 317, Camp Hill, Virginia; and Frank Charles Spizzirri, 106th Ordnance Depot Company.

The Army had to find places for a great number of men who, while not fit for active duty at the front, were still capable of performing work of a military nature and thereby freeing up more fit men for other duties. The United States Guards battalions were mentioned above; men serving in other units in this category included Angelo Carnevale, 5th Limited Services Regiment, and Julian Terranova, Provisional Labor Company, Camp Grant.

Pvt. James Aiello, 38th Machine Gun Battalion, 13th Division, Fort Lewis, Washington, 1918. The silver chevron on Aiello's lower left sleeve indicates he has served at least six months in the United States during the war. Men serving overseas earned a gold chevron for every six months overseas; a single blue chevron indicated less than six months overseas. (*Frank Aiello family*)

4

Overseas Service

In addition to troops stationed stateside, the U.S. Army during the war had men stationed at camps and in the Caribbean, Alaska, Hawaii, and the Philippines. The A.E.F. consisted of troops in France, Belgium, England, and Italy. Later in the war, the U.S. sent forces into North Russia and Siberia. At least 195 of these men went overseas during the war. The date of departure from the U.S. is not known for each man who served overseas, so it is not known who left the U.S. first. That honor should probably go to Pvt. James Potesta, who, as a member of the 18th Infantry Regiment, 1st Division, left the U.S. on June 14, 1917. The 1st Division was the first combat unit sent to France from the United States. Another early departure was Cook Joseph Bagnuola, 149th Field Artillery Regiment, 42nd Division, who shipped out on October 18, 1917. The 42nd Division, made up of National Guard units from twenty-six different states, was one of the first National Guard divisions to arrive in France. The last person to ship out during the war was probably Pvt. Ralph Gentile, who left the U.S. with a field artillery replacement detachment on October 27, 1918; Pvt. Ernest Savalio, 130th Engineer Regiment, who left the U.S. on October 20, is a close runner-up.[1] Private James Baratta left the U.S. two days after the Armistice, on November 13, 1918, as part of Mobile Hospital Unit 102. Most of the rest of the men left the U.S. during the spring, summer, and early fall of 1918.

The American Expeditionary Forces, eventually consisting of about 2 million men, required a vast array of different types of units to function. In addition to the well-known roles of infantry, artillery, and engineers, soldiers performed a bewildering variety of duties in support units. A brief survey of different types of units would include railroad operating and maintenance, water supply, quarry, forestry, refrigeration, laundry and bath, telegraph, butchery, bakery, commissary, supply, veterinary, labor, ordnance repair, and truck units. Soldiers in these units usually served well behind the lines and labored in relative obscurity, day in and day out. Although they and their deeds were unsung, the Allies could not have achieved victory without them.

Cpl. James Potesta, 18th Infantry Regiment, 1st Division. (*Robert R. Porcaro*)

Infantry and Machine-Gun Units

Central to the success of the A.E.F. were the combat units—infantry and artillery—and many of these men served in these units overseas. In war, it is the infantryman who bears the brunt of battle. It is he who must close with the enemy and kill him or force him to flee or surrender. It is he who experiences more than others the misery, terror, filth, and dangers of combat. It is these men who took the fight to the enemy; these were the Doughboys who faced the German machine guns, artillery, poison gas, and rifles; these were the men who suffered the life-changing wounds.

About eighty-five of these men served in forty-three different infantry regiments overseas during the war. Most of them were infantrymen in rifle companies, while others were in machine-gun, headquarters, or supply companies. They served in a variety of Regular Army, National Army, and National Guard divisions (see Summary of Men in Divisions, pp. 56–57).

Men who arrived as replacements in August 1918 had the unenviable duty to assimilate into a close-knit unit of men who had gone through dreadful combat and had suffered losses. When one considers the probable language difficulty that some of the men may have experienced, one can get a feel for the precarious situation facing these men as they approached their first combat experience. The men sent as replacements became, for the most part, members of hard-fighting, tough infantry regiments. The perils of combat are reflected in the fact that eight men assigned to infantry or machine-gun units were killed in action or died of wounds received in action (see Chapter 5).

At least eighteen of these men were wounded or gassed in action. It is possible that others suffered minor wounds or gassing that was not reported to medical personnel. Indeed, probably most men who served in the front lines for any length of time were exposed to gas to some degree. Some of them probably suffered from the effects of this exposure for the rest of their lives. However, if they never reported this, or if they never went to the hospital because of their exposure, they would not be counted as among the wounded/gassed soldiers and would therefore not be awarded a wound chevron to wear on their right sleeve or, later, the Purple Heart Medal. The names and units of those men who were wounded in action appear at the end of this chapter.

General Headquarters had planned for a three-month training period for American divisions. One month would be spent under the tutelage of veteran French or British instructors; during the next month, the units of the division would take turns occupying portions of a "quiet sector," again with French or British units; and during the third month, the American division would occupy a quiet sector on its own. The few Regular Army and National Guard divisions that arrived in France in 1917 and early 1918 received roughly this type of training; National Army divisions (those raised by the draft) arriving in France in the summer of 1918 received nowhere near this type of training.[2] As will be seen by some of the entries below, many draftees in the spring and summer of 1918 were rushed into the front lines. Typically, a man was drafted in late May; by mid-June, he would have been transferred from his initial training and induction unit to a combat division forming for deployment to France; by late July, he would have departed the U.S.; by early August, he would have arrived as part of a depot division; and, finally, by mid- to late August, he would have been assigned as a replacement to a combat unit that had been depleted in strength due to recent casualties.

Thus, after barely three months in service, and with probably the barest minimum of effective training, men were thrust into units preparing for major battle; most of these men would see combat by mid-September after not quite four months in service. The men who arrived in August had to adapt and adjust to the front lines and trenches with minimal training. They were forced to become a part of a combat unit that had, in most cases, already been through the crucible of battle and had formed a cohesion based upon that common ordeal. They had to fit in to a group that would have been naturally wary of "outsiders;" perhaps some men who had difficulty with the English language suffered even more as they tried to blend in and assimilate into a close-knit group.[3]

Artillery Units

Field artillery regiments were normally equipped with 75-mm or 155-mm guns and were assigned to divisions, corps, or armies in the field. As such, they supported infantry assaults throughout France. In addition to the artillery units assigned to each division, there were also artillery units assigned to each corps and army. These units would be used at the corps or army commander's discretion to support his units as needed during an assault. There were also Coast Artillery Corps units overseas during the war. These units were equipped with a variety of types of guns. Some had 155-mm guns; some had larger caliber guns, including 8-inch and 9.2-inch howitzers. Associated with artillery units were artillery parks. An artillery park maintained a stock of artillery ammunition for supply to the advancing units; the park moved forward as the army units advanced. The artillery park also maintained spare guns and performed some repairs.

Engineer and Pioneer Infantry Units

Engineer regiments performed such diverse duties as railroad construction, railroad operation, forestry, water supply, and general maintenance. Engineer regiments that were assigned to divisions normally functioned as modern-day combat engineers. They dug trenches, built and maintained roads, and often manned front-line trenches. Sometimes they accompanied infantry assault waves with Bangalore torpedoes—long metal poles equipped with explosives that were used to breach enemy barbed wire. In some cases, they functioned as infantry.

Men who served in divisional engineer units overseas were Giuseppe Beltrano, 305th Engineer Regiment, 80th Division; Frank Conforti, 101st Engineer Regiment, 26th Division; Charles Joseph Desmonie, 318th Engineer Regiment, 6th Division; Salvatore A. Docimo, 103rd Engineer Regiment, 28th Division; Raffaele Estabelle, 1st Engineer Regiment, 1st Division; Luigi Misasi, 103rd Engineer Regiment, 28th Division; Benjamin E. Potesta, 7th Engineer Regiment, 5th Division; Giuseppe Santelli, 103rd Engineer Regiment, 28th Division; Alfonso Segreti, 4th Engineer Regiment, 4th Division; and Mike Zicarelli, 312th Engineer Regiment, 87th Division.

Men who served in specialist engineer units overseas include Raffaele Aceto, 22nd Engineer Regiment (light railway construction); Nick Peter Algieri, 32nd Engineer Regiment (standard gauge railway construction); Pasquale Carpino, 504th Engineer

Battalion (engineer service battalion); Frank Cicero, 20th Engineer Regiment (forestry); Frank Costabile, 34th Engineer Regiment (supply and shop regiment); Paul Maro, 603rd Engineer Regiment (sappers); Ernest Savalio, 130th Engineer Battalion (general construction battalion); Pietro Francesco Spina, 137th Engineer Battalion (electrical and mechanical battalion); and Giuseppe Tucci, 20th Engineer Regiment (forestry).

Some men were assigned to pioneer infantry regiments. During World War I, pioneer infantry regiments were supposed to serve in much the same capacity as combat engineer units in later wars. Ostensibly trained as infantrymen, their role in combat was to build bridges, build and maintain roads, trenches, and other functions close to the front lines. Their infantry training would be helpful in the event they had to be used in that capacity. In reality, many of these units functioned as general engineer or labor units in France; some pioneer infantry regiments, especially those comprised of African-American soldiers, were called upon to find, exhume, and reinter bodies of men killed in action. Men who served in a pioneer infantry regiment include Paul Adduci, 4th Pioneer Infantry Regiment; Gasparo Bilotti, 4th Pioneer Infantry Regiment; Frank DeLeo, 56th Pioneer Infantry Regiment; Carlo Reda, 5th Pioneer Infantry Regiment; Pietro Ritondale, 53rd Pioneer Infantry Regiment; and John Eugene Segreti, 53rd Pioneer Infantry Regiment.

Ammunition Trains

Each division had an ammunition train assigned to it. The job of the train was to transport artillery and small arms ammunition from supply depots to the divisional ammunition depot. This was a physically and mentally demanding duty; it could be a very hazardous when under artillery and aerial bombardment. Several of these men were assigned to ammunition trains: Louis Micelli, 314th Ammunition Train, 89th Division; Jasper Nudo, 108th Ammunition Train, 33rd Division; Nick Porcaro, 4th Ammunition Train, 4th Division; Vincenzo Salvino, 7th Ammunition Train, 7th Division; and Filiberto Settino, 306th Ammunition Train, 81st Division.

Supply Trains

Closely related to the divisional ammunition train was the divisional supply train. These were responsible for hauling supplies from the forward supply dumps up to divisional dumps. They would consist of either animal-drawn wagons or motor trucks. The following men served in divisional supply trains: Filippo Andrea, 6th Motor Supply Train, 6th Division; Domenico Leonetti, 107th Supply Train, 32nd Division; and Anthony Spizzirri, 311th Supply Train, 86th Division.

Staff and Administrative Positions

All armies in World War I needed an extensive and efficient staff in order to function. Staffs functioned at every level, from General Headquarters down to the company level, to some degree. Each American division contained a staff group called Division

Headquarters Troop. This organization consisted of staff officers supported by a variety of enlisted clerks, couriers, messengers, orderlies and guards.

Medical Units

The Army medical system had to develop a combat footing quickly. By the end of the war, it was efficient enough so that most wounded men had an excellent chance of survival. The medical trail from the front lines to safety and effective medical treatment in the rear could be a long one. Once a man was hit, he would administer first aid to himself if he were able. As soon as possible, a medical aid man from the regimental medical detachment would reach him with proper aid. If he was not ambulatory, stretcher-bearers from the medical detachment, or from the regimental band, would carry him to the battalion aid station. There, the battalion surgeon, usually either a first lieutenant or a captain, would, with the assistance of medical men from the regimental detachment, attend to him. He would eventually be moved back further to the regimental aid and collecting station. From there, the wounded man would be picked up by an ambulance from one of the four divisional ambulance companies and brought back to one of the four divisional field hospitals.

If further treatment were necessary, the wounded man would be brought to an evacuation hospital. The next step brought the wounded man to a base hospital. If necessary, the wounded man could then be transported back to a general hospital or even evacuated to the United States. Some men were in units assigned directly to divisions (sanitary trains, ambulance companies, field hospitals, or sanitary detachments assigned to the infantry companies themselves), while others served in non-divisional units such as evacuation hospitals or base hospitals.

Perhaps unique among these men is Pvt. Frank C. Qualtieri, who actually made two trips to France during and immediately after the war. He deployed to France initially aboard the *Wilhelmina* on September 23, 1918, as part of the Exceptional Medical Replacement Unit No. 36, Camp Grant, Illinois. Then, on January 1, 1919, Qualtieri, in the role of a surgical attendant for a patient, returned to the U.S. aboard the *Princess Matoika*. On January 27, when most men were headed into the U.S., Qualtieri, along with many other men of the Medical Department, returned to France aboard the *Huron*. Qualtieri performed his medical duties again in France until April when he returned to the U.S. aboard U.S.S. *Von Steuben*.

To supply the hospitals and other medical units, the A.E.F. created medical supply depots at all levels. The largest of these were located in what was called the Intermediate Section, that area between the Base Sections and the Advanced Section. The medical supply depots would receive supplies from the Base Sections and then send them out to units in other sections. Eugenio DeBartolo served in Intermediate Medical Supply Depot 2 at Gievres, France.

Veterinary Units

The American Army of World War I was still heavily reliant upon animals for transport. Although some units were motorized, the typical division required horses and mules to haul their artillery pieces, machine guns, ammunition wagons, supply wagons, water carts, rolling kitchens, and machine-gun carts. It is therefore not surprising that there should be Army units specializing in the acquisition and care of these animals. Remount depots were responsible for acquiring and distributing horses. A veterinary detachment was assigned to each division to oversee the care of divisional animals. Of course, there were also veterinary hospitals to care for animals further behind the lines. Only one man, Salvatore Covelli, served overseas with the Veterinary Corps.

U.S. Army Air Service

U.S. Army Air Service units served in England, France, and Italy during the war. There were flying squadrons, support squadrons, repair squadrons, construction companies, and other types of units. Three men served in various U.S. Army Air Service units overseas: Eugenio Abbati (5th Construction Company, England), Carmine Belmonte (1st Construction Company, England), and Andrea Morelli (1107th Aero Replacement Squadron, England).

Cavalry

Horses were also used in cavalry regiments, which were still a reality for the U.S. Army during the war. In the ranks of some of the cavalry regiments were still men who had served in the plains and deserts, men who had participated in cavalry battles during the Indian Wars. The 2nd, 3rd, 6th, and 15th Cavalry Regiments served in the A.E.F.; although some units saw action, they were mainly used to man remount depots, courier service, and straggler patrols. Only one of these men, Sam Aceto (6th Cavalry Regiment), served overseas in such a unit.

Miscellaneous

Following the Armistice, the A.E.F. formed the 3rd Army for occupation duty in Germany. The remaining A.E.F. troops had to await redeployment back to the U.S. Shipping was in just as short supply as it had been before the war. General Pershing, concerned about a decline in discipline, ordered commanders to resume drilling and training. Most men resented having to perform drill and rudimentary combat training. Having just successfully prosecuted a dreadful war, they felt they were entitled to some "down time." By January 1919, Headquarters A.E.F. began to understand the resistance to continued drill; accordingly, they instituted a variety of programs to help the morale of troops waiting for shipment home. Athletic contests, mostly baseball, football, and boxing, were held; unit competitions for the best horses, wagons, and trucks were held; and all types of entertainment and shows, some with soldier talent, were common. Headquarters also created a university system for soldiers who desired to continue their education. Some men could be sent to French or British schools, but the A.E.F. also created the A.E.F. University, staffed by officers, men, and some civilian teachers. Graves Registration Units were responsible to find, exhume, identify, and rebury American soldiers who had been killed or died overseas. The U.S. government created several large cemeteries in several countries in order to inter Americans who had died overseas, and it was a less than pleasant task to find all the myriad small gravesites and exhume the bodies.

The Services of Supply (S.O.S.) had the difficult task of keeping the A.E.F. clothed, fed, equipped, and paid. To do this, they fielded a vast army behind the lines; this army's purpose was to receive, sort, categorized, store, transport, and distribute items as small as wristwatch screws and as large as tanks. They also stored and distributed food; the S.O.S. had a coffee roasting plant and numerous bakeries in the field. To store and process the meat the Army used, many butchery and refrigeration plants were set up behind the lines. Men who served in these types of units, including transportation and divisional support units, and artillery parks (discussed above) included Frank Aiello (Quartermaster Mechanical Repair Unit 310); Joseph Alfano (306th Motorcycle Company); Eugene Brutto (Motor Transport Company 688); Eugene Chesrow (Graves Registration Service Unit 304, 29th Division); Mariano Conforti (V Corps Artillery Park); Emilio Cosentino (Motor Transport Company 318); Francesco Cribaro (I Corps Artillery Park); Frank Fortini (Cook Company 7); Arthur Lucchetti (V Corps Artillery Park); Peter Mele (Butchery Company 344); Gabriele Panza (Mobile Laundry 310, 80th Division); Eugene Potente (Prisoner of War Escort Company 65); Joseph Ritacca (A.E.F. University); Giuseppe Stellato (Cook Company 7); and Saverio Tenuta (Butchery Company 320).

Depot Divisions, Replacement Divisions, and Non-Combat Divisions

Much to the dismay of their commanders and men, upon arrival in France, seven divisions were redesignated as "Depot Divisions." Most of the men in these units were then farmed out as replacements to other divisions to fill up rosters depleted by combat. The men who remained in the divisions were responsible for training and equipping other soldiers to become replacements. Those divisions were the 41st, made up of National Guard troops from the West and Northwest, which became the 1st Depot Division; the 83rd, made up of draftees from Ohio and Pennsylvania, which became the 2nd Depot Division; the 76th, made up of draftees from New England, which became the 3rd Depot Division; the 85th, made up of draftees from Wisconsin and Michigan, which became the 4th Depot Division; the 39th, made up of National Guard troops from the South, which became the 5th Depot Division; the 40th, made up of National Guard troops from the West, which became the 6th Depot Division; and the 31st, made up of National Guard troops from the South, which became the 7th Depot Division. In October 1918, the 40th and 85th divisions were given their old designation back and were sent to be regional replacement divisions in support of a pending offensive of the newly formed U.S. 2nd Army.[4]

In addition to the Depot Divisions, some divisions were, upon arrival in France, designated as "cadre divisions." Men in these units were sent to other units as replacements, and only a small cadre of men remained in the "parent" unit that retained its numerical designation. The 86th Division, made up of draftees from Illinois and a few other states from the Midwest, was one such unit. And the 87th Division, made up initially of draftees from the South, was detailed to perform work behind the lines in the S.O.S. upon their arrival in France in early September, 1918.

Summary of Men in Divisions

As stated above, the brunt of the fighting was borne by riflemen in infantry regiments, and these regiments, supported by artillery, engineer, and other troops, were grouped into divisions. The A.E.F.'s combat record was mostly a record of its divisions. With this in mind, we can analyze the men who were assigned to divisions. Forty-two divisions served overseas during the war.[5] Men in this study served in thirty-two of those divisions. Most of them were replacements sent to these units to fill combat losses. Thus we find heavy representation in the tough, combat hardened Regular Army divisions, in particular the 1st and 3rd Divisions. The 33rd Division, composed initially of Illinois National Guard units, is also well represented here. The 85th and 86th Divisions, both of which received a large number of drafted men from the Chicago area, are represented here in numbers that do not reflect the fact that many of the men went overseas with these two divisions but were later transferred to other divisions as replacements:

1st Division, ten men: 16th Infantry Regiment (one); 18th Infantry Regiment (five); 26th Infantry Regiment (two); 28th Infantry Regiment (one); and 1st Engineer Regiment (one).

2nd Division, three men: 23rd Infantry Regiment.

3rd Division, fifteen men: 4th Infantry Regiment (five); 7th Infantry Regiment (five); 30th Infantry Regiment (two); 9th Machine Gun Battalion (one); 18th Field Artillery Regiment (one); and 76th Field Artillery Regiment (one).

4th Division, seven men: 47th Infantry Regiment (two); 58th Infantry Regiment (one); 59th Infantry Regiment (one); 10th Machine Gun Battalion (one); 4th Engineer Regiment (one); and 4th Ammunition Train (one).

5th Division, three men: 11th Infantry Regiment (one); 60th Infantry Regiment (one); and 7th Engineer Regiment (one).

6th Division, three men: 54th Infantry Regiment (one); 318th Engineer Regiment (one); and 6th Motor Supply Train (one).

7th Division, eleven men: 55th Infantry Regiment (three); 56th Infantry Regiment (six); 8th Field Artillery Regiment (one); and 7th Ammunition Train (one).

26th Division, one man: 101st Engineer Regiment.

27th Division, two men: 106th Infantry Regiment (one) and 104th Field Artillery Regiment (one).

28th Division, five men: 109th Infantry Regiment (one); 111th Infantry Regiment (one); and 103rd Engineer Regiment (three).

29th Division, two men: 115th Infantry Regiment (one) and 115th Field Hospital (one).

31st Division, one man: 117th Machine Gun Battalion.

32nd Division, nine men: 127th Infantry Regiment (one); 128th Infantry Regiment (two); 121st Field Artillery Regiment (five); and 107th Supply Train (one).

33rd Division, twenty-one men: 129th Infantry Regiment (two); 130th Infantry Regiment (seven); 132nd Infantry Regiment (four); 124th Machine Gun Battalion (one); 122nd Field Artillery Regiment (one); 123rd Field Artillery Regiment (two); 124th Field Artillery Regiment (two); 108th Ammunition Train (one); and Headquarters Detachment (one).

35th Division, two men: 138th Infantry Regiment (one) and 139th Infantry Regiment (one).

37th Division, one man: 148th Infantry Regiment.

41st Division, one man: 162nd Infantry Regiment.

42nd Division, two men: 165th Infantry Regiment (one) and 149th Field Artillery Regiment (one).

77th Division, two men: 306th Infantry Regiment (one) and 305th Field Artillery Regiment (one).

78th Division, one man: 312th Infantry Regiment.

80th Division, eight men: 318th Infantry Regiment (one); 319th Infantry Regiment (two); 320th Infantry Regiment (one); 305th Engineer Regiment (one); 313th Field Artillery Regiment (one); 314th Field Artillery Regiment (one); and Mobile Laundry Company 310 (one).

81st Division, two men: 306th Ammunition Train (one) and 306th Sanitary Train (one).

82nd Division, one man: 328th Ambulance Company.

83rd Division, two men: 49th Infantry Regiment.

84th Division, one man: 325th Field Artillery Regiment.

85th Division, six men: 340th Infantry Regiment (five) and Field Hospital 340 (one).

86th Division, seven men: 342nd Infantry Regiment (two); 344th Infantry Regiment (one); 331st Field Artillery Regiment (one); 311th Ammunition Train (one); 311th Sanitary Train (one); and 311th Supply Train (one).

87th Division, two men: 346th Infantry Regiment (one) and 312th Engineer Regiment (one).

89th Division, five men: 353rd Infantry Regiment (two); 354th Infantry Regiment (one); 342nd Field Artillery Regiment (one); and 314th Ammunition Train (one).

90th Division, one man: 344th Field Artillery Regiment.

91st Division, one man: 361st Infantry Regiment.

Service in Siberia

Six men served in Siberia: Carmine Aloe (27th Infantry Regiment), Francesco Bartucci (Siberian Replacement Troops), Francesco (Moris) Costabile (31st Infantry Regiment), Fairy (Fiore) Docimo (Provisional Company 2), Frank Guaglianone (27th Infantry Regiment), and Tony Sansone (Siberian Replacement Troops). These men were assigned to either the 27th or 31st Infantry Regiments. It must be remembered that they participated in an ill-defined mission in a forbidding, desolate foreign land; they engaged in combat against a shadowy foe, and they had to endure questionable allies.

U.S. Navy and U.S. Coast Guard

Eight men served in the U.S. Navy, and one man served in the U.S. Coast Guard. All of these men were volunteers. August Diego Buccieri (U.S.S. *Kearsarge*), William Cara (ship unknown), Salvatore Morelli (U.S.S. *Pamlico*), and Louis Joseph Ruffolo (U.S.S. *George Washington*) served at sea; the others served ashore in various capacities.

Three of the men, Louis Bruno, Eugenio Ferraro, and Anthony Spizzirri, were tailors when they enlisted in the Navy, and they served as tailors at Great Lakes Naval Training Station, Illinois. Since both Bruno and Spizzirri required physical waivers for enlistment with special duty as a tailor, it is apparent that the Navy specifically targeted tailors (among other occupations) in their recruitment drives.[6]

The following men served in the Navy or Coast Guard: Silvio Aiello, U.S. Navy; Louis Bruno, U.S. Navy; August Diego Buccieri, U.S. Navy; William Cara, U.S. Navy; Eugenio Ferraro, U.S. Navy; Salvatore Morelli, U.S. Coast Guard; Louis Joseph Ruffolo, U.S. Navy; Peter Frank Serpe, U.S. Navy; and Anthony Spizzirri, U.S. Navy.

5

Casualties

There are "complete" lists of men who died in service during the war. One such, for the Army, is *Soldiers of the Great War, Volumes I-III*, complied by W. M. Haulsee (Washington, D.C., 1920). The soldiers are listed alphabetically by state, but not much more information is given beyond name, rank, cause of death, and city and state of residence. A similar book, but which gives slightly more information, exists for the Navy. Without further research, there is no way to know who, in these books, were Calabrian men from the Chicago area. A website, published through the United States World War I Centennial Commission, claims to have compiled a list of over 3,000 Italian-born men who died while in the U.S. Army during the war. Using this list as a starting point, I have been able to identify most, if not all, of the Calabrian born men from the Chicago area who died in service with the U.S. Army during the war. Of course, this list does not contain men who were born in the U.S., but it can be considered a fairly complete list.[1]

Unfortunately, there is no central list of men who were wounded. When a man was wounded or gassed he would normally enter into the A.E.F.'s medical system. Medical personnel would make a record of his wound, and this would become part of the hospital records. This record might also reflect in unit records; sometimes company records, such as morning reports, would contain a list of wounded men. But during periods of heavy fighting, this was not always done.

Wounds were annotated in a man's service record, and this information was supposed to be transferred to the statement of service cards made at the end of the war. As stated above, not all of these cards are extant, and those that are can be difficult to obtain. Beginning in 1932, men could apply for the award of the Purple Heart if they could prove they had been wounded or gassed in action. To do this, they could produce their discharge certificate that showed that they had been wounded and awarded a wound chevron. Or they could apply to the War Department to obtain records showing that they had suffered a wound. Clerks created a card for each medal awarded to a veteran, and these award cards are still in the archives. They indicated a man's name, serial number, basic information as to his wound, the date of the award of the Purple Heart, and the medal number, which, at that time, was engraved upon the medal's rim. Of course, not all qualified men applied for a medal.

Thus this record of wounded men is incomplete. Almost certainly, many more men than are recorded here were wounded or gassed. We can still examine this abbreviated sampling and summarize the general findings. Seven of these men were killed in action, and three men died of wounds received in action, for a total of ten combat deaths. Two men died of pneumonia, a complication of the Spanish flu, while serving in stateside training camps, both in the autumn of 1918 when the flu epidemic was raging throughout the world. None of the men stationed overseas died of disease during their time in service. Thus, twelve men died while in service during the war. Nineteen men suffered non-fatal wounds during the war, including one man who also became a prisoner of war. So, excluding the two men who died of pneumonia, we find that twenty-nine men were killed, wounded, or died of wounds during the war. It is interesting to note that of these twenty-nine men, approximately sixteen of them were replacements, while the rest had been original members of their regiment. Two of the men were engineers, one man was in an ambulance company, and one man was in an artillery supply company. Most of the rest of the men were riflemen in line infantry companies. Two of the men in rifle companies were buglers, but they were at the front in combat when they became casualties. Since the list of wounded men is admittedly incomplete, a statistical analysis of number of men wounded per number of men engaged in combat would be misleading. A breakdown by division and regiment gives the following information:

1st Division, six casualties: 16th Infantry Regiment (one wounded); 18th Infantry Regiment (three wounded); 26th Infantry Regiment (one wounded); and 28th Infantry Regiment (one killed).

2nd Division, two casualties: 23rd Infantry Regiment (one died of wounds, one wounded).

3rd Division, eight casualties: 4th Infantry Regiment (one killed, four wounded) and 7th Infantry Regiment (three wounded).

4th Division, one casualty: 47th Infantry Regiment (one wounded).

5th Division, one casualty: 7th Engineer Regiment (one wounded).

7th Division, one casualty: 56th Infantry Regiment (one killed).

27th Division, one casualty: 106th Infantry Regiment (one wounded/prisoner of war).

28th Division, one casualty: 109th Infantry Regiment (one killed).

32nd Division, one casualty: 128th Infantry Regiment (one killed).

33rd Division, four casualties: 130th Infantry Regiment (one killed, two wounded) and 132nd Infantry Regiment (one killed).

77th Division, one casualty: 305th Field Artillery Regiment (one died of wounds).

80th Division, one casualty: 305th Engineer Regiment (one wounded).

82nd Division, one casualty: 328th Ambulance Company (one died of wounds).

Killed in Action, Died of Wounds, Died of Disease

Nicholas Benedetti

Nicholas (Nicola Benedetto) Benedetti was born in Chicago on December 27, 1894. His parents, Alessandro and Anna Maria Benedetti, were from Cosenza. Benedetti was a helper on a wagon and was living in Chicago when he was inducted into the Army. He was a private, serial number 1384188, in Company "G," 130th Infantry Regiment,

33rd Division, when he left for France aboard the Agamemnon on May 16, 1918. The 33rd Division trained with the Australians, British, and French armies; they saw action in defensive sectors prior to their involvement in the Meuse-Argonne Offensive. In late October, the 33rd Division was transferred to the U.S. 2nd Army and participated in the attacks against German positions preparatory to a large-scale advance against Metz, scheduled for November 14. According to the commander of the 130th Infantry Regiment, Colonel John V. Clinnin, Benedetti was "killed by H. E. [high explosive] shell the afternoon of Nov. 10, 1918 about 1 P. M. during raid on Marcheville, France. There is no man in the company who saw him killed or who was near him when he was hit."[2] Thus Benedetti lost his life only one day before the Armistice. It was not until December 22, more than a month after his death and as his family, while anticipating his return, dreaded not hearing anything from him, that Benedetti's mother, Anna Maria Ciambrone, received a telegram informing her of her son's death. The next month, she wrote a poignant letter to the War Department asking to have her son's body shipped to her in Chicago. One may feel a mother's anguish in her closing line: "Trusting that you will soon satisfy a pitiful desire of a proud mother."[3]

Pvt. Nikolas J. Benedetti, 130th Infantry Regiment, 33rd Division. (*Ancestry.com*)

Carmine Broccolo

Carmine Broccolo was born in Bisignano in 1897; he came to the U.S. in 1908 and was living in Chicago when he was inducted into the Army. He was a private, serial number 3071819, when he left for France aboard the *Empress of Britain* on July 14, 1918 as part of the Fort Benjamin Harrison, Indiana, July Medical Replacement Draft. Shortly after arrival in France, Broccolo was sent to the 328th Ambulance Company, 307th Sanitary Train, 82nd Division. The 82nd Division participated in the Saint-Mihiel Offensive and the Meuse-Argonne Offensive. During the latter operation, the 82nd Division advanced against stiff German resistance along the eastern edge of the Argonne Forest. In early October, Broccolo, with a group of men from his company, was acting as a stretcher-bearer for the 327th Infantry Regiment, 82nd Division. According to Pvt. Michael Bishop, also of Broccolo's company, "a shell struck about fifty feet from us, a piece of shrapnel hitting Broccolo on the right side of the head."[4] Broccolo was badly wounded and evacuated to Field Hospital 12, 1st Division, where he died at 7:45 a.m. on October 7.

In January 1919, Broccolo's father, Frank, wrote a plaintive letter to the War Department, asking for particulars of his son's death, requesting information as to how he was identified, and at which hospital he died. Frank Broccolo concluded: "We received our telegram that he died October 7th and two weeks later we got another telegram that he was missing in action since October 10 could you tell me what could be of him."[5] In October 1920, Broccolo's mother, Teresa, wrote to the War Department requesting, among other things, to have a glass or window made in the casket lid, over her son's face, so that should could see him. The War Department replied, declining Mrs. Broccolo's request, and stating that the body was to be shipped home in a metallic lined casket, and that since the body had "been buried for over two years, recognition of the features would be impossible and the viewing of the remains an added trial."[6] After more exchanges of letters, Broccolo's body was delivered to his family in Chicago in 1921.

Pasquale Carravetta

Pasquale Carravetta was born on June 26, 1888, in Lappano. When he registered for the draft, Carravetta was living in Kellettville, Pennsylvania, where he worked as a track foreman. He requested exemption from the draft due to a "rupture." At some point, he moved to Chicago and was drafted into the Army. He was a private, serial number 2061193, assigned to the 2nd Company, Camp Grant April Replacement Draft, when he boarded the *Powhatan* for transport to France on April 30, 1918. He was assigned as a replacement to Company "D," 28th Infantry Regiment, 1st Division. On July 19, during the intense fighting around Soissons, Carravetta was struck by a 37-mm shell and was reported as being killed instantly; however, he is also listed in some records as having died of wounds received in action on July 24. In any case, Carravetta was buried on the field of battle and then exhumed and reburied at the Aisne-Marne American Cemetery in 1922. He was cited for gallantry in action in General Orders No. 1, 1st Division, January 1, 1920.[7]

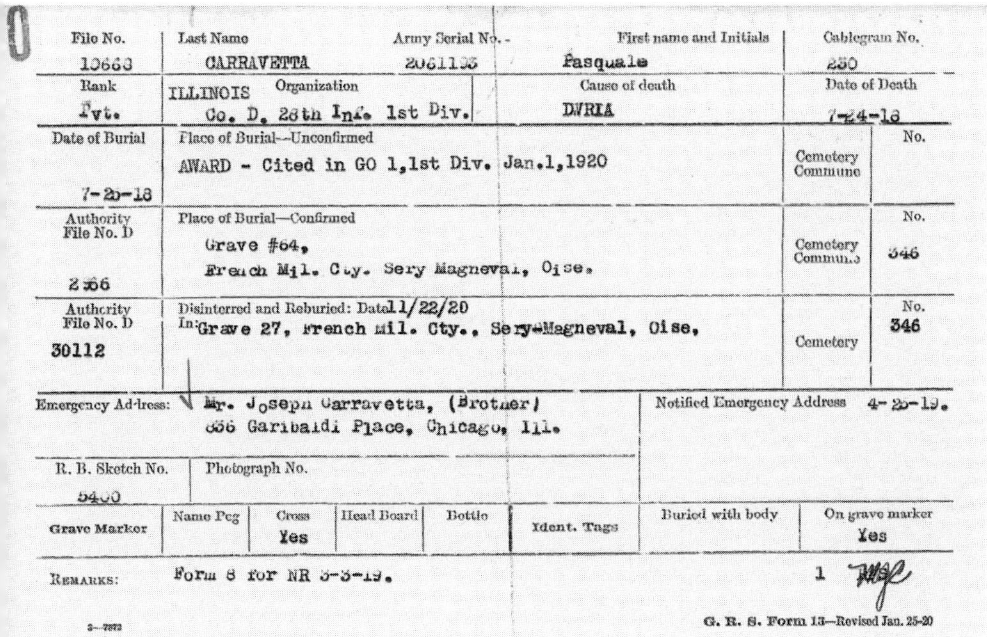

File No. 10663 | Last Name CARRAVETTA | Army Serial No. 2061193 | First name and Initials Pasquale | Cablegram No. 250

Rank Pvt. | ILLINOIS Organization Co. D. 28th Inf. 1st Div. | Cause of death DWRIA | Date of Death 7-24-18

Date of Burial 7-25-18 | Place of Burial—Unconfirmed AWARD - Cited in GO 1,1st Div. Jan.1,1920 | Cemetery Commune | No.

Authority File No. D 2366 | Place of Burial—Confirmed Grave #64, French Mil. Cty. Sery Magneval, Oise. | Cemetery Commune | No. 346

Authority File No. D 30112 | Disinterred and Reburied: Date 11/22/20 In: Grave 27, French Mil. Cty., Sery-Magneval, Oise, | Cemetery | No. 346

Emergency Address: Mr. Joseph Carravetta, (Brother) 336 Garibaldi Place, Chicago, Ill. | Notified Emergency Address 4-25-19.

R. B. Sketch No. 5400 | Photograph No.

Grave Marker | Name Peg | Cross Yes | Head Board | Bottle | Ident. Tags | Buried with body | On grave marker Yes

Remarks: Form 8 for NR 5-5-19. 1

3—7872 G. R. S. Form 13—Revised Jan. 25-20

Front side of Pvt. Pasquale Carravetta's burial card showing his initial burial on the field of battle. He was reburied twice; the reverse side shows his final interment at the Aisne-Marne American Cemetery. (*National Archives*)

Damiano Candelise[8]

Damiano Candelise was born on July 11, 1889 in Rovito, and he came to the U.S. in July 1906. Candelise enlisted in the Regular Army in 1911, and he served in Company "F," 8th Infantry Regiment, in the Philippines. He was discharged at Fort McDowell, California, on December 22, 1913; his character was given as "good." During World War I, he was drafted into the Army and was a bugler, serial number 1098483, in Company "D," 56th Infantry Regiment, 7th Division, at Camp MacArthur, Texas. There, on July 19, Candelise became a naturalized U.S. citizen.

Candelise went overseas with his regiment aboard U.S.S. *Leviathan* on August 3. The 7th Division became part of the U.S. 2nd Army and occupied the front lines near the Saint-Mihiel sector. As part of the preliminary movements associated with the planned attack by the 2nd Army toward Metz, the 7th Division saw combat during October and November.

> [At 10:30 a.m. on November 4, only one week before the Armistice, Candelise] was stationed in a small shelter that he had dug and was in charge of a machine gun. A high-explosive shell burst about two yards from the place where [he] was stationed, almost severing his left leg from his body. He was placed upon a stretcher and carried toward the First Aid station of the First Battalion. He died on the stretcher while being carried there. He was buried at the point where he died, at a place about 700 yards to the right of the First Platoon of Co. D, 56th Infantry.[9]

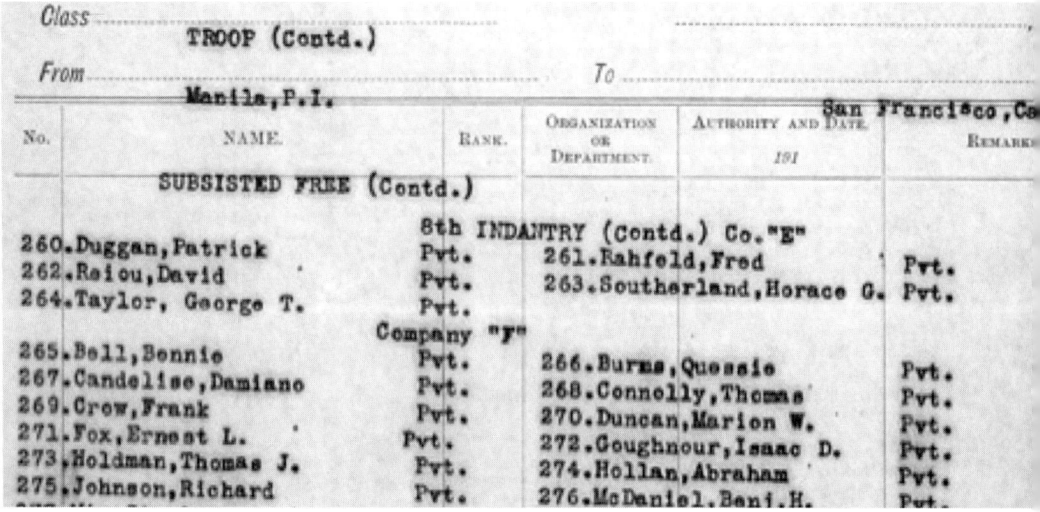

Class
TROOP (Contd.)
From Manila, P.I. To San Francisco, Ca

No.	NAME.	RANK.	ORGANIZATION OR DEPARTMENT	AUTHORITY AND DATE 191	REMARKS

SUBSISTED FREE (Contd.)

8th INDANTRY (Contd.) Co. "E"

260. Duggan, Patrick Pvt. 261. Rahfeld, Fred Pvt.
262. Reiou, David Pvt. 263. Southerland, Horace G. Pvt.
264. Taylor, George T. Pvt.

Company "F"

265. Bell, Bonnie Pvt. 266. Burns, Quessie Pvt.
267. Candelise, Damiano Pvt. 268. Connolly, Thomas Pvt.
269. Crow, Frank Pvt. 270. Duncan, Marion W. Pvt.
271. Fox, Ernest L. Pvt. 272. Goughnour, Isaac D. Pvt.
273. Holdman, Thomas J. Pvt. 274. Hollan, Abraham Pvt.
275. Johnson, Richard Pvt. 276. McDaniel, Benj. H. Pvt.

Detail of the Army transport manifest showing Damiano Candelise's return from the Philippines, U.S.A.T. *Logan*, 1913. (*Ancestry.com*)

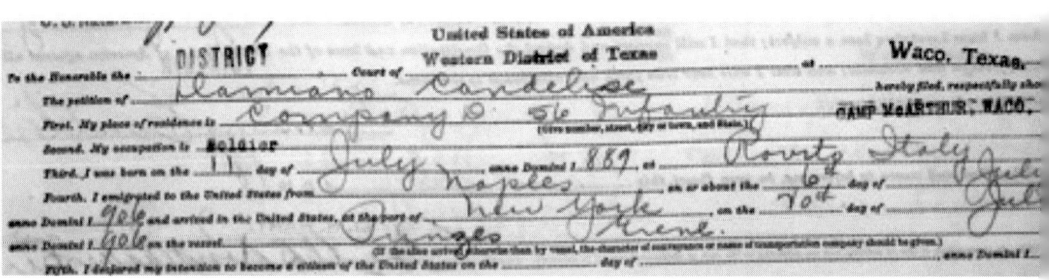

United States of America
To the Honorable the DISTRICT Court of Western District of Texas at Waco, Texas.
The petition of Damiano Candelise hereby filed, respectfully shows:
First. My place of residence is Company D 56 Infantry CAMP McARTHUR, WACO.
Second. My occupation is Soldier
Third. I was born on the 11 day of July anno Domini 1889, at Rovito Italy
Fourth. I emigrated to the United States from Naples on or about the 6th day of ... anno Domini 1906 and arrived in the United States, at the port of New York on the 20th day of ... anno Domini 1906 on the vessel Prinzess Irene.
Fifth. I declared my intention to become a citizen of the United States on the ... day of ... anno Domini

Detail of Bugler Damiano Candelise's Petition for Naturalization, Camp McArthur, 1918. (*Ancestry.com*)

According to the disinterment record, Candelise's left arm was also completely shattered. Candelise's sister, Marie Candelise, expressed the poignancy of her brother's situation in a 1933 affidavit (the dates she mentions are slightly off): "[Damiano] stayed with me from July 30th to Aug. 1918 when he was called to action. There he died, in the year of 1918. Before the papers were signed for peace."[10]

Fiore Filice[11]

Fiore Filice was born in Mongrassano and was living with his brother in Chicago when he entered the Army. He was a private, serial number 2079495, in Supply Company, 305th Field Artillery Regiment, 77th Division, when he sailed for France with his regiment aboard U.S.S. *Northern Pacific* on April 26, 1918. The 77th Division was the first National Army division to sail for France, and it saw a lot of action throughout the summer and fall of 1918. Filice died of wounds received in action, but the date and location are not recorded.

Federico (Fred) Guido

Federico Guido was born on June 26, 1888, in San Fili, and he came to the U.S. in March 1905. He was a tailor living in Chicago when he was inducted into the Army. Guido was a private, serial number 2306584, in Company "L," 128th Infantry Regiment, 32nd Division, when he was scheduled to sail aboard the *Powhatan* on March 22, 1918. It is possible that he was sick or otherwise detained because he missed the *Powhatan* sailing and instead sailed aboard the *Mount Vernon* one week later. Sailing with him were men from a variety of other units; probably all of these men had missed their initial sailing for one reason or another. On the night of August 3, 1918, Guido's regiment was preparing to advance toward the village of Fismes on the Vesle River. He and several other men were

Pvt. Fred Guido, 128th Infantry Regiment, 32nd Division. (*Soldiers of the Great War, via Ancestry.com*)

waiting on a hillside between St. Gilles and Cohen. The night was "so dark one could not see his hand in front of him."[12] According to Pvt. Frances J. Kelly, also of Company "L," a "gas shell came over and part of the casing hit [Guido] in the back of the head."[13] Kelly, Sgt. George W. Strampe, and Pvt. Thompson crawled over to Guido to tell him to put his gas mask on, or to help him to do so, but they found him dead. Guido was buried in a mass grave the next day. Upon disinterring the bodies for reburial or shipment home, Guido's body was not found. Intense investigation throughout the 1920s failed to turn up Guido's grave, and the search was discontinued in 1932. Sadly, Guido's widow, Anna, died in 1922 without experiencing closure on the loss of her husband.[14]

Alessandro Morrone[15]

Alessandro Morrone was born in Marano Marchesato on March 27, 1888, and he came to the U.S. in March 1907, destined for his brother, Giacinto, in Chicago. He was living in Chicago when he registered for the draft. At the time, Morrone was not employed because he had been sick for six months; accordingly, he requested exemption from the draft. He was, however, drafted, probably in May 1918. He was a private, serial number 2826857, in Company "C," Development Battalion 6, 161st Depot Brigade, at Camp Grant, Illinois. Morrone died of lobar pneumonia at Camp Grant Base Hospital at 4 a.m. on October 5, 1918, during the great epidemic that was sweeping the world at the time.

Like most other servicemen of the time, Morrone took advantage of the government provided war risk insurance in the amount of $10,000. As beneficiaries, Morrone designated an even split between his parents living in Italy.

Luigi Perri

Luigi Perri was born in Castrolibero on April 27, 1893; he was an assistant foreman on the Chicago, Burlington, and Quincy Railroad in Chicago when he entered military service sometime in 1917. Perri was a private, serial number 1391161, in Company "G," 132nd Infantry Regiment, 33rd Division, and he went to France in May 1918. By June 21, the 132nd Infantry Regiment began receiving training from British forces. On July 4, well before completion of their training, Companies "A" and "G," 132nd Infantry Regiment, were loaned to the 4th Australian Infantry Brigade to take part in an attack at Hamel and Vaire Woods. When the Australian rolling barrage started, it fell short, landing among the Americans as they formed for the attack.[16] This caused a number of casualties; among them was Pvt. Luigi Perri. The severity of Perri's fatal wound is evident from a later disinterment form that gave remarks concerning wounds received at the time of injury: "Left pelvis, left shoulder blade missing. Lower third of right fibula and upper jaw fractured. Lower jaw missing."[17] In addition, almost all upper teeth were missing. Clearly Perri had suffered a devastating wound.

On July 5, the 132nd's regimental chaplain, 1st Lieutenant John L. O'Donnell, buried Perri near where he fell; the grave was near Bayonvillers, near Vaire Woods. After the war, Perri's brother, Michael, requested that Luigi's body be returned to Chicago for final burial. There then followed a lengthy series of letters and cross-communications involving Michael Perri and another brother in Italy; the final result was that Perri's body was returned to his place of birth, Castrolibero, for final interment.[18]

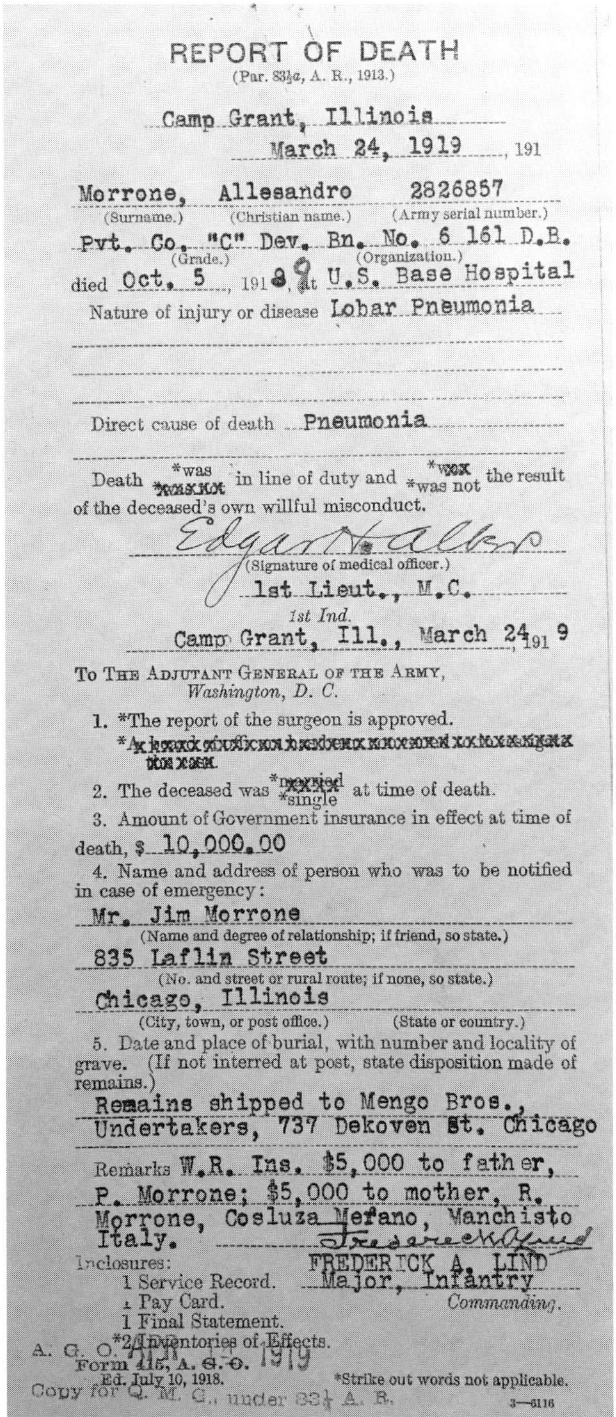

REPORT OF DEATH
(Par. 83½a, A. R., 1913.)

Camp Grant, Illinois
March 24, 1919, 191

Morrone, Allesandro 2826857
(Surname.) (Christian name.) (Army serial number.)

Pvt. Co. "C" Dev. Bn. No. 6 161 D.B.
(Grade.) (Organization.)

died Oct. 5, 1918, at U.S. Base Hospital

Nature of injury or disease Lobar Pneumonia

Direct cause of death Pneumonia

Death *was in line of duty and *was not the result of the deceased's own willful misconduct.

Edgar H. Alker
(Signature of medical officer.)
1st Lieut., M.C.

1st Ind.

Camp Grant, Ill., March 24, 1919

To The Adjutant General of the Army,
Washington, D. C.

1. *The report of the surgeon is approved.

2. The deceased was *single at time of death.

3. Amount of Government insurance in effect at time of death, $ 10,000.00

4. Name and address of person who was to be notified in case of emergency:

Mr. Jim Morrone
(Name and degree of relationship; if friend, so state.)
835 Laflin Street
(No. and street or rural route; if none, so state.)
Chicago, Illinois
(City, town, or post office.) (State or country.)

5. Date and place of burial, with number and locality of grave. (If not interred at post, state disposition made of remains.)

Remains shipped to Mengo Bros., Undertakers, 737 Dekoven St. Chicago

Remarks W.R. Ins. $5,000 to father, P. Morrone; $5,000 to mother, R. Morrone, Cosluza Merano, Manchisto Italy.

Frederick A. Lind
FREDERICK A. LIND
Major, Infantry
Commanding.

Inclosures:
1 Service Record.
1 Pay Card.
1 Final Statement.
*2 Inventories of Effects.

A. G. O. APR 14 1919

Form 415, A. G. O.
Ed. July 10, 1918.
*Strike out words not applicable.

Copy for Q. M. C., under 83½ A. R. 3—6116

Report of Death of Pvt. Alessandro Morrone, 161st Depot Brigade. Morrone died of lobar pneumonia at Camp Grant on October 5, 1918. Morrone wanted his parents to split his life insurance benefit money; note the War Department's effort at recording their address: "Cosluza Merano, Manchisto, Italy." The correct address would be "Marano Marchesato, Cosenza, Italy." (*National Archives*)

Pvt. Luigi Perri, 132nd Infantry Regiment, 33rd Division. (*Back Over There, unsourced*)

Camillo Posterivo[19]

Camillo Posterivo was born on January 6, 1892, in Cervicati. He was a laborer living in Chicago when he was inducted into the Army, probably in May 1918. He was a private, serial number 2822159, in Company "F," 340th Infantry Regiment, 85th Division, previously at Camp Custer, Michigan, when he departed for France aboard the *Corinthic* on July 23, 1918. Posterivo was sent as a replacement to Company "C," 4th Infantry Regiment, 3rd Division. He was killed in action on October 16, 1918, during the Meuse-Argonne Offensive, suffering a fatal wound at the base of his skull. Posterivo is buried in the U.S. National Cemetery at Romagne, France.

Eugenio Scarloto[20]

Eugenio Scarloto (also spelled Scarlato in some documents) was born in August 1889, near Cosenza. He came to the U.S. in May 1906 and settled in Kenosha. On April 8, 1911, he declared his intention to become a U.S. citizen. Scarloto was drafted into the Army on March 29, 1918, and sent to Camp Custer, Michigan, where he became a private, serial number 2035032, in the 7th Company, 2nd Battalion, 160th Depot Brigade. Scarloto listed his uncle, Salvatore Scarloto, with whom he lived in Kenosha, as next of kin. Just a few days later, on April 4, he was sent to Camp Gordon, Georgia, where he was part of the 11th Company, 1st Replacement Regiment, destined to become a replacement for an overseas unit. On May 19 he was transferred to Headquarters, 104th Field Artillery Recruit Detachment, 27th Division, at Camp Stuart, Virginia. It seems that he was now being designated to become a replacement for the 104th Artillery Regiment, part of the 27th Division. However, this assignment was short-lived; on May 24, he was transferred to Company "L," 164th Infantry Regiment, 41th Division. On June 30, he departed the U.S. bound for France.

The 41st Division was made up of National Guard units from the northwestern United States; it had gone to France in late 1917, but, upon arrival, was designated as a depot division. It funneled replacements to other units engaged in combat. Since Scarloto was assigned to the 164th Infantry Regiment while still stateside, he probably went overseas with a detachment of soldiers slated to join the regiment for training and outfitting prior to being sent out as a replacement. Soon after arrival in France in mid-July, Scarloto underwent further training; on August 10, he was sent as a replacement to Company "I," 23th Infantry Regiment, 2nd Division. The 2nd Division was a Regular Army division consisting of one brigade of two Army regiments, and one brigade of two Marine Corps regiments. It suffered high casualty rates and was rated as one of the most effective American divisions in World War I.

Scarloto and other replacements received still more training by the surviving veterans in the 23rd Infantry Regiment. He participated in the Saint-Mihiel Offensive from September 12 to 16; after this, the 2nd Division was sent north to the area west of the Argonne Forest where they participated in the Battle of Blanc Mont in mid-October. Later the division was dispatched to the east to participate in the ongoing Meuse-Argonne Offensive. From November 1 to 11, the 23rd Infantry attacked German positions near the Meuse River. At some point, either during the Blanc Mont action or during the fighting along the Meuse River, Scarloto was wounded in action. Scarloto's statement of service card credits him with participation in the Saint-Mihiel Offensive and "Champagne." The latter was the Battle of Blanc Mont; thus it is unclear precisely when and where he was wounded since no extant records give his date of wounding. It is possible that he was wounded at Blanc Mont in mid-October and then lingered in hospitals until finally succumbing to his wounds more than a month later; it is also possible that he participated in the final stages of the Meuse-Argonne Offensive, being wounded in early November, and that this participation was not recorded in his records.

In any event, he was sent to Evacuation Hospital 19 where he died on November 19, 1918, eight days after the war ended. He was buried the next day at A.E.F. Cemetery No. 84 near Allerey, Saône-et-Loire, France. Although Scarloto's uncle, as next of kin, requested that Eugenio's body be sent to him in Kenosha for final burial, it was discovered that Eugenio had brothers living in Italy and that they were the true legal next of kin. Through a series of misunderstandings and confused letters, the opportunity to have Scarloto's body returned to Kenosha was lost, and he was finally interred in the Saint-Mihiel American Cemetery, Thiaucourt, France.

Gaetano Sorrentino[21]

Gaetano Sorrentino was born in Castrolibero on October 30, 1893. He came to the U.S. in 1911 and settled in Kenosha. He had already declared his intention to become a U.S. citizen and was a laborer at the American Brass Company, living in Kenosha, when he was inducted into the Army on May 26, 1918. Sorrentino was a private, serial number 3329916, assigned to the 35th Company, 161st Depot Brigade, at Camp Grant, Illinois. On August 15, he was transferred to Company "C," 344th Infantry Regiment, 86th Division, which had been training at Camp Grant since the previous September.

The 86th went overseas on September 9; unfortunately, upon arrival, it was stripped of many of its men who were sent to combat units as replacements. Sorrentino was one of those men. On October 6, he was assigned to Company "F," 111th Infantry Regiment,

Final resting place of Pvt. Eugenio Scarloto, 23rd Infantry Regiment, 2nd Division, St. Mihiel American Cemetery, Thiaucourt, France. (*American Battle Monuments Commission*)

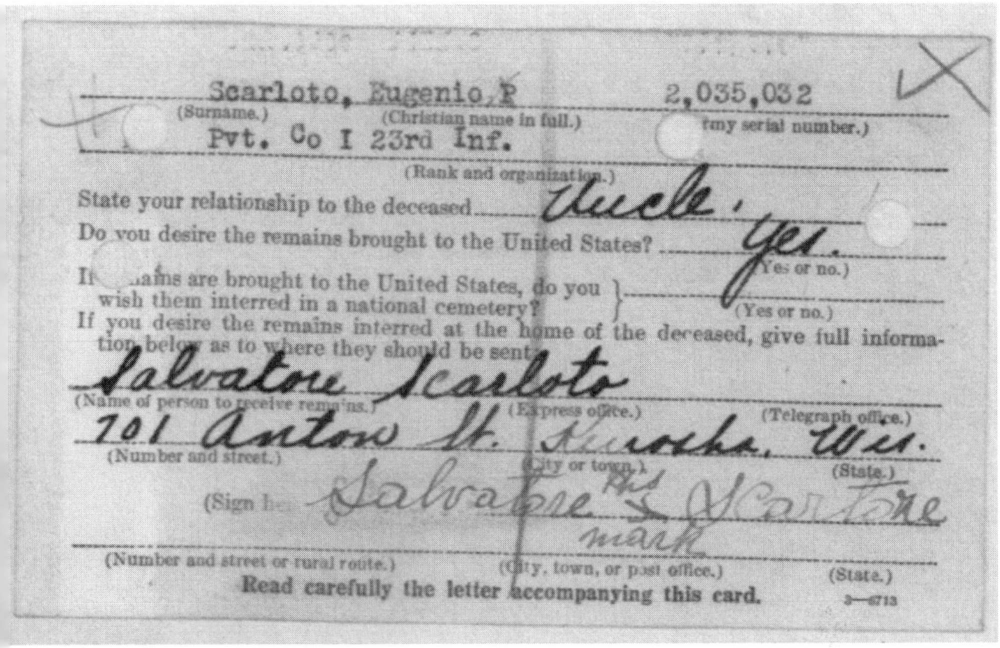

Scarloto, Eugenio P 2,035,032
(Surname.) (Christian name in full.) (Army serial number.)
Pvt. Co I 23rd Inf.
(Rank and organization.)
State your relationship to the deceased Uncle.
Do you desire the remains brought to the United States? Yes.
(Yes or no.)
If remains are brought to the United States, do you wish them interred in a national cemetery? (Yes or no.)
If you desire the remains interred at the home of the deceased, give full information below as to where they should be sent:
Salvatore Scarloto
(Name of person to receive remains.) (Express office.) (Telegraph office.)
701 Anton St. Kenosha, Wis.
(Number and street.) (City or town.) (State.)
(Sign here) Salvatore his mark [illegible]
(Number and street or rural route.) (City, town, or post office.) (State.)
Read carefully the letter accompanying this card. 3—6713

Card filled out by Salvatore Scarloto showing his initial desire to have Pvt. Eugenio Scarloto's remains returned to the United States. (*National Archives*)

28th Division. The 28th Division had originally been comprised of Pennsylvania National Guard regiments; by now it had been infused with draftees and other replacements. It had been engaged in serious combat by the time Sorrentino joined the 111th in the middle of the Meuse-Argonne Offensive. He had minimal time to assimilate and learn what he needed to know to survive in combat. Somewhat unusually, Sorrentino was transferred again, within the division, to Company "F," 109th Infantry Regiment, on November 1, 1918. The 28th Division had been assigned to the new U.S. 2nd Army; in early November, they were poised to commence an offensive with the ultimate aim of taking the city of Metz. In the morning of November 11, just hours before the Armistice, the 109th Infantry Regiment assaulted German positions. Gaetano Sorrentino was killed in action during this advance. Lengthy correspondence between the War Department, Sorrentino's brother, Beniamino, in Kenosha, and his father, Carmine in Castrolibero, resulted in the decision to retain Sorrentino's body in France; he is buried in the Saint-Mihiel Cemetery.

Anthony Spizzirri

Antonio Spizzirri was born on May 16, 1889, in Marano Marchesato, one of at least seven children of Leopoldo Spizzirri and Maria Morrone. He came to the U.S. as part of a family migration around 1910. By 1917, Spizzirri was employed as a tailor with his own shop.

The armed forces, rapidly expanding to wartime strength, were in need of manpower possessing a wide variety of skills. Often, during processing after a man had been drafted (or had enlisted), careful screening determined what skills a man might have that might be of value to the service. Also, recruiters were on the lookout for men with particular skills. This was the case with Spizzirri's enlistment in the U.S. Navy. At America's entry into the war in April 1917, the Navy had only 80,000 men and officers. By the time of the Armistice on November 11, 1918, there were about 533,000 men and officers in the Navy. A great many of those men entered the Navy, or attended other training, at Great Lakes Naval Station, located about 30 miles north of Chicago on the shore of Lake Michigan. Great Lakes Naval Station was the major training base for personnel entering the Navy. With so many men being issued uniforms and fabric equipment at such a rapid pace, it is no wonder that there was a great demand for tailors in the ranks of the sailors. The Navy recruited tailors for special duty in order to fill this need.

Anthony Spizzirri answered this call; he enlisted in the U.S. Navy on April 25, 1918, at Great Lakes Naval Training Station. He listed his brother, Oreste, as his next of kin. Doctors thoroughly examined incoming sailors, and Spizzirri's physical description noted various small scars and moles. He was also recorded as being 5 feet 4.75 inches tall and weighing 179 pounds, with brown eyes and dark brown hair. That he was intentionally recruited as a tailor is indicated by the notation, "Obesity waived for special duty as tailor."[22] Also, the fact that he was enlisted in the rank of fireman first class, with corresponding increased pay, and not as a basic seaman, indicates that he was recruited for his skills.

One of the forms that Spizzirri completed upon his enlistment in April was Navy Form 235, Record of Allotments, Family Allowances, and Insurance of Enlisted Men. On this form, Spizzirri indicated that he wanted no family allotments (i.e., regular payments to family members from his own monthly pay), but he did purchase the government-provided war risk insurance, at the amount of $10,000. Spizzirri listed his sister, Concetta, in Waukegan, Illinois, as his beneficiary and emergency contact. He further stated that his mother was not living.

Following the formalities of a physical exam, official paperwork by the ream, and swearing in, Spizzirri returned to his home in Chicago and was given time to get his affairs in order before reporting for duty. One wonders what provisions he made for his tailor shop; did one of his brothers or perhaps another relative or employee manage the shop in his absence? Or did he simply close the shop for the duration? In any event, Spizzirri returned to Great Lakes Naval Training Station on May 6. At his enlistment, according to another notation on his record, it was agreed that he would remain at Great Lakes for special duty in the tailor shop. Spizzirri probably underwent the normal training for all incoming sailors, although he outranked most of his fellow trainees. It is also possible that his basic training was less thorough than that of ordinary seamen, given that he was to be a landsman in the tailor shop. In any event, he almost certainly would have been called upon early in his career to repair and alter the garments of his "shipmates" or to repair canvas and fabric equipment.

During the late summer and early fall of 1918, a worldwide outbreak of influenza began to take its toll. Where men crowded together in military bases influenza was certain to spread. Sometime in September 1918, Spizzirri was granted liberty and went to visit his family in nearby Chicago. While there, he became ill with influenza and was transferred to the Navy hospital at Great Lakes. While in the base hospital, Spizzirri died on September 29. Thus his service record bears the sad final notation: "Pneumonia

His Bunkie, by A.E.F. combat artist Captain William James Aylward, July 1918. (*111 SC 20063, original in the Smithsonian Institution*)

Broncho. Not in line of duty. Not due to own misconduct. Taken ill while at home on liberty. Buried Chicago, Ill. No effects."

So, at a time when families all over the world were either celebrating or anticipating the return of their loved ones from the war, the Spizzirri family of Chicago was among those who mourned. While other families prepared for joyous holiday feasts, the Spizzirri family was making arrangements for funerals and insurance payments. This is reflected in his service record, where we find that undertaker Frank Tenuta of Waukegan was allowed a claim for $100 for funeral expenses, the maximum allowed, in December 1918. Other financial considerations included the disbursing of Spizzirri's pay and insurance. With a monthly pay of $46.50, less a monthly allotment of $6.90 for life insurance, Spizzirri was due $224.48 at the time of his death. This must have gone to his sister, Concetta, who, along with his brother, Oreste, were listed as next of kin. In January 1919, Concetta was notified that, as beneficiary of Anthony's life insurance, she would receive a monthly payment of $57.50, beginning retroactively to September 1918, and extending through September 1938.

In the early 1920s, Congress provided for adjusted compensation for men and women who had served in the armed forces during the war. This was commonly known as a veteran's bonus, and was to be paid beginning in the 1940s. Concetta applied for this bonus in April 1925. In July, the Navy Department responded by informing Concetta:

> ... no provision is made in the Adjusted Compensation Act whereby a sister may receive the benefits thereof. However, if you can submit evidence in the form of affidavit setting forth the fact that you stood in the place of a mother at least one year before the veteran began his service, your application will be given consideration.[23]

Concetta must have supplied such an affidavit for we find her application annotated, "Evidence as to Loco Parentis furnished Vet. Bureau." In August, the Navy Department determined that Concetta should receive bonus in the amount of $87. This money, both Anthony's military pay balance, the insurance payment, and the bonus, must surely have gone a long way toward easing the life of Concetta during these hard times.

Wounded in Action

Giuseppe Beltrano

Giuseppe Beltrano was born in Cosenza on August 28, 1888; he came to the U.S. in about 1909. In 1917, he was a core maker in a foundry in Racine. Beltrano was drafted on September 21, 1917, among the first men to be inducted. He was a private, serial number 2030365, in Company "F," 310th Engineer Regiment, 85th Division, at Camp Custer, Michigan, until November 5 when he was transferred to the 160th Depot Brigade, also at Camp Custer. Beltrano was promoted to corporal on December 5 but was demoted to private only three months later. On April 25, 1918, Beltrano was transferred to the Engineer Training Regiment at Camp Humphreys, Virginia. He shipped out to France on August 25. Upon arrival, he was assigned to the 116th Engineer Regiment, a unit that supplied replacements to engineer regiments at the front. On October 10, Beltrano was sent to Company "A," 305th Engineer Regiment, 80th Division. The 80th participated in the final push during the Meuse-Argonne Offensive, attacking north toward the Meuse River from November 1 to 6. On November 9, just two days before the end of the war, Beltrano was gassed; since the 80th Division was relieved from the front lines on November 6, it is possible that Beltrano was a victim of latent gas in an area behind the lines, or perhaps his engineer regiment was engaged in support of other units that continued to fight until the very hour of the armistice. He returned to the U.S. aboard U.S.S. *Leviathan* on March 6, 1919, and he was discharged at Camp Grant twenty days later.

Angelo Biscardi[24]

Angelo Biscardi was born in Marano Marchesato or Cosenza around 1888. He came to the U.S. around 1905 and made two trips between his home in Italy and Chicago. In 1915, Biscardi again returned to Italy to pick up his wife and child and bring them to America. While there, Italy declared war on Germany, and Biscardi was caught in the Italian draft. While in the Italian army serving in the Alps, Biscardi was seriously wounded and medically discharged. He came back to Chicago on March 26, 1917, arriving aboard the *Dante Alighieri*, going to his cousin Pietro Ruffolo in Chicago.

Soon thereafter he moved to Kenosha; in 1918, he was employed as a laborer with the American Brass Company. Married, with a child, he claimed exemption from the draft on account of being the sole support of his family and his parents. He was an alien at that time, and he had prior military service as an infantry private in the Italian Army. Despite all this, he was drafted on April 22, 1918, and assigned as a private, serial number 2047634, in the 160th Depot Brigade at Camp Custer, Michigan. In May, he was transferred to Company "F," 340th Infantry Regiment, 85th Division, also at Camp Custer. He went overseas with that unit in July. At some point, he

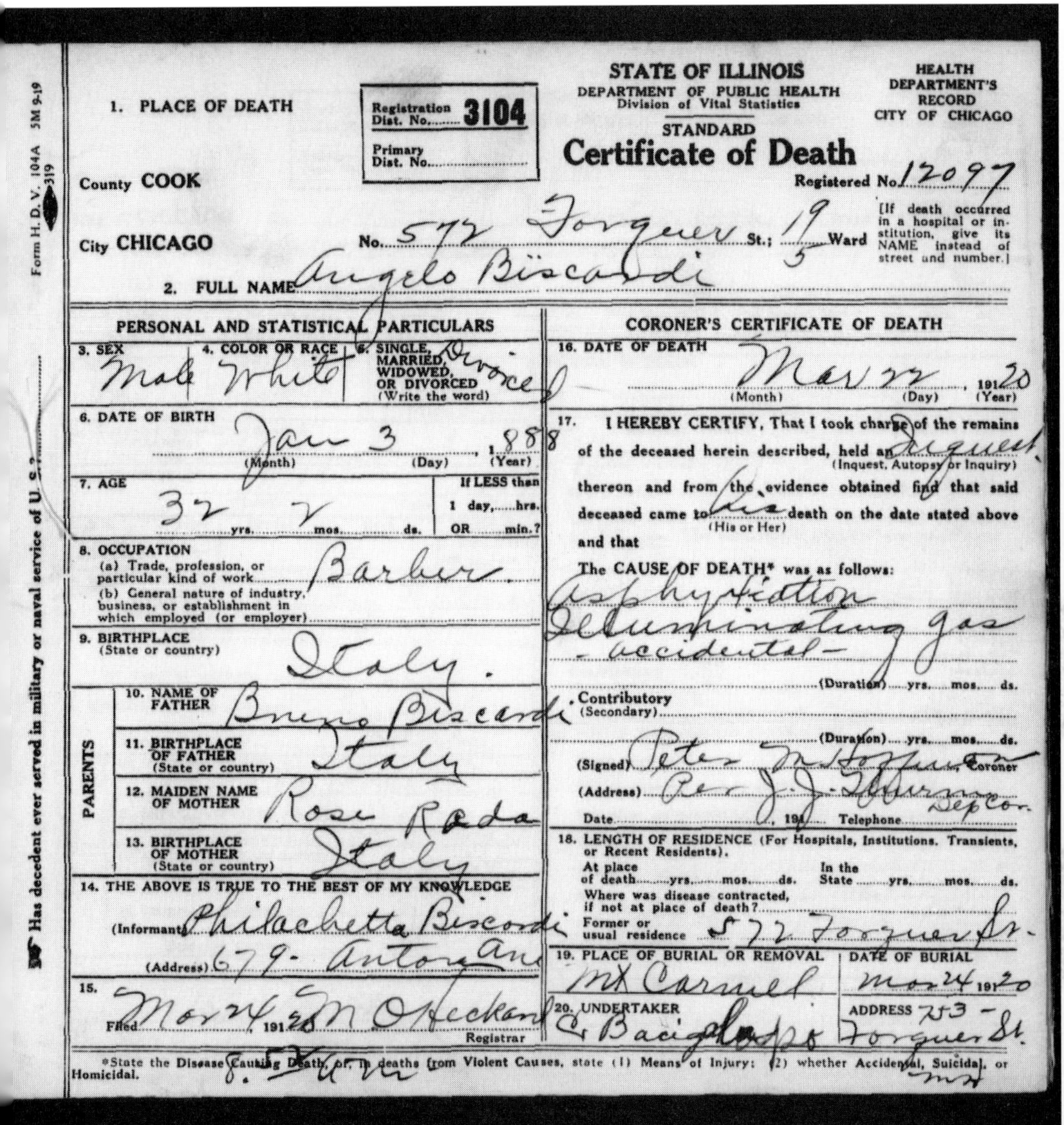

Form H. D. V. 104A 5M 9-19 319

STATE OF ILLINOIS
DEPARTMENT OF PUBLIC HEALTH
Division of Vital Statistics
STANDARD
Certificate of Death

HEALTH DEPARTMENT'S RECORD CITY OF CHICAGO

1. PLACE OF DEATH
Registration Dist. No. 3104
Primary Dist. No.
County COOK
Registered No. 12097
City CHICAGO No. 572 Forquer St.; 19 Ward 5
[If death occurred in a hospital or institution, give its NAME instead of street and number.]

2. FULL NAME Angelo Biscardi

PERSONAL AND STATISTICAL PARTICULARS

3. SEX Male
4. COLOR OR RACE White
5. SINGLE, MARRIED, WIDOWED, OR DIVORCED (Write the word) Divorce
6. DATE OF BIRTH Jan (Month) 3 (Day), 1888 (Year)
7. AGE 32 yrs. 2 mos. ds. If LESS than 1 day, hrs. OR min.?
8. OCCUPATION (a) Trade, profession, or particular kind of work Barber. (b) General nature of industry, business, or establishment in which employed (or employer)
9. BIRTHPLACE (State or country) Italy.
PARENTS
10. NAME OF FATHER Bruno Biscardi
11. BIRTHPLACE OF FATHER (State or country) Italy
12. MAIDEN NAME OF MOTHER Rose Rada
13. BIRTHPLACE OF MOTHER (State or country) Italy
14. THE ABOVE IS TRUE TO THE BEST OF MY KNOWLEDGE
(Informant) Philachetta Biscardi
(Address) 679 - Antonan
15. Filed Mar 24, 1920 M O'Heckard Registrar

CORONER'S CERTIFICATE OF DEATH

16. DATE OF DEATH Mar (Month) 22 (Day), 1920 (Year)
17. I HEREBY CERTIFY, That I took charge of the remains of the deceased herein described, held an Inquest (Inquest, Autopsy or Inquiry) thereon and from the evidence obtained find that said deceased came to his (His or Her) death on the date stated above and that
The CAUSE OF DEATH* was as follows:
Asphyxiation
Illuminating gas
- accidental -
(Duration) yrs. mos. ds.
Contributory (Secondary)
(Duration) yrs. mos. ds.
(Signed) Peter M Hoffman Coroner
(Address) Per J. J. Thurn Dep Cor.
Date 191 Telephone
18. LENGTH OF RESIDENCE (For Hospitals, Institutions, Transients, or Recent Residents).
At place of death yrs. mos. ds. In the State yrs. mos. ds.
Where was disease contracted, if not at place of death?
Former or usual residence 572 Forquer St.
19. PLACE OF BURIAL OR REMOVAL Mt Carmel
DATE OF BURIAL Mar 24, 1920
20. UNDERTAKER C. Baciglappo
ADDRESS 753 - Forquer St.

*State the Disease Causing Death, or, in deaths from Violent Causes, state (1) Means of Injury; (2) whether Accidental, Suicidal, or Homicidal.

Has decedent ever served in military or naval service of U. S.?

Angelo Biscardi's Certificate of Death, 1920. Note cause of death: "Asphyxiation, Illuminating gas, accidental." (*Author's collection*) was promoted to private first class. On August 24, he was assigned as an infantry replacement to Company "D," 4th Infantry Regiment, 3rd Division. On October 6, Pfc. Biscardi was severely wounded during the Meuse-Argonne Offensive. The notation in Biscardi's statement of service card only hints at the horror and suffering he must have experienced: "Bayonet W. rt. Side Sh [shell] W. rt. Eye." He returned to the U.S. in late February 1919 and was sent to military hospitals for convalescence. These hospitals included Fort Sheridan Hospital in Illinois, Marine Hospital, and Drexel Hospital. He was then sent to Camp Grant, Illinois, where, after receiving his final pay of $105.35, he was discharged on April 14. One source indicates that his wife and child died of influenza during his time in service, while another source indicates that he was divorced. In any event, personal and physical tragedy continued to plague him; unable to work at his previous job as a laborer due to his weakened physical condition, he moved to Chicago where he sought work as a watchman. A May 1919 newspaper article states: "Angelo Biscardi, bearing seven wounds received in the war, the *Croix de Guerre*, and honorable discharge papers from the Italian and United States armies, is walking the streets of Chicago seeking employment."[25]

At some point, he found work as a barber in Chicago. Sadly, tragedy struck soon thereafter. Biscardi died at his home in Chicago on March 22, 1920. The cause of death was listed as "Asphyxiation, Illuminating gas—accidental."[26] It is known that many returning servicemen, unable to cope with the horrors of what they had been through and unable to adjust into civilian society, committed suicide throughout the 1920s and 1930s. Perhaps Angelo Biscardi, twice-wounded veteran of two armies, was one such person.

Carmine Chiappetta[27]

Carmine Chiappetta was born in Marano Marchesato around 1888, the son of Saverio Chiappetta and Beatrice Trombino. In 1903, Chiappetta came to the U.S., initially to Chicago, where he worked as a laborer. He stayed for about seven years before returning to Marano Marchesato. There, in 1912, he married Francesca Chiappetta; their first son, Giuseppe, was born in Marano Marchesato in 1913.

As was common with Calabrians seeking to earn money to support their families, Chiappetta left his wife and newborn son in Marano Marchesato and again set forth to the new world aboard the steamship *König Albert*, departing from Naples on May 18, 1913 and arriving in New York on May 30. He stayed in Chicago briefly before making the trip north to Kenosha to join the growing Calabrian community there prior to 1917. In Kenosha, Chiappetta was a laborer at a tannery, living with his brother, Pasquale, a self-employed cobbler, and Pasquale's wife.

Along with thousands of other Kenoshans, Carmine registered for the draft during the first national registration day, June 5, 1917. By that time, he had declared his intention to become a citizen of the United States, and although he listed his wife and child as dependents, he did not claim exemption from the draft. Soon, Chiappetta, along with others, was called to report for physical examination to determine his eligibility for military service. Accordingly, he appeared at a Kenosha examining board on March 4, 1918; there it was determined that he was in good health with physical problems. He weighed 135.5 pounds and was 5 feet 3 inches tall; he had normal physical measurements, no missing teeth, and 20/20 vision in each eye. Found "physically qualified for general military service," he was advised to wait for his call to duty.[28] It was not until May 1918, however, that Chiappetta was called to service.

Along with many other Kenoshans, Chiappetta reported for service on May 26, 1918. He was initially assigned to the 35th Company, 161st Depot Brigade, at Camp Grant, Illinois, as a private, serial number 2825515. On June 13, a large number of men left Camp Grant and boarded trains headed for Camp Custer, Michigan, where they were assigned to units in the newly forming 85th Division. Chiappetta, along with other transferring Calabrians from Kenosha, was assigned to Company "F," 337th Infantry Regiment.

The 85th left the U.S. bound for France on July 23, 1918. The division disembarked at Liverpool, England, and traveled by rail to Southampton. There, the men boarded vessels that carried them to France. The 85th Division was soon redesignated as the 4th Depot Division, charged with sending replacement to combat units. On August 26, Chiappetta was sent to Company "G," 18th Infantry Regiment, 1st Division. The division, a veteran Regular Army division, suffered heavy losses at Soissons in late July; the infusion of new men bolstered the manpower of the regiments, but also provided a training challenge to the veterans in the ranks.

The 1st Division was to be a key part of the first offensive action of by the newly formed American 1st Army under General John Pershing. The Army was to reduce the Saint-Mihiel salient. The 18th Infantry Regiment was to participate in the assault on the flanks of Mont Sec, a large prominence that had given the German Army a clear view of the Allied lines for miles around. The assault was to begin on September 12. The division marched to their jump-off positions in the pouring rain on September 11, the men marching through knee-deep mud in some places. Chiappetta's Company "G" was part of the 2nd Battalion (consisting of Companies "E," "F," "G," and "H") of the 18th Infantry Regiment; the 1st and 2nd Battalions were to be in the assault line with the mission of, once a given line was reached, turning to face west to protect the left flank of the division from possible attack from the Mont Sec area.

The men arrived at their jump-off position in time to witness the start of one of the greatest artillery barrages in history. Beginning at 1 a.m. on September 12, the Allied artillery bombarded the German lines with an overwhelming concentration of fire. At 5 a.m., the artillery switched to a rolling barrage behind, which the infantry assault waves, including Chiappetta in Company "G," followed. Expecting serious resistance, the men advanced against thickly wired positions. Many of the men simply clambered over the barbed-wire obstacles rather than cutting the wire.

The men advanced up to and beyond the first objective, the Rupt de Mad, by 5:30 a.m. At some spots along this stream, the men plunged into the water and crossed, while at others, the engineer regiment threw across prepared footbridges. The men continued on, following the rolling barrage closely. Chiappetta and the rest of the 2nd Battalion wheeled left and faced Mont Sec. The second objective, the wooded slopes of eastern Mont Sec, was reached on time also. As the men advanced into the woods toward the third objective, they encountered the heaviest resistance of the day. They were ordered to advance further, toward the next day's objectives, and this they did, advancing to the Bois-de-l'Étang, Joli Bois, and Bois de Gargantua.

At about 7:30 a.m., Chiappetta went down with a serious wound, a gunshot wound to the head. Years later, he had "a very hazy memory of his wound," according to a doctor.[29] He told the doctor that he remembered, "going over the top and also digging a hole to get into and awoke in hospital. Says he never saw any of his Company again."[30] He also suffered some sort of leg wound. Probably some members of Company "G" saw Chiappetta shot in the head, or perhaps stretcher-bearers who picked him up later saw the severity of his wounds. In any event, he was initially reported as killed in action. But he was very much alive when he was brought into Field Hospital No. 3, where he was given morphine, hot drinks, and hot water. At 5:10 p.m., he was evacuated to Mobile Hospital 39.

There, doctors recorded the following: "Wound 7:30 AM Sept 12/18 by shrapnel.... Penetrating wound upper 1/3 R. thigh outer no exit R. foot very cold ... no plantar upper. II Wound of skull II spattering in area of wound. No depression of cranium observed I thigh right no T.B or fracture observed. W. G. Herman, 1st Lt. M.R."[31]

Chiappetta made his way through the Army hospital system in France before returning to the U.S. aboard the *Pocahontas* on November 7, 1918. In the U.S., he went to various hospitals until his discharge on January 5, 1919. As stated above, Chiappetta had been reported as killed in action. However, at one of the hospitals in France, someone who knew him and knew that he had been listed as killed in action recognized him. The man notified proper channels that Chiappetta was indeed alive. It took a while for that information to make its way through these channels to his family. Chiappetta lived in Kenosha with his family and worked at various jobs after the war. He struggled with physical problems resulting from his horrific, near-fatal injury until his death in Wisconsin in 1955.

Pvt. Carmine Chiappetta, 18th Infantry Regiment, 1st Division, 1919. (*Theresa Van Landuyt*)

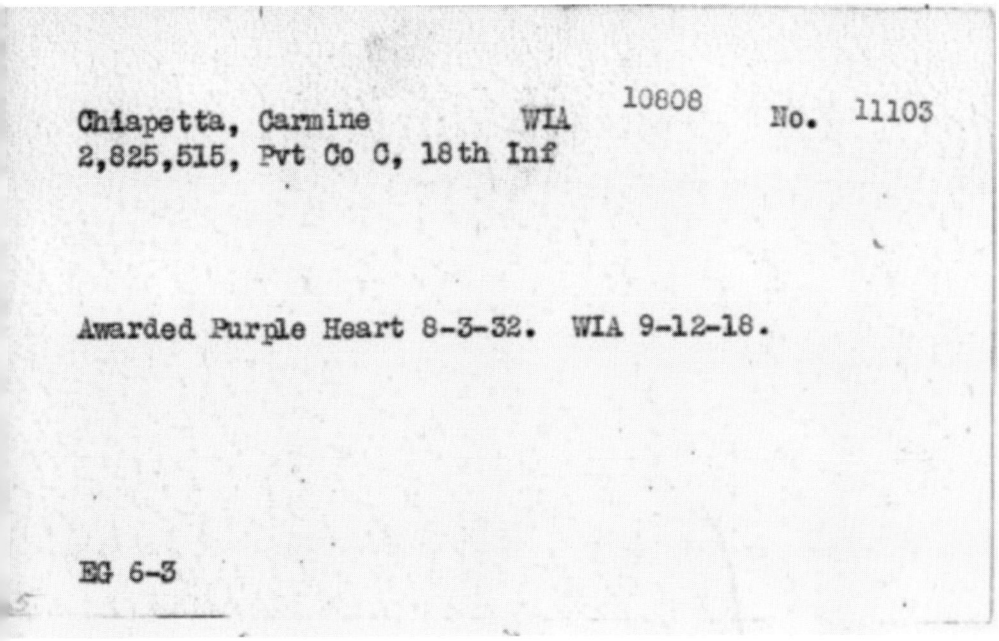

Chiapetta, Carmine WIA 10808 No. 11103
2,825,515, Pvt Co C, 18th Inf

Awarded Purple Heart 8-3-32. WIA 9-12-18.

EG 6-3

Above: Award card showing the award of the Purple Heart to Pvt. Carmine Chiappetta, 18th Infantry Regiment, 1st Division, for wounds received in action, 1932. (*National Archives*)

Below: Award card showing that Pvt. Carmine Chiappetta was cited in General Orders, 1st Division. This allowed him to wear a small Silver Star device on the ribbon of his Victory Medal and, after 1932, the award of the Silver Star Medal. (*National Archives*)

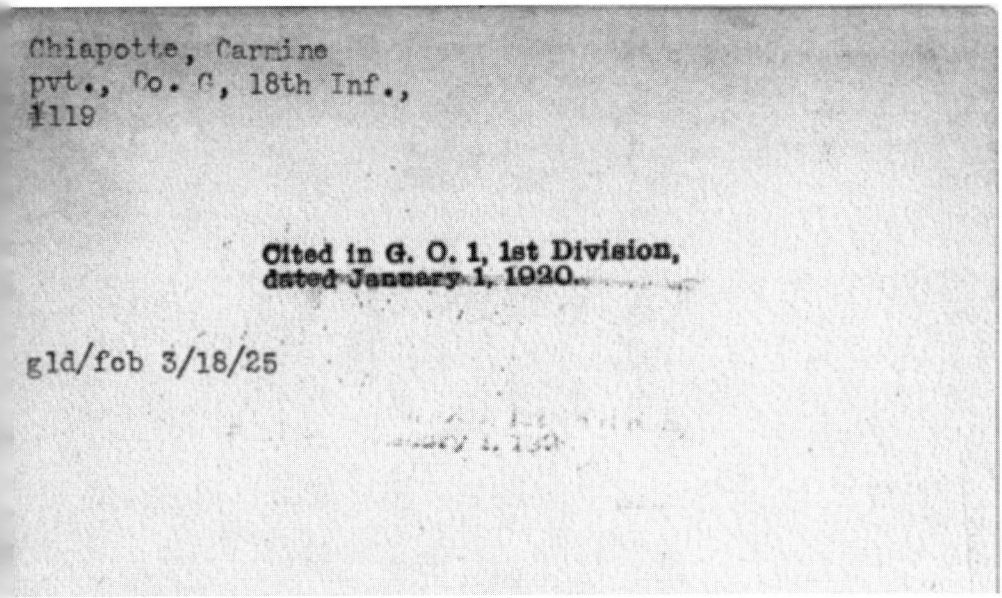

Chiapotte, Carmine
pvt., Co. C, 18th Inf.,
1119

Cited in G. O. 1, 1st Division, dated January 1, 1920.

gld/fcb 3/18/25

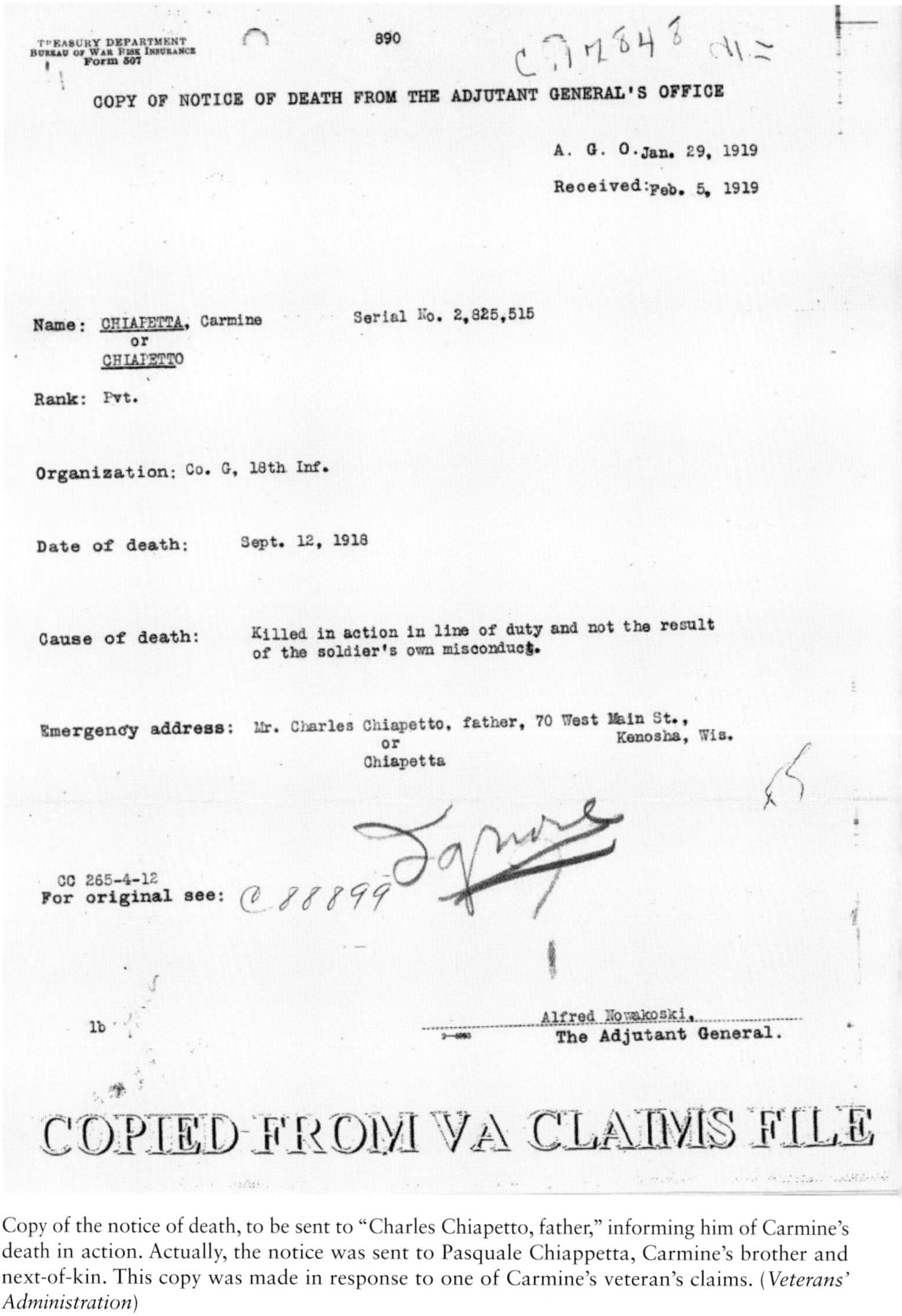

TREASURY DEPARTMENT
BUREAU OF WAR RISK INSURANCE
Form 507

890

C 1784[?]

COPY OF NOTICE OF DEATH FROM THE ADJUTANT GENERAL'S OFFICE

A. G. O. Jan. 29, 1919

Received: Feb. 5, 1919

Name: CHIAPETTA, Carmine or CHIAPETTO — Serial No. 2,825,515

Rank: Pvt.

Organization: Co. G, 18th Inf.

Date of death: Sept. 12, 1918

Cause of death: Killed in action in line of duty and not the result of the soldier's own misconduct.

Emergency address: Mr. Charles Chiapetto, father, 70 West Main St., Kenosha, Wis. or Chiapetta

CC 265-4-12
For original see: C 88899

lb

Alfred Nowakoski,
The Adjutant General.

COPIED FROM VA CLAIMS FILE

Copy of the notice of death, to be sent to "Charles Chiapetto, father," informing him of Carmine's death in action. Actually, the notice was sent to Pasquale Chiappetta, Carmine's brother and next-of-kin. This copy was made in response to one of Carmine's veteran's claims. (*Veterans' Administration*)

Luigi Chiappetta

Luigi (Louis) Chiappetta was born on February 2, 1893, in Marano Marchesato; he came to the U.S. in 1911 and settled in Kenosha. Drafted on May 25, 1918, Chiappetta was assigned as a private, serial number 2825479, to Company "F," 337th Infantry Regiment, 85th Division, at Camp Custer, Michigan. Chiappetta was promoted to private first class on June 22 and went overseas with his regiment in July 1918. On August 25, he was transferred as a replacement to Company "M," 7th Infantry Regiment, 3rd Division. On October 21, he was wounded, degree undetermined, during the Meuse-Argonne Offensive. The 7th Infantry Regiment was heavily engaged throughout the Meuse-Argonne Offensive. Indeed, Benjamin Conforti, a fellow Calabrian and Kenosha resident, was also wounded during the battle. There is a separate entry on Chiappetta's service record stating that he was "gassed at Verdun Sept. 1918." This would have been during the early stages of the Meuse-Argonne Offensive. There is no indication that Chiappetta applied for or received the Purple Heart Medal. Chiappetta probably served with his unit in the Army of Occupation of Germany after the war; he returned to the U.S. and was discharged on April 2, 1919. Luigi's brother, Beniamino, also served in the U.S. Army during World War I.

Beniamino Conforti

Beniamino (Benjamin) Conforti was born on January 2, 1894, in Marano Principato. He came to the U.S. in 1912, and settled in Chicago and Kenosha. He was inducted into the Army at Kenosha on May 26, 1918, and assigned as a private, serial number 2825539, to the 35th Company, 161st Depot Brigade, at Camp Grant, Illinois. On June 13, he was sent to Camp Custer, Michigan, where he became part of Company "C," 337th Infantry Regiment, 85th Division. He went overseas with the division on July 22; on August 25, he was sent as a replacement to Company "I," 7th Infantry Regiment, 3rd Division. The 3rd was in reserved during the St Mihiel Offensive from September 12–16. It was, however, heavily engaged in the Meuse-Argonne Offensive. Benjamin was wounded, degree undetermined on October 12, 1918. He returned to the U.S., arriving on March 24, 1919, and he was discharged at Camp Grant on April 11.

Giuseppe Covelli[32]

Giuseppe (Joe) Covelli was born on October 10, 1894, in Marano Marchesato, the son of Gaetano Covelli and Rachela Orrico. Covelli's father and brothers made several trips to the U.S. before he joined them in Chicago in 1911. By the time he registered for the draft in 1917, Covelli had moved to Kenosha where he worked as a laborer for the Chicago and North Western Railroad. He claimed exemption from the draft on account of being the sole support for his wife and stepchildren; further, he was still an alien and entitled to exemption. All this notwithstanding, he was notified to report for physical examination to determine his health status prior to induction, probably sometime in February 1918. Of medium height, with a stout build, brown eyes, and dark brown hair, Covelli passed his physical and he was ordered to report for induction into the Army.

He entered service on May 30, 1918, reporting to Camp Grant, Illinois, as a private, serial number 2825700, in the 35th Company, 161st Depot Brigade. On June 13, Covelli was one of 2,500 men sent from Camp Grant to Camp Custer, Michigan, where he was assigned to Company "F," 337th Infantry Regiment, 85th Division, which was undergoing training prior to shipment overseas. Covelli left Camp Custer with the division shortly thereafter; the division sailed for France aboard the *Neleus* on July 22, arriving there, after a short stay in England, in early August.

Soon after arrival, the 85th Division was redesignated as the 4th Depot Division and was tasked to train and send men as replacements to combat units that needed to fill regiments depleted by casualties. In August, the division sent a large draft of men to the 1st Division, and Covelli was assigned to Company "G," 18th Infantry Regiment, on August 19, at the end of that regiment's stay in the Saizerais Sector. While there, the regiment suffered two men killed and seven men wounded. The regiment pulled out of the line on August 22. The new men, joining a veteran regiment, undoubtedly felt out of place. Most of the replacements, having been drafted in late spring, had not received adequate training, and they had to be brought up to speed by the veterans quickly.

It is interesting to consider here the state of training and fitness of men in Covelli's situation. General Headquarters, American Expeditionary Forces, had planned for a three-month training period for American divisions. The plan would allow a division, under British or French instructors, to gradually and systematically become accustomed to front line operations. The few Regular Army and National Guard divisions that arrived in France in 1917 and early 1918 received roughly this type of training; National Army divisions (those raised by the draft) arriving in France in the summer of 1918 received less than this. Men such as Covelli were even more at a disadvantage and received nowhere near this type of training.

Many men drafted in late May 1918, for example, were transferred at least once before joining their permanent organization. By early August, they were in France where some of them were sent out as replacement troops to cover combat losses in other divisions. Thus, after barely three months in service, much of which was taken up with travel and administrative matters, and with probably the barest minimum of effective training, men were thrust into units preparing for major battle; most of these men would see combat by mid-September after not quite four months in service.

Men who arrived in August had to adapt and adjust to the front lines and trenches with minimal training. They were forced to become a part of a combat unit that had, in most cases (as in the case of the veteran 1st Division), already been through the crucible of battle and had formed a cohesion based upon that common ordeal. They had to fit in to a group that would have been naturally wary of "outsiders;" perhaps some men who had difficulty with the English language suffered even more as they tried to blend in and assimilate into a close-knit group.

Covelli participated in the Saint-Mihiel Offensive, the first American planned and led action of the new U.S. 1st Army. After the battle, Covelli's regiment rested, re-equipped, and engaged in maneuvers and training. Beginning on September 21, the regiment marched and then road in French *camions* (trucks) to a new location southeast of the Argonne Forest, in preparation for their part in the next battle. The regiment and division were part of army reserve; the men could plainly hear the artillery bombardment along the front, culminating in the terrific opening barrage during the early morning of September 26, the opening of the Meuse-Argonne Offensive. On September 29, the division was ordered north to replace the 35th Division that had suffered in the initial attacks along and east of the Aire River. After a long, rough march, the regiment took over a position preparatory to an assault.

The 3rd Battalion, in the assault wave, took cover in fox holes about a kilometer south of Chaudron Farm; the 2nd Battalion, Covelli's, was in support farther south in a ravine east of the village of Charpentry. The 1st Battalion was in reserve further back. Almost immediately, the 3rd and 2nd Battalions began to suffer from exposure to latent gas in the area, the result of gas bombardment of the previous few days. The men stayed in these precarious positions, exposed to both artillery shelling and gas attacks, until the start of the attack on October 4, 1918.

The 3rd Battalion jumped off just before 5:30 a.m. on October 4, the 2nd Battalion, Covelli's, following in support. Hoping to achieve the element of surprise, the attack started without preliminary artillery bombardment. The ground over which the 18th advanced was a series of wooded hills interspersed with ravines. The assault waves almost immediately came under German machine gun and artillery fire; although in support, the 2nd Battalion caught up with the assault wave near Chaudron Farm and joined the main line. The men advanced and cleared Montrebeau Woods, in which the first German line of resistance was imbedded. Continuing the attack, the battalions moved into the Exermont ravine and cleared part of Exermont. Elements of the 3rd Battalion made it as far as the top of Hill 240, north of Exermont, before coming under severe artillery fire and falling back to the south slopes of Hill 240. There the 3rd Battalion dug in for the night, the 2nd Battalion digging in just south of the road leading out of Exermont.

Due to the severe fighting in the woods, ravines, and hills, both the 3rd and 2nd Battalions were reduced to remnants of companies; they took advantage of the cessation of the day's fighting to reorganize. On October 5, the advance began again. The 3rd Battalion followed the American artillery's rolling barrage up over the top of Hill 240. The men continued down the north slope of the hill, meeting stubborn resistance at the German foxholes in the low ground to the north. The battalions were here subject to machine-gun fire from the left and right, in addition to 77-mm artillery fire. The men were ordered to push forward north of Hill 240, and, in the afternoon of October 5, they made the advance up through the woods on the south slope of Hill 176. Here the men met the same savage machine gun and artillery fire that now prevented further advance for the day. It was during this savage fighting that Covelli was wounded.

The precise nature and type of Covelli's wounds appears differently in the various records. His discharge paperwork, dated February 1919, bears the cryptic, "G.S.W. [gunshot wound] right side face & leg arm." His hospital admission paperwork, dated October 13, 1930, states, "bullet in neck, and bayonet in left forearm, and thigh." A few sentences later, the same document states that the "shot entered back of neck, emerged near right angle of mandible. Bayonet wound in right forearm.... Legs, 2 machine gun bullets..." A 1949 hospital document refers to "a GSW on the right side of his neck ... scars, left forearm and left knee, due to GSW..." A 1950 Veterans Administration document mentions "shrapnel wounds to the face, to the left forearm, and to the right leg ... scars on the face, below the ear, on the left forearm, and on the right leg. They are shrapnel wounds. Apparently the wounds were rather superficial and they do not impair function or cause any symptoms to speak of now... superficial small scars face, forearm and right leg, residuals of shell fragment wounds..." In a 1961 letter, Covelli's doctor, C. C. Davin, states that Covelli "suffered a bayonet wound of the left forearm and shrapnel wound of the right knee."[33]

Covelli's wounds were traumatic and severe, and sometime after his wounding, Covelli was found by litter bearers and taken back to the battalion aid station. As was typical for wounded men, after initial treatment, he made his way back through the hospital system, at one point being in a hospital housed in an old French church. Covelli probably spent the remainder of the war in one of the large A.E.F. base hospitals prior to being sent home aboard U.S.S. *George Washington* on January 12, 1919. Covelli arrived in the United States on January 21; he made his way to the discharge detachment at Camp Grant where he started his service the previous May. At some point, Covelli was advised by authorities to continue his enlistment and receive light duty. Covelli declined, however, and was duly discharged from the Army on February 27, 1919; he received an "excellent" character rating. Covelli made his way back to his family in Kenosha, where he found work as a laborer in mid-April.

Shortly after his discharge, Covelli began experiencing pain and tenderness in the back of his neck at the site of his bullet wound, sometimes for two or three days at a time. This condition was aggravated in cold or damp weather, of which there is no shortage in Kenosha. Covelli became an American citizen in November 1919, taking advantage of a Congressional act that waived certain filing and residency requirements for alien men serving in the armed forces during the war.

Beginning in January 1922, Covelli took advantage of the Vocational Rehabilitation Act, and he began studying to become a machinist at Kenosha Vocational School. In addition, he was granted a monthly stipend of one hundred dollars, later increased to $167.50 on account of his dependents. In April 1924, his rehabilitation was considered complete, and he terminated his training. From that time on, he worked irregularly as a mechanic and laborer in Kenosha until his death in 1976.

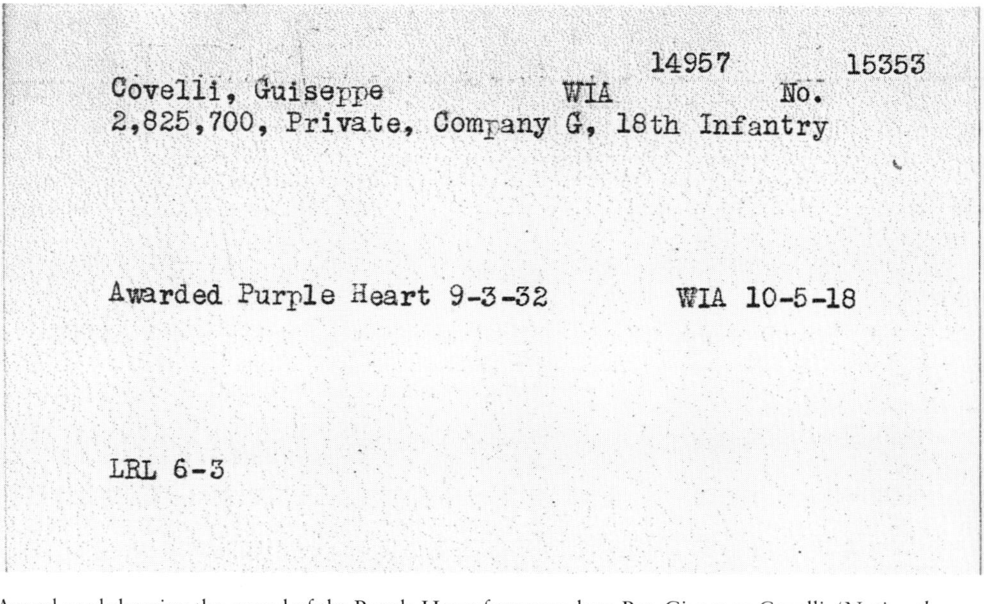

14957 15353
Covelli, Guiseppe WIA No.
2,825,700, Private, Company G, 18th Infantry

Awarded Purple Heart 9-3-32 WIA 10-5-18

LRL 6-3

Award card showing the award of the Purple Heart for wounds to Pvt. Giuseppe Covelli. (*National Archives*)

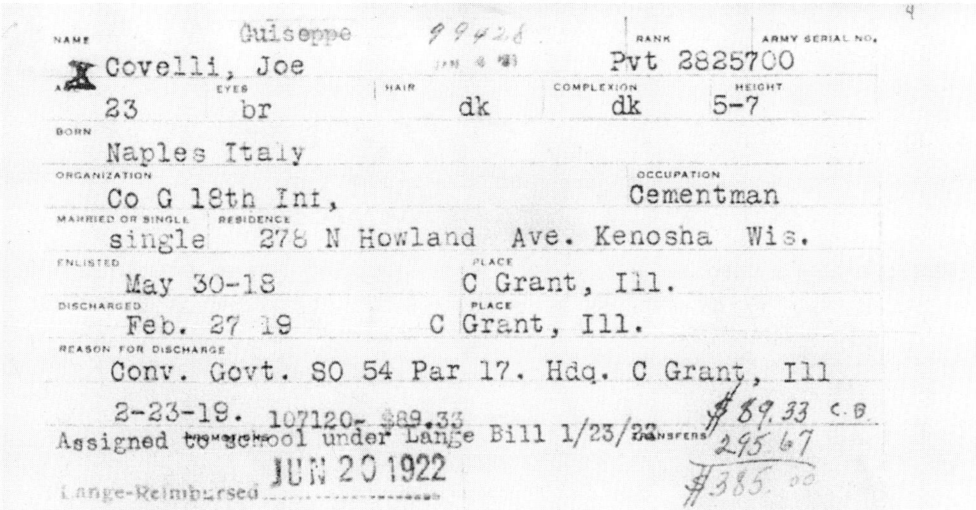

NAME Guiseppe 99428 RANK ARMY SERIAL NO.
Covelli, Joe Pvt 2825700
AGE 23 EYES br HAIR dk COMPLEXION dk HEIGHT 5-7
BORN Naples Italy
ORGANIZATION Co G 18th Inf, OCCUPATION Cementman
MARRIED OR SINGLE single RESIDENCE 278 N Howland Ave. Kenosha Wis.
ENLISTED May 30-18 PLACE C Grant, Ill.
DISCHARGED Feb. 27 19 PLACE C Grant, Ill.
REASON FOR DISCHARGE Conv. Govt. SO 54 Par 17. Hdq. C Grant, Ill 2-23-19.
107120- $89.33
Assigned to school under Lange Bill 1/23/22 TRANSFERS $89.33 C.B. 295.67 $385.00
JUN 20 1922
Lange-Reimbursed

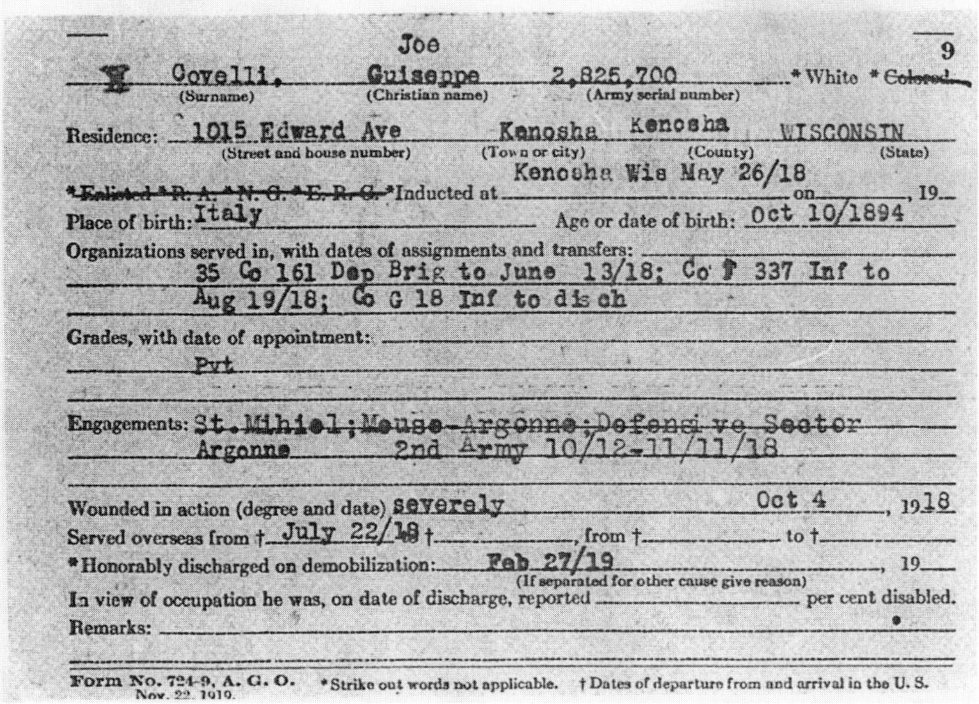

9
Joe
X Covelli, Guiseppe 2,825,700 *White *Colored
(Surname) (Christian name) (Army serial number)
Residence: 1015 Edward Ave Kenosha Kenosha WISCONSIN
(Street and house number) (Town or city) (County) (State)
*Enlisted *R. A. *N. G. *E. R. C. *Inducted at Kenosha Wis May 26/18 on , 19
Place of birth: Italy Age or date of birth: Oct 10/1894
Organizations served in, with dates of assignments and transfers:
35 Co 161 Dep Brig to June 13/18; Co F 337 Inf to Aug 19/18; Co G 18 Inf to disch
Grades, with date of appointment:
Pvt
Engagements: St. Mihiel; Meuse-Argonne; Defensive Sector Argonne 2nd Army 10/12-11/11/18
Wounded in action (degree and date) severely Oct 4, 1918
Served overseas from †July 22/18†, from † to †
*Honorably discharged on demobilization: Feb 27/19, 19
(If separated for other cause give reason)
In view of occupation he was, on date of discharge, reported per cent disabled.
Remarks:
Form No. 724-9, A. G. O. Nov. 22, 1919. *Strike out words not applicable. † Dates of departure from and arrival in the U. S.

Wisconsin veteran's bonus card, top, and statement of service card for Pvt. Giuseppe Covelli, 18th Infantry Regiment, 1st Division. (*Wisconsin Veterans Museum*)

Pvt. Giuseppe Covelli, 18th Infantry Regiment, 1st Division, with friends, *c.* January 1919. (*Theresa Van Landuyt*)

George Imbrogno[34]

George Imbrogno was born in Cosenza on March 8, 1893. He came to the U.S. in 1912 and was a candy maker working for E. J. Brach and Sons in Chicago when he was inducted into the Army on September 21, 1917. Imbrogno was a private, serial number 283634, in Company "E," 344th Infantry Regiment, 86th Division, at Camp Grant, Illinois. On December 17, Imbrogno was transferred to Company "C," 128th Infantry Regiment, 32nd Division, a Wisconsin National Guard unit that was taking on draftees to fill out its rosters. Imbrogno went overseas with the 128th on February 19, 1918. Once in France, Imbrogno was sent to a replacement camp, awaiting assignment. By the end of April, Imbrogno had been sent as a replacement to Company "I," 16th Infantry Regiment, 1st Division. Imbrogno was severely wounded during his regiment's tough fighting near Soissons on July 19. He spent time in various hospitals in France until his return to the U.S. aboard the *Finland* in January 1919; he sailed as a medical and surgical patient requiring no attendant, from Base Hospital 69. Imbrogno was in Convalescent Center Detachment 1 at Camp Sherman, Ohio, when he was discharged on January 27, 1919. Imbrogno moved to Ohio where he was naturalized as a U.S. citizen in October 1919. In 1920, Imbrogno was cited for gallantry in action in 1st Division General Orders No. 1, entitling him to the award of a silver citation star and, later, the Silver Star medal.

Luigi Manna

Luigi Manna was born in Cosenza on February 12, 1887. He came to the U.S. about 1905, and he was a grocer in Kenosha when he entered the Army on April 26, 1918. Manna was a private, serial number 2043960, in the 2nd Company, 1st Battalion, 160th Depot Brigade, at Camp Custer, Michigan. On May 23, he was transferred to Company "F," 340th Infantry Regiment, 85th Division. Manna went overseas with his regiment on July 23. Upon arrival, the 85th Division became a depot division. On August 24, Manna was sent as a replacement to Company "D," 4th Infantry Regiment, 3rd Division. Manna was slightly wounded on October 5 during the Meuse-Argonne Offensive. While the 3rd Division participated in the Army of Occupation, Manna was probably recuperating in hospitals in France. He returned to the U.S. aboard U.S.S. *Von Steuben* on March 23, 1919, as part of the Camp Custer Detachment, 147th Infantry Regiment, 37th Division. This illustrates the practice of dividing men returning to the U.S. into detachments slated to travel to a camp near each man's home of record. Manna's detachment traveled as part of the 37th Division. From Camp Custer, Manna went to Camp Grant, Illinois, where he was discharged on April 15, 1919.

Michael Metagrano[35]

Michael Metagrano was born in Chicago on July 20, 1892, his father, Pasquale Metagrano, was from Marano Marchesato. As a young boy growing up with his parents and siblings on Ewing Street in Chicago's Near West Side Calabrian community, Metagrano experienced some medical problems. Although he avoided most of the normal childhood sicknesses and diseases, he exhibited some developmental delays. His mother remembered that he did not learn to walk until he was four years old; instead, he would crawl on his hands and knees. As a young child, he was often frightened, and he had trouble sleeping unless he was with his mother. Even then, he was plagued by bad dreams of himself falling. When he was school age, Metagrano developed an abscess on his lower left jaw; this caused him a great deal of trouble. Although he attended school from about the age of four to the age of ten when he left school in order to go to work, he had completed only through third grade. This was mostly due to absences attributed to problems with his abscess. Although he did well and got along well with his teachers, he had to repeat some grades due to his absences.

Metagrano had other medical problems. Soon after he had learned to walk, he came down with an unidentified illness. After recovery, he began to be plagued by seizures that caused him to injure himself. When he was eight years old, he suffered a seizure and fell from "the porch of a third story apartment to the roof of a two story building and then on to the ground."[36] He experienced an identical fall later that year, and he suffered a bad leg injury due to a fall while undergoing a seizure. At the age of twelve, while he was playing center field during a baseball game, Metagrano had a seizure and fell, cutting the back of his head and leaving a scar. Another fall resulted in a scar on his left eyebrow. When Metagrano was thirteen, a prominent Chicago surgeon, Dr. Carl Beck, determined that the abscess that had been bothering him was due to bad tooth; surgery soon corrected the problem and left Metagrano with a scar in his mouth.

Metagrano remembered that his father was a big, healthy man. Speaking in 1918 of his father, Metagrano recalled: "I am in no ways like him. I am like my mother. He used to get mad at me, because I didn't go to school, but he never hit me because I was always sick."[37] After leaving school, Metagrano's first job was with the National Biscuit Company where he worked operating a rolling machine at $4 per week. His next job involved pulling cakes out of an oven, with a raise in pay to $9 per week, but the heat caused an increase in his spells so he had to quit the job. Metagrano soon went to another branch of the same company where he worked once again on a rolling machine at $9 per week. On one occasion, when he was eighteen years old, Metagrano suffered a seizure; he later recalled: "[I] lost control of myself, and my hand went between the rollers."[38] This accident resulted in amputation of his right little finger at the middle of the second phalange.

Metagrano had time off work for recovery; when he reported back, however, he was let go, probably because the company feared that he might have another, more serious accident. His next job was as a collar-cutter at a tailor shop at $8 per week. Not caring for this type of work, Metagrano next went to work for the Western Electric Company performing piecework dismantling telephone coin boxes. At this job, he was able to make a minimum of $18 per week and often $20 or more per week. Metagrano had trouble with a drunken foreman, however, and he left this comparatively lucrative job. His next position was with the Northern Pacific Railway where he worked as an interpreter for Italian track laborers in Montana in the early 1910s. He was paid $1.75 per day for the seven months he worked there.

Once back in Chicago, Metagrano secured employment, filling orders for the Sawyer Biscuit Company at $12 per week. The job involved getting materials ready for shipping; according to him, "It was an easy job." He was soon given a raise to $15 per week. Michael later said: "I was not smart enough for shipping clerk ... [but] ... they couldn't touch me on running a machine."[39]

By June 1917, when he registered for the draft, Metagrano was living with his family in Chicago, while working at the Sawyer Biscuit Company as what he called an "order picker." Listed at 5 feet 4 inches tall with a medium build, black eyes, and black hair, his hand injury is noted as being to his left hand instead of his right. Metagrano stated that he was the sole support of his parents (although his father was probably still working at the time), but he declined to request an exemption from the draft.

Sometime soon after his registration, Metagrano was notified to report to Chicago Draft Board Number 43 for a physical examination to determine his fitness to serve in the Army. Despite his childhood sickliness and the fact that he was, as he was later described, "under developed physically," Metagrano was accepted for service and told to get his affairs in order and prepare for service.[40] Undoubtedly, Metagrano never informed the examining board that he was subject to seizures; it is highly unlikely that they would have declared him fit for service if he had informed them.

Metagrano was among the men in the first quota of draftees for the National Army, reporting to Camp Grant, Illinois, on September 19, 1917; he was a private, serial number 2061221, of Company "E," 344th Infantry Regiment, part of the newly forming 86th Division. A follow-up physical exam revealed that Metagrano had black eyes, black hair, and was 5 feet 2.125 inches tall. His missing little finger, and scars resulting from the many falls he experienced during seizures, were also noted, along with tattoos, "MM," on both forearms. The clerks noted everything down to his shoe size: 6½ EE. Over the next few days, Metagrano received vaccinations, including the typhoid vaccination.

Metagrano identified his mother, Antonia, as his next of kin, and in October, he started allotments ($20 per month for nine months and $19 for one month) to purchase Liberty Bonds. All medical and administrative work underway, Metagrano, along with

Pfc. Michael Metagrano, 47th Infantry Regiment, 4th Division, *c.* 1917. (*Margo Metegrano*)

the other young men who were the first to report for duty, began training. At some point, he found time to pose for a photograph in uniform to send to the folks back home.

The men began training for modern warfare. In addition to target practice on newly issued Enfield rifles, the men trained in such auxiliary weapons as the automatic rifle, trench mortars, and machine guns. They dug and lived in trenches and learned about hand grenades and combat liaison. In addition to all this, they learned what all new soldiers must know about drill, regulations, and customs and courtesies. Beginning in October, men were detached from the 86th Division and sent to other camps and units to fill their ranks as they prepared for departure for France. In turn, the 86th received transfers from still other units and from National Army drafts. This mass movement of soldiers between camps and units was common throughout each unit's training time in the United States.

In February and March 1918, the 86th Division supplied 4,000 men to the 4th Division, a Regular Army division undergoing final preparation and training at Camp Greene, near Charlotte, North Carolina. On March 2, 1918, Metagrano was one of those transferees. He was given a "good" character rating by the commanding officer of Company "E," 344th Infantry Regiment, Captain Charles Stephans. Upon arrival at Camp Greene, Metagrano was assigned to Company "C," 47th Infantry Regiment, one of the four infantry regiments in the 4th Division. No doubt some of the newly assigned men had not had as much training as had Metagrano, who, having entered the Army in September, could count almost six months of training experience to his credit. But all the men, whether recent recruits or comparative veterans, had to continue training and develop unit cohesion. With deployment to the combat zone imminent, Metagrano started a $10,000 life insurance allotment, at $6.70 per month. Most soldiers availed themselves of this good opportunity provided by the government.

In May 1918, the regiment proceeded to Camp Mills, New York, to prepare for embarkation. There the men underwent final checks of equipment and service records before leaving the U.S. aboard the transport U.S.S. *Princess Matoika* on May 10, 1918. The ship was crowded; Metagrano recalled: "We were locked up like a lot of sheep." The cramped, weary men were allowed on deck for a couple of hours each day. Although many men later remembered shipboard food as abysmal, Metagrano had "no kick about army food, I am satisfied, for the war anything is good to eat."[41]

Metagrano and his regiment landed at Brest, France, and immediately hiked to Calais. There, according to Metagrano, "the Jerries threw bombs down on us, and there I got my first scare, with the shells coming." From Calais, the men marched to billets in a little village where they were required to remain out of sight and under cover during most of the day: "[German aircraft] were after us all the time, they came in the day, and took pictures and at night came and shelled us. The officers used to say, 'boys lay down on the ground.'"[42]

The regiment began training for duty in the trenches including more rifle and hand-grenade practice. Even in the midst of training, the men found time for diversions. The universal appeal for the Doughboys was *vin blanc* and *vin rouge*—white wine and red wine. Metagrano, whose father annually made wine at home, partook of some wine and beer, but he never got drunk. He recalled: "[I] might feel a little happy, but not drunk.... I saw too many made crazy by it, and I didn't want any court martial for a drink of wine." His seizures recurred in France, and he had them pretty badly. Once, while playing in a baseball game in France, he suffered a seizure and fell, badly cutting his left arm. He was carried into a Y.M.C.A. building for medical attention. Metagrano, along with most young men of this era, had poor dental health. According to him, "I had bum teeth all my life, and had most all of them taken out in France."[43] He had a fine upper plate with several teeth made while in France.

Metagrano's seizure spells came on suddenly, without warning, although heat or extreme excitement seems to have been a catalyst for some spells. The spells manifested themselves by frothing at the mouth (rarely biting his tongue) and falling to the ground, but no loss of sphincter control. The spells lasted for about ten minutes, after which he would have a bad headache. After a spell he usually got up and walked around. He recalled that after a spell he felt "dopey for a while, I can hear what is said, but I can't answer." Sometimes there had been several months between spells, and then he would have two or three a day. "When they come on me," Metagrano remembered, "they come on pretty good and strong."[44]

Metagrano was promoted to private first class on June 1, 1918, shortly after arrival in France. On July 15, 1918, the regiment was ordered to the front. As his regiment moved forward only seven weeks after arrival, with minimal additional training in theater, the men did most of their hiking at night. As was common with American forces throughout the war, the men sometimes rode in trucks. According to Metagrano: "The only time we traveled by day was when we went in at Chateau Thierry, and when they got the Jerries to going we were put on trucks to catch up with them."[45]

On July 24, 1918, the 1st and 3rd Battalions of the 47th were placed at the disposal of the 42nd Division, engaged in halting the German advance at Sergy, near the Ourcq River. The two battalions moved forward to Artois Farm on July 28; the 1st Battalion, with Metagrano's Company "C," went into line on the right of the 167th Infantry Regiment of the 42nd Division. The battalion crossed the Ourcq River and went into line with Companies "D" and "B" in front and Companies "A" and "C" in support.

On July 29, as the men prepared to go over the top, they came under German artillery and aircraft fire. Metagrano recalled: "That was the day I got shot, but I didn't get a chance to shoot at all; I had [an epileptic] spell just before I was shot. The Sergeant ordered me back and I wouldn't go, I told him I wanted to go over the top. The shells were coming over pretty thick, and I got hit in the hand." Metagrano did not know whether an aerial bomb or an artillery shell had hit him; it did not matter because the wound was considered severe, and he was evacuated to an aid station of the 167th Infantry Regiment where he was treated by Capt. W. W. Long and sent to the rear. Later, the sergeant who had ordered Metagrano back just before his wounding found Metagrano at the aid station and said, "'Now are you satisfied you little dago?' and I said I was satisfied." [46] At the aid station, he was given a tetanus shot in the abdomen; he later developed hive-like symptoms in reaction to the shot.

From there, Metagrano was moved to Evacuation Hospital Number 7 and then to American Red Cross Military Hospital Number 5. Metagrano remembered: "There were lots of wounded there, I saw a lot of boys, pretty bad off. I ain't got nothing compared to some of them, I consider myself lucky." Metagrano's own wound was described as a gunshot wound and characterized as "severe" on some field medical tags but "slight" on one tag. On August 5, Michael was sent to Base Hospital Number 8 and soon was

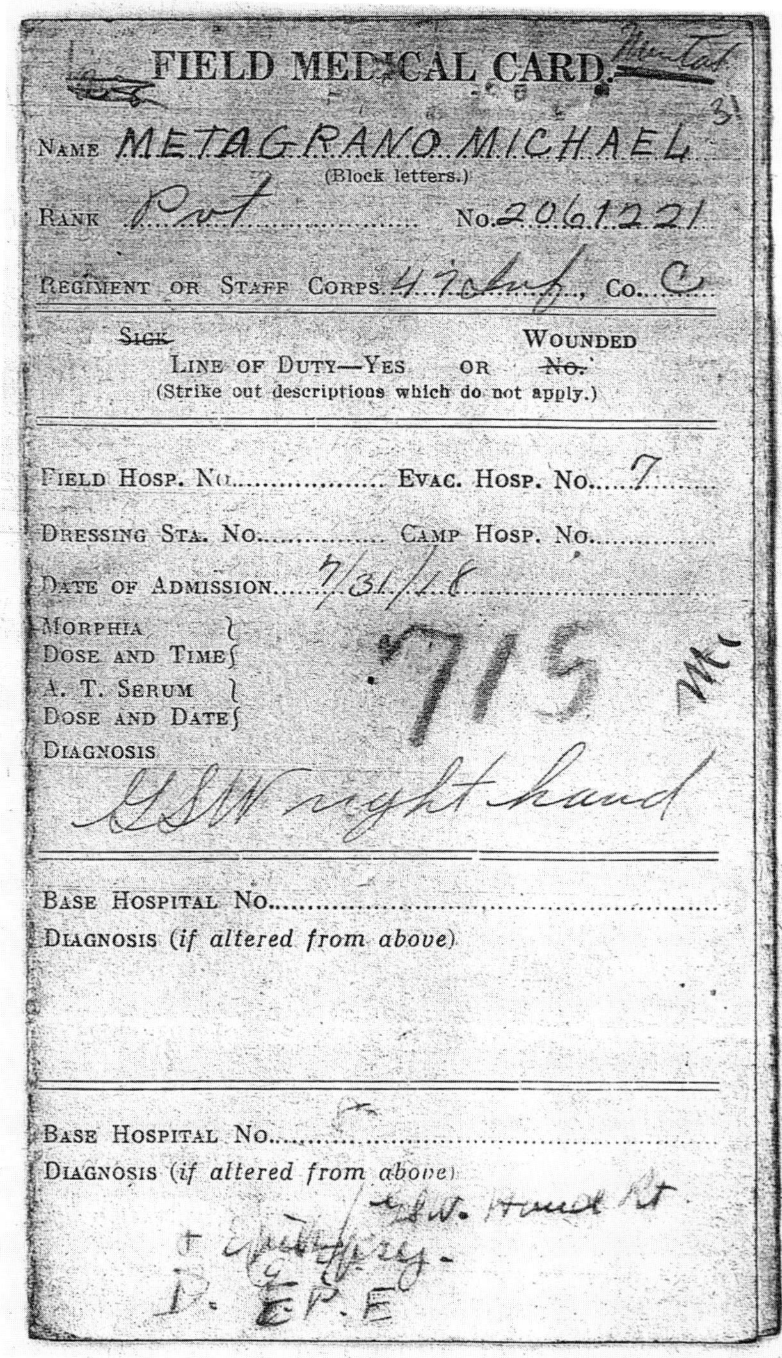

FIELD MEDICAL CARD.

NAME METAGRANO MICHAEL
(Block letters.)

RANK Pvt No. 2061221

REGIMENT OR STAFF CORPS 47 Inf., Co. C

~~SICK~~ WOUNDED
LINE OF DUTY—YES OR ~~NO.~~
(Strike out descriptions which do not apply.)

FIELD HOSP. NO. .... EVAC. HOSP. NO. 7

DRESSING STA. NO. .... CAMP HOSP. NO. ....

DATE OF ADMISSION 7/31/18

MORPHIA DOSE AND TIME

A. T. SERUM DOSE AND DATE

715

DIAGNOSIS

GSW right hand

BASE HOSPITAL NO. ....

DIAGNOSIS (*if altered from above*)

BASE HOSPITAL NO. ....

DIAGNOSIS (*if altered from above*)

G.S.W. Hand Rt

D. E.P.E

Field Medical Card for Pfc. Michael Metagrano, filled out shortly after he was wounded. (*National Archives*) under observation for epilepsy, grand mal. Doctors determined that Metagrano should be sent back to the U.S. and treated for epilepsy. Metagrano did not like the idea; he wanted to stay in the Army or at least work for the government. He had been helping out with wounded soldiers at the Red Cross hospital, and he considered himself a good soldier: "I knew the manual of arms, and was always clean, and alright at inspection, and always did what I was told."[47]

But Metagrano was ordered home; he shipped out aboard the transport U.S.S. *Aeolus* on September 30, 1918. Also aboard this vessel were men who were suffering from psychiatric problems. Metagrano became visibly upset when he remembered the treatment those men were subjected to "Poor fellows who lost their mind, they treated them awful, the meanest captain I ever seen." According to Metagrano, only two Medical Corps men were conscientious in their jobs. He witnessed some acts of cruelty, such as when a Medical Corps man beat a patient with a piece of broom handle, bruising him badly. He remembered that there were "four of five [psychiatric patients] who were very bad, and couldn't understand anything." Two hanged themselves, and one patient begged attendants to let him go up to the deck for fresh air, but they refused to allow him to go. Metagrano, witnessing this, "remonstrated with the Corps man for his roughness," and the Corps man threatened him. After reporting this to a doctor stateside, Metagrano "asked if his telling these things would make it difficult for him to remain in the military service, or to work for the government in some way." So bad was the treatment of patients that two lieutenants who were patients said they would prefer charges when they returned to the states. Despite witnessing such cruelty, Metagrano remembered "we had the best of everything from the Navy people, food and everything." While on the ship, Metagrano had another seizure that lasted ten to fifteen minutes. He "became unconscious, froth at the mouth, bit tongue, gnashed teeth, violent exertions, made noise with mouth. After effects: headache and dizzy."[48]

Upon arrival in the U.S., Metagrano was sent to U.S. Army General Hospital Number 30 at Plattsburg Barracks in northern New York. There he was evaluated for discharge; medical officers examined him and interviewed him. The hospital was located on the shores of Lake Champlain. Once, while Michael and an attendant were walking along the lake shore, someone fired a rifle, and Metagrano "became excited and is reputed by Pvt. St. Rock to have had a convulsion lasting 2 or 3 minutes only—threw arms about, frothed at mouth—felt dazed for about 20 minutes afterward."[49]

On October 16, 1918, Lt. Col. T. D. Woodson, commanding officer of General Hospital Number 30, wrote to Metagrano's half-brother, Thomas Frole, telling him that Metagrano had been admitted for treatment of nervous trouble. Two days later, Thomas wrote to Lieutenant Colonel Woodson requesting information on Metagrano's condition and permission to visit him. Four days after that, Woodson replied, telling Thomas that, although he was free to visit Metagrano at any time, he would recommend postponing any such visit until after the influenza epidemic had subsided. This, he reasoned, would permit greater freedom during the visit.

Metagrano had not heard from his mother since he was at Camp Mills in May 1918. He had received a letter from a cousin informing him that his mother had had a serious operation. In his letter to Lieutenant Colonel Woodson, Thomas Frole made mention of his mother's ill health and requested that any information about Metagrano be sent to him, Thomas, rather than to their mother for fear of shocking her and injuring her further.

Despite his seizure on the lakeshore, Metagrano seemed to be doing better. According to doctors, he was social, willing, and industrious; he was very neat, clean, and orderly in appearance. In conversing with doctors, he was "frank and cooperative, and his estimate of himself as having been a good soldier was easily believed from his general manner so far as conduct was concerned." Metagrano's final diagnosis was "Epilepsy, grand mal type, not in line of duty." On November 25, 1918, Metagrano was brought before a disability board consisting of Capt. Clarence A. Patten and 1st Lt. Edward T. Gibson, both Medical Corps officers, and he was recommended for discharge on a surgeon's certificate of disability. Consequently, Metagrano, who desired to remain in the Army or in government service, was discharged on December 22, 1918; his character was listed as "good." An attendant escorted Metagrano to his home the next day.[50]

By 1920, Metagrano was living with his parents and brother, Thomas Frole, in Chicago. The federal census that year lists his occupation as "military," and his industry as "tax school." It is possible that, due to his disability, Metagrano was attending government-sponsored training in the tax field. In 1920, Congress authorized the creation and award of the World War I Victory Medal, and veterans throughout the United States began to apply for their medal and applicable clasps. In October 1921, Michael sent in his application, claiming a Victory Medal with "France" service clasp. Having served with the 4th Division in combat, Michael was also entitled to the "Aisne-Marne" and "Defensive Sector" battle clasps; he was obviously uninformed, or perhaps misinformed, so his medal issued was with the "France" service clasp.

In 1924, Congress passed the Adjusted Compensation Act that authorized an increased compensation for veterans of the world war. Commonly called the veterans' bonus, it gave men $1 per day for stateside service and $1.25 per day for overseas service, subject to certain constraints, to be paid at a later date. In 1926, Metagrano filed a claim for adjusted compensation, listing his brother, Thomas Frole, as beneficiary. Metagrano's claim was approved for $436 (316 days' stateside service and 144 days' overseas service).

Sometime during the late 1920s, Metagrano must have experienced more medical issues. In early 1929, he was a patient in Unit 6, U.S. Naval Hospital, Great Lakes Naval Base, about thirty miles north of Chicago. He also became aware that he was entitled to battle clasps, rather than the "France" service clasp, for his Victory Medal. Metagrano corresponded with the War Department asking for clarification. While still in the hospital, on February 4, 1929, Michael hand-wrote a letter, on Veterans of Foreign Wars stationery, to Gen. C. H. Bridges, Acting Adjutant General:

> Dear Sir: Your letter of Jan 30th received and am forwarding my victory medal as per request. Was wounded, I think on July 30th, in head and hand and believe am entitled to clasp for Chateau-Thierry drive as well as Aisne-Marne and defensive sector. Hoping this will prove satisfactory, I am, Sincerely [signed] Michael Metagrano [*sic.*].[51]

Action was fairly quick on Metagrano's claim for correct battle clasps; on February 20, 1929, he was approved for the "Aisne-Marne" and "Defensive Sector" battle clasps. One assumes that his Victory Medal with correct clasps was returned to him in a timely manner.

It is not known how much Metagrano was troubled by epilepsy throughout his post-war life. His niece, Ann Metegrano Masesso, remembered him as "a funny, happy

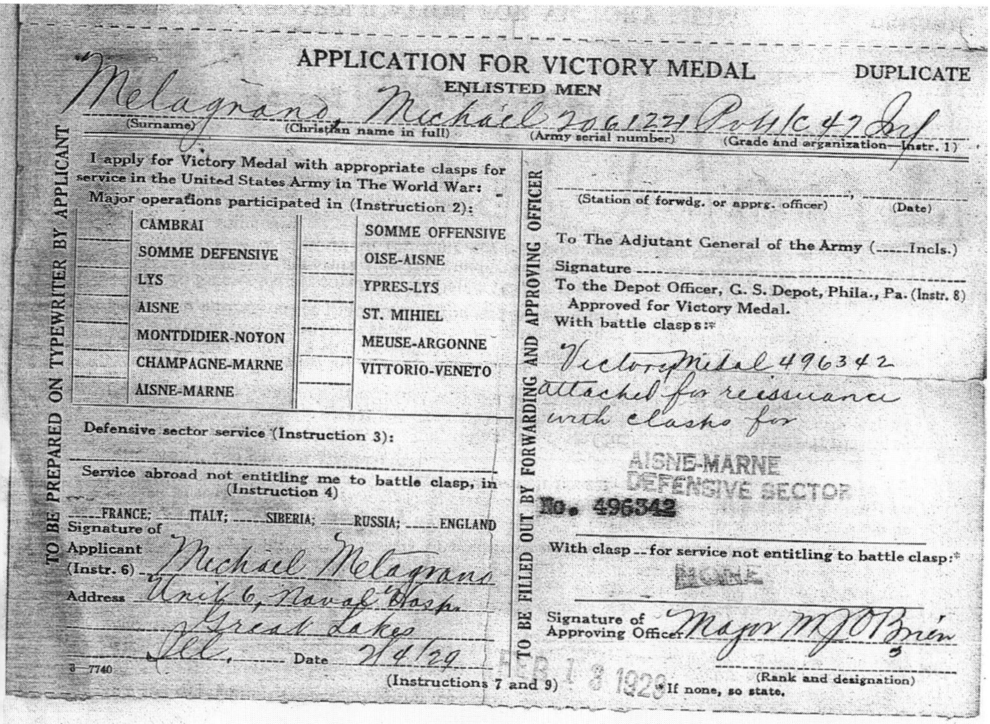

APPLICATION FOR VICTORY MEDAL — DUPLICATE
ENLISTED MEN

Melagrano, Michael 2061221 Pvt 11/C 47 Inf
(Surname) (Christian name in full) (Army serial number) (Grade and organization—Instr. 1)

TO BE PREPARED ON TYPEWRITER BY APPLICANT

I apply for Victory Medal with appropriate clasps for service in the United States Army in The World War:
Major operations participated in (Instruction 2):

	CAMBRAI		SOMME OFFENSIVE
	SOMME DEFENSIVE		OISE-AISNE
	LYS		YPRES-LYS
	AISNE		ST. MIHIEL
	MONTDIDIER-NOYON		MEUSE-ARGONNE
	CHAMPAGNE-MARNE		VITTORIO-VENETO
	AISNE-MARNE		

Defensive sector service (Instruction 3):

Service abroad not entitling me to battle clasp, in (Instruction 4)
----FRANCE; ----ITALY; ----SIBERIA; ----RUSSIA; ----ENGLAND

Signature of Applicant (Instr. 6) Michael Melagrano
Address Unit 6, Naval Hosp. Great Lakes Ill. Date 2/4/29

3—7740 (Instructions 7 and 9)

TO BE FILLED OUT BY FORWARDING AND APPROVING OFFICER

(Station of forwdg. or apprg. officer) (Date)

To The Adjutant General of the Army (-----Incls.)
Signature
To the Depot Officer, G. S. Depot, Phila., Pa. (Instr. 8)
Approved for Victory Medal.
With battle clasps:*
Victory Medal 496342 attached for reissuance with clasps for
AISNE-MARNE
DEFENSIVE SECTOR
No. 496342

With clasp--for service not entitling to battle clasp:*
NONE

Signature of Approving Officer Major M J O'Brien
(Rank and designation)
FEB 18 1929 *If none, so state.

Michael Metagrano's application for the correct clasps for his Victory Medal. (*National Archives*)

person," who "looked hardy."[52] He enjoyed roughhousing with Ann's brothers, to include, much to Ann's mother's chagrin, engaging in simulated sword fights using a bayonet that Metagrano had brought home from the war. On January 31, 1954, Metagrano died of heart trouble at his home in Chicago. He had been suffering from chronic myocarditis, an infection of the heart, for about six years. Shortly after his death, a routine records review revealed the fact that Metagrano had never been awarded the Purple Heart Medal for his wounds. On May 14, 1954, Metagrano was posthumously awarded the Purple Heart. Thus ends the story of an American soldier who, despite a debilitating illness, served his country with honor.

Eugenio Morelli

Eugenio Morelli was born in Marano Marchesato on February 2, 1893. At the time of his entry into the Army, he was living in Racine. He was inducted into the National Army on March 29, 1918, and was a private, serial number 2036880. Morelli went overseas as a member of the 9th Provisional Company, Infantry, a group of replacements, on June 6, 1918. At some point, he was assigned to Company "K," 106th Infantry Regiment, 27th Division. Morelli's regiment fought with the British and participated in taking Mt. Kemmel at a great cost. On September 2, 1918, while his regiment was being relieved on the front lines, Morelli was captured at Mt. Kemmel. He was a prisoner of war in

Left: Pvt. Eugene Morelli, 106th Infantry Regiment, 27th Division. (*Racine County in the World War*)

Below: Back of Pvt. Eugenio's Morelli's veteran's bonus application card, showing his prisoner of war status and wound. Note erroneous listing of "Ramel Hill" instead of the correct Mt. Kemmel. Note also his date of release from Germany, almost a full month after the Armistice. (*Wisconsin Veterans Museum*)

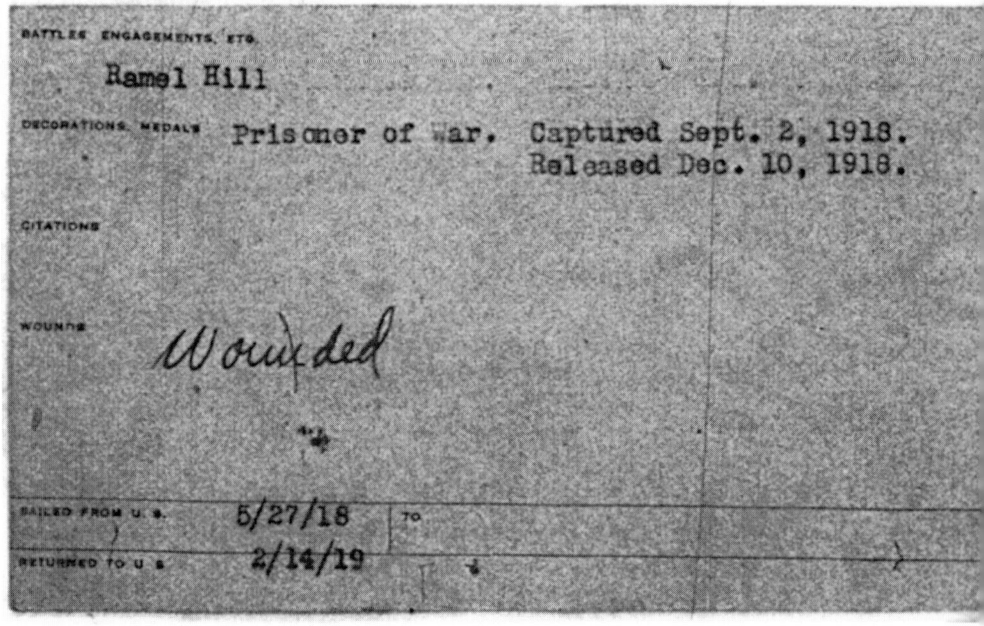

BATTLES ENGAGEMENTS, ETC.
Ramel Hill

DECORATIONS, MEDALS Prisoner of War. Captured Sept. 2, 1918.
Released Dec. 10, 1918.

CITATIONS

WOUNDS
Wounded

SAILED FROM U. S. 5/27/18 TO

RETURNED TO U. S. 2/14/19

Germany until his release after the war, on December 10, 1918. He came back to the U.S. and was discharged on April 25, 1919. His statement of service card also states that he was wounded.

Filiberto Morelli[53]

Filiberto Morelli was born Rosario Filiberto in Marano Marchesato on October 5, 1895; his parents were Vincenzo Morelli and Concetta Orrico. At various times in the early 1900s, Morelli's father, uncle, and other family members lived and worked in Chicago. Trained as a shoemaker, Morelli came to the U.S. in 1913, joining his uncle in Chicago. In 1917, he was a laborer on the Grand Trunk Western Railway, working in Michigan but living in Chicago.

Morelli was drafted during the first draft of men called for the National Army in September 1917, and was assigned first to Company "E," 344th Infantry Regiment, 86th Division, at Camp Grant, Illinois. In late October, 5,400 men from the 86th Division, including 1,100 men from the 344th Infantry Regiment, were transferred to Camp Logan, Texas, to become part of the newly forming 33rd Division, made up largely of Illinois National Guard units and now being augmented by draftees. Morelli was probably one of these men, and he was assigned to Company "C," 108th Engineer Regiment. On January 21, 1918, Morelli was transferred yet again, this time to the 130th Infantry Regiment of the 33rd Division. In February, upon the creation and assignment of serial numbers, Private Morelli was assigned serial number 1388067.

On May 16, Morelli went overseas with the 33rd Division. His regiment served with British and Australian forces during its initial indoctrination to the trenches and combat. During the Meuse-Argonne Offensive, the 130th Infantry Regiment suffered heavily from shelling and gas attacks while occupying the woods on the west bank of the Meuse River. In late October, the division was assigned to the Troyon sector, near Saint-Mihiel. Morelli participated in an attack on November 10 and again on the morning of November 11. He was slightly wounded on the 11th, just hours before the Armistice took effect and all fighting stopped. Morelli returned to the U.S. in May 1919; he was discharged at Camp Grant on May 31.

In March 1923, he became a U.S. citizen in Chicago. The next year, he applied for and received an American passport; his stated desire was to go to Italy to visit. He left, probably in the summer of 1924; it is probable that he never returned to the United States. In 1937, the U.S. State Department determined that he had repatriated himself, and it began proceedings to cancel Morelli's U.S. citizenship. On August 17, 1937, the State Department concluded, "Petitioner established a permanent residence in Italy within 5 years after being admitted citizenship," and it cancelled his citizenship.[54] Morelli had, indeed, married Carmela Giorno in Marano Marchesato, and the couple had started a family there. Morelli died in Marano Marchesato in 1951. As late as the 1990s, Louise Juliani reported seeing a photograph of Morelli in uniform in the house of his son, Orazio, in Marano Marchesato.

Francesco Muto[55]

Francesco Muto was born on February 17, 1890, in Marano Marchesato, the son of Pietro Muto and Gelsomina Cosentino. He first came to the U.S. in 1907, and destined for his cousin, Giuseppe Salerno, in Chicago. Muto stayed for about three years before going back to Italy. He returned to the U.S. again in 1910, going to his cousin, Eugenio DeBartolo, in Kenosha. In 1917, he lived in Kenosha, where he worked as a laborer for the American Brass Company.

Muto was drafted on May 26, 1918; he was a private, serial number 2825575, assigned to Company "G," 337th Infantry, 85th Division, at Camp Custer, Michigan, with which he went overseas in July 1918. On August 17, he was assigned to Company "I," 26th Infantry Regiment, 1st Division, as an infantry replacement. In September, Muto participated in the Saint-Mihiel Offensive with the rest of the 1st Division. During the Meuse-Argonne Offensive, Muto was slightly wounded in action on October 5 as his regiment was engaged in combat during the drive to the Romagne Heights, east of the Argonne Forest. He was also temporarily reported as missing in action. Muto was awarded the Purple Heart Medal on April 18, 1933. After the Armistice Muto served in the Army of Occupation of Germany; he returned to the U.S. in August 1919 and was discharged in early September.

Muto was cited in the 1st Division General Orders and was accordingly awarded a Silver Star Medal. He was also cited for gallantry in action at Soissons from July 18 to 23, 1918. This is problematic, however, because Muto did not arrive in France until early August, and he was not assigned to the 26th Infantry Regiment until August 17. What is clear, however, is that Muto accepted the award of the Silver Star Medal based upon this citation, and he accepted the second award (actually an Oak Leaf Cluster to the first medal) based upon his citation for being wounded in action. Muto's Soissons citation should more accurately have been for gallantry during the Meuse-Argonne Offensive, similar to fellow 26th Infantry Regiment veteran, Antonio Giorno.[56]

Gorski, 2827289	Frank P.	Pvt	I	26th	Wd by enemy shell fire Oct. 8/18
					severe evacuated to Hosp. OAK
Flood, 2724881	Fred M.	Pvt	I	26th	Missing in action since Oct. 7/18.
Smith, 1938836	George A.	Pvt	I	26th	" " " " " 9/18
Muto, 2325575	Francesco	Pvt	I	26th	" " " " " 10/18
Rouse, 2051550	Fay S.	Pvt	I	26th	" " " " " 10/18.
Henry, 3174617	Peter P.	Pvt	I	26th	" " " " " 10/18
Foley, 54400	Joseph	PFC	I	26th	" " " " " 4/18
Dzierkocz, 2725772	Anthony	Pvt	I	26th	" " " " " 4/18
Myers, 3355780	Clyde	Pvt	I	26th	" " " " " 5/18
Hibbler, 2433430	Harry	Pvt	I	26th	" " " " " 5/18
Holbrook, 3485653	Henry D.	Pvt	I	26th	" " " " " 6/18
Petri, 54501	James J.	PFC	I	26th	" " " " " 6/18
Michael, 2720490	Clayton	Pvt	I	26th	" " " " " 6/18
Sanders, 3488025	John E.	Pvt	I	26th	" " " " " 6/18
John, 2053953	Leonard	Pvt	I	26th	" " " " " 7/18
Sigler, 2981150	Ernest W.	Pvt	I	26th	" " " " " 7/18
Casey, 55402	John	Pvt	MG	26th	Wd by ESF Oct. 4/18 sli. evac. to
					Hosp. OAK

Detail of roster showing Francesco Muto as missing in action; note annotation "OK." (*National Archives*)

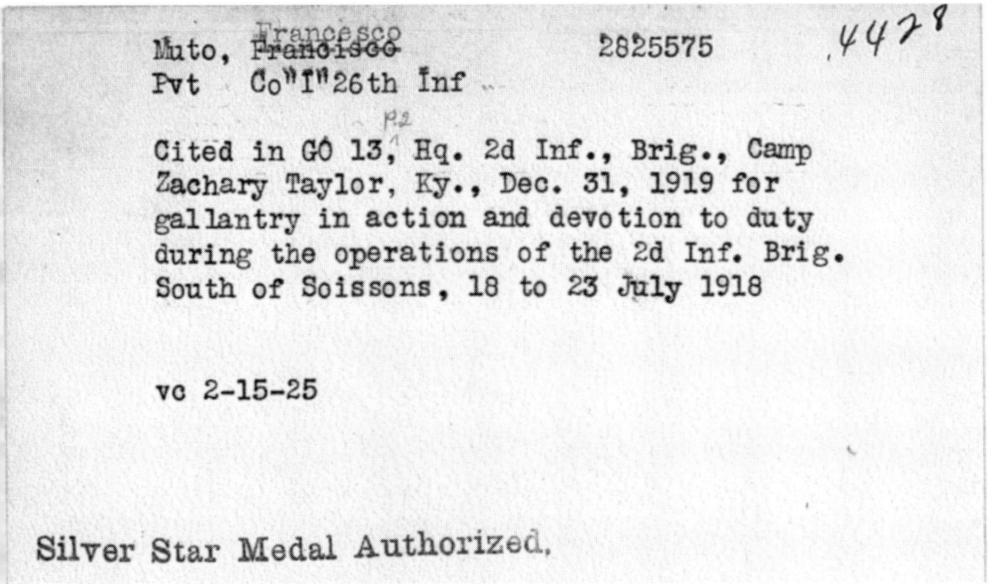

Muto, ~~Francisco~~ Francesco 2825575 4428
Pvt Co"I"26th Inf

Cited in GO 13, Hq. 2d Inf., Brig., Camp Zachary Taylor, Ky., Dec. 31, 1919 for gallantry in action and devotion to duty during the operations of the 2d Inf. Brig. South of Soissons, 18 to 23 July 1918

vc 2-15-25

Silver Star Medal Authorized.

Award card showing Francesco Muto's citation for "gallantry in action" at Soissons, "18 to 23 July 1918." This was an erroneous citation in that he was actually cited for gallantry in action during the Meuse-Argonne Offensive. He was issued Silver Star Medal number 4428, and then given an Oak Leaf Cluster (second award) for being cited for his wounding in action in October 1918. (*National Archives*)

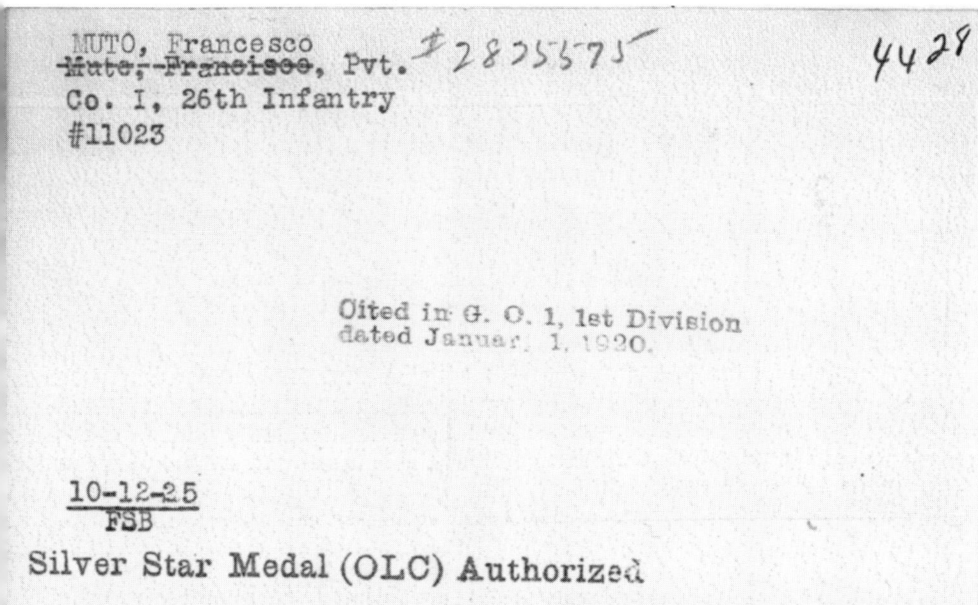

MUTO, Francesco
~~Muto, Francisco~~, Pvt. #2825575 4428
Co. I, 26th Infantry
#11023

Cited in G. O. 1, 1st Division dated January 1, 1920.

10-12-25
FSB

Silver Star Medal (OLC) Authorized

Award card showing the award of an Oak Leaf Cluster to Francesco Muto's first Silver Star Medal. (*National Archives*)

Tony Pellegrino[57]

Tony Pellegrino was born in Marano Principato about February 1890. In 1918, he lived in Kenosha where he worked as a factory laborer. He entered the Army as a private, serial number 2035162, on March 29, 1918. He was assigned to 7th Company, 2nd Battalion, 160th Depot Brigade, at Camp Custer, Michigan. On April 24, he was transferred to Camp Gordon, Georgia, as part of the replacement draft. He was sent overseas as a replacement on June 30 and, upon arrival, was assigned to Company "K," 164th Infantry Regiment, 41st Division, which was then a depot division. On August 10, he was assigned as a replacement to Company "I," 23rd Infantry Regiment, 2nd Division. Pellegrino was in the Marbache Sector until August 24. He then participated in the Saint-Mihiel Offensive (September 12 to 15), Blanc Mont Offensive (September 30 to October 9), and Meuse Argonne Offensive, (November 1 to 4). He was slightly wounded in action on November 4. While recuperating, Pellegrino was transferred to Machine Gun Company, 337th Infantry Regiment, 85th Division; he returned to the U.S. with that unit on April 4, 1919, and was discharged at Camp Grant, Illinois, on April 23, 1919. On October 12, 1932, he was awarded the Purple Heart for the wound he suffered on November 4; his service card also bears the notation that he was also wounded on August 31, but there is no other information on that wound.

Benjamin Potesta[58]

Benjamin E. Potesta was born in Chicago on July 19, 1899; his parents, Raffaele Potesta and Maria Garbarina, were from Grimaldi, Cosenza. Potesta tried to enlist in the Army in 1916, but he was under age and not accepted. After the U.S. declaration of war, Potesta tried again and, at the age of seventeen, was accepted into the Army. Although his initial assignment and location are unknown, he was a private, serial number 1565680, in the 12th Company, June Camp Shelby Automatic Replacement Draft, when he sailed for France aboard the *Grampian* on June 11, 1918. At some point, he was assigned to Company "E," 7th Engineer Regiment, 5th Division. The 5th Division was a Regular Army division that saw combat at Saint-Mihiel and then heavy combat during the Meuse-Argonne Offensive. Engineers from the 7th Engineer Regiment constructed footbridges and pontoon bridges across the Meuse River while under fire in the final few days of the war. Potesta was wounded and as a result suffered the amputation of his left leg at the thigh.

Potesta returned to the U.S. aboard the hospital ship U.S.S. *Mercy* on April 5, 1919. At the time, he was among the litter patients of Base Hospital 69; an annotation next to his name on the transport manifest reads: "AMP LT THIGH." Many of the other men on the manifest seemed to have undergone similar medical treatment. After his return to the U.S., Potesta spent eighteen months in Walter Reed Hospital in Washington, D.C. While there, his parents and brother, Ernest, visited him by train from Chicago. Potesta married Genevieve "Jean" Steibel in about 1922. He died on August 29, 1982, in Hammond, Indiana. Potesta's half-brother, James, also served in the Army and was wounded during the war.

James Potesta[59]

James Potesta was born in Chicago on December 27, 1892; his parents, Raffaele Potesta and Anna Filomena Vaccaro, were from Grimaldi. He was living in Chicago or Indiana

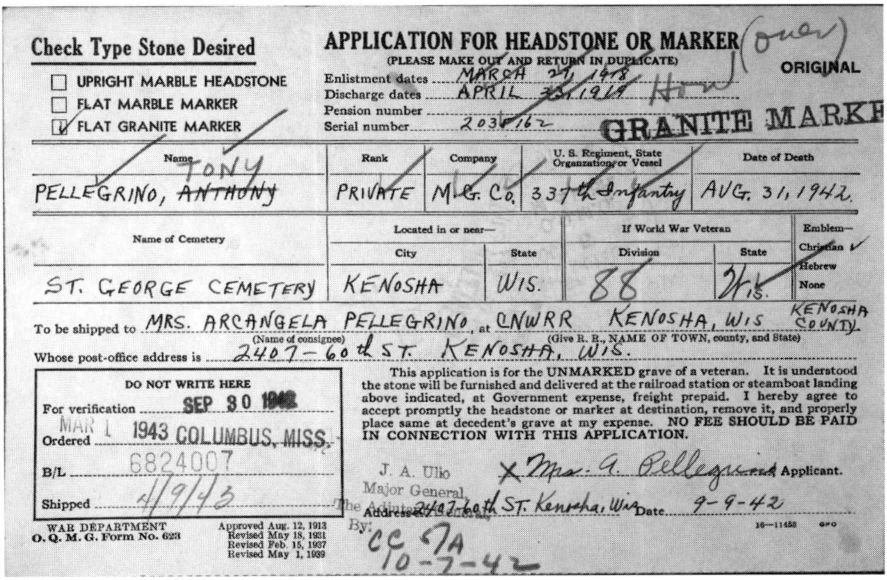

Check Type Stone Desired

☐ UPRIGHT MARBLE HEADSTONE
☐ FLAT MARBLE MARKER
☑ FLAT GRANITE MARKER

APPLICATION FOR HEADSTONE OR MARKER (over)
(PLEASE MAKE OUT AND RETURN IN DUPLICATE)
ORIGINAL

Enlistment dates MARCH 29, 1918
Discharge dates APRIL 25, 1919
Pension number
Serial number 2038162

GRANITE MARKER

Name	Rank	Company	U. S. Regiment, State Organization, or Vessel	Date of Death
PELLEGRINO, ~~ANTHONY~~ TONY	PRIVATE	M.G. Co.	337th Infantry	AUG. 31, 1942.

Name of Cemetery	Located in or near— City	State	If World War Veteran Division	State	Emblem— Christian, Hebrew, None
ST. GEORGE CEMETERY	KENOSHA	WIS.	88	Wis.	Christian ✓

To be shipped to MRS. ARCANGELA PELLEGRINO, at CNWRR KENOSHA, WIS KENOSHA COUNTY
(Name of consignee) (Give R. R., NAME OF TOWN, county, and State)
Whose post-office address is 2407-60th ST. KENOSHA, WIS.

DO NOT WRITE HERE
For verification SEP 30 1942
Ordered MAR 1 1943 COLUMBUS, MISS.
B/L 6824007
Shipped 4/9/43

This application is for the UNMARKED grave of a veteran. It is understood the stone will be furnished and delivered at the railroad station or steamboat landing above indicated, at Government expense, freight prepaid. I hereby agree to accept promptly the headstone or marker at destination, remove it, and properly place same at decedent's grave at my expense. NO FEE SHOULD BE PAID IN CONNECTION WITH THIS APPLICATION.

J. A. Ulio
Major General,
The Adjutant General.
By: CC 7A 10-7-42

X Mrs. A. Pellegrino Applicant.
Address 2407-60th ST. Kenosha, Wis. Date 9-9-42

WAR DEPARTMENT
O. Q. M. G. Form No. 623
Approved Aug. 12, 1913
Revised May 18, 1931
Revised Feb. 15, 1937
Revised May 1, 1939

Front side of Pvt. Tony Pellegrino's Application for Headstone or Marker. Note that his unit is listed as Machine Gun Company, 337th Infantry Regiment (85th Division), and, incorrectly, the 88th Division. While Pellegrino did indeed spend some time in the 337th Infantry Regiment, he saw combat and was wounded while serving in the 23rd Infantry Regiment, 2nd Division. These applications, prepared after the veteran's death, reflected what appeared on whatever paperwork officials had on hand; they do not necessarily show what the veteran's preference might have been, and this is possibly an example. (*National Archives, via Ancestry.com*)

He was awarded Purple Heart 10-12-32
on account of wound received in
action 11-4-18.

RECEIVED SEP 30 1942 O.Q.M.G. M.&R.BR.
RECEIVED OCT 5 1942 O.Q.M.G. M.&R.BR.
AGO OCT 6 1942 DEMOBILIZED PERSONNEL BR.

Reverse side of Pvt. Tony Pellegrino's Application for Headstone or Marker, indicating his wounding and the award of a Purple Heart. (*National Archives, via Ancestry.com*)

Pvt. Benjamin Potesta, 7th Engineer Regiment, 5th Division, 1917. (*Robert R. Porcaro*)

Cpl. James Potesta, 18th Infantry Regiment, 1st Division (left) with friends. (*Robert R. Porcaro*)

Harbor, Indiana, when he enlisted in the Regular Army on April 17, 1917, only one week after America's entry into the war. A little over two months later, on June 14, with only the bare minimum of training, Potesta went overseas as a private, serial number 46114, in Company "B," 18th Infantry Regiment, 1st Division. Thus Potesta was in one of the first groups of men to sail for France. He was promoted to private first class on January 24, 1918, and then to corporal on March 31. Potesta was wounded in action on July 18 during the terrible fighting around Soissons. Potesta, because of his wound, returned to the U.S. before the rest of his division, sailing aboard U.S.S. *South Carolina* on March 5, 1919, as part of the St. Aignan Casual Company 958, Illinois; this was a group of men from various units who were returning to a camp near their homes for discharge. Potesta was discharged on April 2, 1919. Potesta's half-brother, Benjamin, also served in the Army and was wounded during the war.

Santo Saliture

Santo Saliture was born in Rende on March 9, 1894; he was a pressman at the American Brass Company, living in Kenosha, when he was inducted into the Army on April 26, 1918. Saliture was a private, serial number 2043815, in Company "B," 340th Infantry Regiment, 85th Division, at Camp Custer, Michigan. Saliture went overseas with the 85th Division in July 1918; on August 24, he was sent as a replacement to Company "I," 4th Infantry Regiment, 3rd Division. Saliture was gassed on October 5 or 6, 1918, during the Meuse-Argonne Offensive. He returned to the U.S. on April 2, 1919, and he was discharged twenty-two days later.

Peter Scola

Pietro (Peter) Scola was born in Cosenza on November 6, 1893. He came to the U.S. about 1913, and in 1917, he was unemployed and living in Kenosha. Scola was drafted on May 26, 1918; he was a private, serial number 2825565, in the 35th Company, 161st Depot Brigade, at Camp Grant, Illinois. On June 13, Scola was transferred to Company "D," 337th Infantry Regiment, 85th Division, at Camp Custer, Michigan. He went overseas with his regiment on July 22. Upon arrival the 85th Division became a depot division and began to send replacements to other units. On August 24, Scola was assigned as a replacement to Company "H," 7th Infantry Regiment, 3rd Division. On October 5 or 6, during the heavy fighting of the Meuse-Argonne Offensive, Scola was severely wounded "thru stomach and hand." Scola recuperated in hospitals in France while the rest of the 3rd Division went to Germany as part of the Army of Occupation. He returned to the U.S. aboard U.S.S. *Leviathan* as part of the Camp Grant Detachment, 338th Infantry Regiment, on April 2, 1919. Scola was discharged at Camp Grant on April 14 with a 10 percent disability rating.

Gabriel Tarsitano[60]

Gabriel Tarsitano was born on July 28, 1897, in Cosenza, the son of Leopoldo and Rosaria Tarsitano. The Tarsitanos settled in Chicago in the late 1890s or early 1900s. Gabriel Tarsitano enlisted in the Regular Army, probably in 1917. He was a sergeant, serial number 2339717, in Company "K," 4th Infantry Regiment, 3rd Division, when he boarded U.S.S. *Great Northern* for shipment to France on April 6, 1918. The 3rd Division saw heavy combat along the Marne and Aisne Rivers in July and then again during the Meuse-Argonne Offensive. Tarsitano was severely wounded during the Meuse-Argonne Offensive in October or early November. Instead of serving with his regiment in the Army of Occupation of Germany after the war, Tarsitano returned to the U.S. aboard U.S.S. *Aeolus* in December 1918. Tarsitano was attached to the "Sick and Wounded" group in Casual Company 3353 on this vessel. After the war Tarsitano wrote to the family of a fellow soldier in Company "K," Samuel Leo (or Lio), who had been killed by shellfire on September 29, 1918, during the Meuse-Argonne Offensive. Tarsitano wrote that Sam's death "was like losing a brother," and that Tarsitano had himself been wounded a few days later and had been "sent to many different hospitals and then home." Tarsitano lived in Chicago and worked as a mailman; he died in Chicago in 1968.

6

Selected Biographies

Although we have presented a general overview of the military history of these men, a complete accounting could be had only by a review of each man's history. Since space prevents such an undertaking, only a select group of biographies are included here. These examples reflect many different types of military service and the varied history of these men. Some biographies include such minutiae as physical descriptions and military pay details in order to shed light on less-studied aspects of military service during the war. The biographies serve as a memorial to a group of men heretofore without a voice proclaiming their history.[1]

Eugenio (James) Aiello

Eugenio (James) Aiello was born in Marano Marchesato on October 4, 1892, the son of Francesco Aiello and Maria DeBartolo. He came to the U.S. in 1908, joining his brother, Alessandro, in Racine. He was a painter living in Racine when he entered the Army on July 16, 1918, as a private, serial number 3368699. He was in the 8th Company, Motor Transport Detachment, Machine Gun Training Depot, until September 9 when he transferred to Company "B," 38th Machine Gun Battalion, part of the 13th Division forming at Camp Lewis, Washington. The war ended before the 13th Division was sent overseas, and he was discharged on February 8, 1919, at Camp Grant, Illinois. Aiello returned to Italy to be married in 1921. He came back to Racine where he died in 1967.

Frank Aiello

Francesco Maria Carmelo (Frank) Aiello was born in Marano Marchesato on July 1, 1895, the son of Luigi Aiello and Francesca Bartucci. Francesco's father, Luigi, made several trips to the U.S. beginning in 1890. Francesco came to the U.S. in 1912, destined for his brother, Alessandro, in Chicago.

Aiello entered the Army in 1917, and on January 4, 1918, he boarded the Army transport *Mercury* bound for France. He was a private and was part of Provisional Company Number 4, Mechanical Repair Shop 301, a motor repair shop. On July 7, 1919, he boarded the *Imperator* at Brest, France, to return to the United States. At that

Pvt. James Aiello, 38th Machine Gun Battalion, 13th Division, 1918. (*Frank Aiello family*)

time, he was a cook, serial number 222776, in a Quartermaster Corps detachment. The vessel arrived at Camp Mills, New York, on July 13, and Aiello was probably discharged shortly thereafter. Francesco's brother, Silvio, was a Navy veteran of World War I.

Silvio Aiello[2]

Silvio Aiello was born in Marano Marchesato on October 17, 1900, the son of Luigi (Louis) Aiello and Francesca Teresa Bartucci. Luigi had come to the U.S. in the 1890s and had become a U.S. citizen in Chicago on March 21, 1898; he made other round trips between Marano Marchesato and the United States. In 1907, Silvio came to the United States.

Aiello was with his father in Chicago when he enlisted in the Navy at the U.S. Navy Recruiting Station in Chicago on June 12, 1918. On June 16, he was transferred to the U.S. Navy Receiving Ship, Puget Sound, Washington. He was a seaman second class, serial number 1002997. At the time of his enlistment, Aiello gave his birth date as February 17, 1900, which contradicts Italian records. It is possible that he lied about his age since, if he were indeed born in October 1900, as his Italian birth record indicates, he would have been under eighteen years of age at the time of his enlistment and therefore would have required his father's permission to enlist. Upon enlistment, Aiello provided proof of his derivative U.S. citizenship in the form of the naturalization papers of his father, dated 1898—two years before Silvio's birth.

Aiello seems to have had some trouble adjusting to military life. On July 23, we find the following notation in his service record: "Losing liberty pass—Two weeks restriction." Then, a month later, on August 22: "Leaving ranks without permission and attempting to evade drill—10 days restriction, 2nd conduct class." Again, only eight days later, on August 30: "Carelessness in performance of duty—10 Days restriction." On September 9: "Not qualified as marksman, offense above." On February 4, 1919: "AWOL [absent without leave] 15 hrs Jan 14–19. SCM [Special Court Martial] sent. to 30 days conf. and extra [illegible] duties. LP [loss of pay] amtg 107.70. LP as adjudged reduced to 72.90 [illegible] thus reduced is remitted." On March 3: "Failed to confirm rating S2c on acc't of no sea duty." Despite these shortcomings, he was recommended for reenrollment at the time of his release from active duty in early March 1919. At that time, he was given his final pay to include a war discharge gratuity of $60. He was given a final honorable discharge on June 11, 1920; sometime thereafter, he was awarded the Victory Medal without clasp.[3]

After his discharge, Aiello moved to Chicago where he became a salesman for the Gonella Bakery; he would often sit with his wife and other relatives on his front porch, eating an entire loaf of fresh bread with butter. Aiello died in Addison, Illinois, in 1987 and is remembered as "quite a character with a golden heart."[4]

Silvio Aiello, Chicago, *c.* 1920. (*Beverly Adamski*)

Bruno Andrea

Bruno Andrea (the surname was originally Iantria and Iandrea) was born in Marano Marchesato on June 11, 1891, the son of Matteo Andrea and Filomena Chiappetta. He to the U.S. in 1914, destined for his brother, Gioacchino, in Kenosha. Andrea was a part of the first draft for the National Army, arriving at Camp Custer, Michigan, on September 21, 1917. He was a private, serial number 2025531, assigned to the Machine Gun Company, 340th Infantry Regiment, 85th Division. Andrea went overseas with the division on July 23, 1918. The 85th became the 4th Depot Division, and began to send replacements to other combat divisions, although Andrea stayed on as part of the training cadre. On October 20, Andrea was transferred to the Labor Detachment, Quartermaster Corps, 4th Depot Division. He remained in this detachment while the division was redesignated as the 85th Division and sent forward to the Toul sector to serve as a replacement division for the 2nd Army, in preparation for a major offensive in that area. On December 26, Andrea was assigned back to the Machine Gun Company, 340th Infantry Regiment. He returned to the U.S. with the 340th on April 2, 1919, and was discharged at Camp Grant, Illinois, on April 25, 1919. His brother, Filippo (Paul) Andrea, also served in the Army overseas.

Filippo Andrea

Ippolito (Filippo, Paul) Andrea was born May 28, 1894, in Marano Marchesato, the son of Matteo Andrea and Filomena Chiappetta. Andrea was a chauffeur living in Kenosha when he was inducted into the Army on May 1, 1918. He was as a private, serial number 443341, assigned to Company "A," 6th Motor Supply Train, 6th Division. He went overseas with this unit on July 14, 1918, and served in limited combat with the 6th Division. He received credit for the Meuse-Argonne Offensive and Defensive Sector ("Gerardmere Sec."). He returned to the United States on June 22, 1919, and was sent to Camp Grant, Illinois, where he was discharged on July 3, 1919. After the war, Andrea moved back to Kenosha where he worked in the real estate industry; he died in Kenosha in 1958.

Domenico Arvia

Domenico Arvia was born in 1891 in Alessandro del Carretto. He came to the U.S. in May 1903 and was living in Chicago when he was inducted into the Army. Arvia was a private in the 13th Company, 4th Battalion, 161st Depot Brigade, at Camp Grant, Illinois, when he became a U.S. citizen on November 2, 1918. He married after the war and worked as a bookbinder and paper cutter.

Fred Louis Baratta

Fred L. Baratta was born on October 8, 1895, in Chicago, the son of Gaspare Baratta and Maria Antonia Chiappetta, from Marano Marchesato. Baratta was a medical student when he enlisted in the Enlisted Reserve Corps in Chicago on December 21, 1917. He went on active duty on October 3, 1918, and became a private, serial number 985512, in the Medical Department, Camp Crane, Pennsylvania. On November 5, he was assigned to Mobile Hospital Unit 102, and he departed for France on November 13, two days after the armistice. On February 17, 1919, he was transferred to Camp Hospital 33; on June 16, he was assigned as a medical attendant at Segregation Camp,

Base Section No. 5. The Segregation Camp housed men with various communicable diseases and venereal disease. On August 18, he was transferred to casual status, and he returned to the U.S. on August 30. Baratta was discharged from Camp Grant, Illinois, on September 11, 1919.

After the war, he returned to live with his family in Chicago. Baratta completed his medical studies and became a physician. He was the brother of James Dominick Baratta, a fellow World War I veteran.

James Dominick Baratta

James Dominick Baratta was born on July 2, 1893, in Chicago, the son of Gaspare Baratta and Maria Antonia Chiappetta, from Marano Marchesato. Baratta was a shoe salesman living in Chicago when he registered for the draft in 1917; he claimed exemption on account of being the sole support for his wife and two children. Despite this, Baratta was drafted and reported for duty on October 19, 1918, as a private, serial number 4426339. Because of some sort of physical ailment or disability, he was assigned to Company "F," 5th Limited Services Regiment, 161st Depot Brigade, at Camp Grant, Illinois. He was discharged November 30 for physical disability at Camp Grant. For some time after the war, Baratta was a taxi driver in Chicago. He died in Chicago in 1978. James Baratta was the brother of Fred L. Baratta, a fellow World War I veteran.

Luigi Baratta

Luigi Baratta was born in Marano Principato on August 4, 1894; in 1918, he was a laborer living in Kenosha. Despite the fact that claimed exemption from the draft because he was the sole support of his wife and his father, he was inducted into the Army on July 21, 1918. He was assigned as a private, serial number 3715445, to the 3rd Company, 1st Training Battalion, 159th Depot Brigade, at Camp Taylor, Kentucky. He was discharged there on December 1, 1918, and there is an indication on his brief service record that he reenlisted in the Army. He became a U.S. citizen on June 18, 1923, but this was later cancelled because the U.S. State Department had determined that Baratta had moved back to Italy and had, in effect, repatriated himself.

Louis Barbieri[5]

Louis Barbieri was born in Marano Marchesato on May 8, 1893, the son of Michele Barbieri and Carmela Muto. Barbieri came to the U.S. in 1910. Barbieri was living in Chicago, where he plied the trade of barber, the meaning of his Italian surname, when he entered the Army on September 18, 1917. He was a private, serial number 1389588, in Company "H," 132nd Infantry Regiment, 33rd Division. Barbieri trained with the unit and departed for France with it aboard the Army transport *Mt. Vernon* on May 16, 1918. The 33rd Division trained with British, Australian, and French forces in France; they saw plenty of combat including severe fighting along the Meuse River during the Meuse-Argonne Offensive. Major General George Bell, Jr., 33rd Division commander, cited Barbieri for gallantry in action. This would have entitled him to the award of the Silver Star Medal upon creation of the medal in 1932. At some point, Barbieri was promoted to private first class. He departed France with his unit, again aboard the *Mt. Vernon*, on May 9, 1919. After arriving at Camp Mills, New York, the men departed to camps near their home of record for discharge. Barbieri was discharged on May 31, 1919.

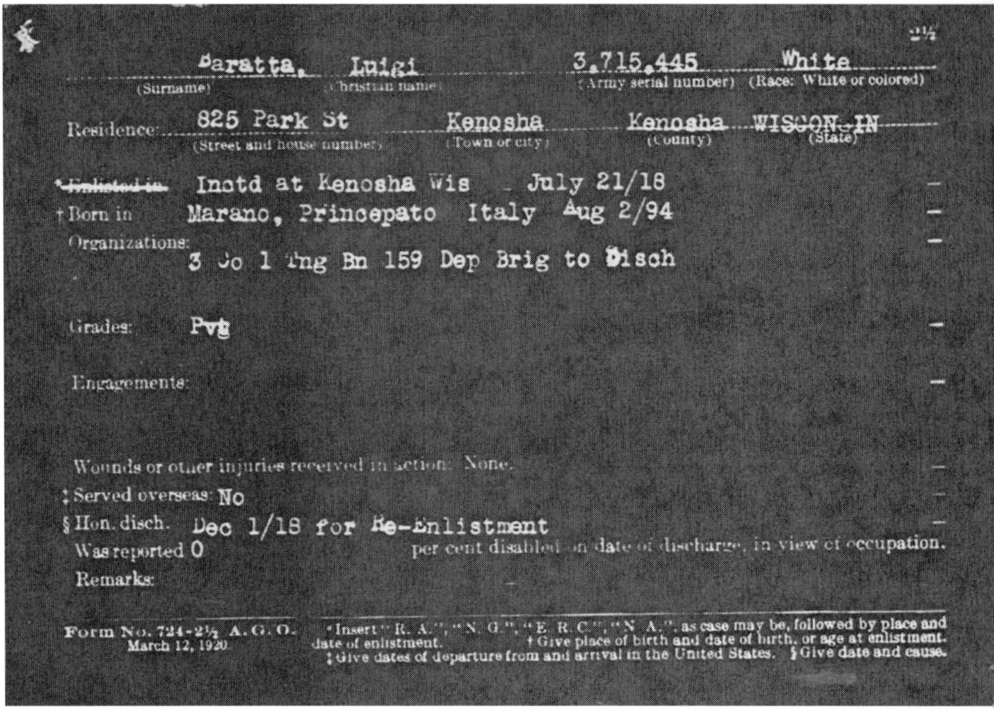

2½

Baratta, Luigi — 3,715,445 — White
(Surname) (Christian name) (Army serial number) (Race: White or colored)

Residence: 825 Park St — Kenosha — Kenosha — WISCONSIN
(Street and house number) (Town or city) (County) (State)

~~Enlisted in~~ Inctd at Kenosha Wis July 21/18

† Born in Marano, Principato Italy Aug 2/94

Organizations: 3 Co 1 Tng Bn 159 Dep Brig to Disch

Grades: Pvt

Engagements:

Wounds or other injuries received in action: None.

‡ Served overseas: No

§ Hon. disch. Dec 1/18 for Re-Enlistment

Was reported 0 per cent disabled on date of discharge, in view of occupation.

Remarks:

Form No. 724-2½ A. G. O. March 12, 1920. — * Insert "R. A.", "N. G.", "E. R. C.", "N. A.", as case may be, followed by place and date of enlistment. † Give place of birth and date of birth, or age at enlistment. ‡ Give dates of departure from and arrival in the United States. § Give date and cause.

Pvt. Luigi Baratta's statement of service card. Notations suggest that Baratta reenlisted after his discharge. (*Wisconsin Veterans Museum*)

Ferdinando Bartucci

Ferdinando Bartucci was born in Marano Marchesato on April 26, 1889, the son of Alessandro (Santo) Bartucci and Gelsomina Tenuta. Alessandro had made at least one trip to the U.S. in the early 1880s, and in 1901, Ferdinando and his father came to the U.S., destined for Chicago.

Bartucci was inducted into the National Army on May 2, 1918, probably at Jefferson Barracks, near St. Louis, Missouri. He was assigned as a private, serial number 479350, in Company "M," 8th Infantry Regiment, 8th Division, at Camp Fremont, California. At some point, he was transferred to Company "D," 25th Battalion, U.S. Guards, at Camp Taliaferro, California, and he was later promoted to cook. The U.S. Guards were formed to guard facilities and camps throughout the United States. Most of the men in these units were deemed unfit for overseas service for physical or other reasons. After the war, he was sent to the 3rd Company, Discharge Detachment at Camp Grant, Illinois, where, on December 29, 1918, he was given his final pay ($23.45) and discharged.

After the war, Bartucci worked as a car cleaner, perhaps referring to work on streetcars or train cars. He died of unknown causes in Chicago on May 15, 1919.

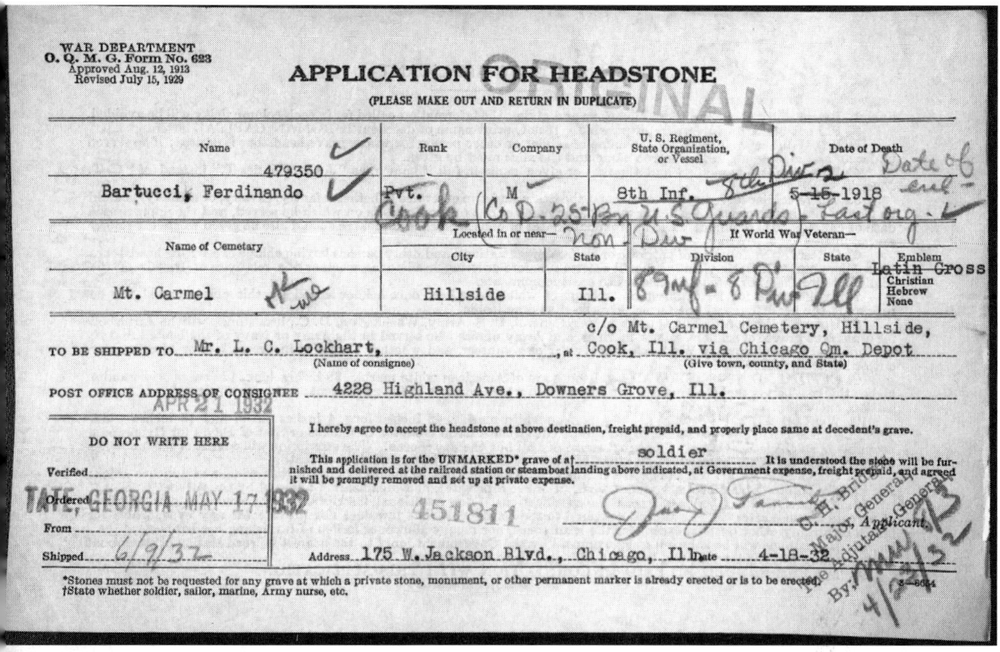

WAR DEPARTMENT
O. Q. M. G. Form No. 623
Approved Aug. 12, 1913
Revised July 15, 1929

APPLICATION FOR HEADSTONE

(PLEASE MAKE OUT AND RETURN IN DUPLICATE)

Name	Rank	Company	U. S. Regiment, State Organization, or Vessel	Date of Death
479350 Bartucci, Ferdinando	Pvt.	M	8th Inf.	5-15-1918

Name of Cemetery	City	State	Division	State	Emblem
Mt. Carmel	Hillside	Ill.			Latin Cross

TO BE SHIPPED TO Mr. L. C. Lockhart, (Name of consignee) at c/o Mt. Carmel Cemetery, Hillside, Cook, Ill. via Chicago Qm. Depot (Give town, county, and State)

POST OFFICE ADDRESS OF CONSIGNEE 4228 Highland Ave., Downers Grove, Ill.

APR 21 1932

DO NOT WRITE HERE
Verified
Ordered TATE, GEORGIA MAY 17 1932
From
Shipped 6/9/32

I hereby agree to accept the headstone at above destination, freight prepaid, and properly place same at decedent's grave.

This application is for the UNMARKED* grave of a† soldier. It is understood the stone will be furnished and delivered at the railroad station or steamboat landing above indicated, at Government expense, freight prepaid, and agreed it will be promptly removed and set up at private expense.

451811

Applicant.

Address 175 W. Jackson Blvd., Chicago, Ill. Date 4-18-32

*Stones must not be requested for any grave at which a private stone, monument, or other permanent marker is already erected or is to be erected.
†State whether soldier, sailor, marine, Army nurse, etc.

Ferdinando Bartucci's Application for Headstone. Note numerous corrections and annotations. (*National Archives, via Ancestry.com*)

Carmine Belmonte[6]

Carmine Belmonte was born on February 12, 1900, in Marano Marchesato, the son of Bruno Belmonte and Filomena Puzzo. He came to the U.S. with his mother and brother in 1911, joining his father in Aurora, Illinois. Bruno was a barber living in Aurora when he enlisted in the Regular Army at Jefferson Barracks, near St. Louis, Missouri, on January 19, 1918. He was sent to Camp Sevier, South Carolina, where he was a private, serial number 1336078, in the Aviation Section of the Signal Corps. On May 17, he was transferred to a detachment of the 1st Construction Company, U.S. Army Air Service. This unit was a bricklaying company composed of bricklayers and other specialized tradesmen. Belmonte left the United States on June 29 aboard the *Mauretania*; it arrived at Liverpool, England, on July 6. The 1st Construction Company was engaged in construction work at various air bases in England into 1919. Belmonte returned to the U.S. on March 19, 1919, and was sent to Camp Grant, Illinois, for demobilization. He was discharged there on April 9, 1919, and he returned home to Aurora. On September 17, he became a U.S. citizen based upon his military service during the war. After the war, he worked as a barber in Chicago and Albuquerque, New Mexico.

Louis Bruno[7]

Mariano Luigi (Louis) Bruno was born in Marano Marchesato on May 14, 1888, the son of Francesco Bruno and Gelsomina Gentile. In the 1890s, Francesco came to the U.S. and began a family-based migration chain in the midst of the overall general commune-based chain migration pattern. In 1899, Louis's older brother, Eugenio, a tailor, came to the U.S. to join his father in Chicago. Louis himself arrived in the U.S. on June 18, 1902, also destined for his father in Chicago. Sometime after this, Francesco journeyed back to Italy, but in April 1910, another brother, Umberto Enrico, continued the family migration chain by coming to the U.S. to join his brothers in Chicago.

Louis and Enrico lived with Eugenio and his wife, May, in Chicago, where the three brothers were employed as tailors. By 1917, at the time of their registration for the draft, Louis and Enrico lived at 814 Madison Street in Chicago, a few blocks from Louis and Eugenio's tailor shop at 673 Madison.

On May 27, 1918, Louis Bruno went to Great Lakes Naval Training Base, just north of Chicago, and enlisted in the U.S. Navy. Because he had special skill as a tailor, he was enrolled as a fireman first class; this rating was higher than what would be given to regular enlistees, and the increased pay reflected the tailor's skill that Bruno brought to the Navy. With blue eyes, brown hair, and a ruddy complexion, Bruno was 5 feet 2.75 inches tall and weighed 116 pounds. His enlistment document bears the notation, "Underheight and underweight waived for special duty," an indication of the Navy's need for tailors in its rapidly expanding ranks.[8]

For the next eight and a half months, Bruno performed his duties as a Navy tailor at Great Lakes Naval Training Center. He had no negative remarks in his record. With the Armistice on November 11, 1918, the Navy began demobilizing. On February 12, 1919, Bruno was released from active duty. Many men who had enlisted in the Navy during the war were given the option, upon release from active duty, of staying in the Naval Reserve, and Bruno availed himself of this opportunity. He returned to civilian life to work as a tailor and start a family in Chicago, proud of having served his country during a time of war.

In 1921, with Congress cutting War Department funding, the Navy notified members of the Naval Reserve that they could no longer fund the Reserve at past levels. Consequently, they discharged many reservists effective September 30 of that year, and Bruno was given an honorable discharge from the Navy at that time. In 1935, Bruno wanted to bring his father back to the United States. In order to do this, he required proof of his citizenship and other documentation pertinent to his military service. To that end, Bruno wrote a poignant letter addressed simply to the "Navy Department" on October 21, 1935:

> Gentlemen: Will you kindly sent me a copy of Honorable Discharge No. 102350. I enlisted in the Office of the Commandant Ninth Naval District Great Lakes Ills. Year 1918. Reported for duty May 25–1918.
>
> Could you also tell me the name of the boat I came on when I enter this Country. I know I landed New York July 2–1902, and Chicago July 4–1902.
>
> The reason I need this information is because I am calling for my Father in Europe and it is necessary to have this information. I do not remember what boat as I was just a minor.
>
> Thanking you in advance for your kindness in the matter I remain Louis Bruno
>
> P. S. Kindly answer immediately as I am anxious to have my Father here for X mas. [*sic.*][9]

A week later, the Chief of the Bureau of Navigation wrote back to Bruno, sending him an application to fill out to obtain a "certificate *in lieu* of discharge." Further, the bureau advised Louis that they were "unable to furnish the information request in regard to your entry into the United States. It is suggested that you communicate with the Shipping Commissioner, Port of New York, giving him all the information that you can furnish."[10]

It is not known how quickly Bruno acted upon this, nor if his father arrived in the United States before Christmas, but he did fill out and return his application for a service certificate on September 10, 1937, almost two years after his initial request. On the application, Bruno dutifully gave all known particulars of his service, to include listing the names of some men with whom he served ("C.P.O. [Chief Petty Officer] Ward, Belvedere, DeLouis, Goldberg, Antoneli"), and declaring that his original discharge certificate was "destroyed thru wear in carrying in pocket," an indication of his pride in his service in the Navy.[11] A few days later, Bruno was furnished with his certificate of service. Bruno died in Chicago on December 9, 1970. His brother, Enrico, served overseas in the 87th Division during the war.

Michele Bruno

Michele (Michael) Bruno was born in Marano Marchesato on November 14, 1890, the son of Giovanni Bruno and Orsola Principe. He lived in the U.S. from 1905 to 1913, and then, following a short stay back in Italy, returned to the U.S. later in 1913. When he registered for the draft in 1917, Bruno was a laborer for the Grand Trunk Railway living in Chicago but working in Bancroft, Michigan. Bruno was living in Kenosha when he entered the Army on May 26, 1918; he was assigned as a private, serial number 2825721, in the 161st Depot Brigade at Camp Grant, Illinois. In June, he was a part of the large contingent of men transferred to Camp Custer, Michigan. Bruno became part of Company "F," 337th Infantry Regiment, 85th Division. He was promoted to private first class on July 15, just before the 85th Division sailed for France.

Bruno was sent as a replacement to Company "F," 139th Infantry Regiment, 35th Division, on October 8. That division had been heavily engaged in the Meuse-Argonne Offensive, and had lost many men. Bruno served with the 139th in the Verdun Sector where they came under enemy artillery fire. He returned to the U.S. on April 24, 1919, and was transferred to Camp Grant for demobilization. He became a naturalized a U.S. citizen there on May 16, 1919, and he was discharged four days later. After the war, Bruno was a machinist at a brass and copper factory in Chicago. He died in 1980 in Elmwood Park, Illinois.

Umberto Enrico Bruno

Umberto Enrico (Enrico Albert) Bruno was born in Marano Marchesato on July 2, 1894, the son of Francesco Bruno and Gelsomina Gentile. He came to the U.S. in 1910, joining his brothers in Chicago. Bruno was a tailor in Chicago when he was drafted during the first call for the National Army, on September 18, 1917; he was a private, serial number 2102250, at Camp Grant, Illinois. Bruno was among a draft of 1,500 men sent from Camp Grant to Camp Pike, Arkansas, in November. There, he became a part of the Sanitary Detachment (medical personnel) of the 346th Infantry Regiment, 87th Division. On May 24, 1918, Bruno applied for and was granted U.S. citizenship on the basis of his service in the Army; at the same time, he changed his first and middle names to Enrico Albert. Sometime thereafter, Bruno was promoted to corporal and sent to Company "K," 346th Infantry Regiment. The division was sent overseas in August and September 1918. The men almost immediately received disappointing news as they became, basically, labor troops. The division was turned over to the Services of Supply and set to work on various projects in the intermediate section. Thus, after almost one year of training, the division was denied the opportunity to fight as an integral unit, and instead it had to perform other essential, though menial, work. Parts of the division returned to the U.S. in December, but Bruno returned on March 31, 1919. He went to Camp Grant where he was discharged on April 17.

Beniamino Caira

Beniamino Caira (Ben Cairo) was born in Marano Marchesato on September 12, 1895, the son of Giuseppe Caira and Carolina Tenuta. He came to the U.S. in 1912, destined for his father in Chicago. In 1917, he lived in Rondout, Illinois, and was a farm laborer for J. Ogden Armour. Caira was inducted into the Army at Libertyville, Illinois, on May 28, 1918; he was assigned as a private, serial number 3485742, to the 69th Company, 6th Infantry Replacement Regiment, Camp Gordon, Georgia. On July 16, he was transferred to the 68th Company, July Automatic Replacement Draft. He went overseas as a replacement on July 24. On August 14, Caira was transferred to 83rd Division, which was also called the 2nd Depot Division, a unit whose purpose was to provide replacements to combat divisions. On September 13, Caira was sent to Company "A," 11th Infantry Regiment, 5th Division. The 11th Infantry Regiment was heavily engaged in October and November 1918, during the Meuse-Argonne Offensive, and it suffered many casualties. Caira's military journey illustrates the path some replacements took: sent overseas with a replacement draft, assigned to a depot division, and finally assigned to a combat division as a replacement. After the war, Caira returned to the U.S. on July 20, 1919. He was discharged six days later at Camp Grant, Illinois. Caira died in Cook County, Illinois, in 1965.

Ferdinando Caira

Ferdinando Caira (Fred Cairo) was born in Marano Marchesato on August 21, 1886, the son of Pasquale Caira and Giuseppina Milone. He arrived in the U.S. in 1902, destined for his uncle, Bruno Caira, in Chicago. Caira was a barber living in Chicago when he enlisted in the Regular Army at Jefferson Barracks, near St. Louis, Missouri, on December 15, 1917. He was assigned as a private, serial number 753442, to Headquarters Company, 14th Battalion, Medical Officers Training Center, Fort Oglethorpe, Georgia. On February 7, 1918, he was transferred to the Evacuation Hospital 5. He went overseas with the unit on May 10, and he was stationed near Paris. Caira returned to the U.S. on February 17, 1919. He was discharged at Camp Grant, Illinois, on March 20, 1919, having become a naturalized U.S. citizen just two days prior. After the war, Caira worked as a barber in Chicago. He died in 1981 in West Chicago.

Leopoldo Caira

Leopoldo Caira (or Cairo) was born on October 5, 1896, in Marano Principato. He was inducted into the Army at Kenosha on August 9, 1918, and was sent to the 57th Depot Brigade at Camp MacArthur, Texas, as a private, serial number 3775687. At some point, he was transferred to the 161st Depot Brigade at Camp Grant, Illinois; he was discharged there on January 3, 1919.

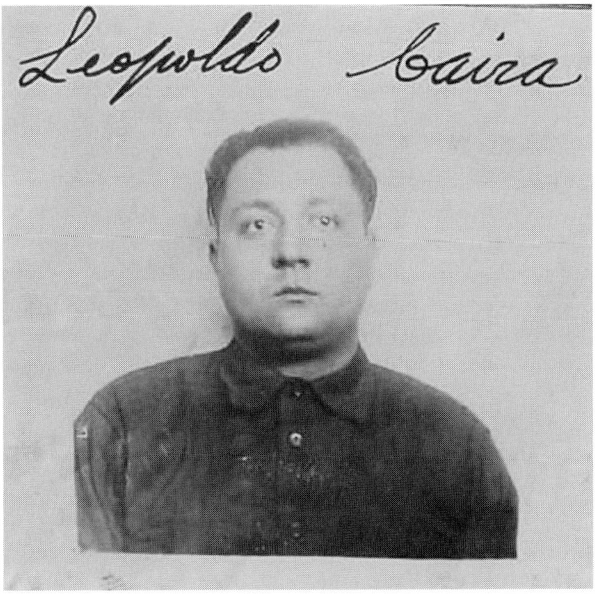

Leopoldo Caira's passport photograph, 1923. (*Ancestry.com*)

Giovanni Caputo

Giovanni Caputo was born in Marano Marchesato in 1888, the son of Raffaele Caputo and Rosina Esposito; he came to the U.S. in 1912. Caputo was employed in the press department at the Black Cat Textiles Company in Kenosha when he registered for the draft. A declarant for United States citizenship, Caputo claimed exemption from the draft on account of the necessity to support his wife. Despite his claim, Caputo was drafted and reported for duty on November 18, 1917. He was a private, serial number 2097657, initially assigned to the Machine Gun Company, 340th Infantry Regiment, 85th Division, at Camp Custer, Michigan. On December 16, 1917, he was transferred to Company "F," 345th Infantry Regiment, 87th Division, at Camp Pike, Arkansas; Caputo was naturalized there on June 1, 1918. On June 19, Caputo was transferred to Company "D," 22nd United States Guards Battalion at Camp Stanley, Texas. On September 19, 1918, he was transferred to 10th Company, 3rd Development Battalion, 165th Depot Brigade, at Camp Travis, Texas. Caputo was discharged from the Army at Camp Travis on December 29, 1918 (or January 1, 1919). Considering Caputo served only stateside, he was well traveled during his year in service.

Pasquale Carpino

Pasquale Carpino was born on January 7, 1890, in Belsito. He came to the U.S. in 1911 and was a baker for the National Biscuit Company in Chicago when he entered the Army. Carpino was a private, serial number 2062020, in Company "A," Washington Barracks Replacement Draft, Engineers (April) when he boarded the *Princess Matoika* for shipment to France on May 10, 1918. Carpino and many others in the same draft, were removed from the vessel, probably due to sickness, and instead sailed aboard U.S.S. *Leviathan* twelve days later as part of Overseas Casual Company No. 181. Upon arrival in France, Carpino was sent to Company "D," 504th Engineer Battalion, an engineer service battalion. He was still a member of that battalion when he boarded U.S.S. *President Grant* for return shipment to the U.S. on May 28, 1919. The ship reached Boston on June 9, and the men were sent to Camp Devens, Massachusetts. Carpino was probably sent to Camp Grant, Illinois, for his discharge shortly thereafter.

Eugene Chesrow (Cesario)[12]

Eugene Chesrow was born on January 1, 1894, in Chicago; his parents were from San Fili. Chesrow's parents were poor, and his father was in poor health; consequently, Chesrow had to work to help support his family. He worked to put himself through college at the University of Valparaiso and then through the Chicago College of Medicine and Surgery, from which he graduated in 1914. Chesrow completed an internship at the Columbus Hospital and was a practicing physician and surgeon when he entered the Army as a physician with the rank of second lieutenant in 1917. On September 8, 1918, Chesrow sailed for France aboard the *Mercury* as part of the Exceptional Medical Replacement Draft Unit No. 39, Camp Hancock. By the time of his return to the U.S. aboard the *Antigone* in July 1919, Chesrow was a first lieutenant in Graves Registration Service Unit 304. Although he resigned his active duty commission in September 1919, Chesrow maintained a commission in the Army Reserve, eventually rising to the rank of lieutenant colonel. He worked in Chicago after the war and was well known locally. Chesrow died in Chicago in 1979.

Beniamino Chiappetta

Beniamino Chiappetta was born in Marano Marchesato on October 3, 1895, the son of Ferdinando Chiappetta and Arcangela Spizzirri. Their other sons were Bruno (born 1887), Carlo (born 1889), and Luigi (born 1893). Carlo and Bruno came to the U.S. in 1905 and 1906, respectively, and Luigi and Beniamino followed in 1911 and 1914, respectively.

In 1918, Beniamino was a laborer living with his brother, Luigi, in Kenosha. Chiappetta was inducted into the National Army on July 21, 1918. He was assigned initially as a private, serial number 3715459, in a development battalion in the 159th Depot Brigade, at Camp Taylor, Kentucky, where he became a naturalized U.S. citizen on August 17. Afterwards, he was transferred to Company "A," 46th U.S. Guards Battalion at Camp Funston, Kansas. He was discharged at Camp Funston on December 11, 1918.

Sometime after his military service, Chiappetta went to Italy for a visit and returned to the U.S. in March 1925, going to his home in Kenosha. Chiappetta must have again returned to Italy because on July 7, 1937, the U.S. State Department had determined that he had "established a permanent residence in Italy within five years after being admitted to citizenship," and had revoked his U.S. citizenship. Chiappetta's brother, Luigi, served with the 7th Infantry Regiment, 3rd Division, and was wounded in action during the war.

Ferdinando Chiappetta

Ferdinando (Fedele) Chiappetta was born on April 11, 1893, in Marano Marchesato, the son of Giuseppe Chiappetta and Fortunata Morrone. Chiappetta was a packer living in Chicago when he entered the Army on June 25, 1918; he was a private, serial number 3278585, in Battery "C," 1st Battalion, 1st Provisional Development Brigade, at Camp Jackson, South Carolina. Chiappetta became a U.S. citizen there in August 1918. At some point, probably for his discharge on January 14, 1919, he was in the 13th Company, 161st Depot Brigade, at Camp Grant, Illinois. Chiappetta died in Chicago in 1963.

Right: Pvt. Ferdinando Chiappetta, 1st Provisional Development Battalion, 1918. (*Ferdinando Chiappetta family*)

Below: Ferdinando Chiappetta's Application for Headstone or Marker. Note numerous corrections and annotations. (*National Archives, via Ancestry.com*)

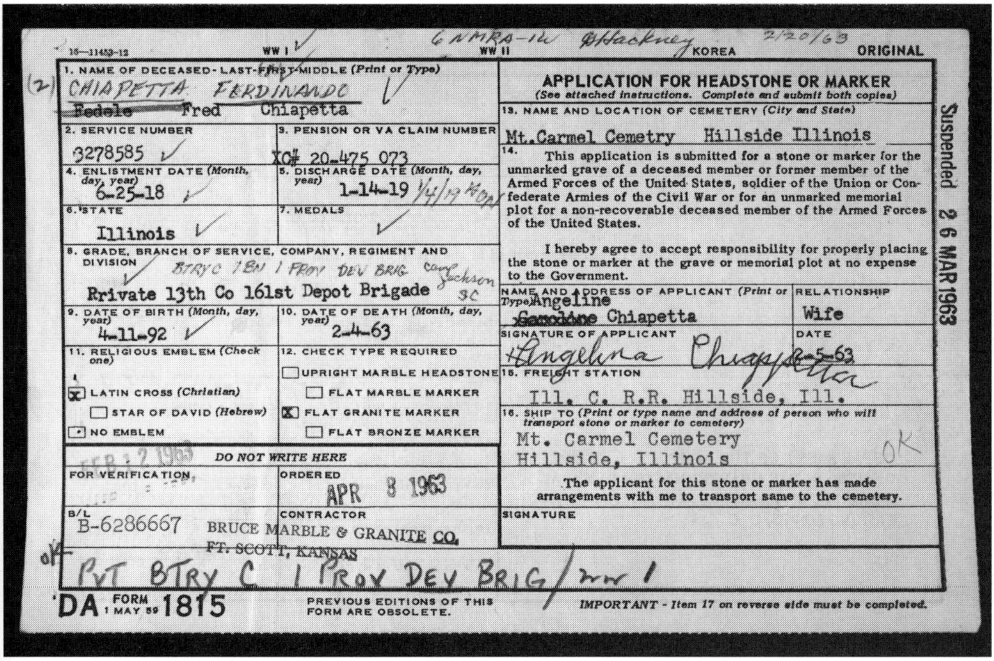

16—11453-12 WW I WW II KOREA ORIGINAL

APPLICATION FOR HEADSTONE OR MARKER
(See attached instructions. Complete and submit both copies)

1. NAME OF DECEASED-LAST-FIRST-MIDDLE (Print or Type)
CHIAPETTA FERDINANDO
~~Fedele~~ Fred Chiapetta

2. SERVICE NUMBER
3278585

3. PENSION OR VA CLAIM NUMBER
XC# 20-475 073

4. ENLISTMENT DATE (Month, day, year)
6-25-18

5. DISCHARGE DATE (Month, day, year)
1-14-19

6. STATE
Illinois

7. MEDALS

8. GRADE, BRANCH OF SERVICE, COMPANY, REGIMENT AND DIVISION
BTRY C 1BN 1 PROV DEV BRIG Camp Jackson SC
Rrivate 13th Co 161st Depot Brigade

9. DATE OF BIRTH (Month, day, year)
4-11-92

10. DATE OF DEATH (Month, day, year)
2-4-63

11. RELIGIOUS EMBLEM (Check one)
[X] LATIN CROSS (Christian)
[ ] STAR OF DAVID (Hebrew)
[ ] NO EMBLEM

12. CHECK TYPE REQUIRED
[ ] UPRIGHT MARBLE HEADSTONE
[ ] FLAT MARBLE MARKER
[X] FLAT GRANITE MARKER
[ ] FLAT BRONZE MARKER

13. NAME AND LOCATION OF CEMETERY (City and State)
Mt.Carmel Cemetry Hillside Illinois

14. This application is submitted for a stone or marker for the unmarked grave of a deceased member or former member of the Armed Forces of the United States, soldier of the Union or Confederate Armies of the Civil War or for an unmarked memorial plot for a non-recoverable deceased member of the Armed Forces of the United States.

I hereby agree to accept responsibility for properly placing the stone or marker at the grave or memorial plot at no expense to the Government.

NAME AND ADDRESS OF APPLICANT (Print or Type) Angeline ~~Caroline~~ Chiapetta
RELATIONSHIP Wife

SIGNATURE OF APPLICANT Angelina Chiappetta
DATE 2-5-63

15. FREIGHT STATION
Ill. C. R.R. Hillside, Ill.

16. SHIP TO (Print or type name and address of person who will transport stone or marker to cemetery)
Mt. Carmel Cemetery
Hillside, Illinois
OK

The applicant for this stone or marker has made arrangements with me to transport same to the cemetery.

SIGNATURE

Suspended 26 MAR 1963

DO NOT WRITE HERE
FEB 12 1963

FOR VERIFICATION

ORDERED
APR 8 1963

B/L
B-6286667

CONTRACTOR
BRUCE MARBLE & GRANITE CO.
FT. SCOTT, KANSAS

PVT BTRY C 1 PROV DEV BRIG / WW I

DA FORM 1 MAY 59 1815
PREVIOUS EDITIONS OF THIS FORM ARE OBSOLETE.
IMPORTANT - Item 17 on reverse side must be completed.

Louis Christian (Cristiano)

Luigi Cristiano (Louis Christian) was born on September 14, 1889, in Carpanzano. He was a bookkeeper and general office worker for the Chicago and North Western Railway, living in Chicago, when he entered the Army. Christian was a private, serial number 1382370, in the Medical Detachment, 129th Infantry Regiment, 33rd Division, when he boarded the *La Lorraine* for shipment to France on May 14, 1918. The 129th Infantry Regiment saw service with the Australians and French before seeing much action during the Meuse-Argonne Offensive. Christian was a private first class when he returned to the U.S. aboard U.S.S. *Leviathan* on May 22, 1919, and was discharged on June 6. Christian died in 1958 in Illinois.

Francesco Conforti

Francesco "Frank" Conforti was born in Marano Marchesato on February 23, 1896, the son of Serafino Conforti and Rosina Cosentino. He arrived in the U.S. in 1912, destined for his brother, Carlo, in Kenosha. Conforti was a machinist at the Simmons Manufacturing Company in Kenosha when he entered the Army on March 29, 1918, being initially assigned as a private, serial number 2040857, to the 160th Depot Brigade at Camp Custer, Michigan. On May 2, he was sent to the Engineers Replacement and Training Regiments at Camp Humphreys, Virginia. There, on June 8, Conforti became a naturalized U.S. citizen. At about the same time he was transferred to Company "F," 116th Engineer Regiment, a replacement regiment assigned to the 41st Division. On June 15, he went overseas as part of the 2nd Company, Camp Humphreys June Automatic Replacement Draft (Engineers). On July 22, he was transferred to Company "F," 101st Engineer Regiment, 26th Division.

Conforti saw much action with this regiment; as a divisional engineer regiment, its duties consisted of building trenches, dugouts, and emplacements for the division's units, and they also sometimes accompanied the attacking infantry regiments. In fact, one half of Conforti's Company "F" accompanied the 103rd Infantry Regiment on during their assault at the beginning of the Saint-Mihiel Offensive on September 12, 1918. The engineers carried wire cutters and Bangalore torpedoes to enable them to breach the enemy's wire entanglements during the attack. During the Meuse-Argonne Offensive, the 101st Engineer Regiment built and maintained roads on the east side of the Meuse River, often while under shellfire.

Conforti returned to the U.S. on April 4, 1919, and was discharged thirteen days later at Camp Grant, Illinois. He received credit for participating in the Aisne-Marne Campaign, Saint-Mihiel Offensive, Meuse-Argonne Offensive, and Defensive Sector. As evidence of the hard service performed by engineers in combat during World War I, Conforti was certified with a 2 percent disability upon his discharge from the Army.

Ignazio Conforti[13]

Ignazio Conforti was born on March 6, 1891, in Marano Marchesato, the son of Serafino Conforti and Angela Ruffolo. Conforti came to the U.S. in 1905, destined for Kenosha, where his brother, Salvatore, an employee at the Nash Motor company, lived. By the time Conforti registered for the draft on June 7, 1917, he was a storekeeper living with his brother and sister-in-law in Kenosha. He claimed exemption because of the necessity to look after his store.

Despite his claim for exemption, Conforti was drafted on May 26, 1918; he was sent to the 161st Depot Brigade at Camp Grant, Illinois. While there, on June 20, 1918, he became a naturalized U.S. citizen. Conforti did well at Camp Grant; on June 9, he was promoted to corporal. On July 12, he was demoted to private, probably in anticipation of his transfer the following day to Company "B," 332nd Machine Gun Battalion, part of the newly forming 86th Division, composed largely of draftees from Illinois and Wisconsin. Conforti was promoted to private first class on August 18, showing once again his adaptation to the military. In early September, the 86th moved to the east coast preparatory to sailing for France and combat with the A.E.F. Upon arrival in France, the 86th Division was stripped of men as they sent replacements to other units engaged in combat. On October 17, 1918, Conforti was sent to Company "C," 9th Machine Gun Battalion, 3rd Division, then heavily engaged in the Meuse-Argonne Offensive. After the war, the 3rd Division served in the Army of Occupation in Germany, and Conforti served there until his return to the U.S. on August 18, 1919. Conforti was discharged from Camp Grant one week later.

On August 25, 1923, Conforti was admitted to the Milwaukee branch of the U.S. National Home for Disabled Volunteer Soldiers, suffering from "T.B. Pul. Chronic Active Mod. Adv," apparently an advanced case of tuberculosis. He was single and listed his brother Salvatore, still living in Kenosha, as next of kin. Sadly, Conforti did not recover, and on February 19, 1924, he died at the hospital. On the same day, his body was delivered to Joseph Cardinal, undertakers, for shipment to Kenosha. Conforti had, on his person at the time, $8.40 in cash and about $12.60 in effects. Those effects were sold at auction on June 26, 1925. They brought only $1.

Leopoldo Conforti

Leopoldo (Leopold or Leo) Conforti was born on July 23, 1896, in Marano Principato, the son of Francesco Conforti and Maria Frisolona. He came to the U.S. with his father in 1911. He was a truck driver or repairer living in Kenosha when he was drafted on October 21, 1918. He became a private, serial number 4303023, in the 63rd Depot Brigade, Camp Dodge, Iowa. On November 4, he was transferred to the November Automatic Replacement Draft at Camp Shelby, Mississippi. After the war, he was transferred to the 16th Company, 161st Depot Brigade, at Camp Grant, Illinois; he was discharged there on December 26, 1918, and he moved back to Kenosha. On October 27, 1942, during World War II, Conforti, by that time living in Chicago, enlisted in the U.S. Army. He served very briefly, being discharged on December 4, 1942. As far as the current research stands, he and Anthony Jerry Desmonie are the only two men in this study to have served during both world wars, although it is possible that Samuel Ritacco also served during both wars.

Louis Conforti

Luigi (Louis) Conforti was born in Marano Marchesato in 1891 or 1893. He came to the U.S. in 1906, and was living in Cicero, Illinois, when he entered the Army on March 25, 1918. He was a private, serial number 1188289, in the 3rd Company, 1st Battalion, 158th Depot Brigade, and 125th Casual Company, both at Camp Sherman, Ohio, before being transferred to Company "C," 344th Field Artillery Regiment, 90th Division. Conforti sailed for France with a detachment of his regiment aboard the

Louisville on July 6. Conforti came back to the U.S. aboard the *Aeolus* on December 16, 1918; at that time, he was a member of the "Fire and S.S. Guard." He was discharged on January 30, 1919. After the war, he moved back to Cicero, where he died in 1936.

Mariano Conforti

Mariano Conforti was born on May 5, 1897, in Marano Marchesato, the son of Giacomo Conforti and Rachela Guido. He came to the U.S. in 1914, destined for his brother, Domenico, in Chicago.

Conforti enlisted in the Regular Army on May 29, 1918, at Jefferson Barracks near St. Louis, Missouri. He was assigned as a private, serial number 3071292, to the Headquarters Company, 18th Battalion, Field Artillery Replacement Depot at Camp Jackson, South Carolina. On August 19, he was transferred to Truck Company "C," 5th Corps Artillery Park; he was promoted to bugler on September 18. Conforti went overseas with the unit on September 23, and he returned to the U.S. on March 29, 1919. He was discharged at Camp Grant, Illinois, on April 22. Conforti reenlisted the following day and, by the time of his final discharge on June 6, 1920, he was a bugler first class with Company "C," 14th Infantry Regiment, 19th Division, at Camp Custer, Michigan. After his military service, Conforti moved to Kenosha where he worked in an automobile factory until his death in 1963.

Emilio Cosentino

Emilio "Emil" Cosentino was born in Chicago on March 23, 1896. Cosentino's parents, Serafino and Filomena Cosentino, from Marano Marchesato, were pioneer Cosenza area immigrants, with Serafino coming to the U.S. in 1881 and Filomena arriving in 1886. Emilio Cosentino was a chauffeur for Dr. Eugene Chesrow (a fellow World War I veteran, see his biography in this chapter) in Chicago when he enlisted in the Quartermaster Enlisted Reserve on September 29, 1917. Cosentino went on active duty on October 13, 1917, and at some point, he was assigned to Motor Transportation Company 318, Motor Supply Train No. 405. He went overseas with this unit aboard the *Megantic* on January 7, 1918. In France, Motor Transport Company 318 served as transportation troops for General Headquarters, A.E.F. When Cosentino returned to the U.S. aboard the *Westshore* on May 20, 1919, he was a corporal, serial number 216537. He was discharged two weeks later. After the war, Cosentino lived in Chicago and Cicero where he worked as a taxi driver until his death in Cicero in 1947.

Francesco (Moris) Costabile[14]

Francesco Mariano (Moris or Morris) Costabile born in Marano Marchesato on February 4, 1893, the son of Tommaso Costabile and Maria Esposito. Costabile came to the U.S. around 1907 and settled with family member in Chicago. On June 16, 1913, Costabile, by then a tailor, enlisted in Troop "M," 2nd Cavalry Regiment, possibly for special duty as a troop tailor. It is interesting to note his "defects at enlistment: Slight corns both feet, flat feet mod. par [partial?] hammer toes, both feet, knock kneed moderate, hyperhidrosis [excessive sweating] mod. both feet."[15] The 2nd Cavalry Regiment had fought the Moros in the Philippines in 1911 and 1912; it is possible that Costabile saw duty in the islands during his enlistment. In any event, he was "honorably discharged March 2, 1915, by purchase."[16] This meant that he paid a certain amount of money to be released from the balance of his enlistment commitment, and he received an honorable discharge (the amount, in 1891, was about $120, no small sum for an enlisted man.)

In June 1917, when Moris Costabile registered for the draft, he was single and employed as a tailor for P. Allevato in Chicago. He claimed to be a U.S. citizen "by act of congress," and listed his mother and father as being completely dependent upon him for support. Costabile also listed his prior service of twenty months and sixteen days as a private in the 2nd U.S. Cavalry Regiment. It is unclear whether he claimed exemption from the draft because on his registration it appears that the word "yes" was written first, but possibly the word "no" was penned over it. Presumably Costabile obtained U.S. citizenship via his earlier military service.

Costabile was back in uniform on May 2, 1918, probably via the draft at Jefferson Barracks, Missouri. He was a private, serial number 479346; he was sent to Camp Fremont, California, where he was assigned to Headquarters Company, 8th Infantry Regiment, 8th Division. His "physical defects" on this occasion consisted of "goiter, obesity, varicose veins, flat feet."[17] On August 1, 1918, Costabile applied for the government-provided life insurance, listing as his beneficiary his wife, "Mrs. Lily Hepperle Costabile," in Oak Park, Illinois. It would appear that he got married between the time of his draft registration in June 1917 and the time of his duty at Camp Fremont.

By the time Costabile was in Camp Fremont, the War Department had agreed to send an American military force to Siberia in order to encourage the struggling government and to protect the people of that area, in addition to guarding Czechoslovakian prisoners who were anti-German and who could be sent to France to bolster allied forces. One of the regiments tapped for this duty was the 27th Infantry Regiment, the Wolfhounds, stationed in the Philippines. Since that regiment was understrength, the War Department authorized the transfer of some 800 men from the 8th Division; one of these men was Costabile who was assigned to Headquarters Company, 27th Infantry Regiment. The men shipped out in August 1918. It is not known how long Costabile was in Siberia or, indeed, his other travels, but he returned to the U.S. on October 6, 1919; since the 27th Infantry Regiment stayed in Siberia until early 1920, Costabile returned early for some reason. He was sent to the Casual Detachment, 1562 Demobilization Group, at Camp Dodge, Iowa, for discharge. After having his final pay tabulated and adjusted, including, along with many other men, an amount due, 38 cents, to the Post Laundry at Fort William McKinley, Philippine Islands, Costabile received his discharge on October 14, 1919.

Costabile's marriage was apparently not a happy or lengthy one; it appears that he was divorced sometime in 1920. At the time, Costabile was the proprietor of a tailor shop. Sometime in the 1920s, Costabile applied for a loan against his adjusted veteran's compensation; there is no indication of how much he received or whether he was able to pay it back. On January 20, 1932, Costabile was murdered. The circumstances of this horrific crime are unknown, but a coroner's inquest jury summed up their findings:

> The unanimous verdict of this Jury is that Morris Costabile came to his death by homicide, the result of eight bullets fired into his head by parties unknown to this Jury. This took place on the Finley Road, three quarters of a mile north of Ogden Avenue in York Township, County of DuPage, State of Illinois.[18]

The fact that Costabile was shot in the head eight times suggests that a message was being conveyed via his murder; it is much more than a robbery, for example. Costabile's ex-wife wrote to the Veterans' Administration requesting information about some claim associated with Costabile's death. The only claim paid appears to be in the amount of $100 to Peter M. Kelly, the Chicago undertaker who took care of the funeral arrangements. This amount was far less than Kelly's annotated expense list. Thus ends the sad story of an Italian immigrant who served his country twice including service during the world war in a hostile and forbidding country in pursuit of ill-defined goals.

Frank A. Costabile

Frank A. Costabile was born in Rende on March 10, 1896. He was a molder at Belle City Malleable Iron Company, living in Racine, when he was inducted into the Army on May 17, 1918. Costabile was assigned as a private, serial number 2863546; at some point, Costabile was promoted to corporal. He went overseas while assigned to Company "L," 34th Engineer Regiment, a supply and shop regiment. Costabile was assigned as a mechanic in the same unit when he returned to the U.S. aboard U.S.S. *America* on July 13, 1919. He was discharged six days later at Camp Grant, Illinois. Less than a month later, on August 20, Costabile reenlisted in the Army at Columbus Barracks, Ohio. Promoted to sergeant on January 26, 1920, Costabile was discharged at Marfa, Texas, on August 19, 1920.

Lawrence Covelli

Lawrence Covelli was born on November 1, 1896, in Marano Principato. He was a laborer living in Kenosha when he was drafted on May 27, 1918. He was sent to Camp Grant, Illinois, where he became a private, serial number 2828941; fairly quickly, he was promoted to corporal in Company "I," 343rd Infantry Regiment, 86th Division. He was naturalized as a U.S. citizen at Camp Grant in June 1918 and went overseas with the division in August. In France, Covelli was transferred to Company "F," 49th Infantry Regiment. He returned to the U.S. in April 1919, and was sent to Fort Leavenworth, Kansas, where, on April 19, he reenlisted in the Army. He was sent with the 49th Infantry Regiment to Fort Snelling, Minnesota, where he served until his discharge on April 18, 1920. Covelli moved back to Kenosha. His initial request for a Wisconsin war veteran's bonus seems to have been denied on account that he was not a Wisconsin resident at time of enlistment; later, this appears to have been corrected and he was paid. Covelli died in Kenosha in 1967.

Frank Cundari

Frank Cundari was born in San Fili in January 1887, the son of Carmine Cundari and Anna Maria Mazzulla; he was a railroad laborer living in Franklin Park, Illinois, when he entered the Army on May 27, 1918. Cundari was a private, serial number 1366846, assigned to Company "A," 123rd Infantry Regiment, 31st Division, a division made up of National Guard units from several southern states, but infused with draftees from around the country. On October 11, 1918, Cundari was preparing to board the Army transport *Harrisburg* for shipment to France with his unit, when he became ill, probably with influenza. He was taken off the vessel and sent to the Base Hospital at Camp Mills, New York, along with at least other members of his company. Cundari was discharged on December 20, 1918. He used his military service for his naturalization in 1936.

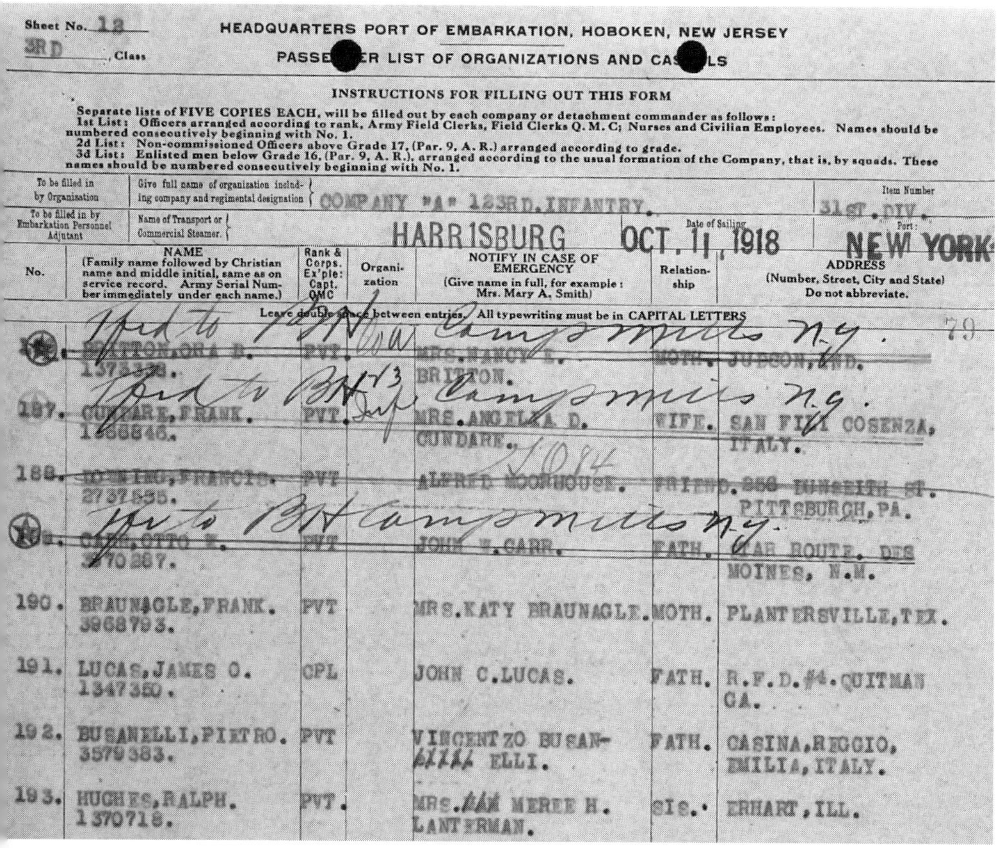

Sheet No. 12

3RD, Class

HEADQUARTERS PORT OF EMBARKATION, HOBOKEN, NEW JERSEY

PASSE[illegible]ER LIST OF ORGANIZATIONS AND CA[illegible]LS

INSTRUCTIONS FOR FILLING OUT THIS FORM

Separate lists of FIVE COPIES EACH, will be filled out by each company or detachment commander as follows:
1st List: Officers arranged according to rank, Army Field Clerks, Field Clerks Q. M. C; Nurses and Civilian Employees. Names should be numbered consecutively beginning with No. 1.
2d List: Non-commissioned Officers above Grade 17, (Par. 9, A. R.) arranged according to grade.
3d List: Enlisted men below Grade 16, (Par. 9, A. R.), arranged according to the usual formation of the Company, that is, by squads. These names should be numbered consecutively beginning with No. 1.

To be filled in by Organization — Give full name of organization including company and regimental designation: COMPANY "A" 123RD. INFANTRY. — Item Number: 31ST. DIV.

To be filled in by Embarkation Personnel Adjutant — Name of Transport or Commercial Steamer: HARRISBURG — Date of Sailing: OCT. 11, 1918 — Port: NEW YORK

Leave double space between entries. All typewriting must be in CAPITAL LETTERS

No.	NAME (Family name followed by Christian name and middle initial, same as on service record. Army Serial Number immediately under each name.)	Rank & Corps. Ex'ple: Capt. QMC	Organization	NOTIFY IN CASE OF EMERGENCY (Give name in full, for example: Mrs. Mary A. Smith)	Relationship	ADDRESS (Number, Street, City and State) Do not abbreviate.
[illegible]	BRITTON, ORA B. 1373338.	PVT		MRS. NANCY E. BRITTON.	MOTH.	JUDSON, IND.
187.	CUNDARE, FRANK. 1868846.	PVT		MRS. ANGELA D. CUNDARE.	WIFE.	SAN FILI COSENZA, ITALY.
188.	[illegible], FRANCIS. 2737535.	PVT		ALFRED MOORHOUSE.	FRIEND.	356 [illegible] ST. PITTSBURGH, PA.
[illegible]	CARR, OTTO E. 3870287.	PVT		JOHN W. CARR.	FATH.	[illegible] ROUTE, DES MOINES, N.M.
190.	BRAUNAGLE, FRANK. 3968793.	PVT		MRS. KATY BRAUNAGLE.	MOTH.	PLANTERSVILLE, TEX.
191.	LUCAS, JAMES O. 1347350.	CPL		JOHN C. LUCAS.	FATH.	R.F.D. #4. QUITMAN GA.
192.	BUSANELLI, PIETRO. 3579383.	PVT		VINCENTZO BUSANELLI.	FATH.	CASINA, REGGIO, EMILIA, ITALY.
193.	HUGHES, RALPH. 1370718.	PVT.		MRS. MERLE H. LANTERMAN.	SIS.	ERHART, ILL.

Detail of the Army transport manifest showing Pvt. Frank "Cundare" (second from the top) being transferred to the Base Hospital at Camp Mills, New York, due to sickness. The surname is usually spelled "Cundari" in Italian records, and that is the spelling Cundari used. (*Ancestry.com*)

Leopoldo (Paul) DeFrancesco

Leopoldo (Paul) DeFrancesco was born in Marano Marchesato in October 1893, the son of Agostino DeFrancesco and Saveria Chiappetta. Agostino made at least one trip to the U.S. in 1890, and other family members came in the early 1900s. Leopoldo came to the U.S. in 1912, destined for his brother in Chicago. DeFrancesco was a laborer for the Michigan Central Railroad in Chicago when he entered the Army on May 2, 1918, at Jefferson Barracks, Missouri. He was a private, serial number 479808, in Company "H," 55th Infantry Regiment, 7th Division, when he went to France aboard U.S.S. *Leviathan* in August 1918. His regiment saw action in France during October and November 1918 as part of the U.S. 2nd Army. DeFrancesco was assigned to Headquarters Troop, 7th Division, when he returned to the U.S. aboard the *Imperator* on June 20, 1919. He was discharged on July 1, 1919. In the early 1930s, DeFrancesco spent some time at the Disabled Veterans Home in Danville, Illinois. He died in Chicago in 1977.

Pasquale DeFranco
Pasquale (Charles) DeFranco was born in 1892 in Marano Marchesato, the son of Michele DeFranco and Maria Loizzo. Pasquale arrived in the U.S. in 1910, along with his brother, Giuseppe (who had been in the U.S. in 1902 and from 1906 to 1908), destined for their cousin, Luigi Puzzo, in Chicago. He was a laborer at the American Brass Company in Kenosha when he was inducted into the National Army on July 21, 1918. DeFranco was assigned as a private, serial number 3715663, in the 159th Depot Brigade at Camp Taylor, Kentucky. DeFranco filed for U.S. naturalization on August 12, and five days later, he became a U.S. citizen. At about this time, he was transferred to the 9th Trench Mortar Battery, part of the newly forming 9th Division at Camp McClellan, Alabama. The unit had finished its training and was preparing for shipment overseas when the war ended. One wonders, even at this late date in the war and with the unit ready for overseas shipment, whether DeFranco and the rest of the 9th Trench Mortar Battery ever got the chance to fire their large, cumbersome mortars. In any event, DeFranco was discharged on February 10, 1919, at Camp Grant, Illinois. After the war, DeFranco lived in Kenosha where he worked as a machine operator until his death in 1968.

Frank DeLeo
Frank DeLeo was born on November 9, 1896, in Gesuiti, part of the larger commune of San Vincenzo la Costa; he was the son of Pasquale DeLeo. He was a baker living in Chicago when he was inducted into the Army. When he went to France aboard the *Cretic* on June 28, 1918, DeLeo was a private, serial number 1626655, assigned to Camp Kearny June Automatic Replacement Draft. Upon arrival in France, DeLeo was assigned to Company "E," 56th Pioneer Infantry Regiment; he returned to the U.S. with his regiment aboard the *Eten* on June 12, 1919.

Francesco (Frank) DeRango
Francesco (Frank) DeRango was born in Marano Marchesato on October 10, 1892, the son of Gabriele DeRango and Maria Greco. He came to the U.S. in 1913 and was living in Chicago when he enlisted in the Regular Army on June 22, 1917. He was a private, serial number 1364416; at some point, he may have been a member of the 124th Field Artillery Regiment, 33rd Division. DeRango was transferred to Camp Wheeler, Georgia, on December 28, 1917, where he became a naturalized U.S. citizen on May 27, 1918. Soon thereafter, DeRango was transferred to Battery "D," 8th Field Artillery Regiment, 7th Division, with which he went to France. DeRango was a private first class when he returned to the U.S. in 1919; he was discharged on June 30, 1919. In early 1942, DeRango was unemployed and receiving a government pension, perhaps for injuries suffered during the war. DeRango died on July 31, 1942, in Chicago.

Carlo DeRose
Carlo DeRose was born in Carolei on April 26, 1896, the son of Salvatore DeRose; he came to the U.S. in June 1912, and was living in Chicago when he entered the Army. DeRose became a naturalized U.S. citizen at Camp Shelby, Mississippi, on December 6, 1918.

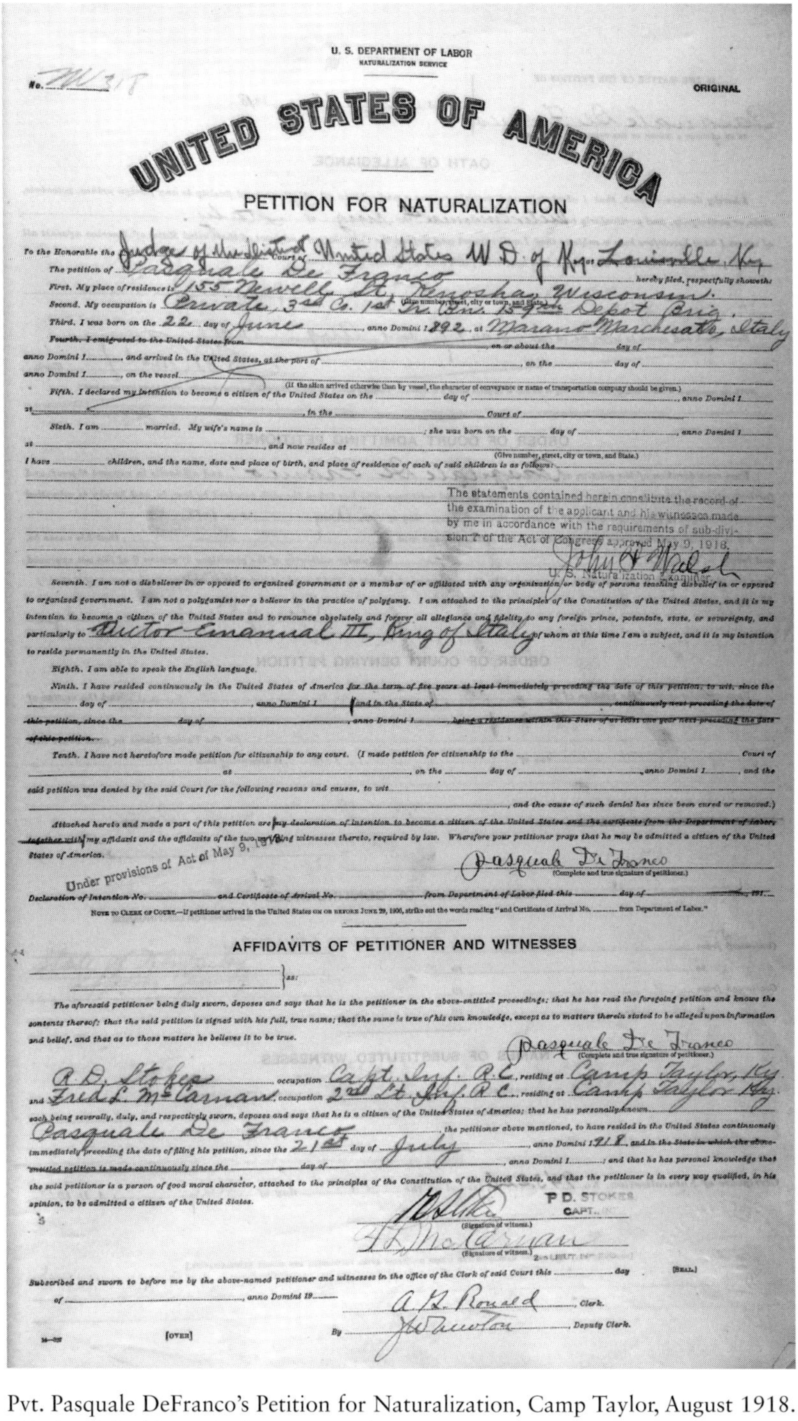

U. S. DEPARTMENT OF LABOR
NATURALIZATION SERVICE

No. M/315 ORIGINAL

UNITED STATES OF AMERICA

PETITION FOR NATURALIZATION

To the Honorable the Judge of the District Court of United States W. D. of Ky. Louisville, Ky.

The petition of Pasquale De Franco hereby filed, respectfully showeth:

First. My place of residence is 155 Newell St. Kenosha Wisconsin.

Second. My occupation is Private 3rd Co. 1st Tr. Bn. 159 Depot Brig.

Third. I was born on the 22 day of June anno Domini 1892, at Marano Marchesato, Italy

~~Fourth. I emigrated to the United States from~~ .... on or about the .... day of .... anno Domini 1........, and arrived in the United States, ~~at the port of~~ .... on the .... day of .... anno Domini 1........, on the vessel ....

Fifth. I declared my intention to become a citizen of the United States on the .... day of ...., anno Domini 1........ at .... in the .... Court of ....

Sixth. I am .... married. My wife's name is ....; she was born on the .... day of ...., anno Domini 1........ at ...., and now resides at ....

I have .... children, and the name, date and place of birth, and place of residence of each of said children is as follows:

The statements contained herein constitute the record of the examination of the applicant and his witnesses made by me in accordance with the requirements of sub-division 7 of the Act of Congress approved May 9, 1918.
John J. Walsh
U. S. Naturalization Examiner.

Seventh. I am not a disbeliever in or opposed to organized government or a member of or affiliated with any organization or body of persons teaching disbelief in or opposed to organized government. I am not a polygamist nor a believer in the practice of polygamy. I am attached to the principles of the Constitution of the United States, and it is my intention to become a citizen of the United States and to renounce absolutely and forever all allegiance and fidelity to any foreign prince, potentate, state, or sovereignty, and particularly to Victor Emanual III, King of Italy of whom at this time I am a subject, and it is my intention to reside permanently in the United States.

Eighth. I am able to speak the English language.

Ninth. I have resided continuously in the United States of America ~~for the term of five years at least immediately preceding the date of this petition, to wit, since the~~ .... day of ...., anno Domini 1........ ~~and in the State of~~ .... ~~continuously next preceding the date of this petition, since the~~ .... day of ...., anno Domini 1........ ~~being a residence within this State of at least one year next preceding the date of this petition.~~

Tenth. I have not heretofore made petition for citizenship to any court. (I made petition for citizenship to the .... Court of .... at ...., on the .... day of ...., anno Domini 1........, and the said petition was denied by the said Court for the following reasons and causes, to wit ...., and the cause of such denial has since been cured or removed.)

Attached hereto and made a part of this petition are ~~my declaration of intention to become a citizen of the United States and the certificate from the Department of Labor, together with~~ my affidavit and the affidavits of the two ~~verifying~~ witnesses thereto, required by law. Wherefore your petitioner prays that he may be admitted a citizen of the United States of America.

Under provisions of Act of May 9, 1918

Pasquale De Franco
(Complete and true signature of petitioner.)

~~Declaration of Intention No. .... and Certificate of Arrival No. .... from Department of Labor filed this .... day of ...., 191....~~

NOTE TO CLERK OF COURT.—If petitioner arrived in the United States on or before June 29, 1906, strike out the words reading "and Certificate of Arrival No. .... from Department of Labor."

AFFIDAVITS OF PETITIONER AND WITNESSES

.... } ss:

The aforesaid petitioner being duly sworn, deposes and says that he is the petitioner in the above-entitled proceedings; that he has read the foregoing petition and knows the contents thereof; that the said petition is signed with his full, true name; that the same is true of his own knowledge, except as to matters therein stated to be alleged upon information and belief, and that as to those matters he believes it to be true.

Pasquale De Franco
(Complete and true signature of petitioner.)

R. D. Stokes, occupation Capt. Inf. R.C., residing at Camp Taylor, Ky.
and Fred L. McCarnan, occupation 2nd Lt. Inf. R.C., residing at Camp Taylor, Ky.
each being severally, duly, and respectively sworn, deposes and says that he is a citizen of the United States of America; that he has personally known Pasquale De Franco, the petitioner above mentioned, to have resided in the United States continuously immediately preceding the date of filing his petition, since the 21st day of July, anno Domini 1918, ~~and in the State in which the above-entitled petition is made continuously since the~~ .... day of ...., anno Domini 1........; and that he has personal knowledge that the said petitioner is a person of good moral character, attached to the principles of the Constitution of the United States, and that the petitioner is in every way qualified, in his opinion, to be admitted a citizen of the United States.

R. D. Stokes
(Signature of witness.)
R. D. STOKES
CAPT. ...

F. L. McCarnan
(Signature of witness.)
2nd LIEUT. INF. ...

Subscribed and sworn to before me by the above-named petitioner and witnesses in the office of the Clerk of said Court this .... day of ...., anno Domini 19.... [SEAL.]

A. G. Ronald, Clerk.
By J. W. Newton, Deputy Clerk.

[OVER]

Pvt. Pasquale DeFranco's Petition for Naturalization, Camp Taylor, August 1918. (*National Archives, via Ancestry.com*)

Carlo DeRose's passport photograph, 1923. (*Ancestry.com*)

Emilio Fallico

Luciano Emilio Fallico was born in San Vincenzo la Costa on November 6, 1895, the son of Domenico Fallico and Filomena Esposito Orrico. He came to the U.S. in 1913 and was living in Racine when he was inducted into the Army on July 25, 1918. Fallico served as a private in the 38th Company, 10th Battalion, 159th Depot Brigade, at Camp Taylor, Kentucky. Fallico became a naturalized U.S. citizen on August 17, 1918, and he was discharged on December 13, 1918. Fallico's 1918 naturalization certificate bears the bold handwritten note: "Vacated—cancelled and set aside, Sept. 20, 1940." Probably Fallico had returned to Italy to live and had thereby abrogated his U.S. citizenship.

Michael Fallico

Michele (Michael) Fallico was born on October 25, 1891, in San Vincenzo la Costa. He was a laborer living in Racine when he was inducted into the Army on September 21, 1917, one of the earliest large induction days. Fallico was a private, serial number 2024510, in Company "D," 340th Infantry Regiment, 85th Division, at Camp Custer, Michigan. On February 25, 1918, he was transferred to Company "B," 58th Infantry Regiment, 4th Division. Fallico sailed for France with his regiment aboard the British ship R.M.S. *Moldavia* on May 6, 1918. Fallico's trip across the ocean was anything but routine.

Fallico had the unusual distinction of surviving the sinking of his transport. The ship was sunk by a torpedo fired by U-Boat *UB-57* as it neared Beachy Head in the English Channel on May 23, 1918. Fifty-four men died in the explosion and subsequent struggle in the water. The 4th Division unit history gives an excellent account of what Fallico and the other survivors experienced:

The explosion tore a gaping hole in the port side of the hull and shattered the compartment where the "B" Company men were sleeping and the ladders leading to the deck above. Nearly all the men in the compartment were killed outright by the explosion. The listing of the ship to port undoubtedly saved those who survived the explosion, enabling them to utilize the uneven surface of the sloping compartment walls in climbing to the next deck above, and from there to the boat deck and rescue.

Fortunately, the engines were not injured by the explosion, and the bursting of a starboard bulkhead caused the ship to resume an even keel. An attempt was made to reach shore, but the water gained rapidly and stilled the ship's throbbing engines within an hour.

The explosion had awakened all on board. Contrary to orders, many of the men had undressed before going to bed in the belief that the submarine danger was practically over, as land had been visible during the entire day. In the darkness and confusion many of them were unable to find their clothes and were forced to go to their boat stations in little more than their underwear—some wore even less.

The dying down of the engines found nearly all the men at their proper boat stations. A decided list to starboard had developed, however, which made the launching of the boats at the port side a very precarious matter. A number of men received a chilly bath during the process, but, eventually, the boats were launched. One of the British destroyers came alongside, and made fast to the starboard side of the Moldavia, taking all the men she could find room for direct from one ship to the other. Another destroyer circled around, picking up those who were in boats and hanging to the life-rafts.

Only two men were lost by drowning, although many unwelcome cold baths were taken by those who tried to climb upon the life-rafts only to overbalance the unwieldy affairs and slide, headlong, back into the sea. One soldier performed this stunt three times before he became convinced of the error of his ways.

After dropping depth bombs over the area in which the Moldavia was struck, three of the destroyer escort and the other five ships of the convoy had scurried away to avoid possibility of further disaster. This left only the two rescuing destroyers with their shivering but thankful burden, to watch the death throes of the stricken vessel. She had settled forward rapidly, her stern slowly rising higher and higher in the air.

Picture, if you will, a glassy, calm sea in the early dawn of that season of the year; a heavily clouded sky through which the sun had not yet made its way, but light enough to make each detail of the tragedy visible to the spectators aboard the little rescue ships; abandoned life boats and rafts bobbing about; here and there a dead body; on the decks of the two waiting destroyers a motley, shivering, awestruck crowd in various stages of dress and undress; a long minute of breathless silence; a lurch; a gurgle; a ponderous gathering of that immense mass of steel, as if for physical effort, followed by the rearing of the stern high in the air; a sickening dive; a seething cauldron in which are tossed bits of wooden wreckage, and the Moldavia was no more. The rescued soldiers, packed on the two destroyers, greeted the final plunge of their ship with a tumult of cheers.[19]

Fallico survived to be promoted to private first class on August 12; he also participated in the Aisne-Marne, Saint-Mihiel, and Meuse-Argonne Offensives as well as serving in the Vesle, Toul, and Meux Defensive Sectors. Fallico was one of the men who opted to receive his discharge while overseas, in his case on July 10, 1919. He returned to the U.S. in the 1920s and lived in Pennsylvania and New Jersey. Fallico became a U.S. citizen in New Jersey using his military service to facilitate the paperwork in 1928.

Eugenio Ferraro[20]

Eugenio Ferraro was born on October 8, 1893, in Marano Marchesato, the son of Giuseppe Ferraro and Luisa Greco. Ferraro's family was, like so many other Cosenza families, part of a family-based migration in the late 1890s and early 1900s. Eugenio came to the U.S. in 1910, joining his brothers, Leopoldo and Rosario, in Kenosha.

At the time of his registration for the draft in 1917, Ferraro was a tailor living in Kenosha. He requested exemption from the draft on account of his support of his parents and sister. Sometime within the next year, Ferraro's feelings about serving in the military changed. Perhaps a Navy campaign to recruit tailors for special duty influenced him. In any event, he declared his intention to become a U.S. citizen on April 11, 1918, and the next day, he traveled 20 miles south to Great Lakes Naval Training Station, Illinois, where he enlisted in the Navy.

Ferraro, with brown eyes, black hair, and a ruddy complexion, 5 feet 6 inches tall, and weighing 141 pounds, gave his occupation as tailor, and he listed his mother in Marano Marchesato as next of kin. He was given the rating as a fireman first class, an increased rating awarded because of his skill as a tailor. He became a naturalized U.S. citizen at Great Lakes, shortly after joining the Navy, on July 2, 1918.

Eugenio served his entire stint in the Navy at Great Lakes. Ferraro worked as a tailor in the Navy, performing alterations and repairs for the thousands of wartime recruits flooding the station. It was like "a regular job; after basic training he didn't live on base, he came home to Kenosha every night. The North Shore railroad had stops at Great Lakes and Kenosha, so it was easy."[21] On his December 31, 1918, Navy evaluation, Ferraro was rated a "4" (on a four-point scale) for both sobriety and obedience. At the time of his discharge on May 26, 1919, he was given a proficiency rating of "3.5," and he was once again rated "4" for sobriety and obedience. Ferraro was discharged from the Navy on May 26, 1919. At that time, he was paid in full, $378.42; this accounted for a little more than three months' back-pay at $46.50 per month (the pay rate for firemen first class), a war service gratuity of $60, mileage pay to Kenosha (at 19 miles, the total was 95 cents), and subsistence ($186.00). Subtracted from that total were allotments for war risk insurance (Ferraro had purchased this government provided insurance in the amount of $10,000 for $6.60 per month, naming his mother as beneficiary), and other miscellaneous deductions.

Shortly after his discharge from the Navy, Ferraro returned to Great Lakes where he was employed as a civilian tailor for the Navy. Sometime after 1920, he settled in Kenosha where he worked "his entire life as a tailor performing alterations and repairs for a number of clothing stores in Kenosha."[22] In 1924, Ferraro applied for compensation adjustment based upon his stateside service in the Navy during the war. He was awarded $350, to be paid after 1944. Ferraro died in Kenosha in 1975. His brother, Serafino, served in the Army during World War I.

Ernest Giordano[23]

Ernesto Vivaldi Giordano was born in San Vincenzo la Costa on May 10, 1890, the son of Pietro Antonio Giordano and Carolina Angelina Mazzulla. He lived in New York from about 1906 to 1913. After a brief visit to Italy, he returned to the U.S. in 1913, going to his uncle, V. Mazzulla, in New York City. Giordano was living in Racine when he was inducted into the Army on March 30, 1918. He was a private, serial number 2037293, when he went to France as part of the Fort Riley Automatic Replacement Draft, Detachment 2, aboard the *Missanabie* on June 11, 1918, not even two weeks after being drafted.[24] While in France, he was assigned to Evacuation Hospital 29, and he received credit for participation in the Champagne-Marne, Aisne-Marne, and Meuse-Argonne Offensives. Giordano returned to the U.S. aboard the *Nansemond* on July 9, 1919; he became a naturalized U.S. citizen at Camp Grant, Illinois, on July 23, 1919, and was discharged two days later.

Sam Giordano

Sam Giordano was born on June 6, 1893, in Cosenza, the son of Santo Giordano and Rose Cundari. He came to the U.S. in 1912 and settled in Kenosha. Giordano enlisted in the Regular Army at Jefferson Barracks, near St. Louis, Missouri, on September 15, 1917. He was a private, serial number 2383087, in Company "D," 60th Infantry Regiment, 5th Division. On April 16, 1918, Giordano, with his regiment, left for France aboard the *Calamares*. In France, Giordano participated in all the campaigns and battles in which his regiment was engaged; he received credit for the Saint-Mihiel and Meuse-Argonne Offensives, along with serving in several defensive sectors. Giordano was promoted to private first class on December 21, 1918, and, with the 5th Division, participated in the Army of Occupation, stationed in Luxembourg. Giordano reenlisted in the Army at Luxembourg on June 24, 1919. He returned to the U.S., probably in late 1919, and was discharged at Camp Gordon, Georgia, in June 1920.

Pvt. Ernest Giordano, Evacuation Hospital 29. (*Racine County in the World War*)

Antonio Giorno[25]

Tommaso Giorno, a twenty-six-year-old laborer from Marano Marchesato, and his newlywed wife, Alessandrina Russo, aged eighteen, arrived in the U.S. on September 11, 1891. They traveled to Kenosha where there was already a burgeoning Calabrian community. Their son, Antonio, was born there on October 20, 1895. A second son, Giuseppe (Joseph), was born in Kenosha on August 15, 1897.

Sometime around 1898, the Giornos returned to Marano Marchesato. In 1910, Antonio came back to Kenosha, and the rest of his family followed in 1912. Giorno was a laborer at the American Brass Company when he was inducted into the Army on May 26, 1918. He was assigned as a private, serial number 2825621, in the 161st Depot Brigade at Camp Grant, Illinois. From the depot brigade, men were fed into the 86th Division, then undergoing final training prior to departure for France; some men were sent from the depot brigade to other units that, like the 86th, were preparing for overseas service. This is precisely what happened to Giorno. On June 13, a large draft of about 2,500 men left Camp Grant, bound for the 85th Division at Camp Custer, Michigan. Giorno was among this number. At Camp Custer, he was assigned to Company "G," 337th Infantry Regiment. Giorno left the U.S. bound for France on July 22, 1918. After a brief stop in England, Giorno arrived in France with his division.

Soon after arrival, the 85th Division was redesignated as the 4th Depot Division and was tasked to train and send men as replacements to combat units that needed to fill up regiments depleted by casualties. The 4th Depot Division sent many replacements to the 1st Division. Giorno, along with fellow Kenoshans Giuseppe Covelli, Frank Muto, and Carmine Chiappetta, was among this group. On August 17, Giorno was one of 1,500 replacements sent to the 26th Infantry Regiment; at that time, the 26th was at Pont-a-Mousson in the Saizerais Sector. While in this relatively quiet sector, the new men had to quickly blend into this veteran regiment and learn from the experienced men. They engaged in limited patrolling in the thick woods, and listening posts were manned day and night. For recreation, the men tended gardens left by their predecessors in the sector; also, the divisional engineers had damned a creek in the area, creating a swimming hole.

On August 22, the 26th left the sector and trucked to Uruffe. On August 26, Giorno, along with at least thirty-six others, became a member of Company "E," in the 2nd Battalion of the 26th Infantry Regiment. Other replacements had joined Company "E" a few days earlier. All these men filled up ranks greatly depleted by combat during July 18–20 at Soissons. So by late August, Giorno, who had been drafted at the end of May, was now in an active, if not particularly dangerous, sector. Barely three months had passed since he had been a civilian; much of his time thus far in the Army had been taken up with administrative issues and travel. This, again, illustrates the precarious position in which replacements found themselves. Men who had been drafted in the spring and summer of 1918 and sent as replacements to combat units rarely had more than two or three months of service before being sent to an active sector; what usually followed quickly enough was actual combat. As stated above, men who had been drafted or enlisted earlier had the luxury of being able to absorb much more training, to include training that gradually exposed them to active sectors and operations.

At Uruffe, the men underwent a ten-day training schedule that included terrain exercises with tanks and artillery rumbling in the background. At the end of August,

Company "E," commanded by Captain Rice McNutt Youell, bore on its roster about 265 men and three officers present for duty. On September 8, the regiment marched to Reine Woods. The going was miserable with knee-deep mud and vehicles of every description blocking the boggy roads. On September 11, the infantry began to move into position for the start of the Saint-Mihiel Offensive, to begin the next day. The 26th Infantry Regiment occupied a 600-meter front on the right of the 1st Division line.

Jump-off was scheduled for 5 a.m. on the 12th. The assault, to be led by the 3rd Battalion on the 26th's front, was preceded by a four-hour bombardment of the enemy's lines. When it let loose, the men watched in awe of the powerful barrage sent over to the Germans. The preparatory artillery firing was imposing and awe inspiring to the men.

At precisely 5:50 a.m., the men went over the top. Things went like clockwork; the initial resistance of occasional shellfire and machine gun fire was less than expected. The regiment reached its first objective before 6 a.m., and then moved to the second. At 11 a.m., following behind a rolling barrage, the infantry reached the day's objective; at noon, the men eagerly consumed their rations of hard bread and bully-beef (canned beef). The regiment was ordered to continue its advance; by the end of the day, they had advanced a total of 8 kilometers while suffering relatively light casualties.

On September 11, the day before the assault, at least three men from Giorno's Company "E" were so ill that they had to report to the hospital. Sometime during the day of the initial assault, Giorno and four others from Company "E" also became so ill that they had to go the rear. It is not known why these men became ill. Probably Giorno, after continued marching in rainy weather through knee-deep mud, suffered from exposure and was weakened. Maybe some sort of fever was passing through the regiment and affected the men whose health was compromised by the weather and continued physical exertion. In any event, Giorno and the others probably reported back to the battalion aid station, and then back through the regimental collecting point and finally to one of the divisional Field Hospitals. It is not known when Giorno again joined the company.[26]

After September 13, the 1st Division was pulled back into reserve. It had advanced 15 kilometers as the crow flies. The 26th Infantry Regiment suffered six killed and ninety-six wounded, and it had captured 350 prisoners. Company "E" reported at least two men killed or died of wounds, twelve men wounded, and three men missing in action. Company "F," also in the 3nd Battalion, reported at least one man killed and at least ten men wounded by shellfire; also, at least four men from that company were reported as missing in action.[27] Following the Saint-Mihiel Offensive, on September 21, the regiment rode all night on French trucks to Neuville, where they spent two uncomfortable days bivouacked in the woods. Later they proceeded to Bulainville where they received a small number of replacements and participated in such training as night marches through the woods and small unit tactics.

The activity of the 26th Infantry Regiment during the Meuse-Argonne Offensive is covered in detail in the author's book *Days of Perfect Hell: The U.S. 26th Infantry Regiment in the Meuse-Argonne Offensive, October–November 1918* (2015). Suffice to say that Giorno participated in the terrible combat experienced by the regiment; indeed, he was cited for gallantry in action for the period October 1–12, 1918. A brief excerpt from the book will give an example of what Giorno experienced. The excerpt describes action on October 4, when the regiment began their attack against well-fortified and well-defended positions. The platoon leader quoted is Second Lieutenant William Mansfield of Company "E," Giorno's company, but it is not known if he was Giorno's platoon leader. It is close enough, however, to give us an example of the fighting Giorno experience.

The attack began with the 1st Battalion in the lead and the 2nd Battalion in support:

> Around 2 p.m., Capt. Youell [the 2nd Battalion commander] gave the order to assault German machine gun positions located at the edge of a woods about 1,000 yards in front of the 2nd Battalion. Youell placed Companies E and F in the assault wave with Companies G and H in support. Lieutenant Bune, commander of Company E, placed his 1st and 3rd platoons in assault and the 2nd platoon in support. Lieutenant Mansfield, commanding the 3rd platoon, once again made the rounds of his men, checking ammunition. Companies E and F were on the high ground south of Exermont Ravine. The fighting to this point had been severe; as Lt. Mansfield recalled, "not too many men in Lt M's Platoon now." Waiting for the order to start the assault, "some of the men [of Company E] from their positions on the reverse slope smoked their cigarettes and would not be present at roll call tomorrow morning."
>
> At H-hour, 3 p.m., the order to move forward came; the men went "over the crest, down the slope, running men falling, shells bursting" as they approached a creek at the bottom of Exermont Ravine. There was a bridge crossing the creek; Lt. Mansfield immediately ascertained that this "enemy-made crossing" was certainly zeroed in by multiple machine guns. The lieutenant shouted to his men to avoid the bridge. Half of the 3rd platoon reached the creek and began to reform, still under severe fire from Germans within 100 yards of them. The men began a heavy return fire. One Company E rifle grenadier at the creek had only two rifle grenades left; with these he made direct hits, and the enemy firing eased up a bit after these "cool, well-directed shots." Mansfield led his men into the creek as some men from Company F, to the right, began a bayonet charge against the Germans on the far side of the creek in their sector. The next thing Lt. Mansfield remembered was being on a French hospital train on his way to the rear with a severe bullet wound in his leg. For his actions on this day, Mansfield received the Silver Star. Capt. Youell, for his extraordinary heroism during this action and some later actions, received the Distinguished Service Cross.[28]

The regiment fought through the rest of the Meuse-Argonne Offensive and were relieved only a few days before the Armistice. After the Armistice, the 1st Division was designated as one of the divisions to make up the new 3rd Army as part of the Army of Occupation in Germany. Giorno served with the 26th Infantry Regiment throughout its stint in Germany as part of the 3rd Army and the Army of Occupation of Germany. Following occupation duty, the division left Germany and went to France to prepare for return to the United States. Giorno arrived back in the U.S. on September 4, 1919. After the various parades that the 1st Division marched in, Giorno was discharged at Camp Grant on September 26.

Giorno earned the Victory Medal with three battle clasps: "St. Mihiel," "Meuse-Argonne," and "Defensive Sector;" he was also entitled to the Army of Occupation of Germany Medal. In addition, he would be entitled to affix a Silver Star device upon the ribbon of his medal, signifying the fact that he was cited for gallantry

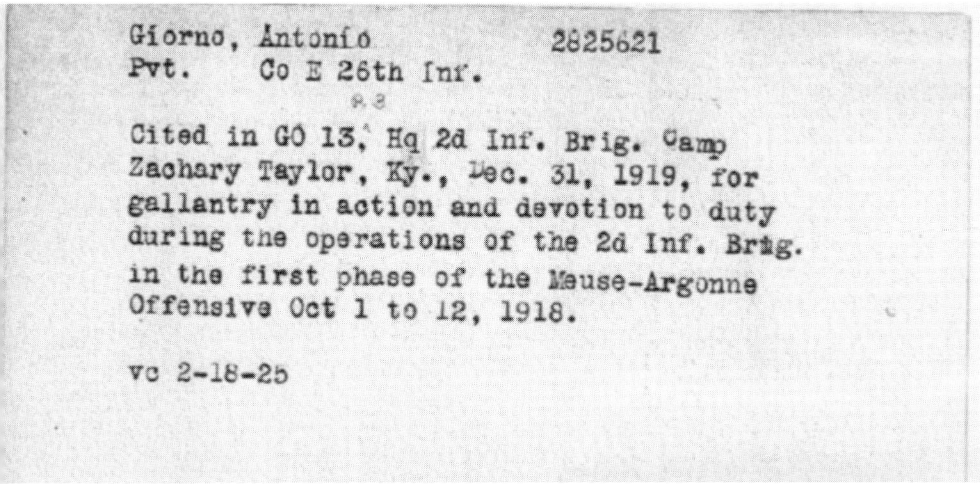

Giorno, Antonio 2825621
Pvt. Co E 26th Inf.

Cited in GO 13, Hq 2d Inf. Brig. Camp Zachary Taylor, Ky., Dec. 31, 1919, for gallantry in action and devotion to duty during the operations of the 2d Inf. Brig. in the first phase of the Meuse-Argonne Offensive Oct 1 to 12, 1918.

vc 2-18-25

Award card showing Pvt. Antonio Giorno's citation for gallantry. This would have authorized him to wear a Silver Star device on the ribbon of his Victory Medal and, after 1932, to receive the Silver Star Medal. (*National Archives*)

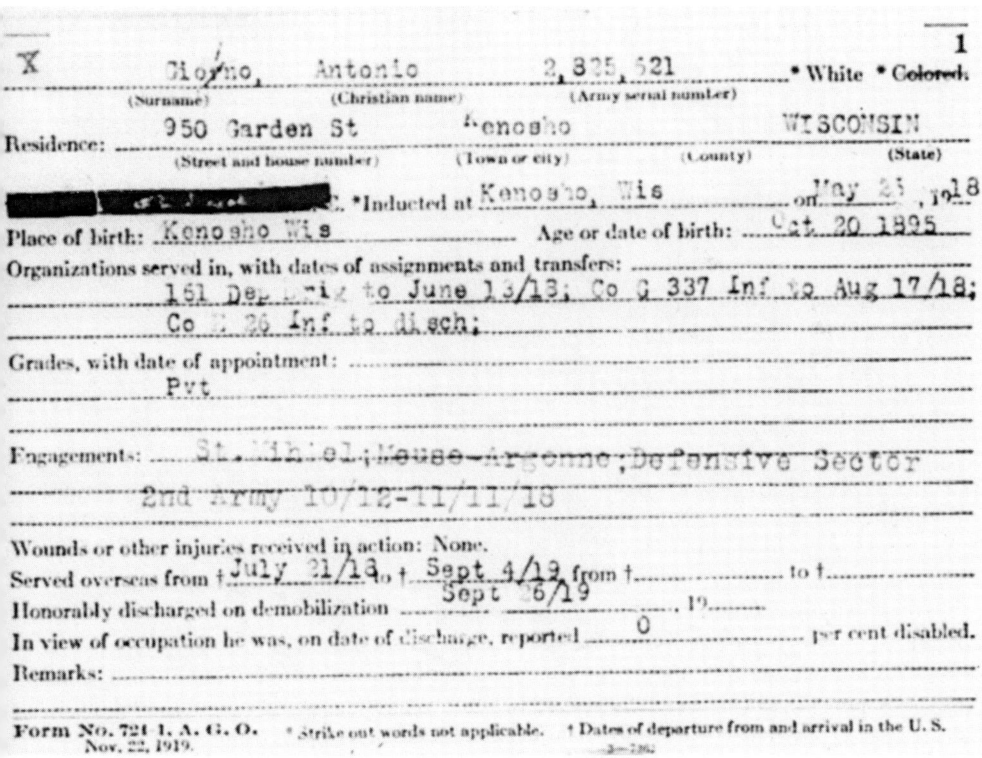

X Giorno, Antonio 2,825,621 * White * ~~Colored.~~ 1
(Surname) (Christian name) (Army serial number)

Residence: 950 Garden St Kenosho WISCONSIN
(Street and house number) (Town or city) (County) (State)

[illegible] *Inducted at Kenosho, Wis on May 25, 1918

Place of birth: Kenosho Wis Age or date of birth: Oct 20 1895

Organizations served in, with dates of assignments and transfers: 161 Dep Brig to June 13/18; Co G 337 Inf to Aug 17/18; Co E 26 Inf to disch;

Grades, with date of appointment: Pvt

Engagements: St. Mihiel; Meuse-Argonne; Defensive Sector 2nd Army 10/12-11/11/18

Wounds or other injuries received in action: None.

Served overseas from † July 21/18 to † Sept 4/19 from † .... to † ....

Honorably discharged on demobilization Sept 26/19, 19....

In view of occupation he was, on date of discharge, reported 0 per cent disabled.

Remarks: ....

Form No. 724-1, A. G. O. Nov. 22, 1919. * Strike out words not applicable. † Dates of departure from and arrival in the U. S.

Pvt. Antonio Giorno's statement of service card. (*National Archives*) in action. That device would later entitle him to the award of the Silver Star Medal, the nation's third highest award for bravery in action, but there is no record that he ever applied for or received that medal. Following his discharge, Giorno moved back to Kenosha and worked for the American Brass Company; he died in Kenosha in 1977.

Joseph Giorno
Joseph Giorno, the son of Tommaso Giorno and Alessandrina Russo, and the brother of Antonio Giorno, was born in Kenosha on August 15, 1897. Giorno was a solderer at the American Brass Company in Kenosha when he was inducted into the Army on October 21, 1918. He was sent to the Recruit Depot, Camp Shelby, Mississippi, as a private, serial number 4303027. On November 4, he was transferred to the 16th Company, 161st Depot Brigade, at Camp Grant, Illinois. There, on December 26, he was given his final pay ($15.69, which included two months' deduction of $13 for war risk insurance) and discharged. Giorno returned to Kenosha and continued working at the American Brass Company. He was a charter member of the Italian American Society in Kenosha and a member of American Legion Post 21. He died in Kenosha in 1980.

Antonio Greco
Antonio Greco was born on January 4, 1891, in Lappano, the son of Francesco Greco and Filomena Conforti. He came to the U.S. in 1903 and was a streetcar conductor living in Chicago when he entered the Army. Greco was a private, serial number 820877, in Battery "A," 62nd Coast Artillery Regiment, when he shipped out for France aboard the *Baltic* on July 14, 1918. Greco was one of the many foreign-born American soldiers who opted to receive his discharge in France; he was discharged at St. Aignan on February 7, 1919, and from there he visited his home town of Lappano until June before returning to the United States.

Giuseppe Greco
Giuseppe Greco was born on November 6, 1892, in Lappano, Cosenza. He was a shoemaker in Racine when he entered the Army in July 1918.

James Greco
Vincenzo (James) Greco was born on April 21, 1896, in Chicago, the son of Giovanni Greco and Francesca Cosentino. Giovanni, and probably Francesca, was from Marano Marchesato; they brought their family to the U.S. in the early 1890s. James Greco was a mechanic living in Racine when he was inducted into the Army on September 21, 1917, part of the first contingent of drafted men for the National Army. He was assigned as a private, serial number 2032124, in Company "F," 310th Engineer Regiment, 85th Division, at Camp Custer, Michigan. On May 13, 1918, he was transferred to Auxiliary Remount Squadron 320. This unit's duty was to receive and supply horses and mules to the combat units in the field. On July 10, Greco was assigned to the 160th Depot Brigade at Camp Custer; on November 2, he was sent to the Infantry Camp at Camp Upton, New York, prior to shipment overseas. Although his statement of service card does not show overseas service, the record of Racine soldiers indicates that he departed the U.S. for France on November 8, 1918, and that he returned on November 13. It is quite possible that he had shipped out and then been recalled upon the Armistice

Above left: Pvt. Joseph Giorno, 161st Depot Brigade, 1918. (*1980 Calendar, Friends of Italian Culture, Kenosha*)

Above right: Pvt. Giuseppe Greco. (*Racine County in the World War*)

Right: Pvt. James Greco, Infantry Replacement Camp, Camp Upton. (*Racine County in the World War*)

taking effect on November 11; even though he had not gotten anywhere near France, this would later entitle him to the "France" clasp to the Victory Medal. Greco was discharged at Camp Grant, Illinois, on January 13, 1919.

Frank Guaglianone

Frank Guaglianone was born in Altomonte on January 6, 1891. He was a tailor-trimmer living in Chicago when he was inducted into the Army on May 2, 1918. Guaglianone was probably among the Chicago-area men who were inducted at Jefferson Barracks, Missouri, and then sent to various training camps. Guaglianone was a private, serial number 479342, when he left the U.S. aboard the *Logan* on May 25, 1919. After a stop at Honolulu, Hawaii Territory, the *Logan* arrived in the Philippines on June 22. The transport then made its way to Vladivostok, Russia; there, Guaglianone was assigned to Company "M," 27th Infantry Regiment, part of the Siberian Expeditionary Forces. Guaglianone served in this inhospitable climate in a confusing, thankless mission before he returned to the U.S. aboard the *Logan* in January 1920. He was discharged on January 12.

Eugenio Guerrieri

Eugenio Guerrieri was born on February 22, 1896, in Rende, the son of Antonio Guerrieri and Luisa Metallo. He came to the U.S. in February 1912, joining his uncle, Luigi Volpentesta, in Chicago. When he entered the Army on June 26, 1918, Guerrieri was a lamp lighter for Nick Geraldi in Chicago. On August 22, when he boarded the *Dante Alighieri* for shipment to France, Guerrieri was a private, serial number 3277957, assigned to the 11th Battery, Camp Jackson August Automatic Replacement Draft. Once again, the short time from induction to embarking, in this case less than two months, demonstrates the meager amount of training that many men experienced before being sent overseas in the summer and fall of 1918. Sometime after arrival in France, Guerrieri was sent as a replacement to Battery "C," 313th Field Artillery Regiment, 80th Division. On May 17, 1919, he boarded the *Zeppelin* for return to the United States. Guerrieri was discharged on June 12, 1919.

Francesco Loizzo[29]

Francesco (Frank) Loizzo was born in Marano Marchesato on March 14, 1895, the son of Antonio Loizzo and Filamena Cosentino. Loizzo came to the U.S. in 1910, going to join his father in Kenosha. Loizzo was a railroad track laborer at the Blodgett Section on the Chicago North Western Railroad, living in Deerfield Township, Illinois, when he was inducted into the Army, probably at Libertyville, Illinois, on February 23, 1918. He was a private, serial number 2078504, in the 161st Depot Brigade at Camp Grant, Illinois. Sometime during the spring, Loizzo was transferred to the 35th Engineer Regiment, a railway shop regiment, at Camp Grant. As he proceeded on his journey overseas, he was sent to Camp Merritt, New Jersey, where he was naturalized as an American citizen on June 7, 1918; he went overseas shortly thereafter.

At the time of his return to the United States on July 3, 1919, Loizzo was assigned to the 51st Company, Transportation Corps. At the time of his discharge, he was assigned to the 141st Company, Transportation Corps. All this suggests that Loizzo was involved with railroad labor as a soldier during the war. A railroad laborer in civil life, Loizzo was a good fit for this duty. Upon his return to the U.S., he was sent to the Demobilization Group at Camp Grant where, on July 12, 1919, he was given his final pay ($72.60) and his discharge. After the war, Loizzo worked as a railroad foreman and as a laborer in a wire rope factory in Kenosha. He died in Hollywood, Florida, in 1980.

Arthur Frank Lucchetti
Arthur Frank Lucchetti was born on April 13, 1897, in Chicago, the son of Antonio Lucchetti and Carmela Spizzirri from Cosenza. Antonio had come to the U.S. in 1883 and Carmela followed about a decade later. Lucchetti was working for the Rock Island Railroad in Chicago when he entered the Army on August 29, 1918. He was a private, serial number 4248100, when he went overseas with Truck Company "A," 5th Corps Artillery Park, less than a month later, on September 23. He returned to the U.S. with the same unit on March 18, 1919, and he was discharged on April 24. After the war, Lucchetti lived in Chicago where he worked as a railway office clerk and then as a law clerk; he died in Chicago in 1986.

Luigi Mandarino
Luigi Mandarino was born in Castrolibero on November 25, 1895. Mandarino came to the U.S. in 1913; he was a railroad laborer living in Chicago when he entered the Army on May 30, 1918. Mandarino was a private, serial number 3073520, when he was naturalized at Camp Funston, Kansas, on June 7, 1918. He was discharged on January 10, 1919, at Camp Grant, Illinois. Interestingly, Mandarino lost his citizenship because the U.S. State Department had determined that he had expatriated himself in 1947, but he returned to the U.S. and reapplied for citizenship in 1951. Two years later, he was approved and became a U.S. citizen once again.

Luigi Mandarino's passport photograph, 1923. (*Ancestry.com*)

Frank Maschio

Frank Maschio was born in Rende on September 15, 1895; he came to the U.S. in 1910 and was a machine hand with a cutlery company, living in Chicago, when he entered the Army on September 26, 1917. Maschio was a private, serial number 2312634, when he went overseas with the Camp Grant Replacement Draft in March 1918. At some point, he was sent as a replacement to Company "H," 23rd Infantry Regiment, 2nd Division. This division had an excellent and extensive combat record. After the war, the division served in the Army of Occupation of Germany. Maschio returned to the U.S. aboard U.S.S. *Virginian* on August 4, 1919; he was discharged eleven days later.

Francesco Miceli

Francesco Miceli was born on May 26, 1892, in Marano Marchesato, the son of Gaetano Miceli and Maria Belmonte. He came to the U.S. around 1910 and settled in Chicago. Miceli was a bookbinder living in Chicago when, on September 4, 1918, he was inducted into the National Army. Assigned serial number 4409744, Private Miceli was sent to Camp Grant, Illinois, where he became part of the 14th Company, 161st Depot Brigade. Miceli was naturalized there on November 2, 1918 (his name appears on the certificate as "Frank Miccilo"). He was discharged at Camp Grant on December 11, 1918. Miceli returned to Chicago where he died in 1952. He is remembered as "a good sweet man who loved car rides on Sundays, loved candies and nuts [and] loved card games. Not a bad bone in his body. Good hardworking man."[30]

Pvt. Francesco Miceli, 161st Depot Brigade, 1918. (*Beverly Adamski*)

Frank Middono

Frank Middono was born on September 15, 1891 or 1892, in Albidona. He was a printing machine operator in Chicago when he was inducted into the Army. Middono served overseas during the war; when he returned to the U.S. aboard the *Mount Vernon* in May 1919, he was a corporal, serial number 1391264, in Company "F," 132nd Infantry Regiment, 33rd Division.

Mariano Mirabelli

Mariano Mirabelli was born in Marano Marchesato on May 15, 1897, the son of Francesco Mirabelli and Francesca Bartucci. He came to the U.S. in 1913 and was living in Chicago when he enlisted in the Regular Army on August 7, 1917. At some point, Mirabelli, a private first class, serial number 736237, was assigned to Company "H," 11th Infantry Regiment, 5th Division. On April 24, 1918, he boarded the *Leviathan* at Hoboken, New Jersey, in preparation to sail overseas. However, Mirabelli and many other men were taken off the ship; their names on the Army transport manifest are lined out and the word "Quarantined" is written in. Apparently there was some sickness, perhaps measles, running through the men at this time. Mirabelli recovered enough to board the *Great Northern* on May 2, as part of the 5th Division casual detachment, made up, no doubt, of men who had missed the first sailing. At some point after arrival in France, he was assigned to Company "A," 165th Infantry Regiment, 42nd Division. This was the famed 69th New York Infantry Regiment of the New York National Guard. When it was federalized and put in the 42nd Division, it was re-designated as the 165th Infantry Regiment. The regiment, and indeed the division, was a hard-fighting, effective unit. It is also possible that Mirabelli had been wounded while serving in the 11th Infantry Regiment and was assigned to the 165th Infantry Regiment for his return to the United States. In any event, Mirabelli returned to the U.S. aboard U.S.S. *Harrisburg* on April 21, 1919, and was discharged on May 14.

Giuseppe Misurelli

Giuseppe Misurelli was born in Rende in September 1890; he was living in Kenosha when he was inducted into the Army in 1918. He was a private, serial number 3365366. Misurelli was promoted to corporal and was assigned to Company "M," 3rd Battalion, Chemical Warfare Service.

Luigi Molinaro

Luigi (Louis) Molinaro was born on October 20, 1894, in Marano Marchesato, the son of Michele Molinaro and Vincenzina Cosentino. He came to the U.S. with his father in 1910 and again in 1913. He was a molder at Racine Mall Iron, living in Racine, when he was inducted into the Army on March 28, 1918. He was assigned initially to Camp Custer, Michigan, as a private, serial number 2035018. Molinaro went overseas on June 30, 1918, and was transferred to Battery "B," 104th Field Artillery Regiment, 27th Division. He participated in the Meuse-Argonne Offensive and Defensive Sector. Molinaro returned to the U.S. on March 13, 1919, and was discharged at Camp Grant, Illinois, on April 5.

Left: Cpl. Giuseppe Misurelli, 3rd Battalion, Chemical Warfare Service, *c.* 1918. (*Misurelli family*)

Below: Louis Molinaro's statement of service card. The 104th Field Artillery Regiment was assigned to the 27th Division, but it supported other divisions during the Meuse-Argonne Offensive. (*Wisconsin Veterans Museum*)

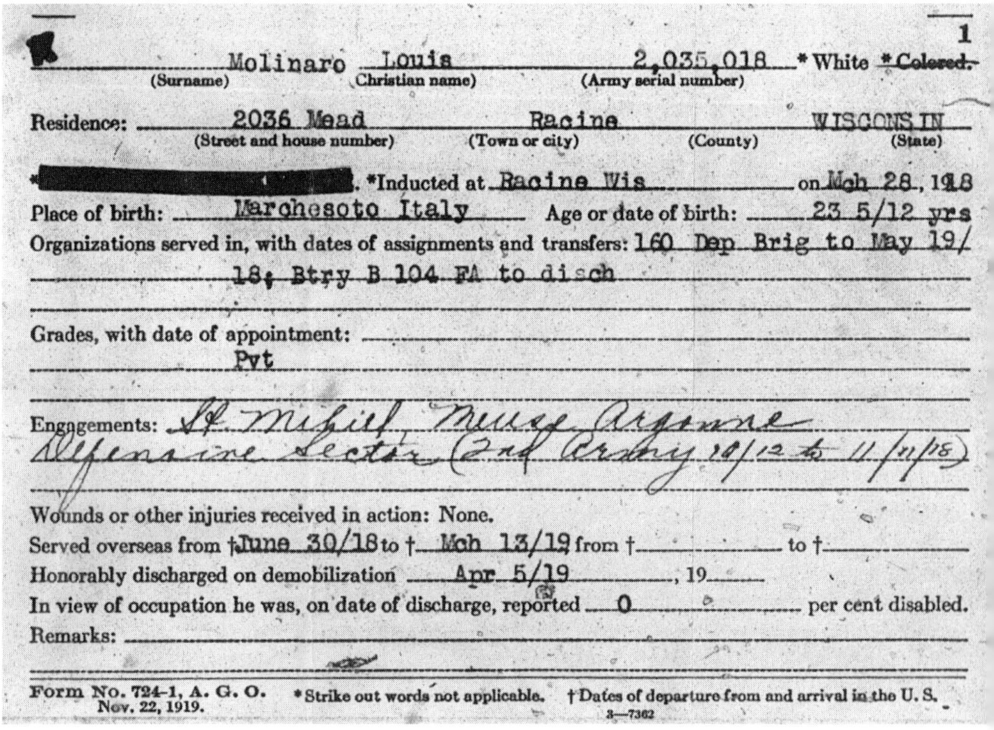

1

Molinaro (Surname) Louis (Christian name) 2,035,018 (Army serial number) *White ~~*Colored.~~

Residence: 2036 Mead (Street and house number) Racine (Town or city) (County) WISCONSIN (State)

[redacted]. *Inducted at Racine Wis on Mch 28, 1918

Place of birth: Marchesoto Italy Age or date of birth: 23 5/12 yrs

Organizations served in, with dates of assignments and transfers: 160 Dep Brig to May 19/18; Btry B 104 FA to di sch

Grades, with date of appointment: Pvt

Engagements: St. Mihiel Meuse Argonne Defensive Sector (2nd Army 10/12 to 11/11/18)

Wounds or other injuries received in action: None.

Served overseas from †June 30/18 to † Mch 13/19 from † to †

Honorably discharged on demobilization Apr 5/19, 19

In view of occupation he was, on date of discharge, reported 0 per cent disabled.

Remarks:

Form No. 724-1, A. G. O. Nov. 22, 1919. *Strike out words not applicable. †Dates of departure from and arrival in the U. S. 3—7362

Michael Molinaro

Michael Theodore Molinaro was born on July 23, 1896, in Beach Park, Illinois. His father, Ferdinando (Fred), was from Marano Principato. At the time of his induction into the Army on August 14, 1918, he was living in Kenosha where he worked as a metal inspector. Private Molinaro, serial number 3478318, was sent to the U.S. Army Training Detachment at Bradley Polytechnic Institute in Peoria, Illinois. No doubt his experience as a metal inspector was noted and needed by the Army. On October 6, he was sent to the 6th Ordnance Supply Company at Raritan Arsenal, New Jersey. His statement of service card also states that he was in unassigned infantry status. At some point, he was sent to Camp Grant, Illinois, where he was discharged on March 29, 1919.

Andrea Morelli[31]

Andrea Morelli was born in Marano Marchesato on January 15, 1888, the son of Giovanni Morelli and Rosalia Ruffolo. Giovanni lived in the U.S. about 1900 to 1904; Andrea then came to the U.S. in May 1906, settling in Chicago. Andrea's father returned to Chicago to join his son in 1906. In 1910, Andrea Morelli was a tailor working for Pietro Pellegrini in Chicago. Morelli enlisted in Company "H," 6th Illinois Infantry Regiment, Illinois National Guard, on August 4, 1911. He transferred to Company "I," 1st Illinois Infantry Regiment, on April 26, 1912, and reenlisted on May 3, 1915. He served with his co-worker, Pasquale (Charles) Pellegrini, in this regiment. During the Mexican border crisis, Illinois troops were mustered and federalized at Springfield, Illinois, on June 19, 1916. Morelli, along with his regiment, left for San Antonio, Texas, in early July. While there, the men went on several long distance marches and engaged in target practice, drill, and other duties. Beginning in September, the Illinois troops began to return home. Morelli returned to Chicago and was discharged on October 4, 1916. Back in Chicago, Morelli continued his work as a tailor, but his life as a civilian was short-lived.

Morelli was inducted into the Army on April 23, 1918 as a private, serial number 1338910. Morelli was at Camp Sevier, South Carolina, when he became a naturalized U.S. citizen on June 14, 1918. He was soon transferred to the Air Service, and on August 15, 1918, he left the U.S. as part of a "Sailmakers Detachment, Air Service." Sailmakers, or, in Morelli's case, tailors, were needed in the Air Service to repair and maintain the fabric skins of World War I aircraft. Upon arrival in England, Morelli was assigned to the 1107th Aero Replacement Squadron, U.S. Army Air Service. He served there from July to late November 1918. Morelli returned to the U.S. as part of the 1st Sailmakers Draft, departing England on November 28 and arriving on December 4, 1918; his final pay voucher, dated December 27, at Camp Grant, indicates: "Arrived in US fr F.S. [Foreign Service] 12/4/18." He was due a refund of $30 for six months' worth of Liberty Loan deductions. After the war, he lived in Chicago.

Salvatore Morelli[32]

Salvatore Morelli was born in Chicago, Illinois, on April 11, 1894, the son of Michele Morelli and Mary Giorno. Michele, and possibly Mary, came from Marano Marchesato. Michele came to the U.S. in 1880, and in 1892, he married Mary in Chicago. Sometime in 1900, Michele and Mary divorced, and their children lived with Mary.

Morelli was a clerk with Wells Fargo in Chicago when, on June 3, 1918, he enlisted in the U.S. Coast Guard at their Chicago recruiting station. Morelli was 5 feet 4.5 inches tall and weighed 134 pounds; he had gray eyes, brown hair, and a light complexion. On June 5, Morelli, with the rank of ordinary seaman, was sent to the New York recruiting office. Leaving that morning at 10:25 a.m., he arrived in New York at 4 p.m.

Morelli worked at the Coast Guard's New York Division, probably in a clerical capacity. His concern for the support of his family is evident in a letter he wrote, through channels, to the "Captain Commandant" of the Coast Guard, dated July 29, 1918:

> Headquarters is advised that upon my enlistment I executed a Class B allotment in favor of my mother, but to this time she has not received any money. It is requested that same be forwarded at the earliest possible time as the money is badly needed at home. [signed] Salvatore Morelli.[33]

The request was duly forwarded; it is not known what action resulted from this letter. Morelli worked in the New York Division until August 10, 1918, at which time he was assigned to the U.S. Coast Guard Academy at New London, Connecticut. During his time in New York, Morelli did his job in an efficient and conscientious manner; his ratings on August 9 were very good. He was given a "4" for his proficiency, "5" for obedience, "5" for sobriety, and a "5" for conduct (this was a five-point scale, differing from the Navy system). His health was listed as excellent. Morelli received identical ratings on a rating dated September 24, 1918, at the Academy.

There may have been an administrative oversight regarding the one-year duration of enlistment on Morelli's enlistment papers because, on September 23, 1918, after only three months and twenty-one days of service, he was honorably discharged only to reenlist the following day "for the period of the war not to exceed three years."

While Morelli was away in service, his brother, Frederick, had to leave school to help provide for his mother who was physically impaired. After the war ended on November 11, 1918, many men who had been stationed stateside began to be discharged, and Mary longed for the return of her oldest son in order to be both a helper and companion to her. Accordingly, Mary wrote to Captain F. G. Crapster, Superintendent of the Coast Guard Academy. Her letter dated November 29, 1918, is given in full:

> Honorable Sir:—
>
> I write to kindly ask you whether it is possible to obtain the discharge of my son, Salvatore Morelli, Third Co. Fort Trumbull, New London, Conn.
>
> I am affected with swollen veins at my legs, and on that account I cannot do much work. My other son Fred is about eighteen years of age, and he is struggling hard to help me. We have no property whatsoever, and no other income but the small amount that my son Fred is able to earn. It is problem for us to secure enough for the absolute necessaries of life.
>
> I have an impression that the services of my son Salvatore are not badly needed now in the Navy, on account of the peace affected; furthermore I know that many of the boys in the Army and Navy are sent home. Salvatore enlisted voluntarily just for the duration of the war. Is it to ask too much now for his release? His return at home would be a blessing to all of us because then he could support the family and Fred could devote part of his time going to school, as he did before.

Thanking you in advance for whatever you will be able to do for us, and hoping to hear from you in the near future, I beg to remain, Yours Respectfully, [signed] Mrs. M. Morelli.[34]

On December 4, before receiving a reply from Captain Crapster, Mary again wrote, this time to the Commanding Officer of the Coast Guard in Washington, D.C. Her letter is given in full:

Dear Sir:

According to newspaper articles, all men in Military Service who have dependents or business to return to or educational course to complete, will be the first to be discharged from the Naval Service.

I am the widowed mother of O.S. Salvatore Morelli at present located at the U.S. Coast Guard Academy, Ft. Trumbull, New London, Conn., and make request for his discharge on the grounds that he is my main support. I have a younger son, who is nineteen years old, who has to the best of his ability been upholding the home since my older boy has been in the Military Services and without a doubt it has proved a very hard task for him, although the Government, as well as my son have been sending money home monthly, to the amount of $25.00 both combined.

It is needless for me to try and further explain the necessity of me asking for the discharge of my oldest son, at once, so that my home can be properly taken care of.

He is enlisted for the duration of the war and has already made request for discharge to his Capt. Commandant.

Trusting you will see this subject in the proper light and act accordingly and thanking you for your interest in this matter, I am yours respectfully, [signed] Mary Morelli.[35]

On December 6, the Coast Guard office in Washington replied to Mary, informing her that, "in order to secure proper action regarding your son, Ordinary Seaman Salvatore Morelli, it will be necessary for him to make request through official channels for his discharge." On December 8, Morelli was transferred from the Coast Guard Academy to the Coast Guard Cutter *Pamlico*, based in Norfolk, Virginia. On December 10, a letter from Coast Guard Division of Operations duly notified Mary that Morelli had just been transferred to the *Pamlico*, and giving her his proper address.

On December 12, Salvatore, probably performing clerical duties aboard the *Pamlico*, wrote a letter to the Coast Guard's "Commodore Commandant," via his ship's commanding officer:

Subject: Discharge, request for.

1. It is requested that I be discharged from the United States Coast Guard on account of the following reasons:

(a) I have a widowed mother depending upon me for support. At present my brother who is about eighteen years of age is trying to maintain the home which of course is proving too hard a tack for him, although I, as well as the Government, am sending home monthly allotment totaling $25.00. This amount includes all of the money that they receive during the month. My mother and brother are the only ones home and have no other way of support except by me. On account of my being away from home

> she was obliged to keep my brother out of school and he will be unable to resume his studies until I return. My mother is unable to work on account of having swollen veins.
>
> (b) I gave up a position which was paying me a good salary and which enabled me to support my family. This position is open for me and I also have a better position in view which will be given me provided I can get my discharge. [signed] Salvatore Morelli.[36]

That same day, the *Pamlico*'s commander, Philip H. Scott, approved Morelli's request and forwarded it on to Washington for final decision. A decision of sorts was forthcoming on December 16 when the Commodore Commandant wrote back to Commander Scott: "You are authorized to discharge Ordinary Seaman Salvatore Morelli when, in your judgment, his services can be spared."[37] Consequently, on December 20, 1918, Morelli received an "ordinary" discharge from the U.S. Coast Guard. His final ratings, from the Academy and from the *Pamlico*, were the same as his previous ratings, and his health at time of discharge was listed as excellent.

Morelli returned to his home on 22nd Street in Chicago where he resumed the care of his mother and brother. At the time of his discharge, Morelli did not receive the $60 bonus that was authorized for military servicemen upon leaving the service. Money still being an issue for Morelli and his family, on February 28, 1919, he wrote to the Navy Department Disbursing Officer:

> Dear Sir:—
>
> Having noticed in the daily Chicago papers that a section of the Revenue Act approved February 24th, 1919 authorizes the payment of a bonus of $60.00 to discharged soldiers and sailors, I herewith put in my claim for said bonus.
>
> Under the date of June 1st, 1918, I enlisted at Chicago into the United States Coast Guard, under supervision of the Navy Department, for the term of one year, then re-enlisted in September for the duration of the war.
>
> Upon the signing of the Armistice my widowed mother put in request for my discharge on the grounds of being her main support, which I received December 20th, 1918. Enclosed you will find both my discharge papers.
>
> Hoping you will see your way clear in forwarding said bonus to me, I beg to remain, Respectfully, [signed] Salvatore Morelli, #12 West 22nd. St. Chicago Ill., Apartment, R.[38]

There is no record that Morelli received this payment, but there is no reason for the Navy Department to deny the legitimate claim. In 1920, Morelli, now a clerk at an express office, was living with his mother and brother at the 22nd Street address. At some point, Morelli began to wonder why he had received an "ordinary" discharge in December. Upon reading an article in the paper that discussed the fact that Navy servicemen who were discharged prior to the expiration of their term of service were entitled to honorable discharges, Morelli wrote the Navy Department asking for a reissuance of an honorable discharge. His letter, dated November 9, 1922, follows:

> Gentlemen:—
>
> Enclosed you will find my Honorable and Ordinary discharges from U.S. Coast Guard which I am forwarding to you so that I many receive an Honorable Discharge which is in accordance with the attached article cut out of one of the newspapers.

> Probably the Ordinary is the only one that I should forward to you but I am sending both and in case the Honorable Discharge is not needed please forward same back to me with the other Honorable discharge in place of the Ordinary one.
>
> Thanking you in advance, Very truly yours [signed], Salvatore Morelli, 14 W. 22nd St., Chicago Ill.[39]

On November 16, 1922, the Navy responded by returning to Morelli his original honorable discharge from September 1918, and a new honorable discharge for his final discharge on December 20, 1918. In addition, by way of demonstrating that the accounting books are never really closed until they balance to the penny, the Navy sent him a "voucher covering clothing credit." Morelli was instructed to sign an enclosure and forward it to the General Accounting Office, Treasury Department, in order to settle the clothing credit, "as it is payable from an old appropriation."[40]

Despite the onset of the Great Depression in 1929, Morelli, still unmarried, owned his own auto garage business in 1930; he lived with his mother and brother at 213 Cullerton Avenue, where they took on four lodgers to supplement the family income. By 1933, Morelli was a service manager for the Wabash Auto Laundry and Greasing Station in Chicago. On October 4, 1933, he wrote a letter, on Wabash Auto Laundry stationary that proclaimed "High Pressure Greasing and Washing, Day and Night Service," to the Navy Department requesting the issuance of a Victory Medal:

> Gentlemen:—
>
> Having served in the World War—a Buddy called my attention to the fact I was entitled to a Victory Medal and a service Button which I have never received. I was discharged from the U.S. Coast Guard ship Pamlico Dec. 20, 1918.
>
> Will you please forward same to me and oblige, [signed] Salvatore Morelli, 2125 S. Wabash Ave., Chicago, Ill.[41]

The medal and lapel button were duly sent to Morelli in a package and letter dated October 19, 1933. Morelli was requested to send a return receipt for the items, which he did a few days later. In the early 1940s, he and his brother were proprietors of Century Music in Chicago. He died in Chicago in 1962.

Clemente Morrone[42]

Clemente Morrone was born in Marano Marchesato on May 24, 1887, the son of Giovanni Morrone and Maria Orrico. Morrone came to the U.S. in 1901, destined for his uncle, Pasquale Orrico, in Chicago. In 1917, Morrone lived in Gary, Indiana, where he was employed as a foreman for the Gary & Interurban Rail Road. Morrone was single, but he requested an exemption based upon the fact that he was supporting his mother in Italy. However, Morrone was notified to report to his draft board on February 12, 1918, for physical examination to determine his fitness to serve in the Army. The resulting examination found Morrone physically fit for general military service. He was 5 feet 4 inches tall with brown eyes, brown hair, and a dark complexion, and he had normal hearing and vision.

Morrone was eventually notified to report for induction on July 23, 1918; at that time, he was enlisted as a private, serial number 3886153. Morrone was sent to

Camp Taylor, Kentucky, as part of the 60th Company, 15th Training Battalion, 159th Depot Brigade, where he underwent more physical examinations and administrative processing. He listed his brother Alexander, then living in Chicago, as his next of kin, and he stated his civilian occupation as a "mechanical helper." He claimed to be the sole supporter of his mother, Mary. His physical exams once again were positive, and he was again certified for general military service by endorsements from four separate officers including Captain C. L. Waymann and Major Val Emiltenberger of the Medical Corps, and Brigadier General Fred T. Austin, commander of Camp Taylor. Morrone continued his training and in processing. He was issued a "recruit toilet kit," and on July 29, he had the Articles of War read to him. The result of his psychological testing revealed him to be "low average." He also started pay allotments, $22 monthly for war risk insurance. Morrone was naturalized as a U.S. citizen on August 17, 1918.

On August 31, Morrone was transferred to the 12th Company, Development Battalion 3, at Camp Taylor; a few days later, on September 5, he was transferred to the Quartermaster Corps at Camp Henry Knox, near West Point, Kentucky. The Army had been training artillerymen at West Point beginning in April 1918. The War Department bought more land in nearby Stithton, and construction of Camp Henry Knox commenced in August 1918. As part of the Quartermaster Corps, Morrone was almost certainly one of the many men living in tents and engaged in the massive construction project. Given his prewar civilian job as a railroad construction foreman, it is easy to understand why he was sent to this project. Although he had had only three years of grammar school, his five years as a foreman were put to good use. At the time of Morrone's transfer, Second Lieutenant Lee T. Rector, commander of the 12th Company, rated his character as "good."

Throughout the fall, Morrone worked in the Stithton–West Point area; at some point, he appears to have worked in the Camp Henry Knox supply office. His ability and devotion to duty were recognized by his promotion to corporal on January 3, 1919. Morrone was on furlough from March 10–18; perhaps he went home to Gary or to Chicago to visit his family. Shortly after his return to Camp Henry Knox, on April 9, 1919, Corporal Morrone received his final pay of $81.40, which included $15.10 travel pay back to Gary, and was discharged from the Army; at this time, his character was judged "excellent."

Ferdinando Morrone

Ferdinando (Fred) Morrone was born in Rende on August 3, 1894, the son of Lorenzo Morrone and Rosaria Principe. He was living in Chicago when he entered the Army on November 6, 1918, just five days before the Armistice; he was perhaps the last Cosenza area immigrant to enter the military during the war. Morrone was a private, serial number 3022523, in the 23rd Company, 2nd Recruit Battalion, at Camp Forrest, Georgia; he was naturalized there on December 7. Morrone was discharged on December 31, 1918.

Giuseppe Napolitano[43]

Giuseppe Napolitano was born on November 1, 1894, in the Parantoro section of Montalto Uffugo, the son of Domenico Enrico and Angelina Napolitano. He came to the U.S. in August 1913, and in 1917, he was living in Deerfield, Illinois, where he worked as a chef at the Old Elm Country Club.

Napolitano was inducted into the Army during the war and was assigned to the School for Bakers and Cooks at Camp Gordon. While there, he perfected his chef skills and was purportedly the private chef for a general. Napolitano became a U.S. citizen at Camp Gordon on July 17, 1918.

Frank Nino[44]

Frank Nino was born in Piane Crati on November 12, 1897. He came to the U.S. in 1905 and settled in Chicago with his father. Although he spent most of his time in Chicago, Nino, infected with wanderlust, spent time in other places; he was a cowboy in Arizona for a time. Nino enlisted in the Army in early May 1918; he was a private, serial number 443810, in Troop "K," 17th Cavalry Regiment, stationed at Camp Harry K. Jones near Douglas, Arizona, when he became a naturalized U.S. citizen on June 17, 1918. The 17th Cavalry Regiment patrolled the still hazardous Mexican border throughout the war. Nino was discharged on March 17, 1919.

Jasper Nudo

Jasper Nudo was born in Castrolibero in 1894, the son of Ralph Nudo. He came to the U.S. in 1912 and settled in Chicago. Nudo was inducted into the Army on March 31, 1918; he was a private, serial number 2086867, in Company "A," 108th Ammunition Train, 33rd Division. He left the U.S. bound for France on May 26, less than two months after his induction. Nudo returned to the U.S. with his unit on May 22, 1919. After arriving at Camp Mills, New York, Nudo was discharged on June 4, 1919. He used his military veteran status to file for U.S. citizenship in Chicago on September 30, 1919.

Eugenio Onofrio

Eugenio Onofrio was born in San Fili on June 29, 1891, the son of Angelo Maria Onofrio and Rosa Esposito; he was a laborer at the Mackie Lovejoy Company, living in Chicago, when he registered for the draft in June 1917. At that time, he claimed exemption from the draft "on account of operation." This, plus the fact that he was an alien and exempt from the draft anyway, had no impact; Onofrio was inducted into the Army. He was stationed at Camp Grant, Illinois, when he became a naturalized U.S. citizen on June 3, 1918. His date of discharge is not known.

Pasquale Pellegrini, Francesco Pellegrini, and Luigi Pellegrini[45]

Pasquale (Charles), Francesco (Frank), and Luigi (Louis) Pellegrini were born in Marano Marchesato in 1890, 1892, and 1896, respectively, the sons of Saverio Pellegrini and Saveria Chiappetta. Each of the sons came to the U.S. (Charles in 1906, Frank in 1909, and Louis in 1911) to join an older brother, Pietro, in Chicago. The sons were all tailors, trained by their father, a master tailor in Italy. The brothers all worked at Pietro's successful tailoring business, and Pietro's wife, Edna Van Kirk, "became a house mother for the Pellegrini boys who came one by one to seek their fortune in America. She housed them, fed them, taught them English, American customs, including personal dress styles and table manners."[46] Other brothers, sisters, and brothers-in-law came and worked with Pietro as their business flourished.

Above left: Pvt. Frank Nino, 17th Cavalry Regiment, *c.* 1918. (*Nino family*)

Above right: Jasper Nudo's passport photograph, 1924. (*Ancestry.com*)

Left: Pvt. Eugenio Onofrio, 161st Depot Brigade (*David and JoAnn Burns, Holland, Michigan*)

The brothers were proud of their adopted country. Charles enlisted in Company "I," 1st Illinois Infantry Regiment, on January 30, 1911. He served until January 30, 1914, and then reenlisted on April 26, 1915. Three weeks later, he became a U.S. citizen at the Superior Court of Cook County in Chicago. During the Mexican border troubles, President Woodrow Wilson ordered the mobilization of the states' National Guard troops. Illinois troops mustered at Camp Dunne (the State Fair grounds) and Camp Lincoln, under the command of Brigadier General D. Jack Foster of the Illinois National Guard. The assembled, mobilized Illinois troops consisted of the First Infantry Brigade (1st, 2nd, and 7th Infantry Regiments); Second Infantry Brigade (3rd, 4th, and 8th Infantry Regiments); the First Field Artillery Regiment; Company "A," First Engineer Regiment; Company "A," Illinois Signal Corps; and Field Hospitals 1 and 2. These units boarded trains and departed for San Antonio, Texas, from June 28 to July 4, 1916. Once in San Antonio, the troops were assigned to the Twelfth Provisional Division under the command of Brigadier General Henry A. Green, a regular Army officer. The infantry regiments took up residence at Camp Wilson, next to Camp Sam Houston.

There, the units made several practice marches to Leon Springs, Landa Park (New Braunfels), and Austin. At other times, the troops participated in training, field exercises, and target practice. Upon orders from the War Department on August 31, 1916, the Illinois troops began to return to Springfield. Charles returned and was discharged on October 4, 1916. The last unit to return to Illinois was the 4th Illinois Infantry Regiment.

Tales of Texas and the border, and of military maneuvers, marches, and "frontier soldiering" might have influenced Charles's younger brother, Louis. Rather than simply enlisting in one of the returned Illinois regiments, particularly the 1st that was based in Chicago, Louis traveled to Fort Sam Houston near San Antonio and there enlisted in Company "E," 4th Illinois Infantry Regiment, on January 8, 1917. The 4th Illinois had been in Texas since the previous July; it returned to Illinois and was mustered out at Fort Sheridan, north of Chicago, on March 15, 1917, the men returning to their homes. Some companies of the regiment were called out in May to preserve order in Mattoon, Illinois, following a tornado. Then, a little later, the entire regiment was dispatched to East Saint Louis, Illinois, for duty during the race riots. Interestingly, the 4th Illinois was made up of men from southern Illinois, and Company "E" was headquartered in Carbondale, Illinois, and it is not known if Louis participated in any of these state call-ups.

The U.S. declaration of war on April 6, 1917, found the brothers living in Chicago and working as tailors for the oldest brother, Pietro. On July 25, the 4th Illinois Infantry Regiment, of which Louis was a member, was mobilized and sworn into federal service, with the companies assembling at their home cities. Louis was mobilized three days later, but it is not known if he went to Carbondale, in southern Illinois, to be with his company or whether he stayed in Chicago. The various companies began recruiting to get up to wartime strength.

On August 1, Louis was promoted to bugler, serial number 1383749. As one of two buglers in Company "E," he would have various responsibilities that, of course, included sounding the myriad bugle calls for the company. The bugler, since he blew reveille early in the morning, rousing the men from their hard-earned slumber, was traditionally, if somewhat jokingly, reviled in the regiment.

In early October, the 4th Illinois journeyed to Camp Logan, Texas, where they soon were redesignated as the 130th Infantry Regiment, part of the 65th Brigade (along with

Bugler Louis Pellegrini, 130th Infantry Regiment, 33rd Division. Photograph taken in Chicago, *c.* 1917 or 1918. (*Andrea Koprcina McGuire and Mark Koprcina*)

the 129th Infantry Regiment), which was part of the 33rd Division, a newly forming division consisting of federalized Illinois National Guard units. Other units in the division were the 131st and 132nd Infantry Regiments (in the 66th Brigade), the 108th Engineer Regiment, and a host of support units. The new units suffered from lack of provisions and a dearth of personnel, but by the end of October, training was underway in all the various duties of an infantry regiment. During October and November, thousands of drafted men were sent to Camp Logan to fill up the ranks of the 33rd Division. Interestingly, many of these transferred men were from the 86th Division, consisting largely of draftees from Illinois.

This training continued despite chronic manpower shortages; training was intensified in March with men attending classes and schools in the evenings. In April, another 7,145 drafted men arrived. Coinciding with this influx, Louis was demoted to private on April 7; probably one of the incoming men outranked him, and room had to be made for the new man. The demotion, however, was only temporary, as Louis was promoted again to bugler on June 10, when the regiment was in France, and he held that rank for the rest of his service.

The 33rd Division received a warning order to be ready to depart for the port of embarkation in late April. On May 3, the 130th left Camp Logan on their way to Camp Upton, New York. On May 16, after final refitting, the regiment departed for France aboard the *Agamemnon*, formerly the *Kaiser Wilhelm II*, a German passenger liner impounded when the United States declared war on Germany. The regiment arrived safely at the port of Brest on May 24, but due to a backlog of unloading, had to wait until May 26 to disembark.

The 33rd Division was the only U.S. division to fight under British, French, and American command. The division saw front line and support service with the Australians and British, and the men suffered the boredom, terror, and filth of the trenches. After joining the American 1st Army in August, the 33rd Division prepared to participate in the Meuse-Argonne Offensive. All along the line, the Allied armies assumed the offensive, hoping this final push would driver the Germans to surrender or seek a peace settlement. For the Americans, the offensive, the largest operation of its kind in U.S. history to that date, was designed to push the Germans back from the area between the Meuse River in the east and the Argonne Forest in the west; the ultimate goal was to reach Sedan in the north, thereby cutting off a major German supply line for its troops in the northwest. The 33rd Division was to be on the extreme right of the line, along the Meuse, with its right flank resting on that river. The attack plan envisioned the entire line moving north, with the 33rd pivoting on its right and ending up along the Meuse, facing the river. It was, in essence, the hinge of the entire line.

On September 25, the 130th moved into final position for the jump-off. The 2nd Battalion marched from Bois de Ville to a ravine in Ruisseau-de-Beaumont, where they and the 3rd Battalion became the 33rd Division reserve. They arrived in position at 1 a.m. on September 26. No sooner had the regiment gotten there than they were ordered forward to the 65th Brigade Advance Post of Command (P.C.). The men marched forward under cover of a smokescreen laid down on the east bank of the Meuse River. The men succeeded in reaching Le Mort Homme without casualties; the regiment was ordered to bivouac in position on Le Mort Homme, and they would receive further orders in the morning. The entire area of Le Mort Homme was under heavy artillery fire. Because of the incoming fire, the battalions were dispersed throughout the area, with the 2nd Battalion and Machine Gun Company occupying a trench system south of Chattancourt. This precaution proved to be a good idea since Chattancourt was bombarded steadily during the night of September 26–27.

On September 26, at about 5:30 a.m., the troops jumped off. For the 33rd Division, the assault troops were the 131st and 132nd Infantry Regiments; the 65th Brigade, including Louis and the 130th Infantry Regiment, remained in reserve south of Chattancourt. At 6:45 a.m. on September 27, the 130th was ordered to join the rear of the column of the 129th Infantry to move to Béthincourt. The 130th departed at 7 a.m., but soon found the roads impassable due to artillery and other vehicles. Col. John V. Clinnin, regimental commander, now ordered the 130th to countermarch back toward the west side of Le Mort Homme. Once there, the men followed a trail to the north side and then set off single file across shell-torn muddy fields to Béthincourt. The regimental transport was ordered to continue on the congested road and work forward as best as they could. The main portion of the regiment, marching across country, arrived at Béthincourt at 2 p.m. on September 27; the 130th formed up behind the 129th. The regimental transport arrived at 6 p.m. and the men enjoyed a hot meal.

At 5 p.m. on September 28, the 65th Brigade commander ordered the 130th's regimental, battalion, and company officers forward to scout the lines of the 320th Infantry Regiment of the 80th Division, which unit the 130th was to relieve. The 320th was in the Bois de la Cote Lemont to the left of the 33rd Division's current line. Louis possibly accompanied his company commander on this expedition. Meanwhile the rest of the regiment moved forward into the Bois d'en Dela. At 10 p.m., the 130th was ordered to begin relieving the 320th. Relief under combat conditions at night was a precarious undertaking fraught with possibilities of disaster. In this case, confusion was evident among the regimental commanders right away. Colonel Clinnin went forward to meet with the commander of the 320th Infantry at his command post at a crossroads south of Bois d'en Dela; the latter officer stated that he had no orders to stand relieved and that he would not withdraw until he received such orders. The 320th's commander arranged to have runners notify Col. Clinnin at his regiment's bivouac in Bois d'en Dela when orders for a relief were received. A heavy rain fell on the men throughout the night; finally, at 5:20 a.m. on September 29, both regimental commanders received positive word of a relief, and such relief began at once.

The 130th moved forward to relieve the 320th in the tangled growth of the Bois de la Cote Lemont. The relief was completed by 2:20 p.m. with some difficulty but minimal casualties; the 320th was disorganized due to them having been heavily gassed, and due to the thick, tangled nature of the woods in which they were. The 1st Battalion occupied the right half of the sub-sector while the 3rd Battalion moved into the Wood Sub-Sector, on the left, in Bois de la Cote Lemont. Louis and Company "E," in the 2nd Battalion, took up support positions with two companies on the north edge of Bois d'en Dela and two companies in Bois de Septsarges. The position was entrenched and wired for defense.

While in this position, in the woods near the bend in the Meuse River, Louis and his fellows in the 130th suffered badly from shelling and gas attacks. They were subject to heavy machine-gun fire from across the Meuse River and from their front and left flank. Artillery from across the Meuse also fired on the men. On night of October 2, 150 gas shells mixed with a heavy bombardment of shrapnel shells plunged into the 130th Infantry Regiment; three men were killed and seven wounded.

On October 4, the 130th assaulted the Teton Trench, south of Brieulles, in an unsuccessful attempt to drive the Germans from that position and help the 4th Division that was held up in the Bois du Fays to the west. On the night of October 9, the 129th Infantry Regiment along with the 3rd Battalion, 130th Infantry Regiment, moved over to the east side of the Meuse River to assist the 131st and 132nd Infantry Regiments which were involved in attacking German forces in an effort to relieve the pressure on the troops on the west side of the river. This left the 130th Infantry Regiment, on October 10, thinly manning a line along the edge of some woods and around the bend in the Meuse River. The infantry units of the 33rd Division west of the Meuse (1st and 2nd Battalions of the 130th Infantry Regiment and assorted machine gun units) then held a dangerous 10-kilometer front along the river. Louis, with his battalion, moved into line to the right of the 1st Battalion, relieving the 129th Infantry Regiment along the river, in the Bois de Dannevoux, the relief being completed at 3:15 a.m. on October 10. Sometime during the night of October 10–11, Louis was gassed and evacuated.

At least twenty-seven men in the 2nd Battalion (the numbers are approximately Company "E"—fifteen; Company "F"—five; Company "G"—seven; no information available for Company "H") were exposed to gas and evacuated. Both of the Company "E" buglers, Louis Pellegrini and Charles Casey, were casualties.[47] The gas exposure was characterized at the time as "slight," but all these men were evacuated; in fact, at the end of November, Louis was still in the hospital and transferred out of his regiment, never to rejoin it. (Louis appears on the roster of Company "E" for October, so it is possible that he came back to the regiment sometime in October and then was subsequently re-evacuated; if so, he would have participated in the combat that his regiment experienced in early November, right up to the day the war ended.) The gassed men were entitled to wear a wound chevron, a gold chevron on the lower right sleeve of the uniform, to indicate that the wearer had suffered a wound in action. This would also entitle Louis to the award of the Purple Heart Medal that would be instituted later, in 1932.[48]

During its two weeks on the west bank of the Meuse, the 130th was subjected to almost continuous machine gun, artillery, and gas fire from their front and flanks. The 130th suffered twenty-seven men killed, and nine officers and 135 men wounded. Louis, as stated, was evacuated and sent to a special gas-treatment hospital. It is not known what, if any, duties Louis had until his departure from France in March 1919, but he was detached from the 130th Infantry Regiment and was probably assigned to hospitals and convalescent regiments. He arrived back in the U.S. on March 24 and was sent to Camp Grant, Illinois, in preparation for his discharge. There, he was assigned as a bugler in the 6th Company, 161st Depot Brigade. Most of the rest of the 33rd Division would not return to the U.S. and be mustered out until May 1919, after participating in welcome-home parades in Chicago. Men like Louis, who had been wounded and returned to the U.S. before the bulk of the division, probably missed out on these parades.

Louis had been paid on February 28, 1919, before he left France, and on April 10, his final pay was issued. This pay included \$60 for regular pay, \$15.90 reimbursement for his war risk insurance allotment, and \$57 travel pay, for a total of \$132.90. Interestingly, he was entitled to travel pay to his place of enlistment, in this case Fort Sam Houston, Texas, although he probably simply caught a train to Chicago after getting his final discharge papers. In addition, he was due $60 war service bonus. And so, on April 10, 1919, Louis was discharged from the Army at Camp Grant. Due to his wounds, he was listed as 10 percent disabled as related to his profession.

While Louis was still on duty in the U.S. at Camp Logan during early 1918, his brothers, Charles and Frank, were notified that they were to report to a local examining board and there to submit themselves for examination to determine their qualification, physical and otherwise, for military service. The men did so, probably in January or February 1918; soon they were notified that they had been accepted for military service, and that they should settle their affairs and be ready to depart. Both men were indeed drafted on May 2, 1918.

The brothers reported to a local board or staging area where they boarded a train for Jefferson Barracks, just south of St. Louis, Missouri. There they were sworn into the U.S. Army with the rank of private. Charles was given serial number 479779 and Frank was given serial number 479753. Sometime in May or June, both men were transferred to Camp MacArthur, near Waco, Texas, to become part of the 7th Division, a Regular Army division that was in the process of building up to wartime strength and training. The 7th received a huge influx of drafted men during this time, making it, in effect, a National Army division, made up largely of draftees. Most of the men received during May and June were from Illinois, Michigan, Pennsylvania, Iowa, and Missouri. These newcomers were placed in provisional companies under Lieutenant Colonel LaMotte; they were, in effect, brought up to speed by being given their inoculations and special training by non-commissioned officers.

Elements of the 7th Division had been undergoing training for a year by the time Charles, Frank, and hundreds of draftees joined in May and June 1918. As with other divisions, the 7th sent thousands of men to other units, and, in turn, received thousands from other units, during this period. This illustrates the difficulties that confronted men, especially immigrants, who were sent to units in the spring and summer of 1918, just prior to their unit departing for overseas service. These men had to absorb a lot of valuable training, and to become a part of a functioning, cohesive military unit, in an incredibly brief period of time. It is a wonder that these men performed as well as they did in combat only a short three months after being drafted.

Frank was assigned to Company "M," 55th Infantry Regiment. Charles was initially assigned to Headquarters Company, 56th Infantry Regiment, and then was reassigned to Company "B" of that regiment on May 24. On June 24, Charles became ill and was sent to the base hospital at Camp MacArthur. He was transferred out of the company on July 13, a few days before the regiment left Camp MacArthur for the port of embarkation. Although family lore states that Charles was sent to France and badly wounded, there is no indication in the available records that such is the case. Rather, he was transferred to the 161st Depot Brigade at Camp Grant, from which unit he received his discharge on December 29, 1918.[49]

But Frank was still with the 55th Infantry Regiment, and on July 15, the 7th Division received a warning order to prepare for departure to the port of embarkation. Beginning on July 18, the various components of the 7th left Camp MacArthur and journeyed to Camp Merritt, New Jersey, for their final preparations for service in France. At Camp

Pvt. Charles Pellegrini, 161st Depot Brigade (standing, center), with friends, *c.* 1918. (*Andrea Koprcina McGuire and Mark Koprcina*)

Merritt, the units prepared for overseas service. The men checked and rechecked unit and personal equipment. Some units required their men to exchange all their personal equipment for new issues; others had to make do with what they had. Also at Camp Merritt, many foreign-born soldiers took advantage of a new law passed by Congress that waived length of residency requirements in order to allow aliens in the U.S. military to become citizens. On July 27, 1918, a few days before shipping out, Frank became a citizen of the United States.

At the port of embarkation, the men were arranged in unit groups and lined up in order according to the passenger manifest. Each man's name was checked at least once prior to boarding. On August 3, most of the 13th Brigade, including Frank and his regiment, boarded U.S.S. *Leviathan* at Hoboken. The *Leviathan* was had been a German ship known as the *Vaterland*; it had been impounded in a U.S. port when the U.S. declared war on Germany and then given to the Navy to use as a troopship. On this trip, the *Leviathan* set the record for the largest number of passengers and crew carried across the Atlantic Ocean to the A.E.F.: a total of 13,558 Army and Navy passengers, Navy crew, and civilians. The vessel arrived at the port of Brest, France, on August 11. The men spent several days at the Pontanezen Barracks before moving to their training area.

On August 17, the division moved to the 15th Training Area near Ancy-le-Franc. Soon thereafter, the 13th Brigade sent 2,000 men as replacements to the 4th and 26th Divisions to replace losses in those divisions, both of which had suffered heavily in recent fighting. It was a bit unusual for a non-depot division to send that many men to other units as replacements. Later that month, the division's artillery departed the area, not to rejoin the division until after the Armistice. The division suffered from a lack of supplies, many of which had been taken from the division upon debarkation, for issue to other units, and a paucity of transport, having only sixty horses, twenty pack mules, and about thirty borrowed motor trucks.

On September 27, the 7th Division moved to the Toul area, in the vicinity of the old Saint-Mihiel salient, as part of the VI Corps, 1st American Army. Due to the lack of transport, the 55th Infantry Regiment "borrowed" and requisitioned any available animals or vehicles in the area, including ox carts and old carriages. General Pershing was in the process of building up the 1st Army in this area in order to prepare for a general offensive while the rest of the 1st Army was engaged in the Meuse-Argonne Offensive to the north and west. The troops in this area, including the 7th Division, would, however, become part of the new U.S. 2nd Army on October 12.

On October 1, while the 55th Infantry Regiment was in the Toul area, Frank was promoted to private first class. Shortly thereafter, the 7th Division relieved the 90th Division in the Puvenelle Sector. All four infantry regiments went into line there, with the 13th Brigade on the right; the 56th Infantry on the far right flank, and Frank's 55th Infantry next in line to the left. The VI Corps, with the 92nd Division (consisting of African-American soldiers) on the right, the 7th Division in the middle, and the 37th Division on the left, was to hold this line defensively and to prepare for offensive operations.

While in this position, Frank and his regiment were subjected to heavy artillery fire, including both high explosives and gas. Frank was in the northern part of Bois de Reppes, on the outpost line with his company, Company "M," 55th Infantry. Suffering from gas attacks, the patrols and outposts in this area were also pulled back into the

Pfc. Francesco Pellegrini, 55th Infantry Regiment, 7th Division. Taken in France, probably in 1918, this photograph shows Pellegrini in heavy marching order. Note the amount of equipment the World War I U.S. infantryman was required to carry. (*Andrea Koprcina McGuire and Mark Koprcina*)

woods. From October 18–31, reliefs within the regiments took place, and Frank took part in active patrolling, including a raid near Preny on October 26. By the end of October, the 1st Army had made significant progress along the Meuse-Argonne front to the north and west of the 7th Division, which was alerted to be ready to exploit any withdrawal of enemy forces from its front. During the first part of November, elements of both the 56th and 55th Infantry Regiments were in action along the 7th Division front. On November 8, elements of the 55th Infantry attacked Hill 323 but were repulsed under heavy enemy artillery fire. On November 10, the day before the Armistice, Frank participated with his regiment in at attack against Hill 323.

Beginning at 5:30 a.m., elements of the 1st and 3rd Battalions moved forward without artillery preparation; they managed to gain the crest by 10:30 a.m. At noon, the enemy made two counterattacks that were driven back. Shortly thereafter, Frank's Company "M," under Lt. James H. Hagan, moved forward with Company "I," relieving Company "D." This relief was completed by 3:30 p.m.; thirty minutes later, Companies "M" and "I" advanced under heavy artillery and machine-gun fire. Later that night, the 34th Infantry Regiment relieved the 55th Infantry Regiment. This operation led to an advance of about 1 kilometer and netted five prisoners and a quantity of enemy munitions, including mortars, machine guns, rifles, and ammunition.

The men in the 7th Division were notified of the Armistice on the morning of November 11, just hours before it was to take effect. An attack had been scheduled for later that morning, but this was called off; artillery, though, continued firing up to the last moment, at 11 a.m. The men patrolled the front line, cautioned against fraternization with the German troops. That night, the doughboys sat quietly in their posts while the German troops, engaged in a great celebration, sent up flares and other pyrotechnics. For the rest of the fall and into winter, the 55th Infantry Regiment was engaged in salvage work in the area, reclaiming, categorizing, and storing the vast quantities of government stores that were prevalent in and around the battlefields.

From October 8 to November 11, the 55th Infantry Regiment lost twenty-nine men killed, twenty-one men died of wounds, and 239 men wounded, for a total of 289 casualties. The 7th Division history gives the following casualty figures for the 55th Infantry Regiment during the war: thirty-eight men killed, 171 men gassed, 153 men wounded, two men captured, two men missing, for a total of 366 casualties.

Following the Armistice, the men also engaged in training and schooling. In an effort to boost the morale of the men, idle for long months after engaging in dangerous and stressful wartime operations, the commanders ensured the men had every opportunity to participate in talent shows and other forms of entertainment. The regiments also fielded football, basketball, baseball, and track teams. Eventually, the 7th Division made its way to Colombey-les-Belles and then to the Le Mans area preparatory to departure for the United States. In June 1919, the regiment made its way west across France, staying once again at Camp Pontanezen. Embarkation from Brest commenced on June 10. The 55th Infantry Regiment reached the Hoboken on June 20, and they proceeded to Camp Merritt, New Jersey. Once there, almost all drafted men were sent to demobilization stations near their home of record.

Frank was sent to the 161st Depot Brigade at Camp Grant. There, together with other men from his regiment who lived in the general area, on June 28, he received his final pay to include $93.20 of back pay and $4.50 travel allowance to Chicago. Subtracted from this was $14 for allotments, plus he had to reimburse the government 65 cents for some trivial debt. When it was all said and done and all the pennies were accounted for, he received his honorable discharge from the Army that same day and probably caught the next train to Chicago.

With the return of the Pellegrini men from overseas, life began to return to some semblance of normal. No doubt Pietro was delighted to have his brothers back to help in the business. The men put away their rifles, pistols, and uniforms and returned to their needles, cloth, and tape measures, hoping to pick up where they left off. The tailor business, started by Pietro in about 1907, eventually involved three locations: 43rd Street, Kimball Building at 25 East Jackson Boulevard, and on the 9th floor of the Westminster Building at 110 South Dearborn Street. Their clientele included many big names in Chicago such as meatpacking industry giant Michael J. Cudahy, retail magnates Marshall Field II and Mr. Goldblatt, movie stars, gangsters (even, reputedly, Al Capone), and Avery Brundage, first president of the U.S. Olympic Committee. At a time when suits cost typically about $20, the Pellegrini brothers could charge between $125 and $200, "which included everything from first measurement through final alterations."[50]

Each brother had a particular skill; Pietro, the founder, was a top manager and sales contact, Charles was the best designer and later top manager when Pietro retired, Frank was the "best cutter in Chicago." Another brother, Eugene, was an "excellent sewer,"

Louis Pellegrini and his daughter Doris, *c.* 1930s. (*Andrea Koprcina McGuire and Mark Koprcina*)

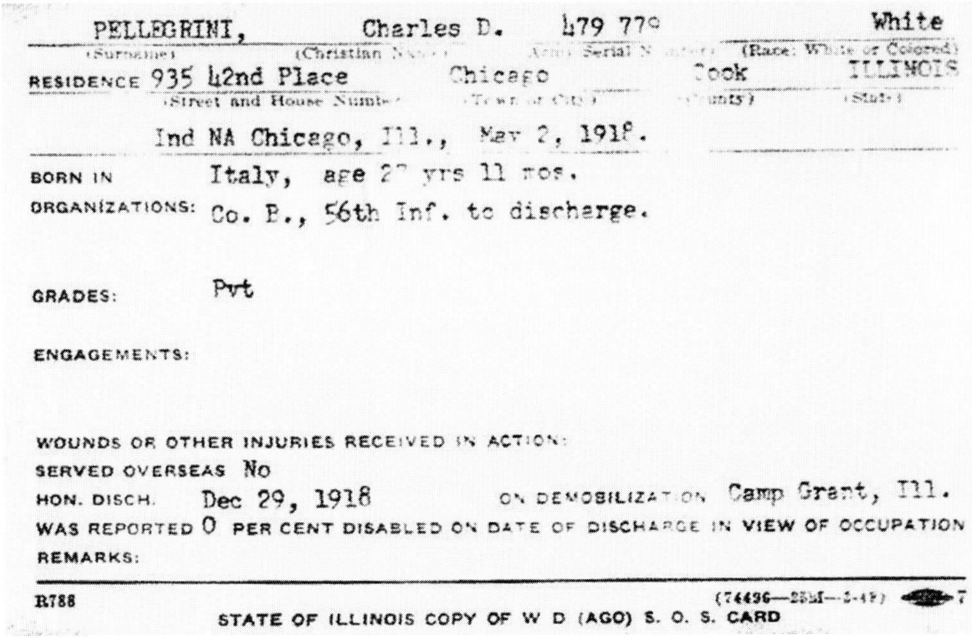

PELLEGRINI, Charles D. 479 779 White
(Surname) (Christian Name) (Army Serial Number) (Race: White or Colored)
RESIDENCE 935 42nd Place Chicago Cook ILLINOIS
(Street and House Number) (Town or City) (County) (State)
Ind NA Chicago, Ill., May 2, 1918.
BORN IN Italy, age 27 yrs 11 mos.
ORGANIZATIONS: Co. B., 56th Inf. to discharge.
GRADES: Pvt
ENGAGEMENTS:
WOUNDS OR OTHER INJURIES RECEIVED IN ACTION:
SERVED OVERSEAS No
HON. DISCH. Dec 29, 1918 ON DEMOBILIZATION Camp Grant, Ill.
WAS REPORTED 0 PER CENT DISABLED ON DATE OF DISCHARGE IN VIEW OF OCCUPATION
REMARKS:
R788 (74496—25M—5-45)
STATE OF ILLINOIS COPY OF W D (AGO) S. O. S. CARD

Pvt. Charles Pellegrini's statement of service card. (*Illinois Adjutant General*)

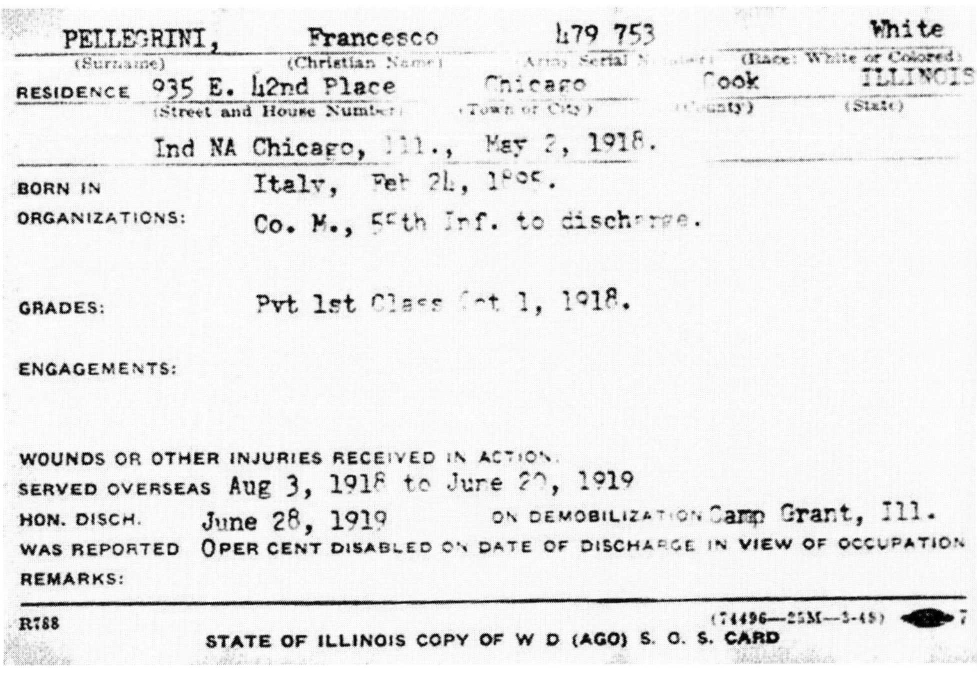

PELLEGRINI, Francesco 479 753 White
(Surname) (Christian Name) (Army Serial Number) (Race: White or Colored)
RESIDENCE 935 E. 42nd Place Chicago Cook ILLINOIS
(Street and House Number) (Town or City) (County) (State)
Ind NA Chicago, Ill., May 2, 1918.
BORN IN Italy, Feb 24, 1895.
ORGANIZATIONS: Co. M., 55th Inf. to discharge.
GRADES: Pvt 1st Class Oct 1, 1918.
ENGAGEMENTS:
WOUNDS OR OTHER INJURIES RECEIVED IN ACTION:
SERVED OVERSEAS Aug 3, 1918 to June 20, 1919
HON. DISCH. June 28, 1919 ON DEMOBILIZATION Camp Grant, Ill.
WAS REPORTED 0 PER CENT DISABLED ON DATE OF DISCHARGE IN VIEW OF OCCUPATION
REMARKS:
R788 (74496—25M—5-45)
STATE OF ILLINOIS COPY OF W D (AGO) S. O. S. CARD

Pfc. Francesco Pellegrini's statement of service card. (*Illinois Adjutant General*)

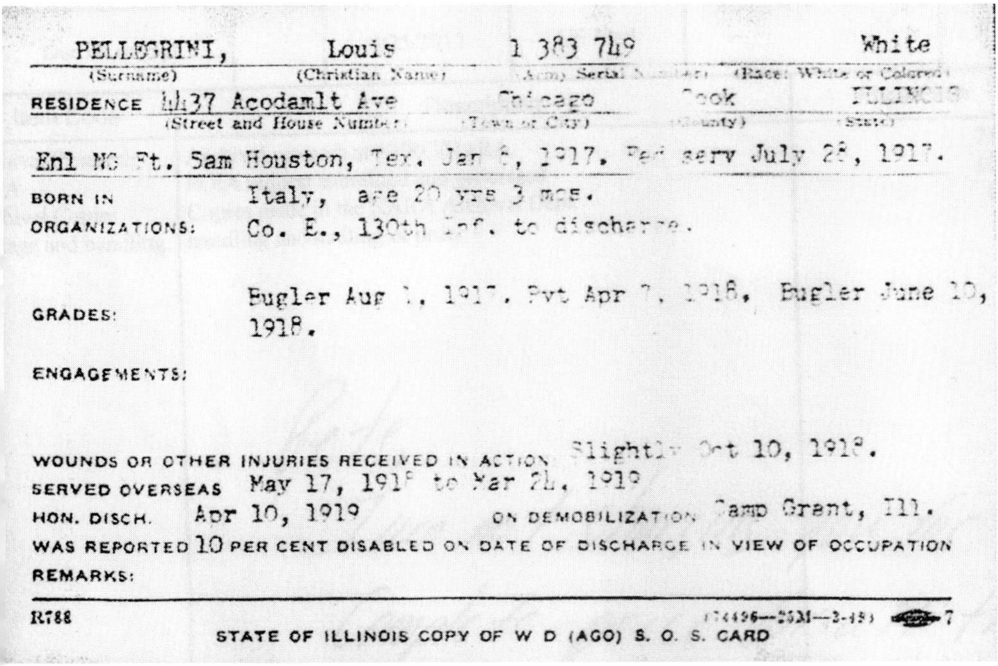

PELLEGRINI, Louis 1 383 749 White
(Surname) (Christian Name) (Army Serial Number) (Race: White or Colored)
RESIDENCE 4437 Acodamlt Ave Chicago Cook ILLINOIS
(Street and House Number) (Town or City) (County) (State)
Enl NG Ft. Sam Houston, Tex. Jan 6, 1917. Fed serv July 25, 1917.
BORN IN Italy, age 20 yrs 3 mos.
ORGANIZATIONS: Co. E., 130th Inf. to discharge.
GRADES: Bugler Aug 1, 1917. Pvt Apr 7, 1918, Bugler June 10, 1918.
ENGAGEMENTS:
WOUNDS OR OTHER INJURIES RECEIVED IN ACTION Slightly Oct 10, 1918.
SERVED OVERSEAS May 17, 1918 to Mar 24, 1919
HON. DISCH. Apr 10, 1919 ON DEMOBILIZATION Camp Grant, Ill.
WAS REPORTED 10 PER CENT DISABLED ON DATE OF DISCHARGE IN VIEW OF OCCUPATION
REMARKS:
R788 (74496—25M—3-43) 7
STATE OF ILLINOIS COPY OF W D (AGO) S. O. S. CARD

Bugler Louis Pellegrini's statement of service card showing his enlistment in the National Guard at Fort Sam Houston, Texas, his wounding during the Meuse-Argonne Offensive, and a consequent 10 percent disability rating. (*Illinois Adjutant General*)

Carmine Iantorno, their brother-in-law, was "one of the best tailors anywhere," and youngest brother, Joe, who joined the group in 1954, was "good at everything."[51] Frank was also known as a "dapper dresser, dashing, handsome [and] a rogue who played the horses, loved women and good whiskey, [with a] marvelous sense of humor."[52] Louis, a "talented tailor," was considered a "fashion plate" for whom ladies swooned.[53] After Pietro retired, Charles left the business in 1951, moving to California. This left Frank, Eugene, and Carmine. But custom tailoring was in decline; by the mid-1960s, the Pellegrini brothers business had closed.

Charles died on March 5, 1963, in Fresno, California. Louis died near Los Angeles on May 22, 1966, and he was buried five days later at the Los Angeles National Cemetery. Frank, the last of the World War I veteran Pellegrini brothers, died on November 18, 1975, in Chicago.

Antonio Perrone[54]

Antonio Perrone was born in San Vincenzo la Costa in 1891 or 1892; he was a laborer living in Kenosha when he enlisted in Company "M," 4th Wisconsin Infantry Regiment, in the Wisconsin National Guard in June 1917. Upon federalization of the National Guard, Perrone's regiment became the 121st Field Artillery Regiment, 32nd Division, and Perrone became a private, serial number 2303906. He went overseas with his regiment on March 4, 1918, and participated in the Aisne-Marne, Oise-Aisne, and Meuse-Argonne Offensives as well as serving in several defensive sectors. Perrone also served as part of the Army of Occupation of Germany. He returned to the U.S. on May 12, 1919, and was discharged at Camp Grant, Illinois, a week later. On November 22, 1920, Perrone reenlisted as a private first class in Company "M," 9th Infantry Regiment. He served for almost two years; he was discharged at San Antonio on March 1, 1922, with a surgeon's certificate of disability. Awarded a monthly pension of $80, Perrone suffered from chronic asthma and other breathing difficulties, possibly as a result of poison gas exposure during the war; he was in and out of veteran's hospitals in the 1920s.

Vincenzo Presta[55]

Vincenzo (Vincent) Presta was born in Marano Principato in 1891, the son of Pasquale Presta and Filomena Rosaria Savaglio. At the time of his induction into the Army on September 21, 1917, he was a photographer living in Kenosha. As part of the first batch of men drafted into the National Army, Presta was assigned as a private, serial number 2024081, to Supply Company, 340th Infantry Regiment, 85th Division, at Camp Custer, Michigan. On November 7, 1917, Presta, a clarinet player, was transferred to the regimental band, Headquarters Company, 340th Infantry Regiment; he was promoted to musician second class on December 6, 1917. He went overseas with the 85th Division on July 24, 1918; the 85th became the 4th Depot Division and sent replacements to other units. In October 1918, the division was again redesignated as the 85th Division and it was sent forward to Toul in preparation for an offensive to be undertaken by the U.S. 2nd Army. Along with some other members of the 85th Division, he was credited with the "Defensive Sector" clasp. He returned to the U.S. on April 2, 1919, and was discharged at Camp Grant, Illinois, on April 23, 1919.

Frank Prete[56]

Frank Philip Prete was born in Rende on August 14, 1894, the son of Alfonso Prete and Mary Martino; he came to the U.S. around 1905. On February 9, 1916, Prete enlisted in Machine Gun Troop, 1st Illinois Cavalry Regiment, Illinois National Guard. In June of that year, President Woodrow Wilson mobilized much of the country's National Guard; Prete and his regiment mobilized on June 19, and they quickly deployed to Texas, serving for the next few months as a guard along the Mexican border. Prete returned home and was demobilized on November 17, 1916.

The U.S. declared war against Germany on April 6, 1917, and within a few months, National Guard units were again federalized. Prete became part of Battery "B," 122nd Field Artillery Regiment, 33rd Division. He was a sergeant, serial number 1375582, when he left for France aboard the British tramp steamer *Kashmir* on May 27, 1918. After training in France, the 122nd left its parent 33rd Division and supported the 1st Division in its attack on the Saint-Mihiel salient on September 12, 1918. Next, the 122nd supported the 91st and 32nd Divisions during the first two phases of the Meuse-Argonne Offensive, from September 26 to October 11. During this time, the regiment was heavily engaged and suffered many casualties. The 122nd went back into line on November 1, supporting the attack of the 89th Division toward the Meuse River. Some guns of Battery "B" advanced with the leading units of infantry in order to give

Pvt. Vincent Presta, 340th Infantry Regiment, 85th Division (back row, left), with family in Kenosha, *c*. 1918. (*Rose Presta Pennington*)

Vincent Presta (second row, far left [holding clarinet]), and the Kenosha American Legion band, *c*. 1930, Kenosha (*Rose Presta Pennington*).

Sgt. Frank P. Prete, 122nd Field Artillery Regiment, 33rd Division, earned the D.S.C. for extraordinary heroism in action, November 1, 1918. (*Illinois in the World War*)

them the best support possible. It was here that Sergeant Prete earned the Distinguished Service Cross (D.S.C.) for extraordinary heroism in action.

Prete's D.S.C. citation reads:

> The President of the United States of America, authorized by Act of Congress, July 9, 1918, takes pleasure in presenting the Distinguished Service Cross to Sergeant Frank P. Prete (ASN: 1375582), United States Army, for extraordinary heroism in action while serving with Battery B, 122d Field Artillery, 33d Division, A.E.F., near Bantheville, France, 1 November 1918. Sergeant Prete three times passed through a heavy barrage and machine-gun fire, while guiding a combat train forward to an advanced artillery platoon.
>
> General Orders: War Department, General Orders 87 (1919).[57]

The 122nd engaged in combat right up to the Armistice on November 11. The regiment served with the 33rd Division as part of the Army of Occupation in Luxemburg until its departure aboard the *America* on May 16, 1919. The regiment arrived at Hoboken, New Jersey, eight days later. After a slight delay at Camp Mills, New York, the regiment returned to Chicago where it participated in a homecoming parade on June 5. Most of the regiment was discharged at Camp Grant, Illinois, three days later. Prete's brother, Armand, also served in the Army during the war.

Gasperto Ritacca

Gaspero Ritacca was born in Montalto Uffugo or Marano Marchesato on July 6, 1897. Ritacca was a crane operator for the American Brass Company in Kenosha when he was inducted into the Army on October 21, 1918. He was assigned as a private, serial number 4303044, in the 14th Company, 161st Depot Brigade at Camp Grant, Illinois.

Cook Giuseppe (Joe) Ritacca, Medical Detachment, A.E.F. University. (*Ritacca family in Kenosha, Wisconsin, and Perth, Australia*)

Ritacca was transferred to Camp Shelby, Mississippi, where he was part of the November Automatic Replacement Draft (NARD). After the Armistice, he was transferred back to Camp Grant where he was discharged on December 6, 1918.

Giuseppe Ritacca

Giuseppe Ritacca was born in Marano Marchesato, on January 1, 1895. In 1917, he lived in Kenosha where he worked as a laborer for the Black Cat Textile Company. He was inducted into the Army on March 29, 1918, and was sent to Company 8, 2nd Battalion, 160th Depot Brigade, at Camp Custer, Michigan, where he was a private, serial number 2038607. On May 1, he was transferred to the Medical Department at Camp Greenleaf, Georgia. Ritacca was sent overseas as part of the Medical Corps on June 7. He was promoted to cook on September 3, 1918, and at some point was transferred to Headquarters Detachment, A.E.F. University, in France. The A.E.F. University was set up after the Armistice to provide education to servicemen who desired to continue their studies. Ritacca returned to the U.S. on June 28, 1919, and was discharged at Camp Grant, Illinois, on July 9, 1919.

Louis R. Rochetto

Luigi (Louis) Rochetto (or, variously, Rucchetto, Rocchetto) was born in Marano Marchesato on May 29, 1895, the son of Alessandro Rochetto and Angelina Greco. At the time of his registration for the draft in 1917, Rochetto was a bookkeeper for the *Chicago Tribune*, living in Chicago. He entered the Army on September 19, 1918, and served in "Detachment 8," U.S. Army Air Service. He became a sergeant and, at the time of his discharge on April 5, 1919, was assigned to Detachment 8, apparently on duty in Chicago.

Louis Joseph Ruffolo[58]

Louis Joseph Ruffolo was born in Racine, Wisconsin, on June 6, 1900, the son of Luigi Ruffolo and Mary Ruffolo, both from Marano Principato. Luigi and Mary were married in 1896 and eventually had ten children in Racine, where Luigi worked as a railroad section foreman.

Ruffolo was a student when, on August 15, 1918, he enlisted in the U.S. Navy at the Navy Recruiting Station in nearby Milwaukee. He was sworn in as an apprentice seaman, serial number 1845163. Ruffolo's category was "Class 4 for general service, United States Naval Reserve Force." His physical examination revealed that he was 5 feet 3.25 inches tall, and weighed 117 pounds; he had brown eyes, black hair, and a ruddy complexion. The Navy Bureau of Navigation issued a waiver for Ruffolo because he was three-quarters of an inch under height for enlistment. He listed his father as his beneficiary, declaring also that Luigi was "partially dependent" upon his son. He also designated his mother as beneficiary for his $10,000 war risk insurance policy.[59]

Administrative and medical paperwork completed, the next day, Ruffolo reported to Great Lakes Naval Training Station, about 45 miles due south of Racine, for training. At Great Lakes, Ruffolo began the normal basic training prescribed for the thousands of incoming sailors who, like him, joined during the war. On October 21, Ruffolo was promoted to fireman third class; the next day, he transferred to U.S.S. *George Washington*. While serving on this ship, Ruffolo was promoted to fireman second class.

F3c Louis Joseph Ruffolo, U.S.S. *George Washington*, *c.* 1918. (*Racine County in the World War*)

The *George Washington* was formerly a German-owned steamship that had been impounded in New York at the start of the war. When the U.S. declared war on Germany, the Navy took control of the vessel and converted it into a transport, U.S.S. *George Washington*, ID-3018. During and after the war, the *George Washington* made eighteen round trips bringing troops to and from France. Ruffolo was part of the crew for many of these trips.

On December 3, 1918, Ruffolo ran into a bit of trouble. He was "slow in obeying orders," and was punished with five days of solitary confinement and a loss of pay amounting to twelve dollars. The next day, President Woodrow Wilson and other members of the American delegation to the Paris Peace Conference departed for France aboard the *George Washington*. For at least some of this journey, it appears that Ruffolo must have been in solitary confinement aboard the vessel. This episode appears to have been the only glitch in Ruffolo's Navy career. The vessel carried other illustrious Americans, including Assistant Secretary of the Navy Franklin D. Roosevelt, to and from France during 1919. President Wilson made one other trip to France aboard the vessel, in March 1919.

Ruffolo's ratings on December 31 were reflective of his previous trouble with obedience. Given a "2.8" for proficiency in rating and a perfect "4" for sobriety, he was stung with a "1" rating for obedience and a non-recommendation for reenrollment. However, three months later, his obedience rating improved. With a "2.6" for proficiency and "4" for sobriety, his obedience score was a perfect "4," and he was recommended for reenrollment. He had similar scores for the rest of his enlistment, except that his proficiency rating edged up to "2.7."

On July 26, 1919, Ruffolo took an examination for promotion to fireman second class. In the test covering fourteen subjects, he scored "3.4" overall for proficiency qualification and was recommended for the promotion that he received on August 1, 1919. At the end of August, he was given five days of leave, the only leave on his record during his service. Ruffolo must have been quite happy with life in the Navy. At some point, he expressed his desire to attend the Naval Academy at Annapolis, Maryland. He made his wishes known through channels, and, on October 9, 1919, U.S. Representative Clifford E. Randall (1st District of Wisconsin) wrote to the Navy Department to request that Ruffolo be given leave to attend an examination to determine his fitness to attend the Academy. Randall wrote:

> Lewis Ruffalo [misspelling in the original] who is now assigned to the Steamship *George Washington*, is very desirous of becoming a candidate for appointment to Annapolis, and if this young man can be furloughed to take this examination at Annapolis on November 1st, I shall greatly appreciate the favor.[60]

The next day, the Navy Department wrote to the commander of the *George Washington* requesting that Ruffolo be given leave to take the test. For once the wheels of administration turned fairly quickly, and Ruffolo was released from active duty on October 30. Ruffolo's final monthly pay at the time was $41; he collected his final pay of $146 and made his way from New York, where the *George Washington* was docked, to Annapolis in time to take the examination. Ruffolo did well on the exam and was admitted to the Naval Academy, to start in the fall of 1920.

By January, 1920, Ruffolo was living with his family in Racine; his father, Luigi, was still a railroad section foreman, and his brothers, seventeen-year-old Theodore and sixteen-year-old Frank, worked as a gate tender and time keeper, respectively, on the railroad. Living with them was one boarder, an Italian railroad laborer who had been in the U.S. since 1884. Ruffolo received his final discharge from the Navy on July 1, 1920; at the same time, he was given an honorable discharge lapel button and United States Navy War Service Certificate number 381390.

During his senior year at the Academy in 1924, while a midshipman first class, Ruffolo received his Victory Medal with "Transport" clasp. Although it appears that Ruffolo attended the Naval Academy four years and had graduated, there is no record of his service as a Navy officer; in fact, a Navy Department memo, dated January 25, 1933, bears the notation: "No service in the Navy prior to 15 Aug 1918 nor subsequent to 1 July 1920." It is not known why he did not serve in the Navy after graduation from the Academy, but perhaps medical issues prevented his commissioning.

On August 9, 1924, Ruffolo applied for an adjustment to his war service credit in anticipation for an eventual payout based on his military service. His stateside service is listed from August 6, 1918, to October 21, 1918; his overseas service from October 22, 1918, to June 30, 1919 (the last day allowable for such credit). The total adjustment came to $322; there is no record as to when he received this payment. At the time of his application, Ruffolo was living in Bethlehem, Pennsylvania.

In 1930, Ruffolo lived at the Cornada Hotel in Chicago, where he worked as a night clerk. Such an employment would be atypical of a Naval Academy graduate who had served as a Navy officer; we can only speculate as to the reason, but perhaps he was medically disqualified from service as an officer and had to rejoin civilian life. Still, with a college degree from the Naval Academy, even at the onset of the Great Depression, one might suspect that Ruffolo would be able to find more lucrative employment than a hotel night clerk. For a time in 1940, Ruffolo was a patient at the veterans' hospital in Shields, Illinois. Ruffolo died on April 27, 1965. His brother, Fred Ruffolo, served in the Students' Army Training Corps at the University of Wisconsin during World War I.

Serafino Ruffolo

Serafino Ruffolo was born in Marano Marchesato on January 19, 1891, the son of Luigi Ruffolo and Maria Provenzano. Serafino was the brother of Pietro Ruffolo, who also was a World War I veteran. Serafino came to the U.S. in September 1909, settling in Kenosha. He was one of the first men drafted on September 21, 1917, and he was assigned as a private, serial number 2025509, in the Supply Company, 340th Infantry Regiment, 85th Division, at Camp Custer, Michigan. On December 1, 1917, he was promoted to wagoner. Ruffolo went overseas with his unit in late July 1918. Once overseas, according to his statement of service card, he became "Military Specialist 10/14/18 trans to Personnel Adj[utant] 12/16/18; To Army Serv[ice] Corps 3/1/9." It appears that he moved from infantry supply duties to administrative and personnel duties fairly quickly. His promotion to battalion sergeant major on May 1, 1919, is evidence of his skill in this work.

The Army Service Corps was made up of all the various labor units that served in the vast area behind the lines. Ruffolo's duty with this headquarters ensured that he would be one of the last men to return from overseas. Ruffolo returned on October 6, 1919, and he was discharged at Camp Dix, New Jersey, five days later. After the war, Ruffolo moved to Kentucky. According to his niece:

> [Ruffolo and his wife, Pearl] lived on a farm in Daviess County, Kentucky, just outside Owensboro. I don't recall ever seeing any crops on this farm as the land was very hilly with many gullies but I often helped Aunt Pearl shell the feed corn so that suggests there was a field of it somewhere on the land. I also don't remember any cows on their land but there was always fresh milk, cream, and butter on the table at every meal so it appears there were some cows somewhere nearby. The couple lived in kind of a ramshackle house but neat and clean by anyone's standards. Aunt Pearl raised Persian cats and had several breeder buildings around the house. My uncle must have raised rabbits as I remember once watching him prepare several for the kitchen.[61]

Given a description of Ruffolo in later life, it is no wonder that he achieved a comparatively high rank. According to his niece:

> [Ruffolo] had a distinctive way of carrying himself that said he clearly was someone to be respected. My recollection is that he stood tall with square shoulders, but I wonder if that was his aura rather than his physical stance. He didn't talk a whole lot but he was the kind of person that everyone listened to.[62]

Giuseppe Santelli[63]

Giuseppe Santelli was born in Belsito on August 23, 1894, and he came to the U.S. in April 1913. He was a machinist living in Chicago when he was inducted into the Army on September 20, 1917. Santelli was a private, serial number 2060965, assigned to the 2nd Company, Camp Grant Automatic Replacement Draft, when he boarded the *Powhatan* for shipment to France in April 1918. Although he was assigned to the infantry, at some point, in France, he was transferred to Company "B," 103rd Engineer Regiment, 28th Division. This unit saw combat during the Meuse-Argonne Offensive. It is possible that Santelli was wounded or otherwise injured. He returned to the U.S. in January 1919 as part of Blois Casual Company No. 343. Blois, France, was a city at which the A.E.F. maintained its reclassification depot. Officers who failed in combat were sent to Blois for reclassification; enlisted men were sent there also, for a variety of reasons. Santelli was in physical class C-2 at the time. He was discharged on February 15, and in May, he became a U.S. citizen using his Army service in order to file the petition.

Luigi Santelli

Luigi Santelli was born in Marano Marchesato on May 11, 1896, the son of Benedetto Santelli and Maria Conforti. Benedetto. Benedetto was among the earliest of the Cosenza area immigrants to come to the U.S., arriving aboard the *Utopia* on March 30, 1882. He returned to Italy and raised his family throughout the 1890s. During the 1890s, the family chain migration continued as two of Benedetto's nephews made two trips each to the United States. In 1900, Benedetto returned to the U.S. with his nephews and two of his sons, Gaetano and Francesco. Luigi followed joined this family-based chain migration, arriving in the U.S. on March 19, 1914, destined for his brother, Francesco, in Chicago.

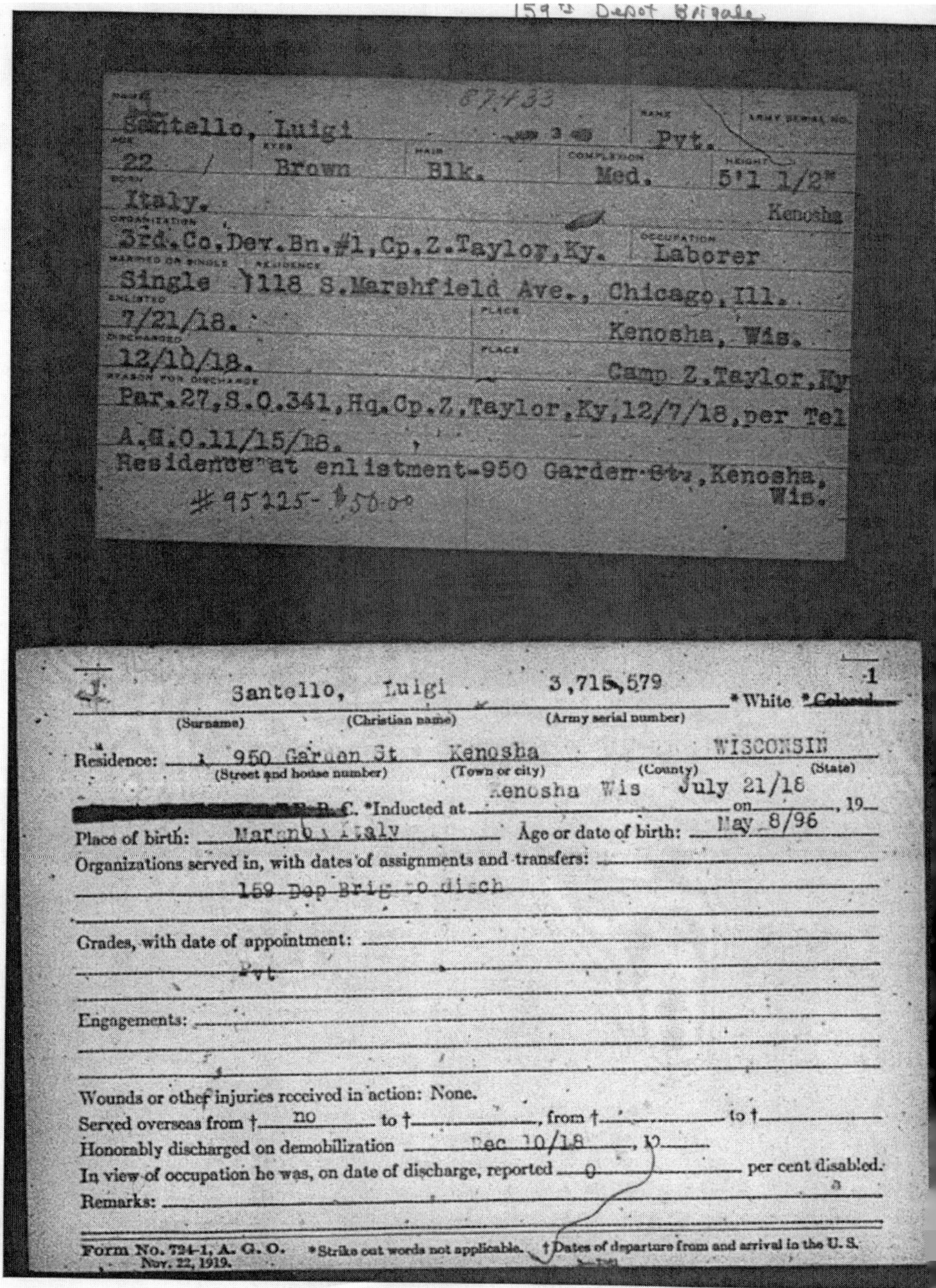

159th Depot Brigade

87433

Santello, Luigi — Pvt.

22 / Brown — Blk. — Med. — 5'1 1/2"

Italy. — Kenosha

3rd.Co.Dev.Bn.#1,Cp.Z.Taylor,Ky. — Laborer

Single 1118 S.Marshfield Ave., Chicago,Ill.

7/21/18. — Kenosha, Wis.

12/10/18. — Camp Z.Taylor,Ky

Par.27,S.O.341,Hq.Cp.Z.Taylor,Ky,12/7/18,per Tel A.G.O.11/15/18.

Residence at enlistment-950 Garden St.,Kenosha, Wis.

#95225-$50.00

Santello, Luigi 3,715,579 (Surname) (Christian name) (Army serial number) *White ~~*Colored~~

Residence: 950 Garden St Kenosha WISCONSIN (Street and house number) (Town or city) (County) (State)

*Inducted at Kenosha Wis on July 21/18, 19

Place of birth: Marsano Italy Age or date of birth: May 8/96

Organizations served in, with dates of assignments and transfers: 159 Dep Brig to disch

Grades, with date of appointment: Pvt

Engagements:

Wounds or other injuries received in action: None.

Served overseas from † no to †, from † to †

Honorably discharged on demobilization Dec 10/18, 19

In view of occupation he was, on date of discharge, reported 0 per cent disabled.

Remarks:

Form No. 724-1, A. G. O. Nov. 22, 1919. *Strike out words not applicable. †Dates of departure from and arrival in the U. S.

Pvt. Luigi Santelli's veteran's bonus application card and statement of service card. (*National Archives*)

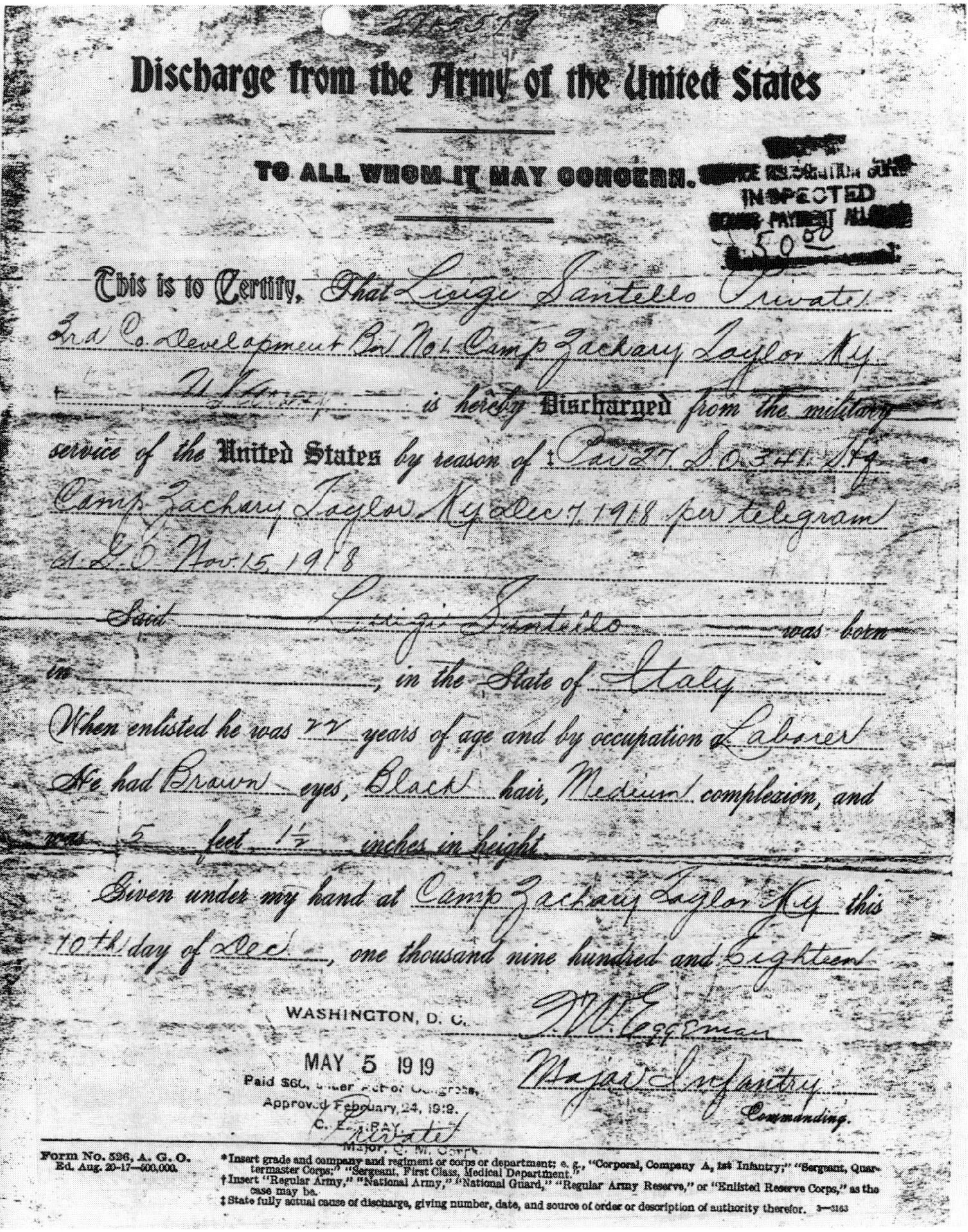

Discharge from the Army of the United States

TO ALL WHOM IT MAY CONCERN.

INSPECTED

BONUS PAYMENT ALLOWED

$50.00

This is to Certify, That Luigi Santello Private 3rd Co. Development Bn No 1 Camp Zachary Taylor Ky. N.A. is hereby Discharged from the military service of the United States by reason of Par 27 S.O. 341 Hq Camp Zachary Taylor Ky Dec 7 1918 per telegram A.G.O. Nov 15 1918

Said Luigi Santello was born in ______, in the State of Italy

When enlisted he was 22 years of age and by occupation Laborer

He had Brown eyes, Black hair, Medium complexion, and was 5 feet 1½ inches in height.

Given under my hand at Camp Zachary Taylor Ky this 10th day of Dec, one thousand nine hundred and Eighteen

WASHINGTON, D. C.

MAY 5 1919

Paid $60, under Act of Congress, Approved February 24, 1919.

C. E. RAY

Major, Q. M. Corps

Private

T. W. Eggeman

Major Infantry

Commanding.

Form No. 526, A. G. O.
Ed. Aug. 20-17—500,000.

*Insert grade and company and regiment or corps or department; e. g., "Corporal, Company A, 1st Infantry;" "Sergeant, Quartermaster Corps;" "Sergeant, First Class, Medical Department."

†Insert "Regular Army," "National Army," "National Guard," "Regular Army Reserve," or "Enlisted Reserve Corps," as the case may be.

‡State fully actual cause of discharge, giving number, date, and source of order or description of authority therefor. 3—3163

Pvt. Luigi Santelli's honorable discharge front side, 1918. (*National Archives*)

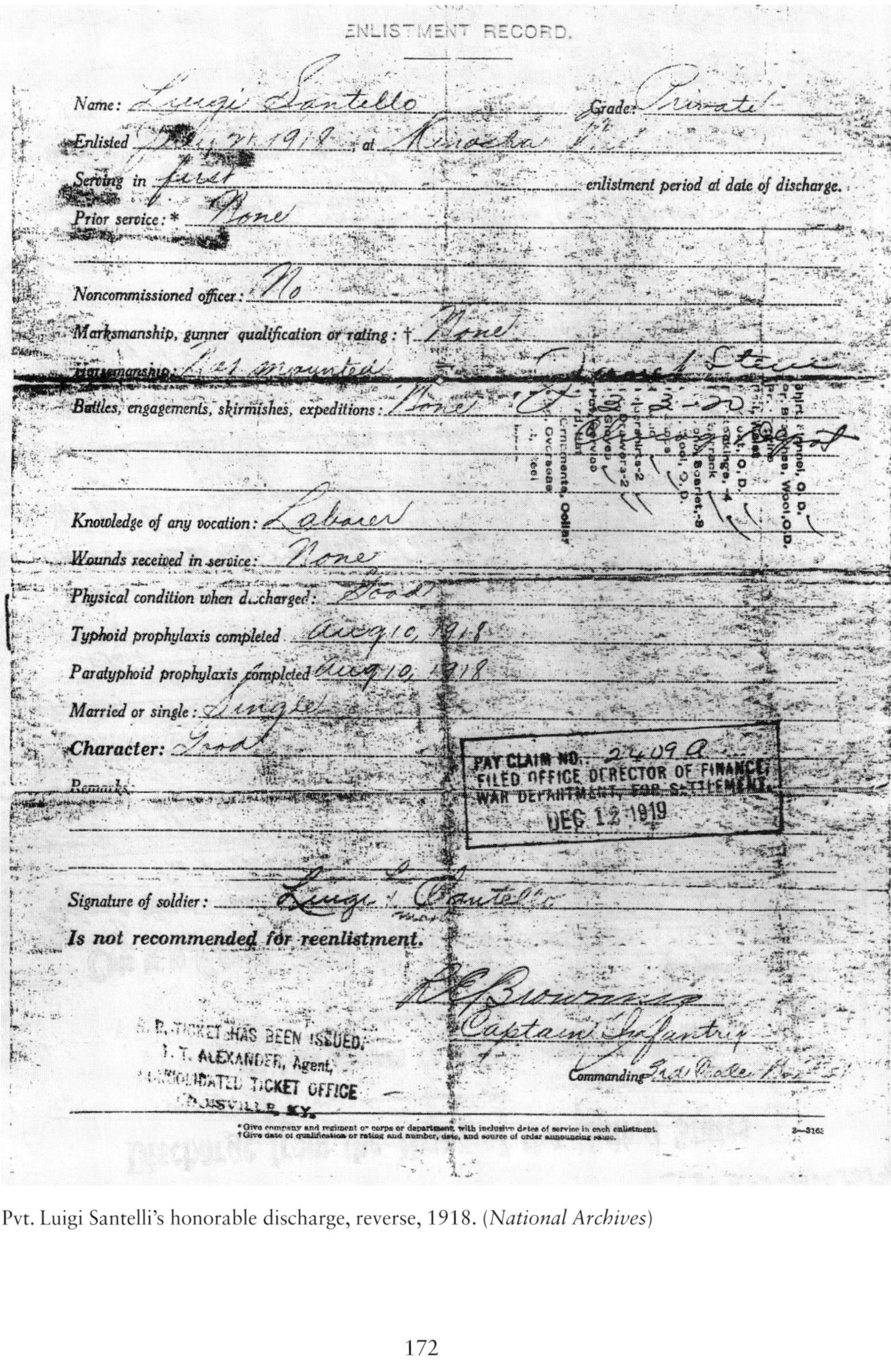

ENLISTMENT RECORD.

Name: Luigi Santello Grade: Private

Enlisted July 2?, 1918, at Kenosha Wis.

Serving in first enlistment period at date of discharge.

Prior service:* None

Noncommissioned officer: No

Marksmanship, gunner qualification or rating: † None

Horsemanship: Not mounted

Battles, engagements, skirmishes, expeditions: None

Knowledge of any vocation: Laborer

Wounds received in service: None

Physical condition when discharged: Good

Typhoid prophylaxis completed Aug 10, 1918

Paratyphoid prophylaxis completed Aug 10, 1918

Married or single: Single

Character: Good

Remarks:

PAY CLAIM NO. 2409 A
FILED OFFICE DIRECTOR OF FINANCE,
WAR DEPARTMENT, FOR SETTLEMENT.
DEC 12 1919

Signature of soldier: Luigi Santello

Is not recommended for reenlistment.

R. C. Browning
Captain Infantry
Commanding

R. R. TICKET HAS BEEN ISSUED,
T. T. ALEXANDER, Agent,
CONSOLIDATED TICKET OFFICE
LOUISVILLE, KY.

*Give company and regiment or corps or department, with inclusive dates of service in each enlistment.
†Give date of qualification or rating and number, date, and source of order announcing same.

Pvt. Luigi Santelli's honorable discharge, reverse, 1918. (*National Archives*)

Santelli was a laborer at the Black Cat Textile Company in Kenosha when he was inducted into the Army on July 21, 1918, and became a private, serial number 3715579, assigned to 3rd Company, Development Battalion 1, 159th Depot Brigade, at Camp Taylor, Kentucky. He was discharged there on December 10, 1918.

In later years, according to his nephew, Albino, who served in the South Pacific during World War II, Santelli joked that he had been drafted and that the Army "sent [him] all the way to Kentucky."[64] Albino Santelli recalled his uncle fondly, saying he was a good man and a "flashy dresser" who was also interested in "wine, women, and song." He also said that Luigi was proud of his service in the U.S. Army, and that he was a long-time member of the American Legion, a veteran's group formed in France for World War I veterans, and later expanded to include all wartime veterans.[65] Santelli died in a Veterans' Administration hospital in Hines, Illinois, in 1974.

Enrico (Harry) Savaglio

Enrico (Harry) Savaglio was born in San Marco Argentano on March 15, 1896, the son of Francesco Savaglio and Costantina Morante. He came to the U.S. in 1913 and settled in Waukegan, Illinois, where he worked as a laborer in a tanning factory. Savaglio entered the Army on June 27, 1918; on August 8, when he became a naturalized U.S. citizen, he was a private in Company "B," 161st Depot Brigade at Camp Grant, Illinois. Savaglio was discharged on February 20, 1919; he died in Waukegan in 1977.

Giuseppe Savaglio

Giuseppe Savaglio was born in January 1891 in Marano Principato. Savaglio was living in Kenosha when he was inducted into the Army on October 22, 1918, and assigned as a private, serial number 3035283, in the 13th Company, New Orleans Coast Artillery Corps. He was discharged on December 17, 1918, at Camp Dodge, Iowa.

Luigi Savaglio

Luigi Savaglio was born on December 12, 1896, in Marano Principato. He was living in Kenosha when he was inducted into the Army on October 21, 1918. Savaglio was a private, serial number 4303046, assigned initially to Company 1, Recruit Detachment, at Camp Shelby, Mississippi. While at there, he became a naturalized U.S. citizen. On November 4, Savaglio transferred to Company 2, Infantry Replacements, also at Camp Shelby. On November 8, he was assigned to 8th Company, November Automatic Replacement Draft (NARD) at Camp Shelby. On December 19, he was transferred to 5th Provisional Battalion, 19th Discharge Company, at Camp Grant, Illinois, where he was discharged on December 28.

Silvio Mariano Savaglio

Silvio Savaglio was born in October 8, 1892, in Marano Principato. He was a barber living in Waukegan, Illinois, when he was inducted into the Army on September 17, 1918. Savaglio was a private, serial number 4423758, in the 2nd Company, 161st Depot Brigade, at Camp Grant, Illinois. He was naturalized as a U.S. citizen on November 20 at Camp Grant, and he was discharged on December 7, 1918. Savaglio died in Kenosha in 1953.

Ernest Scarpelli

Ernest Scarpelli was born on December 10, 1887, in Lappano. He came to the U.S. in 1902 or 1903 and was a laundryman for the Chicago, Milwaukee, and St. Paul Railway in Chicago when he entered the Army on September 22, 1917. Scarpelli was a private, serial number 1377841, in Battery "D," 123rd Field Artillery Regiment, 33rd Division, when he went overseas aboard the *Scotian* on May 27, 1918. He was promoted to private first class during the war and returned to the U.S. aboard U.S.S. *America* on May 24, 1919. He was discharged on June 7 and lived in Chicago after the war.

Francesco Scola

Francesco Andrea Scola was born in Marano Marchesato on July 15, 1886, the son of Antonio Scola and Antonia Ritacca. Scola was a railroad laborer for the Northern Pacific Railway Company, living in Chicago, when he was inducted into the Army on May 26, 1918. He was assigned as a private, serial number 2826875, in the 161st Depot Brigade at Camp Grant, Illinois. Scola became a U.S. citizen there on June 20, 1918. He was discharged on January 8, 1919.

Giuseppe Serpe

Giuseppe (Joseph) Serpe was born on April 27, 1890, in Marano Marchesato, the son of Pasquale Serpe and Fulvia Morelli. Pasquale, Joseph's father, had come to the U.S. in 1890, and settled in Chicago. He probably made at least one round trip back to Italy to bring his family to Chicago. In 1917, Serpe lived with his parents in Chicago; he was employed as a watchman on the Michigan Central Railroad in Michigan City, Indiana. He was already a naturalized citizen, probably on account of his father's U.S. citizenship.

On October 25, 1917, Serpe entered the Army and sometime soon after that he was assigned as a private, serial number 1392636, in Company "D," 124th Machine Gun Battalion, 33rd Division, then training at Camp Logan, Texas. The 33rd went overseas in May 1918, and was assigned to the Australian forces for training

The 33rd Division was engaged in combat during part of the Meuse-Argonne Offensive, from September 26 to about October 24, 1918. The division suffered many casualties while advancing along the west side of the Meuse River. According to a notation on his final pay voucher, Serpe was A.W.O.L. from his unit "fr 10/24/18 to 11/10/18," and again from "11/26/18 to 12/30/18." Absence from one's unit, without leave, during combat is a very serious offense. Serpe's experiences during the fighting along the Meuse might have caused his behavior. Subject to a Summary Court Martial, Serpe was ordered to "forfeit ... 2/3 pay for 6 mos."[66] He returned to the U.S. on May 20, 1919, and was sent to Camp Grant where he was given his final pay and discharged on May 30. Serpe returned to Chicago where for a time he worked as a clerk in a cigar store.

Peter Frank Serpe[67]

Peter Frank Serpe was born in Chicago on February 14, 1897, the son of Francesco (Frank) Serpe and Rosa Chiappetta, both from Marano Marchesato. At the time of his registration for the draft in June 1918, Peter Serpe lived with his family in Chicago, and he was unemployed.

On July 15, 1918, Serpe went to the U.S. Navy Recruiting Station in Chicago where he enlisted in the Navy as a hospital apprentice second class, serial number 1916460. An examination found him to be in good health, 5 feet 4.5 inches tall, and weighing 128 pounds, with brown eyes, black hair, and a ruddy complexion. He listed his mother, Rose, as his next of kin. Serpe was sent to Great Lakes Naval Training Center, north of Chicago, for his training and service. All seemed to go well until December 3, 1918, when Serpe was A.W.O.L. for three days. A summary court martial on January 7, 1919, gave him punishment: "conf. for 20 days with EPD. LOP [loss of pay] $35.90. LOP reduced to $29.40." Serpe was in store for more trouble; on February 2, 1919, he was A.W.O.L. for forty-two hours. Another court-martial, this one on February 15, meted out punishment: "45 days with EPD. LOP $107.70. LOP is reduced to $48.80."

The next series of annotations in his service record display more trouble and confusion. Serpe was "declared a deserter May 27, 1919 account of AOL [probably A.W.O.L.] since April 8, 1919 art. 3604 and 3610 complied with. Effects sold at auction." However, this entry is lined out, and the following note is stamped in the record: "The Bureau, being satisfied that the above named man did not intend to desert, the mark of desertion is removed as erroneous."[68] There is no indication of what had occurred to warrant this absence and the subsequent record notations.

If, as seems likely, Serpe served his first sentence directly after it was handed down, then he must have gone A.W.O.L. the second time almost immediately upon being released from confinement. He must also have then "deserted" after serving his second sentence. Somehow, he must have gotten the impression that he was allowed to leave and go to his home; perhaps this is the explanation of the mark of desertion and its later removal. In any event, Serpe was given an "undesirable discharge," with no recommendation for reenlistment, on August 1, 1919.

Serpe's past was almost the cause of some trouble in the following year. In a letter dated November 8, 1920, addressed to the Chief, Bureau of Navigation, Frank Joy, a detective (whether private or police is unclear), wrote:

> Sir:—On April 8th 1919 Peter F. Serpe deserted at Great Lakes. I have located him and would like paper for his apprehension if he has not already been discharged since desertion. As he is liable to leave his present location at any time I would appreciated an early response [*sic.*].[69]

On November 26, the bureau responded that Serpe "was discharged from the Naval Service August 1, 1919 and his custody is, therefore, not desired." This, then, was the end of any legal threat to Serpe resulting from his supposed desertion. In 1924, Congress passed the Adjusted Compensation Act, providing deferred bonuses to qualified World War I veterans. Perhaps because of his receipt of an "undesirable discharge" Serpe appears to have taken no action to claim this bonus. However, on March 9, 1938, the Navy sent him an application for this bonus. On March 14, Serpe wrote a letter asking for paperwork to prove that he had served in the Navy, presumably preparatory to applying for the bonus. That letter was erroneously forwarded to the War Department, instead of the Navy. The missive was duly sent to the Bureau of Navigation; the bureau on March 28, replied to Serpe, giving him the particulars of his service in the Navy, including his receipt of an "undesirable discharge." Serpe replied on April 12, asking, "am I entitled to a bonus[?] The department send me an application for Adjusted Compensation on March 9, 1938. P.S. World War [*sic.*]."[70] A week later, the Navy confirmed that he was, indeed, entitled to a bonus. Shortly thereafter, Serpe completed the application, which made affidavit of the facts of his service in the Navy during the war; witnesses were Joseph Kotrich, a dentist who had known Serpe for twenty years, and Martin Schupmann, a doctor who had known him for thirty-five years. There is no record showing how much Serpe received for this bonus.

Serafino Serpe

Serafino (Sam) Serpe was born on January 14, 1897, in Marano Marchesato. He came to the U.S. in 1910 and settled in Kenosha. He was inducted into the Army on April 26, 1918, and was assigned as a private, serial number 2048414, in the 160th Depot Brigade, Camp Custer, Michigan. On May 21, he was transferred to Field Hospital 340, 310th Sanitary Train, part of the 85th Division at Camp Custer.

On July 31, Serpe went overseas with the division. Sometime during late October 1918, the 85th Division moved forward to became a regional replacement division for the 2nd Army. Serpe must have deployed forward; his statement of service card bears the notation: "Meuse and Moselle Rivers Nov 9 to Nov 11, 1918." This entitled him to the award of the "Defensive Sector" clasp to his World War I Victory Medal. Serpe returned to the U.S. on April 11, 1919, and he was discharged on April 26 at Camp Grant, Illinois.

Filiberto Settino[71]

Filiberto (Albert) Settino was born on September 21, 1895, in Marano Marchesato, the son of Giovanni Settino and Carmela Chiappetta. He came to the U.S. in 1913, joining his brothers, Luigi, Achille, and Santo, in Chicago. At the time of his registration for the draft in 1917, Settino was a barber living in Chicago.

Sometime in early 1918, Settino was informed that he had been selected to undergo examination to determine his fitness to serve in the military. On March 28, 1918, he appeared at the local draft examination board on Blue Island Avenue to submit to that examination. First, he answered some basic questions about his health. Yes, he considered himself to be "sound and well." No, he had never been "under treatment in any hospital or asylum," nor had he been confined to his "bed at home under a physician's care within the past year." Next he underwent a physical examination that found him to be 5 feet 3.75 inches tall and weighing 112 pounds. His vision was 20/20 in both eyes and he possessed all this teeth. There were no physical abnormalities found, and he was thus certified as being "physically qualified for general military service."

Sometime soon thereafter, he was notified to report for induction into the Army. Earlier drafts of men from Chicago and northern Illinois had reported to Camp Grant, Illinois, for induction and initial training in the 161st Depot Brigade. Settino, however, was an exception to that trend. On June 23, he was inducted at Local Board Number 42 in Chicago and by June 26, he was at Camp Jackson, South Carolina, where he became a private, serial number 2999899, assigned to the 25th Company, 7th Training Battalion, 156th Depot Brigade.

Two days later, Settino, along with other recruits, was once again examined. Military doctors found no change in his condition, and he was also examined for tuberculosis, cardiovascular, and bone problems, all of which came up negative. He also received some vaccinations. A new measurement found him 5 feet 4 inches tall, with brown eyes, black hair, and a fair complexion. This thorough examination also found that he had a scar near his left nipple and one on his left knee. Measurements for military uniform issuance showed that he required a size 7C shoe. He listed his brother, Achille, in Chicago, as his next of kin. A review of his educational qualifications revealed that he had no schooling and that he spoke English and Italian; he was rated "D" for intelligence. It was also noted that he was a barber by trade and that he had run a three-chair barbershop, from which he made $30 per week. In early July, Settino signed up for the government provided war risk insurance that provided for $10,000 to be paid to a serviceman's beneficiary in the event of his death while in the service. This cost each man $6.50 per month. Settino also started a monthly allotment of $15 for family support, probably paid to his mother in Italy.

This preliminary review and examination done, Settino next prepared for training while in the training battalion. It is not know what rudimentary training he received before he was transferred, on July 18, to Company "D," 306th Ammunition Train, part of the newly forming 81st Division at Camp Jackson. At that time, his character was given as "good." The function of an ammunition train was to bring ammunition from supply dumps forward to the divisional artillery units. Lifting, carrying, and hauling these explosives along ruined, crowded roads in the dark of night, often while under enemy bombardment, was mentally and physically draining. The men had to take care of their equipment, whether it was horses, mules, carts and wagons, or motor trucks. All this had to be learned in addition to the basic duties of a soldier, such as customs and courtesies, wearing the uniform, drilling and marching, and marksmanship.

But time was a precious commodity in the summer of 1918; the United States needed to send men and material to France quickly and in large numbers. So, in late July, Settino, along with the rest of the 306th Ammunition Train, moved to Camp Mills, New York, in preparation for deployment to France. Settino was naturalized as a U.S. citizen at Camp Mills on July 30, 1918. Settino sailed with his unit aboard the *Cretic*, an ocean liner converted to troop transport, on August 8; the *Cretic* landed in England on August 19. The men arrived in France about two days later. It is interesting to note that, in less than two months, Settino had gone from being a civilian to being a soldier in France, awaiting combat. Considering that several weeks of this time was given to administrative matters and transportation between stations as well as the lengthy ocean voyage, one might well wonder just how much training Settino and other men received prior to entering combat.

One indication of the paucity of training that was given to men drafted at this time is in Settino's service record. There are no annotations in the sections for Record of Known Distance Rifle Practice or Record of Pistol Firing. Of course, this does not necessarily mean that he did not have such training or practice, but unit histories are replete with references to replacements that had never fired a rifle arriving at combat units in the summer and fall of 1918.

Little is known of Settino's precise activities overseas. Surely he underwent training with his unit at various bases in France. He attended gas school at Vercel, France, where he passed through a gas chamber on October 10, 1918, during the height of the Meuse-Argonne Offensive. Soon after, his unit was engaged in that battle, to that point the largest ever engaged in by United States military forces. His service record bears the notation, "In active sector with Division south of Verdun, November 3 to 11, 1918, inclusive. Meuse-Argonne Offensive." This entitled him to the award of the "Meuse-Argonne" and "Defensive Sector" battle clasps to his Victory Medal, issued to all veterans beginning in 1920. It is not known whether Settino applied for or received this medal.

After the Armistice, Settino participated in the more or less mundane aspects of military life: drill, maintenance of equipment and animals, etc. The men were also allowed such distractions as sports competitions and occasional leave to visit local areas. As an indication of the inevitable laxness that might be expected to follow any military campaign of this magnitude, Settino seems to have ignored some aspects of his duties. On January 11, 1919, he was cited for having "dirty equipment." As punishment, he was "confined to Co. area until equip'nt is cleaned up, and put on K.P. fr 12:00 noon Sat until Sun night." Such a minor blemish was probably to be seen in the records of many men in the A.E.F. On February 18, he was awarded a War Service Chevron, a gold chevron to be worn on the lower left sleeve, each of which indicated six months' service overseas. Men were awarded an additional chevron for each six months' period of service overseas.

On April 10, in recognition of the fact that he had run a three-chair barbershop, Settino was made company barber; he also was designated an "ammunition cannoneer." That the military keeps meticulous records cannot be denied, and Settino's service record bears that out. On April 1, Settino was issued such items as: a belt, an O.D. (olive drab) blanket, brassards, woolen breeches (size 32), a service cap, woolen coat (size 36), woolen drawers, gloves, spiral leggings (called puttees by the men), collar disks or insignia, overcoat, two flannel shirts, two pairs of shoes, four pairs of woolen stockings, two woolen undershirts, and a toilet kit. Some purely military articles issued included a standard model 1910 mess kit consisting of a meat can, cup, knife, fork, and spoon, condiment can, brush and thong, canteen cover, cartridge belt, gun sling, haversack, oiler and thong case, pack carrier, first aid pouch, gas mask, helmet, rifle cover, and rifle (serial number 637729). Various items of tent equipment completed his kit. In May, Settino turned in many of these items prior to departure from Europe.

Prior to his leaving France, Settino made affidavit of his home of record, for future travel pay purposes. On June 9, he boarded the *Roanoke* and sailed for the United States. The grateful soldiers aboard the *Roanoke* arrived at Charleston, South Carolina, on June 22. On June 24, shortly after arrival at Camp Jackson, Settino was transferred to the Camp Grant Detachment. This group consisted of men at Camp Jackson who lived in the northern Illinois area and who would be discharged from Camp Grant, comparatively near their homes. At that time, Settino's character was given as "excellent." On July 2, Settino, along with many other men from the 306th Ammunition Train and related units, was given his final pay (amounting to $76.20 in his case) and his discharge from the U.S. Army.

In another display of its meticulousness and thoroughness, the Army performed various audits of its payroll in the postwar period. Many men were given various types of back pay. There must have been some type of problem with Settino's wartime $15 monthly family allotment because he was issued a check for $166 in repayment of the allotment, covering almost the entire period of its life, August 1, 1918, to his discharge on July 2, 1919.

In 1924, Congress authorized an increased compensation for veterans of the World War. Commonly called the veterans' bonus, it gave men about $1 per day for stateside service and about $1.25 per day for overseas service, subject to certain constraints. On November 4, 1924, Settino made application for the bonus, attesting to his service on the prescribed affidavit witnessed by Louis Scaramuzzo and Silvio Belgioiello (who was himself a veteran, having served from Kenosha). The calculated amount due was $391.25; he listed his daughter, Carmella, in Chicago, as beneficiary. It was this application, which listed Settino's birth as March, 1897, that started a minor paperwork flurry seeking to determine Settino's actual date of birth. One office, probably the Adjutant General's office, made reference to the application, stating: "Date of birth shown therein as March 1897. Records this office show age time of enl was 23 yrs and date of birth as July 21, 1896: Sept 23, 1889."[72]

The Adjutant General's office, on November 22, sent a letter to Settino discussing this inconsistency and requesting "satisfactory evidence in proof of the correct date of your birth," in the form of one of a list of items including birth certificate, baptismal certificate, affidavit of parent, certified extract from a family bible, among other things. It is fairly certain that Settino had none of these things at hand, although a certified birth certificate from Marano Marchesato could have been gotten with some effort. On January 14, 1925, it was determined that March 23, 1897 was Settino's correct date of birth. Presumably he was authorized his bonus at that time. Strangely, in 1966, another date of birth, September 21, 1895, which is probably the actual date of birth, appears on a Veterans' Administration form requesting information on Settino's record. Even this form gives the notation: "Enl age: 23 yr 5 mo," which, of course, contradicts the stated birth date. Settino worked in a factory after the war; he died at Melrose Park, Illinois, in 1973.

Benedetto Sicilia

Benedetto Sicilia was born on January 10, 1895, in Marano Marchesato, the son of Francesco Sicilia and Filomena Porro. Members of the extended Sicilia family had begun to immigrate from Marano Marchesato to the U.S. beginning in the early 1880s and continuing throughout the 1890s when several of Benedetto's cousins journeyed to Chicago. Others went to Springfield, Illinois. These men, and others of the Sicilia clan, were birds of passage, making many trips between Italy and the U.S. over a period of many years.

Members of another branch of the Sicilia family began a migration chain in the early 1900s. Several of Benedetto's cousins and his uncle, aunt, and brother had settled in Kenosha and Chicago by the time he came to the U.S. in 1913 with still other cousins. Sicilia was a laborer at the N. R. Allen and Sons tannery in Kenosha when he was inducted into the Army on August 26, 1918. He was a private, serial number 3546062, assigned to the 19th Company, 5th Training Battalion, 158th Depot Brigade, at Camp Sherman, Ohio.[73]

The war ended on November 11, 1918, and soon the stateside Army units began their peacetime drawdown. On December 6, 1918, Sicilia was assigned to Company "A," Development Battalion No. 6, 158th Depot Brigade. He drew his final pay, $44.10, and then received his discharge. Along with hundreds of other men, Sicilia returned to Kenosha to continue his life. Sometime in 1919, Sicilia was awarded a Wisconsin veterans' bonus, the amount of which was determined by each man's length of service, and on overseas service. Sicilia's bonus came to $50, probably the minimum amount awarded.

In 1920, Sicilia lived with his brother and uncle in Kenosha, but he soon returned to Italy to be married. On June 25, 1921, in the neighboring village of Marano Principato, he married Innocenza Nigro. Benedetto and Innocenza started a family in Marano Principato. Sadly, on January 29, 1926, in Marano Marchesato, Benedetto Sicilia died, the death resulting from adenoma of the left kidney. While in service, Sicilia had taken advantage of the war risk insurance program, administered by the Treasury Department and made available to servicemen. It provided for $10,000 death benefit for the soldier's designated beneficiary. At the time of his enrollment, Sicilia had designated his father, Francesco, as beneficiary. Upon discharge from the Army, Sicilia elected to keep this insurance in effect. After his marriage, Sicilia named his wife, Innocenza, as his beneficiary, and she filed for a pension based upon her deceased husband's wartime U.S. military service. In 1947, 1949, and 1951, Innocenza filled out bilingual Veterans' Administration claims forms certifying, for each year previous, that she remained the widow of Benedetto, and she had no children under eighteen years of age. She also

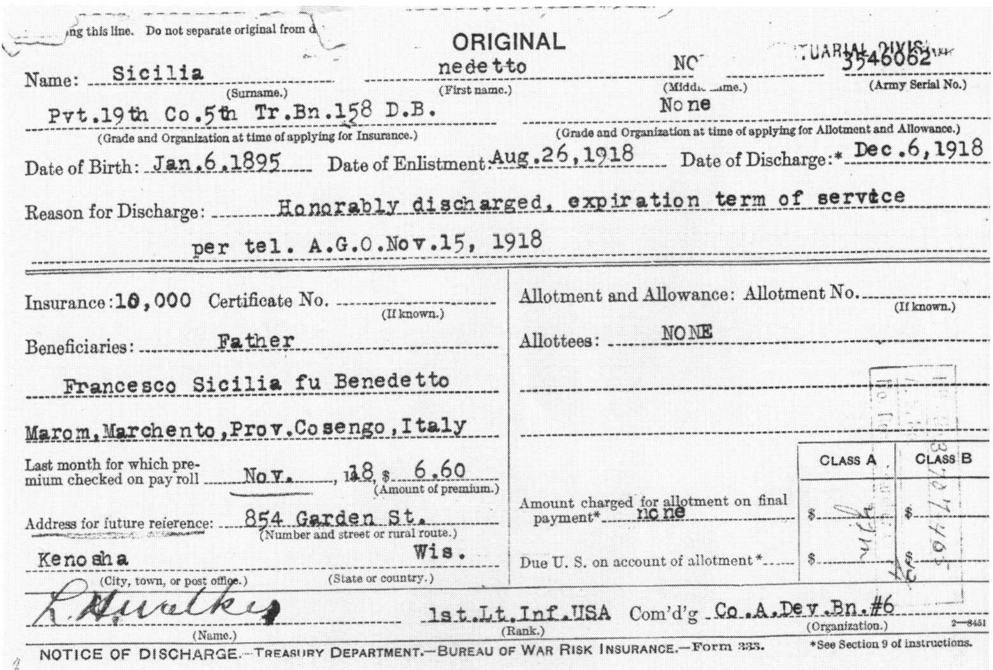
ng this line. Do not separate original from d

ORIGINAL

Name: Sicilia (Surname.) nedetto (First name.) NO (Middle name.) 3546062 (Army Serial No.)

Pvt.19th Co.5th Tr.Bn.158 D.B. (Grade and Organization at time of applying for Insurance.) None (Grade and Organization at time of applying for Allotment and Allowance.)

Date of Birth: Jan.6.1895 Date of Enlistment: Aug.26,1918 Date of Discharge:* Dec.6,1918

Reason for Discharge: Honorably discharged, expiration term of service per tel. A.G.O.Nov.15, 1918

Insurance: 10,000 Certificate No. (If known.)

Beneficiaries: Father Francesco Sicilia fu Benedetto Marom,Marchento,Prov.Cosengo,Italy

Last month for which premium checked on pay roll Nov., 18, $ 6.60 (Amount of premium.)

Address for future reference: 854 Garden St. (Number and street or rural route.) Kenosha (City, town, or post office.) Wis. (State or country.)

Allotment and Allowance: Allotment No. (If known.)

Allottees: NONE

	CLASS A	CLASS B
Amount charged for allotment on final payment* none	$	$
Due U. S. on account of allotment*	$	$

L. Hurlkes (Name.) 1st.Lt.Inf.USA (Rank.) Com'd'g Co.A.Dev.Bn.#6 (Organization.) 2—8451

NOTICE OF DISCHARGE.—TREASURY DEPARTMENT.—BUREAU OF WAR RISK INSURANCE.—Form 333. *See Section 9 of instructions.

Pvt. Benedetto Sicilia's application for War Risk Life Insurance, 1918. Note that his beneficiary, Benedetto's father, is listed as "Francesco fu Benedetto," which means, in Italian, "Francesco, son of the deceased Benedetto." His address is given as "Marom, Marchento, Prov. Cosengo, Italy." The actual address should read: "Marano Marchesato, Prov. Cosenza, Italy." (*National Archives*)

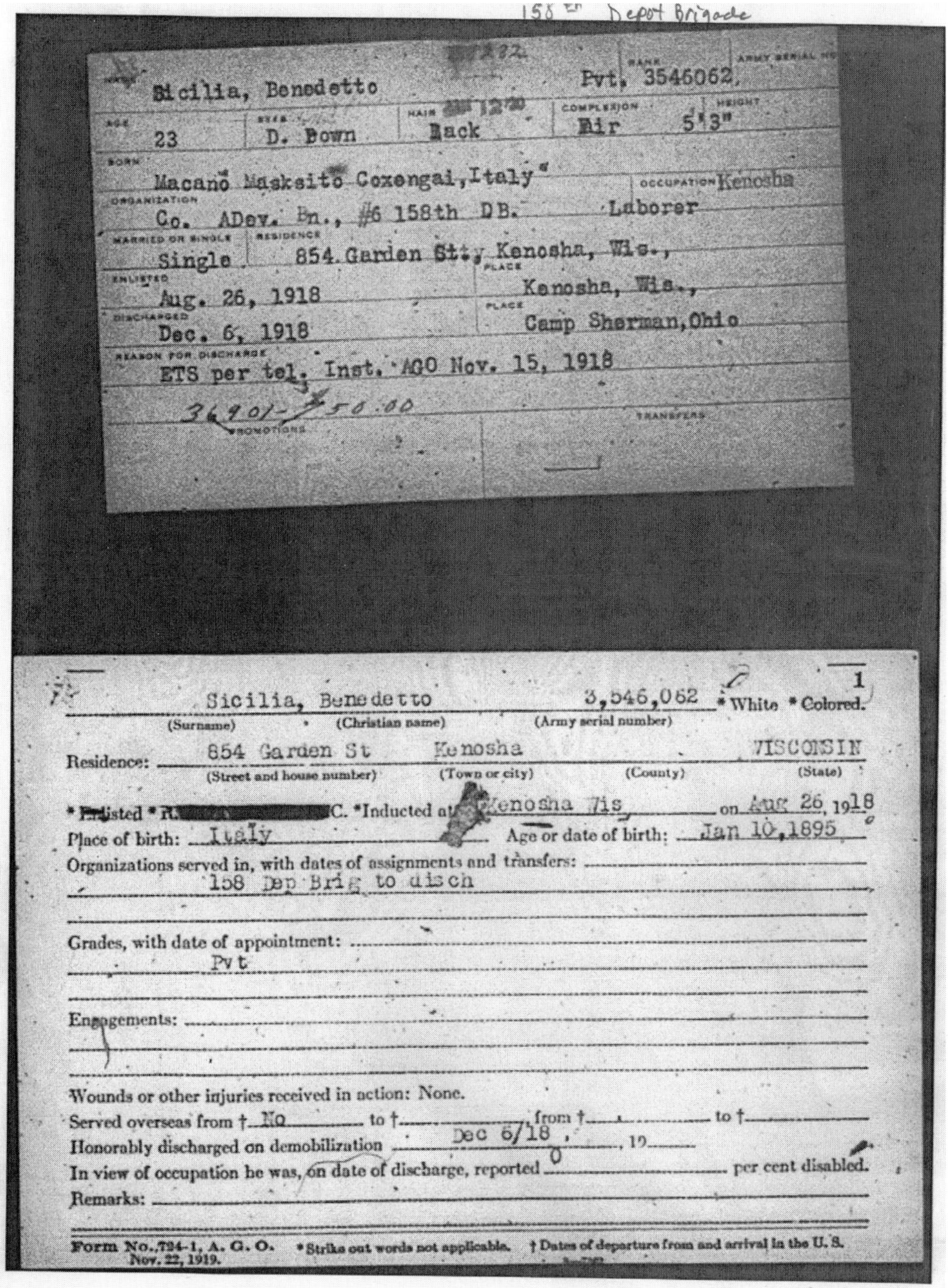

158th Depot Brigade

NAME Sicilia, Benedetto — RANK Pvt. — ARMY SERIAL NO. 3546062

AGE 23 — EYES D. Bown — HAIR Back — COMPLEXION Fair — HEIGHT 5'3"

BORN Macanô Maskeitô Coxengai, Italy — OCCUPATION Kenosha Laborer

ORGANIZATION Co. A Dev. Bn., #6 158th DB.

MARRIED OR SINGLE Single — RESIDENCE 854 Garden St., Kenosha, Wis.,

ENLISTED Aug. 26, 1918 — PLACE Kenosha, Wis.,

DISCHARGED Dec. 6, 1918 — PLACE Camp Sherman, Ohio

REASON FOR DISCHARGE ETS per tel. Inst. AGO Nov. 15, 1918

36901- $50.00

PROMOTIONS — TRANSFERS

Sicilia, Benedetto 3,546,062 * White * Colored. 1

(Surname) (Christian name) (Army serial number)

Residence: 854 Garden St Kenosha WISCONSIN

(Street and house number) (Town or city) (County) (State)

* Enlisted * R.A. * N.G. * E.R.C. *Inducted at Kenosha Wis on Aug 26 1918

Place of birth: Italy Age or date of birth: Jan 10, 1895

Organizations served in, with dates of assignments and transfers:

158 Dep Brig to disch

Grades, with date of appointment:

Pvt

Engagements:

Wounds or other injuries received in action: None.

Served overseas from † No to † from † to †

Honorably discharged on demobilization Dec 6/18, 19

In view of occupation he was, on date of discharge, reported 0 per cent disabled.

Remarks:

Form No. 724-1, A. G. O. Nov. 22, 1919. *Strike out words not applicable. † Dates of departure from and arrival in the U. S.

Pvt. Benedetto Sicilia's veteran's bonus application card statement of service card. (*Wisconsin Veterans Museum*) certified that she had no income and no property other than "a small two room house occupied by a relative of my deceased husband who does not pay any rent." She had received gratuitous assistance in filling out at least the 1947 forms from the American Legion, Department of Italy. No records have been found after 1951.

This story illustrates the blood and economic ties between the United States and Italy. The fact that there was a U.S. war veterans group, the American Legion, with a separate department in Italy is evidence the many Italian American veterans of World War I who returned to Italy following their wartime service, as had Benedetto Sicilia. Indeed, one wonders how active this Italian branch of the American Legion was during World War II, when America and Italy were no longer allies, but temporary enemies instead. Calabria in the 1920s through the 1940s was a harsh place to live. Sicilia's widow must have struggled to survive. The 1951 form shows that she received a $42 payment, not much money if that is one's sole income for the year.

Anthony Francis Spizzirri

Anthony Francis Spizzirri was born in Chicago on April 5, 1895, the son of Domenico Spizzirri and Teresa Lucchetti; both Domenico and Teresa were from villages near Cosenza and had come to the U.S. in the mid 1880s and early 1890s.

Anthony Spizzirri was a utility man living in Chicago when he was drafted into the National Army on May 27, 1918. He was sent to Camp Grant, Illinois, where he became a private, serial number 2826245, assigned to Company "E," 311th Supply Train, part of the 86th Division. At some point, Spizzirri was promoted to corporal. The 86th Division went to France in August 1918, and upon arrival, the division sent men as replacements to other combat divisions at the front. The 86th was skeletonized, but the 311th Supply Train remained intact and supported the remainder of the division while in France. Spizzirri returned to the U.S. on June 27, 1919. Along with perhaps hundreds of others from his division, he was sent to the demobilization group at Camp Grant. There, on July 8, he was given his final pay of $70.10, which included a deduction of $4 for an allotment and included $4.50 for travel pay to Chicago. After the war, Spizzirri worked as a post office clerk in the Chicago area.

Francesco Spizzirri

Francesco (Frank) Spizzirri was born on July 12, 1894, in Marano Marchesato, the son of Alessandro Spizzirri and Concetta Magro. Spizzirri came to the U.S. with his mother and brothers in 1909, going to join his father in Chicago. He was an order-filler with the Sheppard Strasheim Company, living at in Chicago, when he was inducted into the Army on July 29, 1918. He was assigned as a private, serial number 2757468, in Guard and Fire Company 317, Quartermaster Corps, at Camp Hill, Virginia. Spizzirri was discharged from the Army at Camp Hill on December 10, 1918. He was the brother of Pietro (Peter) Spizzirri, a fellow World War I veteran.

Pietro Spizzirri

Pietro (Peter) Spizzirri was born on July 22, 1896, in Marano Marchesato, the son of Alessandro Spizzirri and Concetta Magro. Spizzirri came to the U.S. with his mother and brothers in 1909, going to join his father, Alessandro, in Chicago. Spizzirri was inducted into the Army on April 28, 1918, and was assigned as a private, serial number 2816945, in Company "I," 3rd Infantry Regiment, at Camp Eagle Pass, Texas. The 3rd Infantry Regiment spent the war patrolling the still-dangerous Mexican border. Spizzirri was given a dependency discharge there on August 23, 1919. He is also recorded under the name Peter Carlo Spitz. He was the brother of Francesco (Frank) Spizzirri, a fellow World War I veteran.

Francesco Tenuta

Francesco Tenuta was born on January 18, 1893, in Marano Principato. He was a bar maker living in Kenosha when he was inducted into the Army on September 21, 1917. Tenuta was a private, serial number 2025587, in the Machine Gun Company, 340th Infantry Regiment, 85th Division, at Camp Custer, Michigan. On December 17, Tenuta was promoted to private first class; less than a month later, on January 8, 1918, he was promoted to corporal. However, on May 22, he was demoted to private, only to be promoted again, to private first class, on June 5. He departed for France with the 85th Division on July 24, 1918. Tenuta was assigned as a replacement to Company "A" (or possibly Company "C"), 10th Machine Gun Battalion, 4th Division, during the Meuse-Argonne Offensive, on November 5, 1918. After the Armistice, Tenuta served with the 4th Division as part of the Army of Occupation in Germany. He returned to the U.S. on July 27, 1919, and he was sent to Camp Grant, Illinois, where he was discharged on August 19.

Giovanni Tenuta

Giovanni Tenuta was born on February 20, 1887, in Marano Principato. He was an "auto driver" living in Kenosha when he was inducted into the Army on May 26, 1918. Tenuta was a private, serial number 2825661, in Company "I," 344th Infantry Regiment, 86th Division, at Camp Grant, Illinois. He departed for France with the 86th Division on September 8, 1918. The 86th was used as a replacement pool upon arrival in France. Tenuta was assigned as a replacement to Company "C," 318th Infantry Regiment, 80th Division, during the Meuse-Argonne Offensive, on October 1, 1918. He served in the Meuse-Argonne Offensive with his regiment from November 1–7, 1918. Tenuta returned to the U.S. on May 27, 1919, and he was sent to Camp Grant where he was discharged on June 10. Tenuta lived in Kenosha after the war, and he died on December 22, 1954.

Raffaele Tenuta

Raffaele Tenuta was born in Marano Marchesato on September 29, 1894. He came to the U.S. in 1912, and he was a fireman on the Illinois Central Railroad, living in Chicago, when he was inducted into the Army in February or March 1918. Tenuta was a private, serial number 950380, in the 11th Company, 3rd Development Battalion, at Camp Logan, Texas, when he became a naturalized U.S. citizen on November 22, 1918. He was discharged at Camp Grant, Illinois, on January 9, 1919, at which time he assigned to the 4th Company, 1st Infantry Replacement and Training Regiment. After his military service, Tenuta moved back to Chicago and resumed working for the Illinois Central Railroad; he died in Chicago in 1952.

Pvt. John Trotta, 66th Field Artillery Regiment, 96th Division. (*A Taste of Memories from Columbus Park*)

John Trotta

John Trotta was born on April 14, 1893 or 1894, in Rota Greca. He came to the U.S. in 1910, and he was working in a freight house in Chicago when he was inducted into the Army on May 23, 1918. Trotta was in Battery "E," 66th Field Artillery Regiment, part of the newly created 96th Division. The artillery regiments for the 96th were forming at Camp Kearny, California. He became a U.S. citizen while stationed there on November 14, 1918. He was discharged on December 29.

Giuseppe Tucci

Giuseppe Tucci was born on June 4, 1892, in Paterno Calabro. He was a railroad laborer living in Chicago when he entered the Army on October 3, 1917. He was a private, serial number 191648, in Company "C," 503rd Engineer Service Battalion, when he left the U.S. aboard the *Aeolus* on November 26, 1917, with less than two months of training. In France, he was sent to the 3rd Engineer Service Company, part of the 20th Engineer Regiment, a forestry unit responsible for forestry and lumber activity for the entire A.E.F. Tucci returned to the U.S. aboard the *Zeelandia* on May 23, 1919; he was discharged on June 2. On September 2, 1919, Tucci became a U.S. citizen using his military service to file the paperwork, but he later lost his citizenship because he moved back to Italy.

Dominick Volpentesta

Dominick Joseph Volpentesta was born on December 17, 1890, in Chicago the son of Luigi Volpentesta and Maria Giraldi, both of whom were from Rende. Volpentesta was a tailor living in Chicago when he was inducted into the Army on September 20, 1917, part of the first batch of drafted soldiers. He was probably sent to Camp Grant, Illinois, where he became a private, serial number 2064005. In November, Camp Grant sent thousands of men to fill up the ranks of the 33rd Division in Camp Logan, Texas; Volpentesta was among them, assigned to the 131st Infantry Regiment. He served overseas with the Headquarters Troop, 33rd Division, and he returned to the U.S. on May 17, 1919. He was sent to the Casual Detachment of the 2nd Training Battalion, 161st Depot Brigade, at Camp Grant for his discharge, which he received on May 30, 1919. He lived in Chicago after the war, working as a tailor. Sometime after 1930, he changed his surname to Testa; he died in 1956.

Domenick Wells (Domenico Guido)

Domenick Wells was born Domenico Guido on July 4, 1896, in Marano Principato, the son of Domenico or Eugenio Guido and Carmina Baratta. He came to the U.S. in 1910, destined to join his brothers, Gaetano and Annunziato, in Racine. Wells was a shoemaker living in Racine when he was inducted into the Army on October 25, 1918. He was a private, serial number 5037151, in Company "A," Development Battalion, Camp Shelby, Mississippi. Wells was discharged on January 3, 1919, at Camp Grant, Illinois. He was admitted to the Veterans Hospital in Milwaukee for two days in February 1927, under observation for tuberculosis; his actual diagnosis is unknown. Wells died in Racine in 1948.[74]

Pvt. Dominick Volpentesta, 33rd Division, *c.* 1918 or 1919. (*Tony Molinaro, Carol Stream, Illinois*)

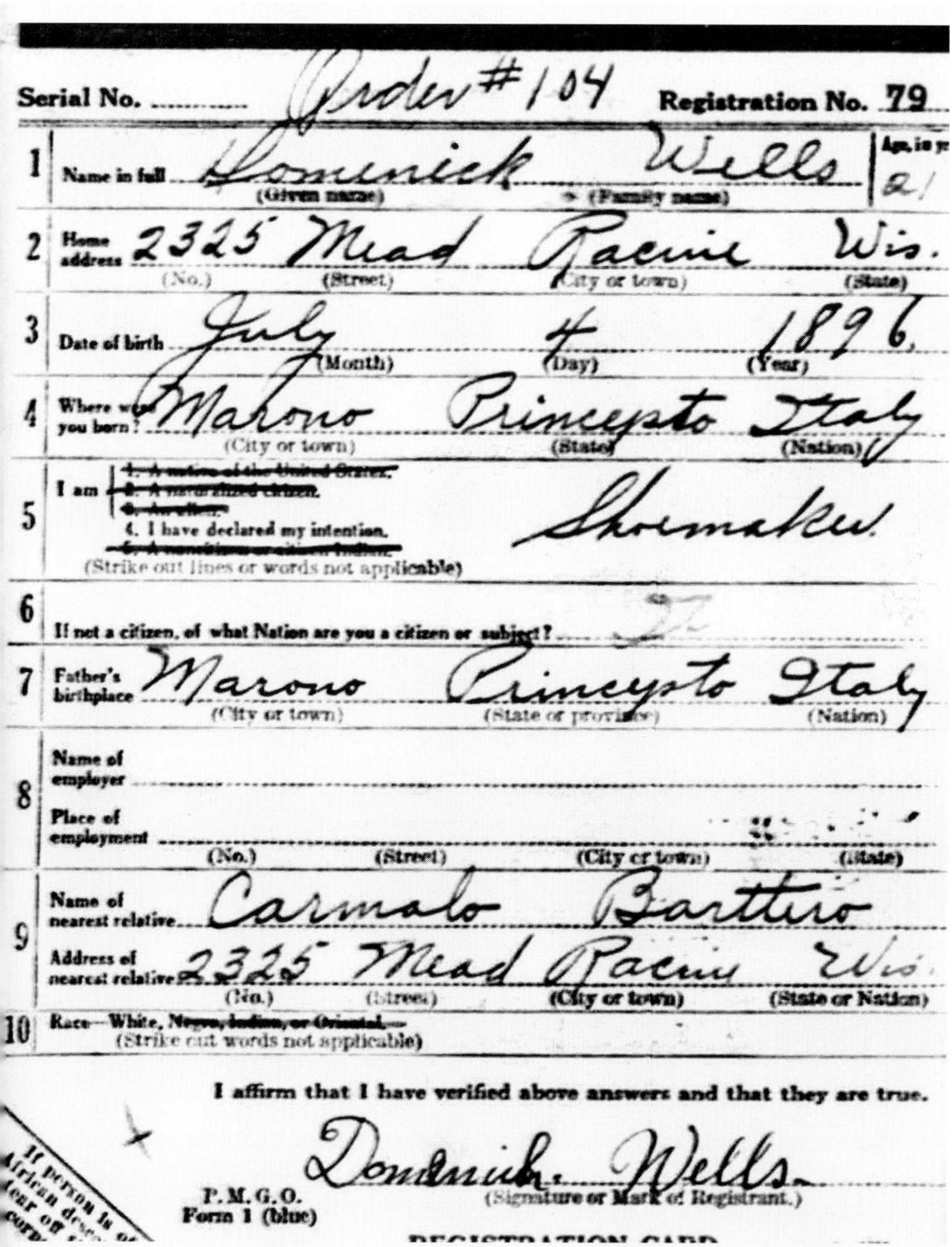

Serial No. Order #104 Registration No. 79

1 Name in full Domenick Wells (Given name) (Family name) Age, in yrs 21

2 Home address 2325 Mead Racine Wis. (No.) (Street) (City or town) (State)

3 Date of birth July 4 1896 (Month) (Day) (Year)

4 Where were you born? Marono Princepto Italy (City or town) (State) (Nation)

5 I am ~~1. A native of the United States.~~ ~~2. A naturalized citizen.~~ ~~3. An alien.~~ 4. I have declared my intention. ~~5. A noncitizen or citizen Indian.~~ (Strike out lines or words not applicable) Shoemaker

6 If not a citizen, of what Nation are you a citizen or subject?

7 Father's birthplace Marono Princepto Italy (City or town) (State or province) (Nation)

8 Name of employer

Place of employment (No.) (Street) (City or town) (State)

9 Name of nearest relative Carmalo Barttiro

Address of nearest relative 2325 Mead Racine Wis (No.) (Street) (City or town) (State or Nation)

10 Race—White, ~~Negro, Indian, or Oriental,~~— (Strike out words not applicable)

I affirm that I have verified above answers and that they are true.

Domenick Wells (Signature or Mark of Registrant.)

P.M.G.O. Form 1 (blue)

REGISTRATION CARD

If person is of African descent tear off this corner.

Draft registration card for Domenick Wells (Domenico Guido). (*National Archives, via Ancestry.com*)

Mike Zicarelli

Mike Zicarelli was born on May 6, 1895, in Rende. He was a trunk maker in Racine, when he entered the Army. Zicarelli was a private, serial number 2121468, in Company "E," 312th Engineer Regiment, 87th Division, when he boarded the *Caronia* for shipment to France on August 24, 1918. Much to the disappointment of the men in the division, the 87th Division worked at various labor and construction projects behind the lines in France. Zicarelli was promoted to corporal, and he returned to the U.S. aboard the *Dakotan* on June 25, 1919.

Cpl. Mike Zicarelli, 312th Engineer Regiment, 87th Division. (*Racine County in the World War*)

Epilogue

Taken as a whole, the military history of these men reflects the general history of American soldiers during the war. They served in every capacity, in all types of units, except the Marine Corps. Some were in the service even before the war began, while others joined immediately after the U.S. entered the war. Still others were drafted during the war, some reporting for duty during each draft day, from the first in September 1917 to the last, less than a week before the Armistice. They served honorably with a few glitches in their record. Men who went overseas served in every capacity, from support units well behind the lines to infantry units engaged in fierce combat in many campaigns. Some of them suffered life-changing physical wounds, and we will never know how many suffered psychological wounds that were invisible to all, but keenly felt by the men. Many men were wounded, one was taken prisoner, and twelve made the supreme sacrifice.

Appendix I

A book such as this is very data-heavy. Fully citing each bit of data would quickly bog down the reader in a morass of URLs, government microfilm numbers, file numbers, folder and box numbers, and any number of other "metadata." To avoid this while maintaining academic rigor and integrity, I have decided to omit many citations from the biographies section of the book. I have included a few that fall outside of the general categories of those listed below. The military service information presented here can be found in the statement of service cards (Wisconsin or Illinois) or military service records (National Personnel Records Center, National Archives and Records Administration, St. Louis, Missouri). Any information regarding residence or occupation in 1917 or 1918 usually comes from the draft registration card; sometimes this information is gleaned from the military statement of service cards. Any personal data for decennial years (1900, 1910, 1920, 1930, and 1940) comes from U.S. census data via Ancestry.com. Information regarding immigration, naturalization, and passports comes via Ancestry.com; some immigration data comes from a database compiled and maintained by the author. Examples of full citations appear below. This method will allow for fact verification while preserving a pleasant reading experience. Sufficient information is included here to allow interested readers to pursue more research.

Birth, Death, and Marriage Records

Microfilmed birth, death, and marriage records for many of the Cosenza villages are available from the Family History Library (Latter Day Saints Church). Specific citations will vary based upon the type of record and the Calabrian village. A sample citation of a record from Marano Marchesato, one of the Cosenza villages, appears below. The "Families from Marano Marchesato" website, created by Lisa Perkins, contains some indexes to records from that village.

Sample citation for several microfilms for Luigi Santelli's biographical sketch:
Family History Library microfilms: No. 1468239, *Nati, processetti, notificazioni, matrimoni, morti*, 1852–1858; No. 1641041, *Matrimoni* 1866–1900; No. 1608134,

Nati, 1866–1883; No. 1608135, *Nati*, 1884–1900; No. 1642125, *Nati*, 1901–1907. See also: "Families from Marano Marchesato, Cosenza, Calabria, Italia" webpage URL: www.rootsweb.ancestry.com/~ilfmm/index.html.

Transcripts of Italian vital statistics records for San Fili and San Vincenzo La Costa are found on the following website: sanvincenzolacostagenealogy.blogspot.com.

Draft Registration Records

Draft registration cards are available through several sources, but the Ancestry.com database is the most efficient and convenient. Specific citations will vary depending upon the registrant's residence. Researchers should not have trouble using the Ancestry.com database to find specific registrants. Data pertaining to a registrant's residence, occupation, and overall status as of June 1917 likely comes from the draft registration card.

The general citation for draft registrations found on Ancestry.com is Ancestry.com. *U.S., World War I Draft Registration Cards, 1917–1918* (database online). Provo, UT, USA: Ancestry.com Operations Inc., 2005; Original data: United States, Selective Service System. *World War I Selective Service System Draft Registration Cards, 1917–1918*. Washington, D.C.: National Archives and Records Administration. M1509, 4,582 rolls. Imaged from Family History Library microfilm.

Military Service

After the war, the War Department mandated the creation of statement of service cards for each person who served in the military during the war. Created by clerks from each man's service record, the cards were sent to the Adjutant General's office of the state where each veteran lived at the time they entered service. These cards, sometimes easily available and sometimes not, are a miniature military biography of each soldier. Statement of service cards for Illinois soldiers are stored in the Illinois Adjutant General's Office, Springfield, Illinois. Cards for Wisconsin residents are in Wisconsin Adjutant General's Office: *Regimental Muster and Descriptive Rolls, World War I*, Wisconsin Veterans Museum, Madison, Wisconsin.

Due to a fire at the National Personnel Records Center in 1973, information from the National Archives in St. Louis, Missouri, is mostly limited to final pay vouchers. In a few cases, more complete records were saved and reconstructed. U.S. Navy records at the archives are in good shape and easily available.

Applications for veterans' headstones for deceased veterans contain personal and military information; the citation appears below: Ancestry.com. *U.S., Headstone Applications for Military Veterans, 1925–1963* (database online). Provo, UT, USA: Ancestry.com Operations, Inc., 2012; Original data: *Applications for Headstones for U.S. Military Veterans, 1925–1941*. Microfilm publication M1916, 134 rolls. ARC ID: 596118. Records of the Office of the Quartermaster General, Record Group 92. National Archives at Washington, D.C.

The Beneficiary Identification Records Locator Subsystem (B.I.R.L.S.) Death File provides some very basic military service information. Sometimes it is the only indication of military service to be found. The citation is: Ancestry.com. *U.S., Department of Veterans Affairs BIRLS Death File, 1850–2010* (database online). Provo, UT, USA: Ancestry.com Operations, Inc., 2011; Original data: *Beneficiary Identification Records Locator Subsystem (BIRLS) Death File*. Washington, D.C.: U.S. Department of Veterans Affairs.

The records of National Soldiers' Homes also contain personal and military service information: Ancestry.com. *U.S. National Homes for Disabled Volunteer Soldiers, 1866–1938* (database online). Provo, UT, USA: Ancestry.com Operations Inc., 2007; Original data: Historical Register of National Homes for Disabled Volunteer Soldiers, 1866–1938; (National Archives Microfilm Publication M1749, 282 rolls); Records of the Department of Veterans Affairs, Record Group 15; National Archives, Washington, D.C.

An important source for Army transport information is U.S. Army Transport Service, Passenger Lists, 1910–1939: Ancestry.com. *U.S., Army Transport Service, Passenger Lists, 1910–1939* (database online). Lehi, UT, USA: Ancestry.com Operations, Inc., 2016; Original data: *Lists of Incoming Passengers, 1917–1938*. Textual records. 360 Boxes. NAI: 6234465. Records of the Office of the Quartermaster General, 1774–1985, Record Group 92. The National Archives at College Park, Maryland.

Lists of Outgoing Passengers, 1917–1938. Textual records. 255 Boxes. NAI: 6234477. Records of the Office of the Quartermaster General, 1774–1985, Record Group 92. The National Archives at College Park, Maryland.

Some military and personal information can be found on passport applications: Ancestry.com. *U.S. Passport Applications, 1795–1925* (database online). Lehi, UT, USA: Ancestry.com Operations, Inc., 2007. Original data: *Selected Passports*. National Archives, Washington, D.C.

A list of about 3,000 Italian American soldiers who died during World War I is available at *Back Over There*, a tribute website: www.worldwar1centennial.org/index.php/back-over-there.html.

Information for Racine County veterans can be found in an excellent and comprehensive history: Haight, Capt. Walter L. *Racine County in the World War: A History*. Racine, WI: Walter L. Haight and Frank P. Haight, 1920.

For information regarding units (location, dates of service, etc.), *United States Army in the World War, 1917–1919, Organization of the American Expeditionary Forces*, Volume I (Washington, D.C.: Center of Military History, United States Army, 1988, available online via history.army.mil) is invaluable; I have used it extensively to flesh out information on various obscure units.

Passenger Lists

Passenger lists for ships arriving in the United States can be found in the Ancestry.com database; the Ellis Island database is also available online. The citations vary based upon year, port of arrival, and, of course, each individual. Specific citations will give page and line numbers for each passenger; researchers should not have any difficulties using the database to find individual soldiers.

Appendix I

U.S. Census Data

The 1900, 1910, 1920, and 1930 United States censuses are valuable sources of information. In particular, the 1930 census schedule indicates whether the resident was a veteran. As with other records, specific citations vary depending upon where the person lived. The citations appear below:

1900: Ancestry.com. *1900 United States Federal Census* (database online). Provo, UT, USA: Ancestry.com Operations Inc., 2004. Original data: United States of America, Bureau of the Census. *Twelfth Census of the United States, 1900*. Washington, D.C.: National Archives and Records Administration, 1900. T623, 1854 rolls.
1910: Ancestry.com. *1910 United States Federal Census* (database online). Lehi, UT, USA: Ancestry.com Operations Inc., 2006.; Original data: Thirteenth Census of the United States, 1910 (NARA microfilm publication T624, 1,178 rolls). Records of the Bureau of the Census, Record Group 29. National Archives, Washington, D.C. For details on the contents of the film numbers, visit the NARA web page.
1920: Ancestry.com. *1920 United States Federal Census* (database online). Provo, UT, USA: Ancestry.com Operations, Inc., 2010. Images reproduced by FamilySearch; Original data: Fourteenth Census of the United States, 1920. (NARA microfilm publication T625, 2076 rolls). Records of the Bureau of the Census, Record Group 29. National Archives, Washington, D.C. For details on the contents of the film numbers, visit the NARA web page. Note: Enumeration Districts 819-839 are on roll 323 (Chicago City).
1930: Ancestry.com. *1930 United States Federal Census* (database online). Provo, UT, USA: Ancestry.com Operations Inc., 2002; Original data: United States of America, Bureau of the Census. *Fifteenth Census of the United States, 1930*. Washington, D.C.: National Archives and Records Administration, 1930. T626, 2,667 rolls.

Appendix II

This list shows the names of each man in this study; they are listed under the city where each man lived upon entry into military service.[1] The format gives each man's name, serial number, rank, and unit, where this data is known. The serial number is given, when known, to enable researchers to pursue information on individual soldiers. It is important to remember that men served in more than one unit during their stint in the military; only one unit per man is given here. The reader will also notice differences in nomenclature for the various units; these designations are recorded here generally as they appear in official documents. The biographies of men whose names appear in bold type are featured in either the casualties or selected biographies chapters.

Aurora, Illinois

BELMONTE, Carmine, 1336078, Pvt., 1st Construction Company, U.S. Army Air Service

Blue Island, Illinois

CISTARO, Ralph, 480646, PFC, Co. "C," 56th Infantry Regiment, 7th Division

Chicago, Illinois

ADDUCI, Paul, 4248248, PFC, Co. "M," 4th Pioneer Infantry Regiment
AIELLO, Frank, Camp Grant, 1918
AIELLO, Frank, 222776, Cook, Mechanical Repair Shop 301, Quartermaster Corps, A.E.F.
AIELLO, Silvio, 100-29-97, S2C, U.S. Navy Receiving Ship, Puget Sound
ALGIERI, Nick Peter, 2088725, Pvt., Co. "D," 32nd Engineer Regiment
ALOE, Carmine, 477271, Pvt., Co. "H," 27th Infantry Regiment
ANDREA, Frank, Camp Grant, 1918
ANGIO, Frank, Pvt., Co. "E," Development Battalion 2, Camp Gordon
ARENA, Angelo, Pvt., Machine Gun Co., 129th Infantry Regiment, 33rd Division
ARNONE, Mike Frank, Pvt., Co. "B," 19th Infantry Regiment, 18th Division

ARVIA, Domenico, Camp Grant, 1918
BAGNUOLA, Joseph, 142942, Cook, Battery "F," 149th Field Artillery Regiment, 42nd Division
BARATTA, Fred Louis, 985512, Pvt., Mobile Hospital Unit 102
BARATTA, James D., 4426339, Pvt., 161st Depot Brigade
BARBIERI, Luigi, 1389588, PFC, Co. "H," 132nd Infantry Regiment, 33rd Division
BARTUCCI, Ferdinando, 479350, Cook, Co. "D," 25th U.S. Guards Battalion
BARTUCCI, Francesco, 477015, Pvt., 13th (or 31st) Infantry Regiment
BARTUCCI, Joseph, Camp Funston, 1918
BARTUCCI, Salvatore, 480546, Pvt., Co. "B," 56th Infantry Regiment, 7th Division
BELMONTE, Eugene, 3022399, Pvt., 23rd Co., 2 Recruit Battalion, Camp Forrest
BENEDETTO, Nicola (BENEDETTI), 1384188, Pvt., Co. "G," 130th Infantry Regiment, 33rd
BIAFORE, Samuel, 745528, Pvt., Co. "K," 54th Infantry Regiment, 6th Division
BIANCO, Antonio L., 302nd Cavalry Regiment
BILOTTI, Gasparo, 4248090, PFC, Co. "K," 4th Pioneer Infantry Regiment
BILOTTI, Giacomo, 3072112, Sgt., Machine Gun Troop, 311th Cavalry Regiment
BOMICINO, Joseph Samuel, 1383059, PFC, Co. "A," 130th Infantry Regiment, 33rd Division
BROCCOLO, Carmelo, 3071819, Pvt., 328th Ambulance Company, 82nd Division
BRONO, Alessandro, Pvt., Co. "K," 343th Infantry Regiment, 86th Division
BRUNETTI, John, 982753, Pvt., Co. "G," 8th Depot Battalion, Signal Corps
BRUNO, Louis, 113-79-02, F1C, U.S. Navy, Great Lakes Naval Training Station
BRUNO, Umberto Enrico (Enrico Albert), 2102250, Cpl., Co. "K," 346th Infantry Regiment, 87th Division
BRUNO, Louis, 2826598, Pvt., Co. "C," 8th Development Battalion, Camp Grant
BRUNO, Louis, 4249667, Pvt., Co. "B," 5th Anti-Aircraft Machine Gun Battalion
BRUTTO, Eugene, 681424, PFC, Motor Transport Company 688
CAIRA, Ferdinando (CAIRO, Fred), 753442, Pvt., Evacuation Hospital 5
CAIRA, Giovanni, 1368855, PFC, Co. "A," 117th Machine Gun Battalion, 31st Division
CANDELISE, Damiano, 1098483, Bugler, Co. "D," 56th Infantry Regiment, 7th Division
CANDREVA, Raffaele, 2822773, Pvt., Co. "M," 342nd Infantry Regiment, 86th Division
CAPALBO, Annibale, Pvt., 3rd Co., 1st Development Battalion, 156th Depot Brigade
CAPPARELLI, Frank, 2822302, Pvt., Co. "C," 130th Infantry Regiment, 33rd Division
CAPPARELLI, Frank Sam, 2822067, Pvt., Co. "C," 3rd U.S. Guards Battalion
CARA, Dominick J., 492187, Pvt., 89th Company, Transportation Corps
CARA, William, 120-36-35, WT, U.S. Navy
CARDAMONE, Diego (Dan), U.S. military, 1918–1919
CARNEVALE, Angelo, Pvt., Co. "E," 5th Limited Service Regiment
CARPINO, Pasquale, 2062020, Pvt., Co. "D," 504th Engineer Battalion
CARRAVETTA, Pasquale, 2061193, Pvt., Co. "D," 28th Infantry Regiment, 1st Division
CARUSO, Joe, 1382763, Pvt., HQ Co., 130th Infantry Regiment, 33rd Division
CASALINO, Antonio, 2828584, Pvt., Machine Gun Co., 56th Infantry Regiment, 7th Division
CAVA, Salvatore (Sam) Paul, U.S. military, 1918

CESARIO, Joseph, 2827045, Pvt., 21st Co., 6th Provisional Battalion
CESARIO, Raffaele, 3748583, Pvt., Co. "B," 312th Infantry Regiment, 78th Division
CHESROW (CESARIO), Eugene Joseph, 1Lt, Graves Registration Service Unit 304
CHIAPPETTA, Ferdinando, 3278585, Pvt., Co. "C," 1st Battalion, 1st Provisional Development Brigade
CHIAPPETTA, Gennaro, 2822811, 2nd Co., 1st Training Battalion, 161st Depot Brigade
CHIAPPETTA, Luigi, 480024, Pvt., Co. "A," 55th Infantry Regiment, 7th Division
CHRISTIAN (CRISTIANO), Louis, 1382370, PFC, Medical Detachment, 129th Infantry Regiment, 33rd Division
CIANNI, Dominick, 561569, PFC, Co. "L," 59th Infantry Regiment, 4th Division
CICERO, Frank, 191252, PFC, 2nd Engineer Service Co., 20th Engineer Regiment (Forestry)
CONFORTI, Frank, 1378511, Mus. 1c, HQ Battery, 124th Field Artillery Regiment, 33rd Division
CONFORTI, Vincenzo, 2458794, Mus. 3c, Band, Coast Artillery Corps, Fort Williams, Maine
CONTE, Salvatore, Camp Dix
CORRADO, John Peter, 2826278, Pvt., Co. "I," 161st Depot Brigade
COSENTINO, Alessandro, 2826895, Pvt., 148th Infantry Regiment, 37th Division
COSENTINO, Emilio, 216537, Cpl., Motor Transport Company 318
COSTABILE, Moris (Francesco), 479346, Pvt., HQ Co., 27th Infantry Regiment
COSTABILE, Pasquale, 3689636, Pvt., 19th Co., 5th Battalion, 163rd Depot Brigade
COVELLI, Salvatore, 2827002, Pvt., Veterinary Corps, Detachment AED 301
CRIBARI, Domenico, U.S. military, 1918
CRIBARO, Francesco, Truck Company Number 5, I Corps Artillery Park
DEBARTOLO, John, 3017087, Pvt., 1st Co., 1st Recruit Battalion, Camp Forrest
DEFRANCESCO, Paul, 479808, Pvt., Co. "A," 55th Infantry Regiment, 7th Division
DELEO, Frank, 1626655, Pvt., Co. "E," 56th Pioneer Infantry Regiment
DEPASQUALE, Antonio, 3277587, Pvt., Co. "A," 319th Infantry Regiment, 80th Division
DERANGO, Eugenio, 2087678, PFC, Co. "L," 353rd Infantry Regiment, 89th Division
DERANGO, Francesco (Frank), 1364416, PFC, Battery "D," 8th Field Artillery Regiment, 7th Division
DEROSE, Carlo, Pvt., Camp Shelby
DOCIMO, Fairy (Fiore), 479097, Pvt., Provisional Company 2 (Siberia)
DOCIMO, Salvatore A., 2085672, Mec, HQ Co., 103rd Engineer Regiment, 28th Division
FELICE, Frank, Camp Taliaferro, California
FILICE, Fiore, Pvt., Supply Co., 305th Field Artillery Regiment, 77th Division
FERRARO, Francesco, Pvt., 14th Co., 161 Depot Brigade
FORTINI, Frank, 2826795, PFC, Cook Company 7, Army Service Corps Detachment
GALLO, Eugene (James), U.S. military, 1918
GAUDIO, Raffaele, Pvt., Co. "B," Development Battalion 1, 157th Depot Brigade
GRECO, Angelo A., 2828804, Pvt., Quartermaster Corps, Camp Johnston
GRECO, Antonio, 820877, Pvt., Co. "A," 62nd Artillery, Coast Artillery Corps

GRECO, Eugene, U.S. Army, 1918–1919
GRECO, Eugenio, 2826850, Pvt., HQ Co., 7th Infantry Regiment, 3rd Division
GRECO, Joseph, 1390510, PFC, Co. "K," 132nd Infantry Regiment, 33rd Division
GRECO, Joseph, Pvt., Machine Gun Co., 19th Infantry Regiment, 18th Division
GRECO, Ralph, 2088873, Pvt., Battery "C," 123rd Field Artillery Regiment, 33rd Division
GUAGLIANONE, Frank, PFC, Co. "M," 27th Infantry Regiment
GUERRIERI, Eugenio, 3277957, Pvt., Battery "C," 313th Field Artillery Regiment, 80th Division
GUIDO, Federico (Fred), 2306584, Pvt., Co. "L," 128th Infantry Regiment, 32nd Division
IANTORNO, Louis, U.S. Army, 1918–1919
IMBROGNO, George, 2833634, Pvt., Co. "I," 16th Infantry Regiment, 1st Division
LATO, Antonio, U.S. military, 1918–1919
LIO, Serafino, 2816909, Pvt., 4th Co., 3rd Development Battalion, Camp Logan
LITRENTI, James, 823054, Pvt., Co. "B," 62nd Artillery, Coast Artillery Corps
LOIZZO, Giuseppe Salvatore, 2826689, Pvt., 4th Co., 1st Regiment, Replacements
LUCCHETTI, Arthur Frank, 4248100, Pvt., Truck Co. "A," V Corps Artillery Park
MALITO, Louis, 2822744, Pvt., Co. "D," 354th Infantry Regiment, 89th Division
MANDARINO, Angelo, 838742, Pvt., Co. "C," 52nd Ammunition Train, Coast Artillery Corps
MANDARINO, Luigi, Camp Funston
MARABELLO, Louis, 2826913, PFC, Co. "F," 111th Infantry Regiment, 28th Division
MARO, Paul, 2816915, Pvt., Co. "C," 603rd Engineer Regiment
MASCHIO, Frank, 2312634, Pvt., Co. "H," 23rd Infantry Regiment, 2nd Division
MAZZUCA, James E., 2094913, Pvt., Co. "C," 80th Infantry Regiment, 15th Division
MAZZUCA, Michele Giovanni, 4129223, Pvt., 2nd Battery, October Artillery Replacements
MAZZULLA, Frank, 3073742, Pvt., HQ Co., 162nd Infantry Regiment, 41st Division
MELE, Peter, 2999852, Pvt., Butchery Company 344
MELE, Umelo, 1388984, Pvt., Co. "D," 320th Infantry Regiment, 80th Division
METAGRANO, Michael, 2061221, PFC, Co. "C," 47th Infantry Regiment, 4th Division
MICELI, Francesco, 4409744, Pvt., 14th Co., 161st Depot Brigade
MICELI, Gaetano, 2077351, Cpl., Co. "C," 18th U.S. Guards Battalion
MICELI, Louis, 2816921, Pvt., Co. "B," 314th Ammunition Train, 89th Division
MIDDONO, Frank, 1391264, Cpl., Co. "F," 132nd Infantry Regiment, 33rd Division
MINERVINI, Gaetano, 626554, PFC, 4th Co., Discharge Detachment, Camp Grant
MINERVINI, Leonardo, Camp Grant
MIRABELLI, Mariano, 736237, Pvt., Co. "A," 165th Infantry Regiment, 42nd Division
MONACO, Armand, Camp Grant
MONACO, Rudolph Eugene, Pvt., Students' Army Training Corps, University of Chicago
MORELLI, Andrea, 1338910, Pvt., 1107th Aero Replacement Squadron
MORELLI, Filiberto, 1388067, Pvt., 130th Infantry Regiment, 33rd Division
MORELLI, Mike, Camp Grant
MORELLI, Pasquale, 3072201, Pvt., Battery "F," 67th Field Artillery Regiment, 95th Division

MORELLI, Salvatore, 135-411, OS, U.S. Coast Guard, U.S.S. *Pamlico*
MORRONE, Alessandro, 2826857, Pvt., Co. "C," 6th Development Battalion, 161st Depot Brigade
MORRONE, Ferdinando Fred, 3022523, Pvt., 23rd Co., 2nd Recruit Battalion
NACCARATO, James, 2055853, PFC, HQ Co., 49th Infantry Regiment, 83rd Division
NINO, Frank, 443810, Pvt., Troop "K," 17th Cavalry Regiment
NUDO, Jasper, 2086867, Pvt., Co. "A," 108th Ammunition Train, 33rd Division
ONOFRIO, Eugenio, Camp Grant
ORLANDO, Luigi, U.S. Army, California
PANGER, John, 2999869, Pvt., Battery "C," 124th Field Artillery Regiment, 33rd Division
PANKER, Laurence, 2821121, Pvt., 12th Co., Development Battalion 3, Camp Logan
PANZA, Gabriele, 2826438, Pvt., Mobile Laundry Company 310, 80th Division
PELLEGRINI, Charles, 479779, Pvt., 161st Depot Brigade
PELLEGRINI, Francesco, 479753, PFC, Co. "M," 55th Infantry Regiment, 7th Division
PELLEGRINI, Louis, 1383749, Bugler, Co. "E," 130th Infantry Regiment, 33rd Division
PERRI, Frank, 2826914, Pvt., Co. "K," 344th Infantry Regiment, 86th Division
PERRI, Joseph, Co. "M," 3rd Provisional Battalion
PERRI, Joseph Michele Francesco, Pvt., Camp Dix
PERRI, Luigi, 1391161, Pvt., Co. "G," 132nd Infantry Regiment, 33rd Division
PERRI, Tony Frank, 2069081, PFC, Chemical Warfare Service, O&T Center
PONTILLO, Eugene, 3280735, PFC, Battery "B," 18th Field Artillery Regiment, 3rd Division
POSTERIVO, Camillo, 2822159, Pvt., Co. "C," 4th Infantry Regiment, 3rd Division
POTESTA, Sam, 1389384, Pvt., Co. "C," 132nd Infantry Regiment, 33rd Division
PRETE, Armand, U.S. Army, 1917
PRETE, Frank P., 1375582, Sgt., Battery "B," 122nd Field Artillery Regiment, 33rd Division
QUALTIERI, Frank C., 2828577, Pvt., Medical Department
REDA, Carlo, Co. "A," 5th Pioneer Infantry Regiment
RENDE, Frank, 2087699, Pvt., Co. "M," 353rd Infantry Regiment, 89th Division
RICCHIO, Giuseppe, 66 Field Artillery Regiment, 96th Division
RITACCO, Samuel, 1550747, Pvt., Battery "C," 76th Field Artillery Regiment, 3rd Division
RIZZO, Gennaro, U.S. Army, 1918–1919
ROCHETTO, Louis R., 3376047, Sgt., Det. 8, U.S. Army Air Service
ROSSI, Eugenio, Coast Artillery Corps, Maine
RUFFOLO, Luigi, 428552, Pvt., Co. "H," 21st Infantry Regiment, 16th Division
SALERNO, Frank Lewis, 283162, PFC, Supply Co. 128th Infantry Regiment, 32nd Division
SALERNO, Mike, 2826927, Sgt., Quartermaster Corps
SALVINO, Vincenzo, 481845, Pvt., Co. "C," 7th Ammunition Train, 7th Division
SANTELLI, Giuseppe, 2060965, Pvt., Co. "B," 103rd Engineer Regiment, 28th Division
SANZONE (SANSONE), Tony, 477431, Pvt., Siberia
SANZONE (SANSONE), Vincenzo, Co. "A," 70th Engineer Battalion (Railway Construction)
SAVAGLIO, James Rocco, 2061230, Cpl., Co. "C," 47th Infantry Regiment, 4th Division

SCARPELLI, Bartolo, 1382758, Mec, HQ Co., 130th Infantry Regiment, 33rd Division
SCARPELLI, Ernest, 1377841, PFC, Battery D, 123rd Field Artillery Regiment, 33rd Division
SCOLA, Frank (Francesco), 2826875, Pvt., 161st Depot Brigade
SEGRETI, Alfonso, 2059973, PFC, Co. "B," 4th Engineer Regiment, 4th Division
SEGRETI, Giuseppe, 2082107, PFC, Co. "E," 342nd Infantry Regiment, 86th Division
SEGRETI, John Eugene, 2999898, PFC, Co. "E," 53 Pioneer Infantry Regiment
SERPE, Giuseppe, 1392636, PFC, Co. "D," 124th Machine Gun Battalion, 33rd Division
SERPE, Peter F., 191-64-60, HA2c, U.S. Navy, Great Lakes Naval Training Station
SETTINO, Albert Filiberto, 2999899, Pvt., Co. "D," 306th Ammunition Train, 81st Division
SPINA, Pietro Francesco, 2062079, Pvt., Co. "C," 137th Engineer Battalion (Electrical and Mechanical)
SPIZZIRRI, Albert Anthony, 3279338, Pvt., Co. "B," 138th Engineer Regiment, (Railway Construction)
SPIZZIRRI, Anthony, 116-89-75, F1c, U.S. Navy, Great Lakes Naval Training Station
SPIZZIRRI, Anthony, 2826245, Cpl., Co. "E," 311th Supply Train, 86th Division
SPIZZIRRI, Frank, 2757468, Pvt., Guard and Fire Co. 317, Quartermaster Corps
SPIZZIRRI, Frank Charles, 3277218, Pvt., 106th Ordnance Depot Company
SPIZZIRRI, Peter, 2816945, PFC, Co. "I," 3rd Infantry Regiment
SPIZZIRRI, Raymond C., 3277274, PFC, 70th Co., 18th Battalion, 1st Replacement & Training Troops
SPROVIERO, Ippolito Paul, Camp Grant
STELLATO, Giuseppe, 2081218, Cook, Cook Company 7, Army Service Corps
TARSITANO, Gabriel, 2339717, Sgt., Co. "K," 4th Infantry Regiment, 3rd Division
TENUTA, Alexander, 4417002, Pvt., 35th Co., 161st Depot Brigade
TENUTA, Raffaele, 950380, Pvt., 4th Co., 1st Regiment, Replacements
TROTTA, John, 498512, Pvt., Battery "E," 66th Field Artillery Regiment, 96th Division
TUCCI, Giuseppe, 191648, Pvt., 20th Engineer Regiment (Forestry)
VIZZA, Eugene, 273431. Pvt., Co. "A," 127th Infantry Regiment, 32nd Division
VOLPENTESTA, Dominick J., 2064005, Pvt., Headquarters Detachment, 33rd Division
ZICCARELLI, Frank L., 2067739, Sgt. Maj., Ambulance Co. 344, 311th Sanitary Train, 86th Division

Cicero, Illinois
CAPALBO, Mariano, 4411359, Pvt., 7th Co., 161st Depot Brigade
CONFORTI, Louis, 1188289, Pvt., Battery "C," 344th Field Artillery Regiment, 90th Division

Deerfield, Illinois
LOIZZO, Frank, 2078504, Pvt., 141st Company, Transportation Corps
NAPOLITANO, Giuseppe, School for Bakers and Cooks, Camp Gordon

East Chicago, Indiana
DELUCA, Peter, U.S. military, 1918
SCAVELLO, Antonio, Pvt., 325th Field Artillery Regiment, 84th Division

Elmhurst, Illinois
MISASI, Luigi, 2078546, Pvt., Co. "D," 103rd Engineer Regiment, 28th Division

Franklin Park, Illinois
CUNDARI, Frank, 1366846, Pvt., Co. "A," 123th Infantry Regiment, 31st Division

Gary, Indiana
MORRONE, Clemente, 3886153, Cpl., Quartermaster Corps

Harvey, Illinois
RITONDALE, Pietro, 3286435, Pvt., Co. "G," 53rd Pioneer Infantry Regiment

Highwood, Illinois
DEBARTOLO, Alessandro, 2816964, Pvt., Co. "K," 306th Infantry Regiment, 77th Division
DEBARTOLO, Eugenio, 494651, Pvt., Co. "E," 14th Infantry Regiment
GRECO, Eugenio, 1380238, PFC, Co. "B," 129th Infantry Regiment, 33rd Division
GRECO, Salvatore, 270267, Cook, Co. "F," 18th Infantry Regiment, 1st Division

Indiana Harbor, Indiana
PARISI, Giacomo; Pvt., 25th Co., 7th Battalion, 159th Depot Brigade
POTESTA, Benjamin E., 1565680, Pvt., Co. "E," 7th Engineer Regiment, 5th Division
POTESTA, James, 46114, Cpl., 18th Infantry Regiment, 1st Division

Joliet, Illinois
GAMMUTO, Filippo, 428758, Pvt., Co. "M," 48th Infantry Regiment, 20th Division
GENTILE, Salvatore F., 1561229, PFC, Co. "B," 150th Infantry Regiment, 38th Division
LOIZZO, Gaetano, 2854026, Pvt., 306th Sanitary Train, 81st Division
PIRARO, Louis, Camp Wheeler
RENDE, Gaetano, 1374943, Pvt., Co. "G," 138th Infantry Regiment, 35th Division
TEDESCO, Tommaso Antonio, 1373862, Pvt., Co. "F," 7th Infantry Regiment, 3rd Division

Kenosha, Wisconsin
ACETO, Louis, 3365339, Pvt., Machine Gun Training Center, Camp Hancock
ACETO, Pasquale, 10296, Pvt., Supply Co., 340th Infantry Regiment, 85th Division
ACETO, Raffaele, 2097645, Pvt., Co. "A," 22nd Engineer Regiment (Light Railway Construction)
AIELLO, Pasquale, 2025529, Pvt., Machine Gun Co., 340th Infantry Regiment, 85th Division
AMADEO, Francesco, 2077595, Pvt., Co. "B," 25th U.S. Guards Battalion
ANDREA, Bruno, 2025531, Pvt., Machine Gun Co., 340th Infantry Regiment, 85th Division
ANDREA, Filippo, 443341, Pvt., Co. "A," 6th Motor Supply Train, 6th Division
BALSANO, Semo, 2097650, Pvt., Co. "I," 13th Replacement Regiment
BARATTA, Luigi, 3715445, Pvt., 3rd Co., 159th Depot Brigade

BELGIOIELLO, Silvio, 3896769, Pvt., 159th Depot Brigade
BISCARDI, Angelo, 2047634, PFC, Co. "D," 4th Infantry Regiment, 3rd Division
BOCCI, Paul, 2029633, Pvt., 2nd Development Battalion, Camp Gordon
BOMBI, Bruno, 2303844, Pvt., Battery "A," 121st Field Artillery Regiment, 32nd Division
BONARETTI, Albert, 1128738, PFC, 25th Construction Company U.S. Army Air Service
BONARETTI, Amedeo, 4414183, Pvt., 161st Depot Brigade
BOTTINO, Beniamino, 3775697, Pvt., Officers Training Camp
BRUNO, Michael, 2825721, PFC, Co. "F," 139th Infantry Regiment, 35th Division
BRUNO, Rosario, 3365324, PFC, 28th Co., 3rd Group, Machine Gun Training
BUCCIERI, August Diego, Seaman, U.S. Navy, U.S.S. *Kearsarge*
CAIRA, Leopoldo, 3775667, Pvt., 57th Depot Brigade
CAIRO, Domenico, 2039769, PFC, Base Hospital 27
CAIRO, Ralph, 4303019, Pvt., November Automatic Replacement Draft
CAMMIRIRE, Gaetano, Pvt., Battery "A," 121st Field Artillery Regiment, 32nd Division
CAPUTO, Giovanni, 2097657, Pvt., 165th Depot Brigade
CELEBRE, Giuseppe, 3896742, Pvt., Development Battalion 1
CHIANELLI, Peter, 3715689, PFC, Quartermaster Corps
CHIAPPETTA, Beniamino, 3715459, Pvt., Co. "A," 46th U.S. Guards Battalion
CHIAPPETTA, Carmine, 2825515, Pvt., Co. "G," 18th Infantry Regiment, 1st Division
CHIAPPETTA, Louis, 2825497, PFC, Co. "M," 7th Infantry Regiment, 3rd Division
CINELLI, Gaetano, 3369244, Pvt., General Service Infantry
CONFORTI, Benjamin, 2825539, Pvt., Co. "I," 7th Infantry Regiment, 3rd Division
CONFORTI, Francesco (Frank), 2040857, Pvt., Co. "F," 101st Engineer Regiment, 26th Division
CONFORTI, Ignazio, 2825495, Cpl., Co. "C," 9th Machine Gun Battalion, 3rd Division
CONFORTI, Leopold, 4303023, Pvt., November Automatic Replacement Draft
CONFORTI, Mariano, 3071292, Bugler, Truck Co. "C," V Corps Artillery Park
CONFORTI, Peter, 3281646, Pvt., Co. "A," 319th Infantry Regiment, 80th Division
COVELLI, Giuseppe, 2825700, Pvt., Co. "G," 18th Infantry Regiment, 1st Division
COVELLI, Lawrence, 2828941, Cpl., Co. "F," 49th Infantry Regiment, 83rd Division
CUNDARI, Raffaele, 3365348, Pvt., 161st Depot Brigade
CUNTARI, Eugenio, 2043643, Pvt., 16th Co., 4th Battalion, 160th Depot Brigade
CUNTORI, Francesco, 3715652, Pvt., 159th Depot Brigade
DATILLO, Albert, 3446519, Pvt., 151th Depot Brigade
DEBARTOLO, Eugenio, 2038516, PFC, Intermediate Medical Supply Depot 2
DEFRANCO, Pasquale, 3715653, Pvt., 9th Trench Mortar Battery, 9th Division
DEROSE, Eugenio, 3896766, Pvt., 311th Co., Development Battalion
DESMONIE, Anthony Jerry, U.S. military
DESMONIE, Charles Joseph, 881102, PFC, Co. "B," 318th Engineer Regiment, 6th Division
DESMONIE, Louis, 2189543, PFC, Supply Co, 342nd Field Artillery Regiment, 89th Division
ESTABELLE (COSTABILE), Raffaelo, 2034151, Pvt., Co. "E," 1st Engineer Regiment, 1st Division

FELICE, Alexander, 3418473, Pvt., Casual Detachment, S.P.D.
FERRARO, Eugenio, 150-43-89, F1c, U.S. Navy, Great Lakes Naval Training Station
FERRARO, Serafino, 2825526, Pvt., 12th Co., Development Battalion 3, Camp Logan
GAUDIO, Francesco, 3896779, Pvt., 809th MTC
GEPALLA, Antonio, 2303861, Pvt., Battery "A," 121st Field Artillery Regiment, 32nd Division
GIORDANO, Sam, 2383087, PFC, Co. "D," 60th Infantry Regiment, 5th Division
GIORNO, Antonio, 2825621, Pvt., Co. "E," 26th Infantry Regiment, 1st Division
GIORNO, Joseph, 4303027, Pvt., Recruit Depot, Camp Shelby
GUIDO, Alessandro, 2038956, Pvt., Co. "A," 115th Infantry Regiment, 29th Division
GUIDO, Salvatore, 3365345, PFC, 53rd Depot Brigade
IMBROGNO, Pasquale, 2825642, Pvt., Co. "H," 361st Infantry Regiment, 91st Division
LEONETTI, Domenico, 251049, PFC, Co. "B," 107th Supply Train, 32nd Division
LORATTO, Gilberto, 3690559, Sgt. 1c, Service Park Unit 515, Motor Transport Corps
LUPO, Michele, 3365329, Pvt., Medical Department
MANNA, Luigi, 2043960, Pvt., Co. "D," 4th Infantry Regiment, 3rd Division
MARRAZZO, Emilio, 2825566, Cpl., Co. "H," 18th Infantry Regiment, 1st Division
MARRAZZO, Francesco, 3715678, Pvt., Battery "D," 27th Field Artillery Regiment, 9th Division
MATALLO, Michael, 2825588, Pvt., Quartermaster Corps Salvage Company
MATERA, Emil, 2039880, Pvt., 115th Field Hospital, 104th Sanitary Train, 29th Division
METALLO, Giuseppe, Pvt., 1917
MISURELLI, Giuseppe, 3365366, Cpl., Co. "M," 3rd Battalion, Chemical Warfare Service
MOLINARO, Michael, 3478318, Pvt., 6th Ordnance Supply Company
MORELLI, Agostino, 3715621, Mus1c, HQ Co., 27th Field Artillery Regiment, 9th Division
MUTO, Francesco, 2825575, Pvt., Co. "I," 26th Infantry Regiment, 1st Division
NICASTRO, Luigi, 3368795, Pvt., Motor Transport Department, Machine Gun School
NOTO, Carmine, 2761204, PFC, 336th Guard and Fire Company
PARISE, Dominick, 2303902, Pvt., Battery "A," 121st Field Artillery Regiment, 32nd Division
PASSIRELLI, Serafino, 2072809, Pvt., 2nd Co., 161st Depot Brigade
PELLEGRINO, Tony, 2035162, Pvt., Co. "I," 23rd Infantry Regiment, 2nd Division
PERRONE, Antonio, 2303906, Pvt., Battery "A," 121st Field Artillery Regiment, 32nd Division
PIRRI, Giuseppe, 3715625, Pvt., Field Artillery Central Officers Training School
POSTERARO, Camillo, 2383155, Pvt., Evacuation Hospital 30
POTENTE, Eugene, 2035123, Cpl., Prisoner of War Escort Company 65
PRESTA, Salvatore, 3715727, Pvt., 9th Trench Mortar Battery, 9th Division
PRESTA, Vincent, 2024081, Mus. 2c, HQ Co., 340th Infantry Regiment, 85th Division
PRINCIPE, Eugene, 4303042, Pvt., Camp Shelby
PRINCIPE, Francesco, Pvt., 3rd Co., 1st Training Battalion, 159th Depot Brigade
REDA, Natale, 3418478, Pvt., 3rd Co., Discharge Detachment
RITACCA, Gaspero, 4030344, Pvt., November Automatic Replacement Draft

RITACCA, Joseph, 2038607, Cook, A.E.F. University
RUFFOLO, Frank, 3715695, Pvt., 9th Trench Mortar Battery, 9th Division
RUFFOLO, Luigi, 2825644, Pvt., 161st Depot Brigade
RUFFOLO, Peter, Pvt., Machine Gun Co., 340th Infantry Regiment, 85th Division
RUFFOLO, Serafino, 2025509, Bn. Sgt. Maj., Army Service Corps
RUFFOLO, Simone, 2825622, Pvt., 161st Depot Brigade
SALERNO, Giuseppe, 3715619, Pvt., Battery "F," 27th Field Artillery Regiment, 9th Division
SALITURE, Santo, 2043815, Pvt., Co. "I," 4th Infantry Regiment, 3rd Division
SANTELLI, Luigi, 3715579, Pvt., 3rd Co., 159th Depot Brigade
SAVAGLIO, Alessandro, 2041194, Pvt., 160th Depot Brigade
SAVAGLIO, Emil, 4414148, Pvt., 161st Depot Brigade
SAVAGLIO, Giuseppe, 3035283, Pvt., 13th Co., New Orleans Coast Artillery Corps
SAVAGLIO, Luigi, 4303046, Pvt., November Automatic Replacement Draft
SAVALIO, Ernest, 2035109, Pvt., Co. "B," 130th Engineer Battalion (General Construction)
SCARLOTO (SCARLATO), Eugenio, 2035032, Pvt., Co. "I," 23rd Infantry Regiment, 2nd Division
SCOLA, Peter, 2825565, Pvt., Co. "H," 7th Infantry Regiment, 3rd Division
SERPE, Serafino, 2048414, Pvt., Field Hospital 340, 310th Sanitary Train, 85th Division
SESSO, Benjamin, 3715435, Pvt., 3rd Co., 159th Depot Brigade
SICILIA, Benedetto, 3546062, Pvt., 19th Co., 158th Depot Brigade
SICILIA, Emil, 3715473, Mus. 1c, Battery "C," 27th Field Artillery Regiment, 9th Division
SORRENTINO, Gaetano, 3329916, Pvt., Co. "F," 109 Infantry Regiment, 28th Division
SPALLATO, Francesco, 2097731, Pvt., Co. "D," 20th U.S. Guards Battalion
STURINO, Costantino, U.S. military
TENUTA, Francesco, 2025587, PFC, Co. "C," 10th Machine Gun Battalion, 4th Division
TENUTA, Giovanni, 2825661, Pvt., Co. "C," 318th Infantry Regiment, 80th Division
TENUTA, Paul, 3715431, Pvt., 3rd Co., 1st Training Battalion, 159th Depot Brigade
TENUTA, Pietro, Pvt., U.S. Army, 1918
TENUTA, Saverio, 2825668, PFC, Butchery Company 320
TURCO, Benedetto, 2033090, Cpl., Co. "A," 42nd Machine Gun Battalion, 14th Division
VELARDI, Gaspare, 3369406, Wagon Co., Quartermaster Corps
VENA, Leopold Paul, 3715443, Pvt., 3rd Co., 1st Training Battalion, 159th Depot Brigade
VENA, Luigi, 3775709, Pvt., Co. "G," 30th Infantry Regiment, 3rd Division
VENCI, Antonio, 3715474, Pvt., 3rd Co., 1st Training Battalion, 159th Depot Brigade
ZAZZARO, Michele U., Pvt., Medical Department

Melrose Park, Illinois
IMBROGNO, Robert D., 480291, PFC, Co. "B," 56th Infantry Regiment, 7th Division
MOLEZZI, Eugenio, 480292, Pvt., Co. "A," 56th Infantry Regiment, 7th Division
ORLANDINI, Francesco, Pvt., 129th Infantry Regiment, 33rd Division

Racine, Wisconsin

ABBATI, Eugenio, 1336375, PFC, 5th Construction Company, U.S. Army Air Service
ABBATI, Francesco, Pvt., HQ, Camp Taylor
ACETO, Antonio, 3446639, Pvt., Field Hospital 246, 12th Sanitary Train, 12th Division
ACETO, Eugenio James, 3546341, Pvt., Casual Company, Camp Sherman
ACETO, Sam, 1004427, PFC, Troop "M," 6th Cavalry Regiment
AIELLO, Eugenio (James), 3368699, Pvt., Co. "B," 38th Machine Gun Battalion, 13th Division
AIELLO, Salvatore (Sam), Pvt., Co. "A," 41st Infantry Regiment, 10th Division
ALFANO, Joseph, 782813, Cook, 306th Motorcycle Company
BELTRANO, Giuseppe, 2030365, Pvt., Co. "A," 305th Engineer Regiment, 80th Division
CARUSO, Santo, 1st Co., 1st Development Battalion, Camp Grant
CHIAPPETTA, Joseph, 3892506, 42nd Co., 11th Battalion, 159th Depot Brigade
COSENTINO, Frank, 547833, Pvt., Co. "K," 30th Infantry Regiment, 3rd Division
COSTABILE, Frank A., 2863546, Cpl., Co. "L," 34th Engineer Regiment
DERANGO, Achille, Pvt., 153th Machine Gun Battalion
DERANGO, James, Pvt., Co. "B," 120th Engineer Regiment (Standard Gauge Railway Shop)
DEROSE, Raffaele, 3446678, Pvt., Base Hospital 5
DEROSE, Rosario, 2039302, PFC, Medical Detachment 2
FALLICO, Emilio, Pvt., 38th Co., 10th Battalion, 159th Depot Brigade
FALLICO, Michael, 2024510, PFC, Co. "B," 58th Infantry Regiment, 4th Division
FUCILLA, Joseph, 5276137, Pvt., Students' Army Training Corps, University of Wisconsin, Madison
GAGLIARDO, Rosso, 3546438, Pvt., 158th Depot Brigade
GENTILE, John, 3446690, Pvt., Evacuation Hospital 12
GENTILE, Ralph, 3892362, Pvt., Battery "F," 314th Field Artillery Regiment, 80th Division
GIORDANO, Ernest, 2037293, Pvt., Evacuation Hospital 29
GRECO, Giuseppe, Pvt., U.S. Army, 1918
GRECO, James, 2032124, Pvt., Infantry Camp
MAGALDI (MIGALDI), Salvatore, Pvt., Co. "C," Development Battalion, 159th Depot Brigade
MOLINARO, Louis, 2035018, Pvt., Battery "B," 104th Field Artillery Regiment, 27th Division
MORELLI, Eugenio, 2036880, Pvt., Co. "K," 106th Infantry Regiment, 27th Division
NACCARATO, Angelo, 2097440, Pvt., Co. "A," 19th U.S. Guards Battalion
PAGLIARO, Antonio, Pvt., 46th Co., 12th Battalion, 4th Regiment, 159th Depot Brigade
PALAZZO, Paolo, Pvt., 42nd Co., 11th Battalion, 159th Depot Brigade
PORCARO, Nick, 2024559, PFC, Co. "C," 4th Ammunition Train, 4th Division
PRESTA, Gaetano, 3896894, Pvt., 37th Co., 10th Battalion, 159th Depot Brigade
RUFFOLO, Fred, 5276028, Pvt., Students' Army Training Corps, University of Wisconsin, Madison
RUFFOLO, Joseph Raymond, 3892541, Pvt., 159th Depot Brigade
RUFFOLO, Louis Joseph, 184-51-63, F2c, U.S. Navy, U.S.S. *George Washington*

SCARPELLI, Tom, Bugler, Columbus Barracks
SERPE, Luigi, Camp Custer
VALENTE, Rocco, Pvt., Co. "E," 46th Infantry Regiment, 9th Division
WELLS (GUIDO), Domenick, 5037151, Pvt., Co. "A," Development Battalion, Camp Shelby
ZICARELLI, Mike, 2121468, Cpl., Co. "E," 312th Engineer Regiment, 87th Division

Rondout, Illinois
CAIRA (CAIRO), Ben, 3485742, Pvt., Co. "A," 11th Infantry Regiment, 5th Division

Waukegan, Illinois
SAVAGLIO, Harry (Enrico), 3337022, Pvt., Battery "D," 331st Field Artillery Regiment, 86th Division
SAVAGLIO, Silvio, 4423758, Pvt., 2nd Co., 161st Depot Brigade

Wilmette, Illinois
TERRANOVA, Julian, Pvt., Provisional Labor Company, Camp Grant

Unidentified Cosenza-area men from Kenosha, friends of Pvt. Giuseppe Covelli, probably early or mid-1919. The man at right wears an overseas chevron on his lower left sleeve, indicating between six months and one year of overseas service; he also wears a wound chevron on his lower right sleeve, indicating he had been wounded in action. (*Theresa Van Landuyt*)

Endnotes

Introduction

1. For information on Pvt. Covelli, see Belmonte, P., *Calabrian-Americans in the U.S. Military During World War I: Cosenza-Area Immigrants*, Volume 1 (Kindle Direct Publishing, 2017), pp. 93-99.
2. In this book, the term "Italian/Calabrian American" refers to someone who had been born in Italy/Calabria or who had at least one parent who had been born in Italy/Calabria. In some cases I refer to the Cosenza area as the Cosentino.

   Efforts to determine precise numbers of Italian Americans who served during the war are bedeviled at the outset by a dearth of records and imprecise definitions. During World War I, the War Department recorded each soldier's place of birth, but this data was probably not tabulated in any systematic way. When discussing percentages, it is helpful to know whether one is addressing the percentage with respect to all of the U.S. military or, as is often the case, to just the U.S. Army (thereby excluding the Navy, Marine Corps, and Coast Guard).

   An early estimate came from George Creel, head of the Committee on Public Information during the war. According to Creel, "[m]ore than 300,000 Italians figure on the Army list..." (Schiavo, G., *Four Centuries of Italian American History* [New York: The Vigo Press, 1952], p. 327) Historian Giovanni Schiavo, using figures provided by the Adjutant General's Office concerning war veterans who had applied for an adjusted compensation (bonus), gives a figure of about 89,000. (*Ibid.*) Schiavo's figure, however, does not take into account the fact that not all veterans applied for an adjusted compensation. In 1965, Michael Musmanno asserted: "It has been estimated that about 400,000 American soldiers with Italian names served under the Stars and Stripes in World War I" (Musmanno, M., *The Story of Italians in America* [Garden City, NY: Doubleday & Co., 1965], p. 141). In a similar vein, in 1992, Jerre Mangione and Ben Morreale stated: "In World War I, when Italy was an ally of the Americans, about 12 percent of the U.S. Army was made up of Italian immigrants and (to a lesser extent) their American-born sons" (Mangione, J., and Morreale, B., *La Storia: Five Centuries of the Italian American Experience* [New York: HarperCollins, 1992], p. 340). For neither of these assertions is there any reference or source cited. Of course, it would be extremely difficult to come up with anything approaching an authoritative figure for the number of Italian Americans who served during the war. Even a comprehensive survey of rosters, lists of wounded men, and lists of men receiving awards would give a figure skewed by the types of units surveyed. For example, many Italian Americans served in such stateside units as development battalions and depot brigades in the final few months of the war.

3. Vecoli, R., *The Formation of Chicago's "Little Italies,"* Journal of American Ethnic History, Vol. 2, No. 2 (Spring, 1983), pp. 5–20 [www.jstor.org/stable/27500267?seq=1#page_scan_tab_contents]
4. I have made one exception to this geographic limitation. Frank Conforti served overseas as a musician first class in the 124th Field Artillery Regiment, 33rd Division. Conforti was a musician living and working in Beloit, Wisconsin, about 95 miles northwest of Chicago. On the Army transport manifest for his trip to and from France, Conforti listed his uncle, Frank Scarpelli, of Chicago, as his next of kin. I surmise that Conforti had solid ties to Chicago, and he is included in this group of men. No doubt other men, as yet unfound, are in the same situation.
5. Such is the case with Domenic Wells, who was born Domenico Guido in Marano Principato. His father changed the surname to Wells; the author more or less stumbled upon Wells in his research. Wells served stateside during the closing days of the war.

Chapter 1

1. For Spizzirri's date of immigration, see Ancestry.com. *Chicago, Illinois, Voter Registration, 1892* (database online). Provo, UT, USA: Ancestry.com Operations Inc., 2001, as well as various U.S. census records on Ancestry.com. See also Sturino, F., *Forging the Chain* (Toronto: Multicultural History Society of Ontario, 1990), p. 96. Sturino gives Spizzirri's place of birth as San Vincenzo la Costa, but the present author has found U.S. and Italian records that show his place of birth as Rende, near Cosenza.
2. Sturino, *op. cit.*, gives an excellent account of the nature of immigration from the province of Cosenza, Calabria.
3. Familial relationships are sometimes easily established, but often supporting evidence must be found, especially for distant relationships. The data here is based upon extensive research conducted by the author and others in Italian civil records and United States records.
4. Service information for the Spizzirri brothers comes from their respective Veterans Administration Claims index cards, National Archives, St. Louis, Missouri.
5. This quotation comes from an unsourced newspaper obituary in a public family tree on Ancestry.com. In the following paragraphs, Jerry Desmonie's information is from Ancestry.com, *U.S., Find A Grave Index, 1600s–Current* (database online). Provo, UT, U.S.A: Ancestry.com Operations, Inc., 2012. For Joseph Desmonie, see Ancestry.com. *U.S., Find A Grave Index, 1600s–Current* (database online). Provo, UT, U.S.A: Ancestry.com Operations, Inc., 2012, and Ancestry.com. *U.S., Headstone Applications for Military Veterans, 1925–1963* (database online). Provo, UT, U.S.A: Ancestry.com Operations, Inc., 2012. See also statement of service cards, Wisconsin Veterans Museum, Madison, Wisconsin.
6. The birthplace of Samuel Biafore from Chicago, who served overseas with the 54th Infantry Regiment, 6th Division, and Field Hospital 38, 6th Division, is not known. Some of his census data shows Colorado as a birthplace, while others show Italy. His parents came from San Giovanni in Fiore, and he is tallied under that town in this study. See various records on Ancestry.com.

Endnotes

Chapter 2

1. For the number of Italians who returned to Italy to serve in her armed forces, as well as the number of Italians to serve in the U.S. Army during the war, see Musmanno, M., *The Story of Italians in America* (Garden City, NY: Doubleday & Co., 1965), p. 141.
2. See Ancestry.com, *U.S, World War I Draft Registration Cards, 1917–1918*, information page.
3. Faulkner, R., *Pershing's Crusaders: The American Soldier in World War I* (Lawrence, KS: University Press of Kansas, 2017), is an excellent review of the American Army in World War I.
4. The information on the men in this paragraph comes from their respective statement of service cards, Wisconsin Veterans Museum, Madison, Wisconsin.
5. Not all of the men whose data is reflected in this table are among the subjects of this book; some of them lived outside the Chicago area. See Belmonte, P., *Calabrian-Americans in the U.S. Military During World War I, Cosenza-Area Immigrants*, Volume 1 (2017), for more information on men from these two villages.
6. For Aceto and the other men in this paragraph, see their respective Wisconsin statement of service card. See also Barnes, A., and Belmonte, P., *Forgotten Soldiers of World War I: America's Immigrant Doughboys* (Atglen, PA: Schiffer Books, 2018), p. 45.
7. The sections on divisions and regiments are adapted from Belmonte, P., *Days of Perfect Hell: The U.S. 26th Infantry Regiment in the Meuse-Argonne Offensive, October–November 1918* (Atglen, PA: Schiffer Books, 2015), pp. 12–14.
8. Of the 389 men in this group, thirty were U.S.-born citizens, seventeen had already been naturalized before May 1918, and three men left before the law was passed and subsequently died overseas. This leaves a total of not more than 339 men who were eligible to take advantage of the new naturalization act. The pertinent part of the 1918 law states: "[A]ny alien serving in the military or naval service of the United States during the time this country is engaged in the present war may file his petition for naturalization without making the preliminary declaration of intention and without proof of the required five years' residence within the United States..." [www.loc.gov/law/help/statutes-at-large/65th-congress/session-2/c65s2ch69.pdf].
9. Pvt. Andrea Morelli, 1107th Aero Replacement Squadron, U.S. Army Air Service, was probably the first non-combat soldier to return to the United States. Morelli returned from England in late November 1918.
10. It is possible that Pvt. Frank Guaglianone, 27th Infantry Regiment, returned to the U.S. from Vladivostok, Russia, as late as January 1920.

Chapter 3

1. An excellent account of the construction of these camps and the training of draftees is Barnes, A., *To Hell With the Kaiser: America Prepares for War, 1916–1918*, Volumes 1 and 2 (Atglen, PA: Schiffer Books, 2015). Volume 1, pp. 146–150, 229–233, discusses the construction of the camps and the general plan to send National Guard divisions to the southern states while training National Army divisions in the northern states. For concise contemporary information on American divisions, including general information in subsequent paragraphs, see Beamish, R. J., and March, F. A., *America's Part in the World War* (Philadelphia: The John C. Winston Company, Publishers, 1919), pp. 551–603.

2. For information on depot brigades see, *Training Regulations for Depot Brigades*, Training Circular No. 23 (Washington: Office of the Adjutant General, 1918). For more on foreign-born soldiers in development battalions, see Barnes, A., and Belmonte, P., *Forgotten Soldiers of World War I: America's Immigrant Doughboys* (Atglen, PA: Schiffer Books, 2018), pp. 42–45, 48–50.
3. See Beamish and March, *op. cit.*, pp. 551–603.
4. *Ibid.*, p. 561. The information on the men in the 9th Trench Mortar Battery comes from the author's research of Kenosha men reflected on their Wisconsin statement of service cards.
5. Fucilla went on to become a distinguished professor of Romance languages and a researcher of Italian surnames. His book, *Our Italian Surnames* (reprinted by the Genealogical Publishing Company, 1998), is vital to Italian surname research.

Chapter 4

1. James Greco apparently left the U.S. bound for France on November 8, 1918, three days before the Armistice. His ship returned to the U.S. on November 13 without reaching France. See Haight, W. L., *Racine County in the World War: A History* (Racine, WI: Walter L. Haight and Frank P. Haight, 1920), p. 508.
2. Faulkner, R., *Pershing's Crusaders: The American Soldier in World War I* (Lawrence, KS: University Press of Kansas, 2017), pp. 325–327.
3. For a detailed discussion and analysis of the case of some men from Kenosha who ended up as replacements, see Barnes, A., and Belmonte, P., *Forgotten Soldiers of World War I: America's Immigrant Doughboys* (Atglen, PA: Schiffer Books, 2018), pp. 78–80. See also the biography of Giuseppe Covelli (in Chapter 5) for a discussion of his case.
4. Beamish, R. J., and March, F. A., *America's Part in the World War* (Philadelphia: The John C. Winston Company, Publishers, 1919), pp. 551–603.
5. This total takes into account the 92nd and 93rd Divisions, which were composed of African-American enlisted men, but it does not include the 8th, 10th, and 11th Divisions, each of which sent small advanced detachments to England and France just prior to the Armistice. In categorizing these men, I included the 49th Infantry Regiment in the 83rd Division because it was assigned to that division briefly overseas. I have omitted some men assigned to some divisional support units. For example, I did not include a man assigned to Graves Registration Service Unit 304, part of the 29th Division, in that division's totals, nor did I include some men in butchery and bakery units that supported divisions.
6. The U.S. Army Air Service also recruited tailors, among other specialist occupations including photographers, bricklayers, and carpenters.

Chapter 5

1. See the *Back Over There* website: www.worldwar1centennial.org/index.php/back-over-there.html. *Soldiers of the Great War* is available on Ancestry.com. The Navy version, *Officers and Enlisted Men of the United States Navy Who Lost Their Lives During the World War, From April 6, 1917 to November 11, 1918* (Washington: Government Printing Office, 1920), is available via books.google.com. For the Wisconsin men listed here, see statement of service cards, Wisconsin Veterans Museum, Madison, Wisconsin. For all men in this

chapter, the usual Ancestry.com sources, such as census and draft registration records, provided basic background information. See Appendix I for more information.

2. See Benedetti's Burial File, National Archives, St. Louis, Missouri. Benedetti's given and surname are spelled differently in the various documents consulted.
3. *Ibid.*
4. See Broccolo's Burial File, National Archives, St. Louis, Missouri.
5. *Ibid.*
6. *Ibid.*
7. For the circumstances of Carravetta's death, see the testimony of Private Howard Strouse, Company "D," 28th Infantry Regiment, in Carravetta's Burial File, National Archives, St. Louis, Missouri; First Division Museum at Cantigny has other records for Carravetta. Carravetta's burial card: National Archives Record Group 92.
8. See Ancestry.com sources for Candelise's prior service and general background. See also, Belmonte, P., *Calabrian-Americans in the U.S. Military During World War I: Cosenza-Area Immigrants*, Volume 3 (Kindle Direct Publishing, 2017), pp. 100–101.
9. For the circumstances of Candelise's death, see the testimony of First Lieutenant Charlton M. Theus, Company "D," 56th Infantry Regiment, in Candelise's Burial File, National Archives, St. Louis, Missouri.
10. See Candelise's Burial File, National Archives, St. Louis, Missouri.
11. Filice's surname is spelled in a variety of ways; the Army transport manifest gives his name as "Fiori Fillici." I have used the spelling that his brother, Aurelio Filice, with whom he lived, used.
12. See Guido's Burial File, National Archives, St. Louis, Missouri.
13. *Ibid.*
14. *Ibid.*
15. See Morrone's Burial File, National Archives, St. Louis, Missouri.
16. See also: Davis, A., *The Story of the 132d Infantry, A.E.F.* (N.p., *c.* 1919), unpaginated.
17. See Perri's Burial File, National Archives, St. Louis, Missouri.
18. For a more complete account, see Barnes, A., and Belmonte, P., *Forgotten Soldiers of World War I: America's Immigrant Doughboys* (Atglen, PA: Schiffer Books, 2018), pp. 161–166.
19. See Posterivo's Burial File, National Archives, St. Louis, Missouri. See also American Battle Monuments Commission, *WWI, WWII, and Korean War Casualty Listings* on Ancestry.com.
20. See Scarloto's Burial File, National Archives, St. Louis, Missouri. For a more complete account, see Barnes and Belmonte, *op. cit.*, pp. 155–162.
21. See Sorrentino's Burial File, National Archives, St. Louis, Missouri.
22. See Spizzirri's Burial File and Naval Service Records, National Archives, St. Louis, Missouri. Unless otherwise specified, quotations herein are from his Burial File.
23. See Spizzirri's Burial File, National Archives, St. Louis, Missouri.
24. Some information courtesy of Vickie Zagame, one of Biscardi's relatives.
25. Newspaper article, "Man Who Fought Under Two Flags Seeks Job Here," *The Chicago Daily Tribune*, 25 May 1919, Section Two, page 21, scanned copy courtesy Vickie Zagame.
26. State of Illinois, Certificate of Death number 12097, copy in the author's possession.
27. For information on the 18th Infantry Regiment see Chastaine, B., *History of the 18th U.S. Infantry, First Division, 1812–1919* (New York: The Hymans Publishing Company, n.d.). For information on the 1st Division see The Society of the First Division, *History of the First Division During the World War, 1917–1919* (Philadelphia: The John C. Winston Company, 1922).

28. Chiappetta's Veterans Administration claims file contains information about his military service, wounding, and post-war medical treatment; partial copy in the author's possession.
29. See Chiappetta's claims file, Department of Veterans Affairs, Milwaukee Regional Branch, Milwaukee, Wisconsin.
30. *Ibid.* Apparently a machine-gun bullet struck the top left part of Chiappetta's head a glancing blow and broke his skull without penetrating the skin. The size of the wound would variously be described as 1 inch square, 1 centimeter square, etc. A physician's report dated January 1919, stated: "Hit by machine gun bullet, destruction of bone about 1 inch in diameter on or about coronal section left side of skull. Scar extending deeply and depressed." Other information and documents provided by Chiappetta's granddaughter, Christine Chiappetta Thorsen.
31. *Ibid.*
32. For information on the 18th Infantry Regiment see Chastaine, *op. cit.*, especially pp. 73–98. For information on the 1st Division, see The Society of the First Division, *op. cit.* For information on the 86th Division, see *The Official History of the Eighty-Sixth Division* (Chicago: States Publication Society, 1921).
33. Much of the information about Covelli's wound comes from his claims file, Department of Veterans Affairs, Milwaukee Regional Branch, Milwaukee, Wisconsin. Some information comes from his statement of service card, Wisconsin Veterans Museum, Madison, Wisconsin.
34. For Imbrogno's service information, see Ancestry.com, *Ohio Soldiers in WWI, 1917–1918* (database online). Provo, UT, USA: Ancestry.com Operations Inc., 2005. Original data: *The Official Roster of Ohio Soldiers, Sailors, and Marines in the World War, 1917–18*. Columbus, OH, USA: The F.J. Heer Printing Co., 1926. Despite being from Chicago, Imbrogno's information was recorded in this book of Ohio veterans. For silver star citation, First Division Museum at Cantigny, Wheaton, Illinois.
35. Metagrano's military service records were salvaged from the 1973 fire, and they provide a rare glimpse into the situation involving a wounded soldier who was also suffering from epilepsy; much of what follows is from his service record. The surname is spelled in a variety of ways in American documents and transcriptions. Indeed, Margo Metegrano, Michael's grandniece, spells her surname differently than other members of the extended family. For clarity, for all family members, I have used the surname spelling used by Michael. For date of birth see "Mikey Metagran", Return of a Birth, Cook County, Illinois, birth certificate, Ancestry.com. See various passenger lists, birth, death, and marriage records at Ancestry.com. For aspects of the 47th Infantry Regiment history, see Pollard, J. E., *The Forty-Seventh Infantry: A History, 1917–1918, 1919* (Saginaw, MI: 1919), pp. 32–33, available on-line, Internet Archive, archive.org. For the 86th Division, see *The Official History of the Eighty-Sixth Division* (Chicago: States Publication Society, 1921), pp. 18–21. A version of Metagrano's biography appeared in Belmonte, P., "'I wanted to go over the top': Pfc. Michael Metagrano, a Doughboy's Story," *Military Collector and Historian*, winter, 2015.
36. See Metagrano's military service record, National Archives, St. Louis, Missouri.
37. *Ibid.*
38. *Ibid.*
39. *Ibid.*
40. *Ibid.*
41. *Ibid.*
42. *Ibid.*
43. *Ibid.*

44. *Ibid.*
45. *Ibid.*
46. *Ibid.*
47. *Ibid.*
48. *Ibid.*
49. *Ibid.*
50. *Ibid.*
51. *Ibid.*
52. Ancestry.com, message to the author from Margo Metegrano, October 7, 2014.
53. Family information supplied by Louise Juliani in miscellaneous correspondence with the author. Unit history information is found in *Illinois in the Great War: An Illustrated History of the Thirty-Third Division*, Volume II (Chicago: States Publications Society, 1921). See also statement of service card, Illinois Adjutant General's office, Springfield, Illinois.
54. Naturalization information is found in National Archives and Records Administration (NARA); Washington, D.C.; *Soundex Index to Naturalization Petitions for the United States District and Circuit Courts, Northern District of Illinois and Immigration and Naturalization Service District 9, 1840–1950 (M1285)*; Microfilm Serial: *M1285*; Microfilm Roll: *127*, available on Ancestry.com.
55. See unit records, Company "I," 26th Infantry Regiment, 1st Division, Record Group 120, National Archives.
56. See award cards, National Archives, St. Louis, Missouri.
57. See award card for the Purple Heart, National Archives, and statement of service card, Wisconsin Veterans Museum, Madison, Wisconsin.
58. In addition to the standard Ancestry.com sources, see email from Robert R. Porcaro, grandnephew of Benjamin Potesta, and Deena Porcaro Hill, Robert's daughter, to the author, January 13 and 14, 2019.
59. In addition to the standard databases on Ancestry.com, see email from Robert R. Porcaro, grandnephew of James Potesta, and Deena Porcaro Hill, Robert's daughter, to the author, January 30, 2019. Also see information provided by First Division Museum at Cantigny, copies in the author's possession.
60. In addition to the standard Ancestry.com sources, I am indebted to World War I historian and author James Carl Nelson who provided me with quotes from Tarsitano's letter to Leo's parents; the letter appeared in the Lykens, Pennsylvania *Standard* on October 17, 1919. Leo, who was only eighteen years old at the time of his death, lived in Hazelton, Pennsylvania, and his parents were from the Cosenza-area.

Chapter 6

1. Some of these men are featured in one or more volumes of the author's series, *Calabrian Americans in the U.S. Military During World War I: Cosenza-Area Immigrants*, Volumes 1–4 (Kindle Direct Publishing, 2017 and 2018). For the Wisconsin men listed here, see statement of service cards, Wisconsin Veterans Museum, Madison, Wisconsin. For men from Racine, see also Haight, W. L., *Racine County in the World War: A History* (Racine, WI: Walter L. Haight and Frank P. Haight, 1920). For a few of the Illinois men, see statement of service cards, Illinois Adjutant General's Office, Springfield, Illinois. For each man, the standard records available on Ancestry.com have been consulted; thus not every man's biography is

fully covered in these endnotes. See Appendix I for more information. Men from the Rende area (consisting of the villages of Castrolibero, Cerisano, Marano Marchesato, Marano Principato, Monalto Uffugo, Rende, San Fili, San Vincenzo la Costa) are well represented in this section for two main reasons. First, immigrants from this precise area settled in large numbers in the Chicago area. Second, the author has extensively researched the biographies of these men.

2. Correspondence with Beverly Adamski, Silvio Aiello's grandniece. Birthdate also per transcripts of index of Marano Marchesato vital records, via Rootsweb. See also *Beneficiary Identification Records Locator Subsystem (BIRLS) Death File*. Washington, D.C.: U.S. Department of Veterans Affairs, which gives October 17, 1900 for Silvio's date of birth. For service information, see Aiello's service record, National Archives, St. Louis, Missouri.
3. See Aiello's service record, National Archives, St. Louis, Missouri.
4. Personal correspondence with Beverly Adamski, Aiello's grandniece.
5. Some of Barbieri's service information is found on his petition for naturalization, Ancestry.com. For a notice of his citation for bravery, see *Illinois in the World War*, Volume I (Chicago: States Publications Society, 1920), p. 364. His name appears in many documents as Barberi.
6. For information on the 1st Construction Company, see *Gorrell's History of the American Expeditionary Forces Air Service, 1917–1919*. National Archives and Records Administration (N.A.R.A.), M990, RG 120 (available on Fold3.com). See also, Belmonte, *op. cit.*, Volume 1, pp. 51–53.
7. For information on Louis Bruno and his family, see Marano Marchesato, Civil Records, LDS Microfilm Number 1608135, *Nati*. Courtesy "Families from Marano Marchesato" website. See passenger list and census data available on Ancestry.com.
8. See Bruno's service record, National Archives, St. Louis, Missouri.
9. *Ibid.*
10. *Ibid.*
11. *Ibid.*
12. See *The Selected Directory of Italians in Chicago*, available at archive.org. Chesrow's military service information is via Ancestry.com.
13. See *U.S. National Homes for Disabled Volunteer Soldiers, 1866–1938*, records available on Ancestry.com.
14. See Costabile's service record, National Archives, St. Louis, Missouri. Costabile's Illinois death certificate gives an erroneous date of birth (February 2, 1893). Other military service information is found on Ancestry.com sources.
15. See Costabile's service record, National Archives, St. Louis, Missouri.
16. *Ibid.*
17. *Ibid.*
18. *Ibid.* Costabile's postwar personal information is included in his military service records probably due to the fact that a monetary claim was filed on the basis of his service, and copies of civilian records were appended to his service records.
19. Bach, C. A., and Hall, H. N., *The Fourth Division, Its Services and Achievements in the World War, Gathered from the Records of the Division* (Garden City, NY: The Country Life Press, 1920), pp. 43–44. Other information is from Fallico's statement of service card, Wisconsin Veterans Museum, Madison, Wisconsin.
20. For information on Ferraro's naturalization, see Eugenio Ferraro, Declaration of Intention on file at the University of Wisconsin-Parkside Archives and Area Research Center, Kenosha,

Wisconsin. For service information, see Ferraro's service record, National Archives, St. Louis, Missouri.

21. Rudolph Ferraro (Eugenio Ferraro's son), Kenosha, Wisconsin, telephone interview with the author, January 16, 2013.
22. *Ibid.*
23. San Vincenzo la Costa genealogy website (see Appendix I). See also Giordano's statement of service card, Wisconsin Veterans Museum, Madison, Wisconsin.
24. Haight, *op. cit.*, p. 507. It seems odd that he would depart for France after less than two weeks in the Army, but that is entirely possible.
25. Giorno family information via Ancestry.com sources; some 26th Infantry Regiment information via Fullerton, B., *The Twenty-Sixth Infantry in France* (N. p., 1919), photocopy in the author's possession, as well as Belmonte, P., *Days of Perfect Hell: The U.S. 2th Infantry Regiment in the Meuse-Argonne Offensive, October-November 1918* (Atglen, PA: Schiffer Books, 2015).
26. See morning report of Company "E," 26th Infantry Regiment, for September 12, 1918, Record Group 120, National Archives.
27. 26th Infantry Regiment records, Record Group 120, National Archives.
28. Belmonte, 2015, *op. cit.*, pp. 54-55.
29. See Loizzo's service record and final pay voucher, National Archives, St. Louis, Missouri.
30. Beverly Adamski, Orland Park, Illinois (Miceli's granddaughter), telephone conversation, January 2013, and message to the author via Ancestry.com, January 17, 2013. On his veteran's headstone application, Miceli's name is erroneously recorded as "MacIleo." See also Belmonte, P, *Calabrian-Americans in the U.S. Military During World War I: Cosenza Area Immigrants*, Volumes 1 and 4 (Kindle Direct Publishing, 2017 and 2018).
31. See Morelli's final pay voucher, National Archives, St. Louis, Missouri.
32. See Morelli's service record, National Archives, St. Louis, Missouri.
33. *Ibid.*
34. *Ibid.*
35. *Ibid.*
36. *Ibid.*
37. *Ibid.*
38. *Ibid.*
39. *Ibid.*
40. *Ibid.*
41. *Ibid.*
42. See Morrone's service record, National Archives, St. Louis, Missouri. His service record is one of the few that survived the fire at the National Personnel Records Center.
43. See Napolitano's grandson's Montalto Uffugo website. The site gives a birthdate of November 11, 1892; naturalization and draft registration documents give slightly differing dates. See www.montaltouffugo.net/index.html.
44. Personal correspondence with Gail Cannova, February 2019.
45. In addition to the usual Ancestry.com sources for naturalizations, passports applications, censuses, draft registrations, etc., I have consulted many other sources. General information about the Pellegrini family is from Foley, B., *A Short History of the Pellegrini Family in Pictures, Words, and Charts* (2002; a copy of this unpublished monograph, provided by Andrea Koprcina McGuire, is in the author's possession) in addition to my own extensive research in microfilmed and online records. Information about the Illinois National Guard

on the Mexican border is from *Roster of the Illinois National Guard on the Mexican Border, 1916–1917* (N.p., 1927, via Hathitrust.org). Information about the 33rd Division and its units are from *Illinois in the World War*, Volume I, *op. cit.* (1920), American Battle Monuments Commission, *33d Division Summary of Operations in the World War* (U.S. Government Printing Office, Washington, D.C., 1944), Cochrane, R. C., *The 33rd Division Along the Meuse, October 1918* (U.S. Army Chemical Corps Historical Office: Washington, D.C., 1958), and unit records, including rosters and morning reports, from National Archives, Record Group 120. Information about the 7th Division and its units are from Fell, E. T., *History of the Seventh Division, United States Army, 1917–1919* (Philadelphia: George H. Buchanan Company, 1927) and American Battle Monuments Commission, *7th Division Summary of Operations in the World War* (U.S. Government Printing Office, Washington, D.C., 1944). See also Charles Pellegrini, Francesco Pellegrini, and Louis Pellegrini, military service records, including final pay vouchers, National Archives, St. Louis, Missouri; statement of service cards, Illinois Adjutant General's Office, Springfield, Illinois; Andrea Koprcina McGuire (Louis's granddaughter), Facebook message to the author, May 15, 2013, and information from her aunt, Amelia Lucchetti (Louis's niece), in Bridgeport, Illinois.

46. Foley, *op. cit.*, p. 2.
47. See morning reports for Company "E," 130th Infantry Regiment, 33rd Division, Record Group 120, National Archives.
48. See unit records, 130th Infantry Regiment, 33rd Division, National Archives.
49. Charles Pellegrini's family information sheet contained within Foley, *op. cit.*, also claims that Charles was badly gassed in action. His statement of service card shows no overseas service, and service only with the 56th Infantry Regiment, so it is obviously incomplete. It would very unusual, but not be unprecedented, for a man to be badly gassed and return home for discharge by the end of 1918.
50. Foley, *op. cit.*, unpaginated section.
51. *Ibid.*
52. Francesco (Frank) Pellegrini's family information sheet contained within Foley, *op. cit.*
53. Louis Pellegrini's family information sheet contained within Foley, *op. cit.*
54. For information on Perrone's reenlistment and illnesses, see *U.S. National Homes for Disabled Volunteer Soldiers, 1866–1938*, records on Ancestry.com. See also Perrone's statement of service card, Wisconsin Veterans Museum, Madison, Wisconsin.
55. Miscellaneous email correspondence with Presta's grandniece, Rose Presta Pennington.
56. Passenger list, draft registration, B.I.R.L.S., public family tree, and naturalization records at Ancestry.com. For Illinois National Guard service, see *Roster of the Illinois National Guard on the Mexican Border, 1916–1917*, (1925), via hathitrust.org.
57. Award citation: valor.militarytimes.com/recipient.php?recipientid=14166. See also *Illinois in the World War*, Volume I (1920).
58. See Louis Joseph Ruffolo's service records, National Archives, St. Louis, Missouri.
59. *Ibid.*
60. *Ibid.*
61. Email correspondence with Mary Jane Ruffolo, February 4, 2013.
62. *Ibid.*
63. See Santelli's naturalization petition on Ancestry.com for his dates of service. The Army transport manifests are unclear as to his precise date of return to the U.S., and as to the vessel upon which he sailed. It appears to have been the *Caronia*.

64. Personal correspondence with Albino Santelli (Luigi Santelli's nephew), dated September 1996, and February 10, 1997. Also, Albino Santelli, telephone interview with the author, March 23, 2013. Other items include Declaration of Intention, Petition for Naturalization, and Certificate of Naturalization, all on Ancestry.com, and State of Illinois Medical Certificate of Death in Santelli's Veterans Administration claims paperwork.
65. Personal correspondence with Albino Santelli (Luigi Santelli's nephew), dated September 1996, and February 10, 1997.
66. See Serpe's final pay voucher, National Archives, St. Louis, Missouri.
67. See Peter Serpe's military service records, National Archives, St. Louis, Missouri.
68. *Ibid.*
69. *Ibid.*
70. *Ibid.*
71. Settino's service record is one of the few that survived the 1973 fire at the National Personnel Records Center (now the National Archives) in St. Louis, Missouri; accordingly, I have used it extensively for his biography; all quotations and military information are from this source. Although Settino was naturalized at Camp Mills in 1918, he also underwent naturalization proceedings on June 18, 1920, at which time he lived at 708 West Taylor Street in Chicago. It is unclear why there should be two separate records for his naturalization.
72. See Settino's military service record, National Archives, St. Louis, Missouri.
73. See Sicilia's Veterans Administration claims, National Archives, St. Louis, Missouri. Some military service and family history information via the authors research in Italian civil records and Ancestry.com sources. See also Sicilia's statement of service card, Wisconsin Veterans Museum, Madison, Wisconsin.
74. When or why the Guido family adopted the name Wells is not known. It appears to have been used by the family early in the twentieth century. Some Ancestry.com public family trees show Domenico's father's name as Domenico while others show it as Eugenio.

Appendix II

1. Some men could rightly be listed under more than one city (Chicago or Kenosha, or Racine and Kenosha, for example) because they moved between those cities around the time of their entry into the military. I have chosen only one city for each man here, however.

Bibliography

American Battle Monuments Commission, *7th Division Summary of Operations in the World War* (Washington, DC: U.S. Government Printing Office, 1944)

American Battle Monuments Commission, *33d Division Summary of Operations in the World War* (Washington, D.C.: U.S. Government Printing Office, 1944)

Arlacchi, P., *Mafia, Peasants, and Great Estates: Society in Traditional Calabria* (Cambridge: Cambridge University Press, 1983; online version via books.google.com)

Bach, Col. C. A., and Hall, H. N., *The Fourth Division, Its Services and Achievements in the World War, Gathered from the Records of the Division* (Garden City, NY: The Country Life Press, 1920)

Barnes, A. F., *To Hell With the Kaiser: America Prepares for War, 1916–1918*, Volumes 1 and 2 (Atglen, PA: Schiffer Books, 2015).

Barnes, A. F., and Belmonte, P. L., *Forgotten Soldiers of World War I: America's Immigrant Doughboys* (Atglen, PA: Schiffer Books, 2018)

Beamish, R. J., and March, Ph.D., F. A., *America's Part in the World War* (Philadelphia: The John C. Winston Company, Publishers, 1919)

Belmonte, P. L., *Days of Perfect Hell: The U.S. 26th Infantry Regiment in the Meuse-Argonne Offensive, October–November 1918* (Atglen, PA: Schiffer Books, 2015)

Belmonte, P. L., *Calabrian-Americans in the US Military During World War I: Cosenza Area Immigrants*, Volumes 1 through 4 (CreateSpace, 2017, 2018)

Chastaine, Capt. B., *History of the 18th U.S. Infantry, First Division, 1812–1919* (New York: The Hymans Publishing Company, n.d.)

Cochrane, R. C., *The 33rd Division Along the Meuse, October 1918* (U.S. Army Chemical Corps Historical Office, Army Chemical Center, Maryland, 1958)

Davis, Col. A., U.S. Army, *The Story of the 132d Infantry, A.E.F.* (no publishing data, but probably Luxembourg, 1919)

Faulkner, R. S., *Pershing's Crusaders: The American Soldier in World War I* (Lawrence, KS: University Press of Kansas, 2017)

Fell, Capt. E. T., compiler, *History of the Seventh Division, United States Army, 1917–1919* (Philadelphia: George H. Buchanan Company, 1927)

Foley, B., *A Short History of the Pellegrini Family in Pictures, Words, and Charts*, (unpublished paper, 2002)

Fullerton, B., *The Twenty-Sixth Infantry in France* (Frankfort, Germany: Martin Flock & Co., 1919)

Haight, Capt. W. L., *Racine County in the World War: A History* (Racine, WI: Walter L. Haight and Frank P. Haight, 1920)

History of the 101st United States Engineers, American Expeditionary Forces, 1917–1918–1919 (Cambridge, MA: Voluntary Committee of the Regiment, 1926).

Illinois in the World War, Volume I (Chicago: States Publications Society, 1920)

Mangione, J., and Morreale, B., *La Storia: Five Centuries of the Italian American Experience* (New York: HarperCollins Publishers, 1992)

Murray, C. T., *A Taste of Memories From Columbus Park* (Madison, WI: Greenbush Remembered, 1992)

Musmanno, M. A., *The Story of the Italians in America* (Garden City, New York: Doubleday & Co., Inc., 1965)

Pollard, J. E., *The Forty-Seventh Infantry: A History, 1917–1918, 1919* (Saginaw, MI: 1919)

Roster of the Illinois National Guard on the Mexican Border, 1916–1917 (N.p., 1927)

Schiavo, G., *Four Centuries of Italian American History* (New York: The Vigo Press, 1952)

Sturino, F., *Forging the Chain: Italian Migration to North America, 1880–1930* (Toronto: Multicultural History Society of Ontario, 1990)

The Official History of the Eighty-Sixth Division (Chicago: States Publication Society, 1921)

The Society of the First Division, *History of the First Division During the World War, 1917–1919* (Philadelphia: The John C. Winston Company, 1922)

United States Army in the World War, 1917–1919, Organization of the American Expeditionary Forces, Volume I (Washington, D.C.: Center of Military History, United States Army, 1988, available on-line via history.army.mil)

Vecoli, R. J., *The Formation of Chicago's "Little Italies,"* Journal of American Ethnic History, Vol. 2, No. 2 (Spring, 1983), pp. 5–20 [www.jstor.org/stable/27500267?seq=1#page_scan_tab_contents]

Woodward, D. R., *The American Army and the First World War* (Cambridge: Cambridge University Press, 2014)